# YESTERDAY CAME SUDDENLY

*Also by Francis King and published by Constable*

The Ant Colony
Visiting Cards
Secret Lives (novella in the Secret Lives collection)

# YESTERDAY CAME SUDDENLY

an autobiography by

## Francis King

CONSTABLE · LONDON

First published in Great Britain 1993
by Constable and Company Limited
3 The Lanchesters, 162 Fulham Palace Road
London W6 9ER
Copyright © 1993 by Francis King
The right of Francis King to be
identified as the author of this book
has been asserted by him in accordance
with the Copyright, Designs and Patents Act 1988
ISBN 0 09 472220 X
Set in Monophoto 11pt Ehrhardt
by Servis Filmsetting Limited, Manchester
Printed in Great Britain
by St Edmundsbury Press Limited
Bury St Edmunds, Suffolk

A CIP catalogue record for this book
is available from the British Library

*To Peter Day*

*best of friends*

I look into my glass,
And view my wasting skin,
And say, 'Would God it came to pass
My heart had shrunk as thin!'

For then, I, undistrest
By hearts grown cold to me,
Could lonely wait my endless rest
With equanimity.

But Time, to make me grieve,
Part steals, lets part abide;
And shakes this fragile frame at eve
With throbbings of noontide.

Thomas Hardy

# Contents

# ILLUSTRATIONS

Except where indicated, all photographs come from the author's private collection

*Part I*

# — 1 —

# *A Taste of Salt*

Sometimes, when I am thinking of my father with a particular intensity – usually during one of those stretches which each night disrupt my sleep like jagged reefs intermittently impeding the passage of a ship across an otherwise tranquil lagoon – I taste a brine-like salt on my lips. It is literally the taste of him, as I knew it all those years ago in my country of birth, Switzerland, in my country of childhood residence, India, and in my country of education, England. 'Kiss your father goodnight,' my mother would tell me; and with a leaden reluctance I used to cross over to the chair in which he would be reading or doing a crossword and place my lips on his forehead. I would taste that salt. He would never kiss me in return; he would merely respond by putting an arm round my shoulder or by patting me on the back. 'Goodnight, boy,' he would sometimes say; but more often he would say nothing.

Since he was not merely a confident rider but also a daring polo-player, I cannot remember a time when he did not own at least one horse. He would hold out a hand, palm upwards, to one of these horses or to the pony which he had bought for me in the hope, fruitless as it turned out, that I should eventually acquire his own equestrian skill. The animal would then at once begin to lick his palm, its tongue scraping like emery paper over flesh unnaturally red. But when, with some trepidation, I held out my own hand, not even the pony, ridden by me every day, showed any interest. 'It's the salt,' my father explained. 'My hands are salt, yours are not.'

That salt, I eventually realized, like the flush not merely of his palms but also of his cheeks, was a symptom of his illness. Although my father's body was so strong, wiry and hard, he was none the less slowly dying of tuberculosis. It was this which had taken him from India to Switzerland in the hope of a cure, with the result that I was born there, in 1923, in a hotel in Adelboden; and it was this which presented one obstacle after another – surmounted (as I now see) with exemplary courage – to a career first in the Indian Police and then in the Intelligence Bureau, of which he was Deputy Director at the time of his death.

That was a time, in the Thirties, when tuberculosis was still 'the white plague', regarded by many people with the same irrational horror as Aids today. One of my earliest childhood memories, dating from my fifth year, is of a hurried departure, after only a night or two, from a luxury Swiss hotel in which, as guests of my well-

15

to-do German grandmother, we had been planning to stay for two weeks. My mother had confided in an English couple, also staying in the hotel, that my father had just come out of a sanatorium. They had passed on this information to some fellow English guests. A deputation had then confronted the manager: it was 'dangerous' to have a TB sufferer scattering his germs about the hotel; either he must go or they would go. The manager, clearly a sensible and decent man, assured them that the director of the sanatorium had told my father, when releasing him, that he was no longer infectious. The guests would not listen. Embarrassed, ashamed, apologetic, the manager asked my father to leave. At the next hotel, my mother was more discreet.

Throughout my childhood, I was always aware of the precarious state of my father's health. A thermometer was not merely a glass tube with mercury in it but a magician's wand, which could wholly transform our previously happy and tranquil lives. 'I'm going to take your temperature,' my mother would say. Impatiently my father would shake his head. 'No, no! I'm all right. I'm perfectly all right.' But my mother, so obdurate where my father's health was concerned even if so yielding to him in all other matters, would insist. I see them now. He is sitting on the edge of his bed or on a chair, the thermometer jutting upwards out of his mouth, as the cigarettes which he chain-smoked similarly jutted. He looks irritable, even petulant. His right leg jigs up and down. My mother frowns down at him, protective and, yes, puzzled, I do not know why. Sometimes, after she has held the thermometer up to the light, she says, with a sigh of relief, 'Nothing' and then begins to shake it vigorously, as though to expunge all memory of those minutes of dread. Sometimes she says, 'Yes, I thought it was up. You can't go to work. I'll send a message to Dr Cameron to come and see you.'

Although death was never mentioned, I seemed to be aware of its inevitability by the time that I was eight or nine. For a few weeks my father was in a sanatorium not in Switzerland but by a lake among the foothills of the Himalayas. My mother, my sister and I – by then my two older sisters were at school in Switzerland – stayed in a nearby farmhouse, the owner of which, a fiercely outspoken, tough but kind widow, took in boarders.

Because my father was then deemed to be infectious, only my mother made the trek up the hill to the sanatorium to visit him.

'Why are you leaving us?' I used to demand of her. I was then seven.

'I have to see Daddy.'

'Why can't we come?' my five-year-old sister would then ask. 'I want to come, I want to come!' At that she would begin to sob.

Either the landlady or her handsome, simple-minded son would then try to distract us – wouldn't we like to look at the newly hatched chickens, see the pigs being fed, play on the swing in the orchard? These prospects rarely consoled us.

My father eventually joined us on the farm. His suit hung on him, the collar of his shirt looked at least two sizes too large. He was tender and affectionate to me as he had rarely been before. I was delighted and yet awed by the change. Leaving my mother and sister behind, we used to go for walks together. 'Not too fast, not too fast!' This former athlete would now soon grow breathless. He would halt and point with his stick. Did I know the name of that mountain over there? And that one? And did I know what bird that was? And the name of that butterfly? He was always eager to educate me; and as with some stern but much-loved master, I was terrified of forgetting the lessons learned from him.

Sometimes, motionless except for the shaking of his shoulders, he would start to cough, on and on and on, while, with increasing panic, longing to rush away, I would wait for him. Then he would take a small blue bottle out of the pocket of his jacket, unscrew the lid and spit into it. He would screw the lid back. Many years later I read of this kind of bottle in Thomas Mann's *The Magic Mountain* – a 'Blue Peter' it is called in the Lowe-Porter translation.

Not surprisingly tuberculosis filled me with dread for many years, long after the discovery of antibiotics had emptied sanatoria. When, in the Sixties, I was living in Japan, I consulted a lung specialist about a persistent cough and loss of weight. Having sounded me thoroughly, he put his head on one side, drew in his breath and then expelled it on a long 'Sah!' Finally he said, 'Maybe tuberculosis.' Couldn't he be sure, one way or another? He shook his head. I must have an X-ray. Now? No, not now, he replied. It was Friday afternoon, I must wait until after the weekened. I passed that weekend in a state of anxiety as acute as if he had told me that he suspected cancer. In the event, there was nothing seriously wrong.

Because of the precariousness of my father's health during my formative years, I have always suffered from undue anxiety about any illness, however trivial, suffered by myself or anyone close to me. Sometimes I see myself laboriously spinning away at my life, as a spider spins away at its web. The web is extraordinarily tensile and tenacious. But some careless passer-by can easily rip a hole in it or destroy it altogether. At other times I feel as if life were a matter of picking one's way over the thinnest crust of earth above a sleeping volcano. At any moment, the earth may give way or the volcano erupt.


No doubt it was his illness which made my father suffer from a chronic morbidity; and no doubt my father infected me with that chronic morbidity, though not, mercifully, with the illness itself. When I was eight, he would often take me for walks through the mouldering ruins and the then well-kept grounds of the Residency in Lucknow. It was here that the British had held out with remarkable heroism against the Indians during the Mutiny, later to exact a hideous revenge. There were innumerable tablets commemorating the dead. My father would read their inscriptions to me or, occasionally, make me read them to him. Here was a girl of eleven who had been shot by a sniper. Here was a mother who had been buried, with her two children, aged two and three, under falling masonry. He would point with his stick. 'Now whose grave is that?' If I gave him the correct answer, he was approving: 'Good boy! *Good* boy!' If I gave him the wrong answer or stood in panicky silence, he would cry out impatiently, 'Oh, come on! Come *on*!'

Sometimes, instead of taking me to the Residency for a walk, he would take me to the cemetery. Some of the gravestones, particularly those from the nineteenth century, had verses carved on them. He would know all such verses by heart; and he would expect me similarly to know them. Anyone who has visited such a cemetery in India will have been oppressed by the youth of so many of the people buried in it: girl brides who succumbed to typhoid, cholera or puerperal fever; subalterns killed by an assassin or in some petty skirmish; children dead almost as soon as they were born. From these graves, as much as from my father's illness, I received a sense of the ephemerality of human existence.

It was not only disease which threatened my father and so, by association, also my mother, my sisters and me. One day, in Allahabad – I must then have been four – my father came home with red patches on his throat. He spoke in a husky whisper. Two of his men had dragged some small-time, long-sought gangster into his office, having arrested him in the bazaar. My father told them that there was no need to hold the gangster; they should bring him a chair on which to sit during his interrogation. When the two policemen let him go, the gangster at once sprang at my father, gripping his throat with both hands. It was with difficulty that the two policemen prised him off.

In the hill station of Naini Tal, my father sat down to his usual luncheon with us. Curry was served; and since he liked his curry extremely hot, he ate a different one from ours. Luncheon over, he mounted his horse and, attended by a syce, made his way back down the hill to his office. Suddenly, he was taken violently ill outside the house of some friends. He staggered into the house while the syce, showing admirable presence of mind, mounted the horse and galloped to the surgery of the doctor to summon his aid. Those were days when, in India, few private houses possessed telephones. The doctor managed to save my father's life. So violent had been the attack that he suspected that poison had been the cause. This suspicion was confirmed when it was discovered that the cook had vanished, never to reappear or be traced.

Violence of this kind also extended to people close to us. In the hot weather, my father and mother endured a punishing journey across India from Naini Tal to Murree, after learning that the husband of one of my father's sisters, a major in the Indian Army, had been murdered by a sepoy. The murderer had intended to kill not my uncle but another officer, then absent. Why had he wanted to kill the other officer? It was never revealed at the time – there was open talk of promotion denied to the sepoy, there were also whispers of some kind of sexual imbroglio – and I have never been able to discover the truth since. When my father and mother returned to Naini Tal with the distraught young widow and her two little sons, John and Colin Haycraft, they merely told me that my Uncle Billy had died. Although only five, I was precociously already able to read. Some weeks later, thumbing through a copy of the *Illustrated London News*, recently arrived, I saw a picture of my uncle and, with mounting horror, spelled out, word by word, the account of his death. Perhaps my father would also be murdered in the same way, I thought. Perhaps we should all be murdered.

Once, when we were out for a drive in the car, a hostile crowd suddenly surrounded it, beating on its sides and its bonnet and then, when my father had been obliged to halt it in order not to run anyone over, rocking it from side to side. My father pulled a handful of coins out of his pocket and threw them in a wide arc across the road. The crowd abandoned the car to scavenge for them. My father drove on. I was full of admiration both for his quick-wittedness at the time and for his total composure afterwards.

My father was not merely a man of action; he was also an intellectual. Some years ago, in the course of a lecture at the English Centre of PEN, Salman Rushdie declared that, in sending out its administrators, England had unloaded on to India 'rubbishy second-raters'. The ignorance of this astounded me. In the years of British rule men who passed out at the top in the Civil Service examinations would often opt for service in India. My godfather had been a Farsi scholar; my father an Urdu one, with in addition a lifelong passion for Latin and Greek literature and for English poetry. This passion for English poetry he transmitted to me. I can remember how, on one of our walks, this time on Beachy Head during one of his leaves from India, he suddenly halted and recited into the fierce wind: 'My heart aches and a drowsy numbness pains . . .' I was then eleven, and had already spent three years at private school 'back home'. From time to time he would set me the task of learning a poem. One of these, a favourite of his and now of mine, was Flecker's 'The Old Ships':

> I have seen old ships sail like swans asleep
> Beyond the village which men still call Tyre,
> With leaden age o'ercargoed, dipping deep
> For Famagusta and the hidden sun
> Which rings black Cyprus with a lake of fire . . .

I can still hear his voice declaim the poem; I can still myself recite it from beginning to end.

At the time I was often resentful at thus being obliged, not merely at my private school but even during holidays with my parents, to learn poetry by heart. Now I am grateful, and sorry for the pupils of today, in general absolved from all such rote learning. What my father forced me to learn, often irritably correcting me as I recited it to him – 'No, no, not "*Will* I compare thee to a summer's day?" – shall, shall, *shall*' – has remained with me, like some invisible trust fund, on which I have been always able to draw in need. The importance of such an invisible trust fund was brought home to me when I was International President of PEN. Repeatedly writers who had spent years in prison, with little or no access to books, told me how they had recited either to themselves or to their fellow prisoners poetry which they had learned in their youth. It had been an unfailing support to them, as, in circumstances far less dire, it has been an unfailing support to me.

My father's own father had forced him to learn by heart passages in Latin from the *Aeneid* when he was only five. This grandfather of mine had been a judge in Madras. In his early fifties, still a bachelor, he retired, returned to Europe, and there married the daughter, only eighteen years old, of an impoverished German aristocrat. Somehow, during his years in India, he had become rich. How? I have never been able to discover. Did he brilliantly invest his savings? Or, as a judge, did he find other, less reputable means of accumulating money? Within some twenty years, travelling in his retirement about Europe, he had fathered ten children. Since he treated my father with all the severity of a Victorian paterfamilias – making him endure daily cold baths at an early age, beating him for the smallest transgression – it is to my father's credit that the only severity which he ever showed me was a verbal one. Cousins, a girl and a boy, often used to come and stay with us. When the cousins, along with my sister and myself, were discovered in some wrongdoing, their otherwise equable father, a railway engineer, or their formidable mother, Aunt Amie, my mother's oldest sister, would beat them; but neither my father nor my mother would ever lay a hand on my sister and myself. Only once, exasperated beyond endurance because I insisted on making a noise when he was trying to listen to a Beethoven quartet on the wind-up gramophone, my father pulled off his slipper and whacked my behind three times with it. I was far too amazed to feel any pain.

It is difficult now to convey that, by the standards of his time, my father was the same sort of liberal as his friend Malcolm Darling, often said to be the prototype of Fielding in E.M. Forster's *A Passage to India*, or Malcolm Hailey (later Lord Hailey), Governor of the United Provinces for much of the period of my father's service there. My father would freely use phrases such as 'wog', 'black as your boots' and 'a touch of the tar-brush'. I can remember him once reciting a limerick – whether of his own authorship or someone else's I do not know – over a luncheon table in a restaurant and how we all, children, aunts and uncles, laughed uproariously at it:

> There was a young man of Sydenham
> Who lost his best pants with a quid in them.
> He found them again
> Down Petticoat Lane,
> But there wasn't a quid but a Yid in them.

Yet, unlike the majority of his colleagues, he was interested in the art and literature of India and he had many Indian friends. One of these Indian friends, a Christian whose brother-in-law was the first Governor of Bombay after Independence, became my godmother.

When I was thirteen, in the year before his death, my father found me reading Christopher Isherwood's *Mr Norris Changes Trains* and took it away from me. It was 'wonderfully entertaining pornography', he said, but I was neither young enough nor old enough to read it. This last remark illustrated his often expressed belief that pornography had no deleterious effect on either children or adults, but only on adolescents. Needless to say, I procured another copy of Isherwood's novel, which I read in secret. The only effect it had on me was a beneficial one: it gave me an early literary lesson in the use of irony and the merits of concision. Oddly, my father also forbade me to read Warwick Deeping's best-selling *Sorrel and Son* – 'it's pornography and it's tripe, and I won't have you reading either.' Today, most people would agree with only the second of these objections to the book.

My father had both a love and an admiration for Kipling, whom (in common with many Indians) he believed to have understood India and the Indians far better than E.M. Forster. He transmitted his love and admiration to me. When I was a precocious child of nine, due within a few weeks to be sent back 'home' to be educated, I was browsing in my father's library and so somehow came on the story, 'Baa, Baa, Black Sheep', about Kipling's sufferings when, a remittance child such as I myself was about to become, he was boarded with a family in England. I was filled with apprehension, even terror. But fortunately the relatives who took charge of me, although sometimes negligent or impatient, were never unkind.

When the time came to send her children back to England, my mother, like most other English mothers in India at that period, was confronted with a terrible dilemma. Was she to accompany them and make a home for them; or was she to stay with her husband? My mother decided (and I am sure that she was right) to stay with her husband. The wife of one of my father's colleagues was travelling back to England at the same time and I was therefore placed in her charge for the long sea voyage. My mother had planned to accompany us on the train from Lucknow to Bombay but then abandoned the idea, since my father was once more ill. That she should opt to stay with him, rather than come to see me off on the ship, filled me with anger and grief. As, late at night, the train moved out of the station, my mother, clutching my hand, ran beside it. I felt that eventually, so strong was her grasp, either I should be yanked out of the carriage or my arm would be severed. Finally, at the end of the platform, she let go. I have no memory of whether my father was at the station or not. Presumably he was too ill to be there. Something of my anger and grief remained with me. She had abandoned me for him. He would always be her first choice.

I had always been a mother's boy, perhaps inevitably since my father was so often absent because of either illness or the work which he took so seriously. If I was jealous of my father, I think that he was also jealous of me, resenting it if my mother made too much fuss over me ('Oh, stop worrying about the boy! He's only got a common cold'), spent too much time with me ('Do hurry up! We're going to be late yet again'), or was too generous to me ('What's the use of giving him a watch like that? He'll only break it'). It was over my mother's absence, not my father's, that, alone in the cabin which I shared with the wife of my father's colleague, I wept secret, scalding tears; and when, from school in England, I wrote letters beginning 'Darling Mummy and Daddy', it was really only to my mother that I was speaking.


I was thirteen when my father spent his last leave in England. To his and my own delight, I had just won a scholarship to Harrow. Then, all at once, he told me that he had decided that Harrow was not the right school for me. He wished me to go to Shrewsbury instead. Since among public schools Harrow was then regarded as second only to Eton, I was at first astounded and then furious. Why, why, why? I demanded. My father explained. Even more than Eton, Harrow catered for the sons of rich fathers. He was not a rich father, and I should therefore feel at a constant disadvantage. I protested loudly and then, when that failed to change his mind, I sulked. Now, in retrospect, I see that he was right. At my private school, most of the boys were the sons of rich fathers. On Parents' Days, we all used to sit on the wall which separated the school grounds from the road and watch the Rolls Royces, Bentleys, Daimlers and Armstrong Siddeleys arriving. When my Uncle Charlie turned up in an ancient two-seater Morris Cowley with a dickey, an ironic cheer went up. I was deeply ashamed.

During that last leave, much of it spent in Hereford, my father yet again fell ill and had to go into hospital in London to have an operation. It was typical of his gallows humour that he should be delighted to find that the three medical men in charge of him were called Cutler, Ripman and De'Ath. Refusing a lengthy convalescence, he boarded the P. & O. liner to return to India on the date originally fixed. My mother and two elder sisters, now grown up, were with him. My sisters told me that he was in the highest of spirits, amusing and charming everyone with whom he came into contact. (Long after his death, people who had known him would say one of two things about him to me. The first was: He was such fun. The second was: He was such wonderful company.) Then, on board a small motor boat that was taking passengers ashore at Port Said, he began to cough on the thick, black fumes belching out from the ancient engine and suddenly had a haemorrhage. Although he reached India, he died soon after.

By then I had started my first term at Shrewsbury. Since it was thought that anxiety over my father would make it even more difficult for me to settle down, this last illness was concealed from me. Yet I knew, knew with absolute certainty, even while I was struggling to come to terms with the ferocious discipline of Shrewsbury in the early Thirties, that far away, in that now remote part of the world, a lost paradise which had once been so familiar to me, my father was dying. Because of that certainty and despite efforts of rationalist friends to convince me otherwise – my father had been seriously ill, it was natural enough that I should have anticipated his death, they tell me – I have always had an unshakeable belief in extra-sensory perception.

I was undressing for bed, when a monitor entered the dormitory and told me that the housemaster wished to see me in his study. 'I wonder what you've done,' he gloated, clearly supposing that I was being summoned for a beating. I pulled on the clothes which I had just taken off. So it's happened, I thought, with a bleak composure. It's happened.

The housemaster, Hope-Simpson, a decent, unemotional, inarticulate bachelor, clearly dreaded his task.

'I'm afraid I've some bad news for you,' he said when, with unusual gentleness, he had told me to sit down.

I nodded.

'I expect you knew that your father had been ill. Very ill. Very, *very* ill.'

He paused, reaching for a silver cigarette box on the table between us and momentarily holding it out to me before hurriedly withdrawing it and himself extracting a cigarette.

Again I nodded.

'Well – I'm afraid – I'm afraid I have to tell you . . . He's died.'

Yet again I nodded.,

He stared at me in a wondering disbelief. Perhaps I had not taken in what he had told me? 'You'll miss him. Of course you'll miss him. But you must be brave – for your mother's sake.'

This last was something that my relatives, who came to visit me in Shrewsbury in the days that followed, also repeatedly told me. It puzzled me. Why could one not be brave merely for one's own sake?

Eventually the housekeeper, Miss Fry, also unusually gentle, arrived to take me to the guest-room in which it was agreed that I should sleep that night. She looked at me with the same wondering disbelief as Hope-Simpson had done. I was still totally composed. I had shed not a tear.

'I expect you'd like a hot-water bottle,' she said. 'And I'm going to bring you a mug of Ovaltine. A hot drink is always comforting, isn't it?'

I thought of the freezing dormitory, its windows open by decree, however cold the weather. I was glad not to be in it.

In bed, I hugged the hot-water bottle to me. Then, as though its warmth were at long last thawing out something frozen within me, I began first to snuffle and then to sob. I must eventually have been overheard by Hope-Simpson and Miss Fry. I could hear their voices in the passageway.

'He's crying,' he said. 'Do you think we ought . . .?'

'Crying will be good for him,' she replied, wiser than he. 'Let's leave him to it.'

Eventually I fell asleep, to awake, in the small hours, to find my bed damp and cold. For a horrified moment I thought that I had wet it. Then I realized that the bottle had leaked. I tried to go to sleep again but could not do so. Shivering I got up, dragged a blanket and the eiderdown off the bed, and went over to an armchair by the window. Intermittently I dozed.

When Miss Fry arrived with a cup of tea and two biscuits, she surveyed the bed and the chair.

'I'm afraid I had an accident,' I said.

She looked momentarily cross. Then she said, 'Oh, don't worry!' Clearly she assumed that I had wet the bed.

'It was the hot-water bottle. It leaked.'

'Oh, gosh! Oh, golly! It's not been used for donkey's years. Oh, I *am* sorry! How awful for you.'

My grief for my father was real; it was also deep. But then, as that winter term dragged on, an emotion even more real and even deeper coalesced with it. This was guilt. From time to time, in the weeks while my father was dying at the house of my Uncle Billy (Napper, not Haycraft) and Aunt Amie in Ratlam, I had sometimes mused on the changes which would occur in my life and in the lives of my mother and my sisters after he had gone. My mother would come to England, she would make a home for us, we should all be happy together. Later, all these things happened. My mother did, indeed, return to England; previously dependent on innumerable servants, she did indeed make a home for us on the cruelly diminished income which her pension provided; and we were indeed happy – I far, far happier than I had been during those years of being a remittance child in the charge of relatives or friends of the family, and as happy as I have ever been since. Reflecting on how in my musings I had anticipated all the changes which would follow on the death of my father, I began to persuade myself that somehow I had caused that death merely by thinking about it. The guilt intensified. It became almost unbearable. Years later, when I spoke of this guilt to a psychiatrist friend, he told me that he often encountered it among his patients. One of them, a middle-aged spinster, had even attempted suicide after her invalid mother, whom she had selflessly tended for many years, eventually died. The spinster had persuaded herself that, because in her darkest hours she had thought, 'Oh, if only she would *go*!', she had somehow hastened that going.


I have often wondered how different my life would have been if, instead of dying of tuberculosis, my father had recovered from it. I should have passed my school and university years in greater affluence; and I should no doubt have initially felt less ill at ease in a man's world if he had been on hand to do such things as introduce me to his tailor, arrange for me to become a member of his club, and speak to the right people when I embarked on a career. But our relationship would certainly not have been wholly easy. I have no doubt that, just as he took pride and pleasure in my scholastic achievements, he would have gone on doing so. Himself a thwarted writer – from time to time he would contribute light verse to such papers in India as the *Times of India*, the *Pioneer* and the *Statesman* – he would also have been delighted that I eventually achieved some success as a novelist. But, unlike my mother, he would have been appalled by my extreme left-wing views in my youth, and by my refusal to join the Officers' Training Corps at Shrewsbury and my subsequent conscientious objection to the war.

Even more he would have been appalled by my homosexuality – of which, I suspect, he had a disquieting prescience, in the manner of fathers and mothers, even in my early youth. 'Take your hand off your hip! Anyone would think you were a nancy boy,' he chided me once. At my seventh birthday party, he crept up behind me with a cracker and pulled it over my neck. When I burst into admittedly unnecessary tears – I had felt no pain, only shock – he had exclaimed in disgust, 'Oh, for God's sake! What's the matter with you? You're not a *girl*!' Yet, though so perspicacious about my sexuality, he could also be strangely innocent. When we were staying in Eastbourne – I was then eleven – one of my father's friends, a retired Indian Army colonel, a bachelor, began to take an inordinate interest in me. I was uneasily aware, despite a lack of sexual knowledge such as few boys of that age would suffer from today, that there was something wrong with the relationship. But as the colonel bought me sweets and books, treated me to ice-creams in cafés on the front, took me swimming, took me to the cinema, my father seemed totally unaware of what was going on. 'I don't want to go out with him,' I would say, unable to explain, since I did not know, why I felt this; and my father would then say something like, 'Don't be a little ass! You want to go swimming, don't you? I'm far too busy to take you. Go on – go, go, go!'


Four years ago I decided to travel out to India to visit my father's grave. My mother, then ninety-six, spoke to me of it: 'It's in this cemetery on a hillside. It's such a beautiful place. You cannot imagine. There are hills all around it, green hills even when the weather is hottest, and it's all so peaceful, unbelievably peaceful.'

It was dusk when my travelling companion, Diana Petre, and I approached Ratlam in our hired car. The outskirts of the town were squalid beyond words. There were stark factories, the smoke from their chimneys staining the sky a bilious yellow, and all around them there were sheds, little more than hutches, constructed out of wood, cardboard and corrugated iron. 'How hideous it all is!' I exclaimed; and almost at the same time Diana pointed excitedly and cried out, 'There! There it is! There!'

I could only just decipher the battered sign on the wall: 'Protestant Cemetery'.

Diana and I clambered out of the car; then, with her usual tact, she wandered off, away from me, leaving me to find the grave alone. The grass was yellow and dusty. In the distance, a small boy was striking out with a stick at the rumps of a herd of emaciated cows, their udders swinging as they bucked and skittered away from him.

I found the grave. The grass had been cut around it. The stone was in place and free of moss. Later, I was to learn that Eurasian Christians from a nearby church still tended the place.

I stared at the grave. I felt the tears coming, unexpected, to my eyes. One ran down to my mouth. I tasted its salt.

Strangely, I felt nearer to my father then in his death than at any time during his life.

When I returned to England, the first thing that my mother asked me was whether I had visited the grave. Yes, I said, yes, I had visited it.

'Isn't that a perfect spot?'

'Yes, perfect. Absolutely perfect.'

# — 2 —

# *Remittance Child*

Strangely, I have found that, although it is easier to describe mental or physical pain than happiness, it is happiness that is easier to relive. Closing my eyes, I am once again a child of seven exulting in the skill involved in hitting a tennis ball with a racket against the high garden wall of our house in the Indian hill station of Naini Tal; once again lying out on the beach of Vouliagmeni, the country around still undefiled by property developers, with the late spring sunshine blissfully warm on my upturned face; once again biting into the flesh, fizzing with juice, of a pear which, in my pyjamas, I have reached up to pick from a tree in my Kyoto garden as yet another long, beautiful day breaks. But of many of the most disagreeable events of my life I have, perhaps mercifully, only the faintest of recollections.

In the case of two of these events, both from my childhood, an area of memory has been totally obliterated. When I was four, my older sister Pamela, then eight, and I were playing in Naini Tal with the English bull-terrier bitch which belonged to our neighbours. Obese, with doleful, red-rimmed eyes and the waddling gait of a sailor just disembarked after a lengthy voyage, she was so good-natured that she would carry me round on her back, wagging her tail. A few days later she had developed rabies and, to our intense grief, had to be shot. When had we last played with her? my father asked us. Had she licked either of us? Because then, as now, I found it extremely difficult to lie, I told him the truth. We had played with her on that day when we had later gone to a children's party at Government House; and, yes, she had licked me on the face, as she often did. My sister denied that she had even touched the bitch. She had merely sat on the wall while I had romped with her, she said. In telling this falsehood, she was totally unaware of the terrible risk which she was running. In the case of rabies, inevitable death can enter by the smallest crack in the skin.

It was therefore I alone whom my mother took to the Pasteur Institute in Kasaouli. I remember clearly the long journey by hired car, during which the successive hairpin bends caused me to be repeatedly sick; the hotel bedroom shared by my mother and myself, and my first ride on a pony up to the Institute, she striding out beside me; the friendly doctor who lifted me up on to a couch and then told my mother to pull down my trousers and lift up my shirt. After that, darkness descends, as though the bulb of a film-projector had suddenly died. In those days rabies injections, jabbed daily into the stomach for a fortnight on end, were extremely painful; and they were particularly painful for a child since the smallness of the area inevitably meant that the needle tended to home in on approximately the same already swollen spot. Eventually I had to be dragged out from the hotel by our Indian bearer and carried up the hill to the Institute in his arms. I was held down on the couch. I struggled. I screamed. Since it was essential during the course of treatment not to do anything energetic, my mother then taught me to knit. I still knit from time to time, finding the rhythmic click-click-click of the needles extraordinarily soothing to the nerves. When I was International President of PEN there was an elderly Scandinavian woman who would often take out her knitting at our assemblies of delegates. At moments of tension or boredom during these sessions – the second more frequent than the first – I used to wish that I could follow her example.

Just as the painful memory of those anti-rabies shots – which for many years gave me a terror of being injected – has been wholly expunged, so has that of the journey which took me, away from my mother, my father, my sister and the Indian servants who had constantly petted and pampered me, to Bombay. Since, as I have related, my mother could not accompany me, she sent our Indian bearer, and it was from him that she learned the story, to pass it on, many years later, to me.

That night he had knelt beside my bunk on the train, begging me to sleep. But in a trance-like daze, I had merely lain motionless, my eyes wide open. When he spoke to me, I made no response. The next day, he coaxed me to eat. But I refused everything. The family friend, Mrs Bayard, who was taking me back to England eventually lost her patience. I can imagine her saying to me, 'Oh, for heaven's sake, you have to eat something. Come on!' I can imagine her saying to the bearer in Hindustani, 'You'd better leave him alone. Oh, leave him alone!' As the bearer recounted all this to my mother, he burst into tears. He was devoted to us – 'I sometimes think that he really cared for you more than for any of his own children so far away in his village,' my mother often remarked to me.

Mrs Bayard and I shared a cabin. Even in ordinary circumstances, to share a cabin with a nine-year-old boy would be a source of inconvenience and therefore of irritation to any woman. Here the circumstances were not normal. Soon after the boat had set sail, Mrs Bayard was swept up in what in those days was called 'a shipboard romance' with a young, unmarried Army officer, returning to England on leave. She herself was returning to be with a teenage daughter who, like my father, had been afflicted with tuberculosis and was eventually to die of it in a Swiss sanatorium. Perhaps it was to escape from her desolation over her daughter's illness that she started the affair. At all events, I can sympathize with her, burdened with a child not even her own at a time when she wished to give all her attention to a love-affair.

The officer – about whose physical appearance I can remember nothing but the efflorescence of thick, red hair not merely on his chest but also on his shoulder-blades – was sharing a cabin with an elderly businessman. It was necessary therefore that the cabin shared by Mrs Bayard and myself should be the place of assignation for the lovers. 'Oh, do go and play up on the deck! Go on! And don't come back, I'll come up and fetch you!' Her voice had the scrape of a rusty razor. She was probably saying to herself and even to him, 'What on earth possessed me to take on this child?' Alone and disconsolate, I used to wander round and round the deck. There was a swimming-pool but I have no recollection of ever swimming in it. Briefly I made friends with a group of Australian children, with loud voices, sturdy legs and hair bleached white by the sun. Perhaps I did not show sufficient enthusiasm or skill for their rough, rowdy games. At all events they had soon become contemptuous of me, mimicking what they called my 'posh' accent and responding with a dismissive 'Oh, for Christ's sake stow it!' or a sarcastic 'You don't mean to say?' if I ventured a remark. Two bony, pallid women missionaries used to call me over to their deck-chairs from time to time, offering me mint humbugs from a tin which they carried around with them and questioning me, with a faint air of disapproval, about my family and, with a disapproval far more positive – no doubt they had guessed what was afoot – about the whereabouts of Mrs Bayard. 'She leaves you to spend a lot of time on your own,' one of them would say; and 'She's hardly the motherly type, is she?' would put in the other. Mrs Bayard would refer to them contemptuously as 'the mint humbugs'.

One night a cry awoke me. I jerked up in the upper bunk. My first thought was that Mrs Bayard had been taken ill. I looked over the side of the bunk. Surely there were two people down there? But with no light except the moonlight through the porthole, I could not be sure.

'Turn over! Go to sleep again!'

'I thought –'

'Go to sleep again!'

I turned over and went to sleep again.

Many years later I told this story to L.P. Hartley, as something that might amuse him. But he was deeply shocked. 'Oh, what a terrible thing! It must have had the most awful psychological effect on you.'

'No, I don't think so. Not at all. I'd no idea what she and he were up to, none whatever.'

Clearly he did not believe me.

At Marseilles my German grandmother was to meet me, to take me back to Switzerland, where she had briefly come to rest in the course of her nomadic life. Mrs Bayard was to travel on to England by sea. Although I had no clear recollection of my grandmother, whom I had not seen for almost four years, I began to long for the moment when Mrs Bayard handed me over to her. No doubt Mrs Bayard was also longing for that moment. I repeatedly visualized my grandmother and me walking hand in hand down the gangway; sitting facing each other in the first-class carriage of the train which would whisk us off to the chalet which she had rented near Montreux; stepping out on to a Swiss platform with snow-capped mountains all around us.

My grandmother never met me. I was dressed in a grey flannel suit which the Indian tailor in Naini Tal had made for me; my hair had been cropped by the ship's barber and what was left of it had been plastered to my skull with Anzora; my two cases had been packed. Mrs Bayard and I sat in the ship's lounge and waited. And waited. And waited. 'Oh, this is too bad!' Mrs Bayard exclaimed more than once to me. 'It's too bad!' she exclaimed to fellow passengers who expressed surprise that I had not been 'collected' (the word, suggesting that I was merely a parcel, only added to my despair). 'Hasn't she collected the little blighter yet?' Mrs Bayard's lover arrived to demand of her. I began to whimper.

Eventually the ship sailed on, with me aboard. Couldn't I disembark alone and wait for my grandmother on the quay? I had suggested. I was told not to be so silly. Two days later my parents received a cable: HAVE MISSED SHIP STOP FRANCIS ON WAY TO ENGLAND STOP MUDDLED DATES STOP PLEASE ADVISE STOP VERY WORRIED. My parents were more than very worried; they were frantic. Mrs Bayard was furious. She now would not speak to me, except to snap some instruction.

After all these years I still remember with gratitude the kindness of the captain. He learned from Mrs Bayard of what had happened. In front of me she said, 'I've absolutely no idea what to do with him in England. I have to see to my daughter, she's very ill with TB, you know. And I have a round of visits to make. I can't lug him around with me. Out of the question!' The captain told me that, if no relative came to Tilbury to claim me, he would take me to his house in Greenwich. He had a daughter about my age and a son who was a year or two younger. I'd be happy there. I could stay as long as I liked.

Did he really mean that?

I do not know. At all events I believed him.

In my early, autobiographical novel *Never Again*, I wrote, with the blithe egotism of novelists, about this voyage and Mrs Bayard's love-affair. Not surprisingly perhaps, she then ceased to have anything more to do with my mother, who had been one of her closest friends.


In the saloon of the docked ship I uttered a cry of joyful disbelief. Then I raced towards a woman in a fur coat and cloche hat. I jumped up at her, I threw my arms around her. 'Mummy! Mummy!' But it was not my mother but her sister, my Aunt Hetty, whom I had never met. They were extraordinarily alike, with high cheekbones, broad foreheads and deep-set eyes which enabled them to retain their beauty into old age. Because of that physical similarity to my mother, I was always to feel a close attachment to this aunt, even though her character and my mother's were so different. Aunt Hetty could be vain, demanding, selfish. She could also be amusing, charming, kind. The one man whom she had ever wholly loved had been a regular soldier, killed in the First World War. When she met him, she was already married to a fellow officer of his in the Gunners, Charles Bingham, one of whose relatives, Lord Clanmorris – for a time in MI5 but better known to the public at large as the detective story writer John Bingham – was to become a friend of mine. At the outbreak of war, the two young officers apparently told each other that whichever of them survived would 'look after' Hetty. What would happen if both of them survived, Aunt Hetty did not reveal when, only eleven, I heard the story from her. We were sitting side by side on her bed. A small crocodile attaché case, a wedding present to her from my mother, lay open on her lap. In turn, with hesistant melancholy, she took from the case a blurred sepia photograph of a skinny young subaltern in uniform and a peaked hat, the shadow of which masked most of his face; a packet of letters, tied up with ribbon; a cigarette case; a signet ring; a frayed regimental tie. Apart from the letters, written to her from the trenches, all these relics had come from his mother, she told me – 'That was decent of her, wasn't it?' Did Uncle Charlie know of the contents of the case? I never learned.

Uncle Charlie had come back from the war suffering so badly from the effects of having been gassed on the Somme that he remained an invalid for the rest of his life. Until her middle years Aunt Hetty suffered from epileptiform seizures, the last of which occurred when she learned of my father's death. Because of this disability, my mother, her younger by two years, was obliged, when barely into her teens, to accompany her everywhere in the Indian town of Ghorakpur, for fear of an attack. Thus, early in her life, my mother's role was set; it was she who, sturdy, staunch and steadfast, was typecast to look after others.

At first, I was lodged with the younger of my mother's two brothers, Philip, and his second wife, Aunt Mickie, in their small flat in Talgarth Mansions, Barons Court. Over the site of this block of flats in a once tranquil road, cars now rush, nose to tail, towards the M4. As a young man Uncle Philip had been a handsome charmer; and even after cancer had necessitated the amputation of one of his legs in early middle-age, so he remained. He never boarded a bus without speaking to the conductor; and, if the bus was a local one, then the likelihood was that he and the conductor would greet each other by name. 'And 'ow are we today, Mr Read?' 'Mustn't complain, Fred, mustn't complain! But this damp is always bad for my rheumatism.' I was fretted with impatience when, in the paper shop, the tobacconist's or the shoemaker's, he would carry on some interminable conversation about nothing at all. 'Your uncle always has the time of day for everyone,' a waitress in the local ABC remarked to me approvingly, as Uncle Philip hobbled off to the lavatory, leaving me to finish my beans on toast. He seemed to me to have the time of several days for anyone disposed to loiter and chat.

In India he had embarked on what had seemed likely to prove a brilliant career as a barrister, such as his by then dead father had had before him. But his first wife Elsa, whom I never knew but whom my Read relatives always characterized, with disapproval, as 'artistic' and, with even more disapproval, as 'highly strung', soon decided that she hated the country and set about persuading Uncle Philip to return 'home' with her. Departing, Uncle Philip lacked the courage to tell either my mother, who was extremely close to him, or my grandmother that he was planning to settle in England for good; with the result that for a long time, at great expense to my grandmother, his office, which had been his father's office, was kept open for him. In England he had a far less successful career as a minor civil servant. When I knew him, he was always generous to me, my sisters and my cousins, slipping us now a half-crown and now a ten-shilling note, which he would neatly fold and refold into a wad the size and thickness of a train ticket of those days, or taking a horde of us to the ninepennies at the Kensington or Hammersmith Cinema. As a young man he had borrowed money off both his mother and my mother, which he never repaid. My mother adored him but nonetheless never forgot this debt – 'There were many times when I could have done with that money,' she would still say many, many years after his death.

Uncle Philip had a single son by Elsa, my cousin Peter. Whereas, in the straitened circumstances of her widowhood, my mother was determined that, whatever the financial sacrifices involved, I should have a university education, Uncle Philip took Peter, a boy of intelligence, away from his public school at the earliest possible age and placed him in Barclays Bank.

Like myself in my early years, Aunt Mickie was one of those people who feel warmth but find it difficult to radiate it. She was also extremely strait-laced, wearing her propriety like inviolable stays. This made things difficult for her with the Reads, who were given both to extravagant gushing and to the telling of jokes about drunkenness, lavatories and even, with elaborate recourse to *double entendre*, sex. Aunt Mickie, like all my Read relatives at that time, was a Christian Scientist. Of Christian Science, my father used to say, 'It's not Christian and it's not science. It's just bosh.' But, bosh or not, it certainly helped my Uncle Philip and my Uncle John to overcome the terrible effects of their war experiences. To me it has always seemed the best of religions for people who imagine that they are ill and the worst of religions for those who are really ill. My Christian Science relatives all eventually ended their lives in the hands of the doctors and surgeons whom they had previously boycotted, taking the drugs which they had previously shunned. Then to the fear of imminent death was added a burden of guilt: it was, they were convinced, because of 'error' and a failure to 'hold the right thoughts' that they were now unable to cure themselves and so had to rely on others to attempt to cure them.

Of his war experiences, my Uncle John, my mother's oldest brother, never ceased to talk. This eminent barrister was haunted by them; and when, near the close of his life, he lapsed into a depression so profound that he would barely answer any question put to him, it was, I am sure, because the unsheddable weight of them had at last crushed his gallant but sensitive spirit. One of Uncle John's stories, told to me when I was only nine or ten, was of standing with a fellow officer in the trenches – 'There was this whizz and a bang, not a particularly loud bang, and suddenly he was headless, propped up there headless. And I was covered in blood, somehow there was even his blood in my mouth. How it got there,' he went on with jocular desperation, 'I cannot imagine. Perhaps I had been gaping at another of his tall stories.' When at the age of fourteen I decided that I was a pacifist and refused to join the Officers' Training Corps at Shrewsbury, I should guess that the pathetic relics in Aunt Hetty's attaché case, Uncle John's tales of the horrors of the trenches and Uncle Charlie's effortful wheezing, gasping and coughing from his gas-ravaged lungs were in large part the reason.

From Aunt Mickie and Uncle Philip I was passed on to Aunt Hetty and Uncle Charlie, who were then living, with their only child, Rosemary, in a boarding-house in Earls Court. So began a life of school terms alternating with holidays spent shuttling between relatives, often in boarding-houses. No one, not even Uncle Charlie, who all too obviously liked me no more than I liked him, was ever cruel to me or even spoke to me harshly; but when an already grown-up cousin, Philip, told me, in one of the dark, malevolent fits of rage to which he was prone, 'You'd better get it into your head once and for all that you're living with us on sufferance!', I knew that that was, essentially, the truth. On every occasion when I travelled in a taxi with these relatives, I noticed that it was I, not one of their children, who was expected to take one of the two tip-up seats. When Aunt Hetty paid the cabbie, she had a way of saying, 'Now let me see – that's four shillings for us and sixpence extra for Francis.' I felt no resentment at this. It was as well to face the fact: I was an extra in their lives. From these years of living as an extra, I learned the arts of pleasing and placating. Chameleon-like I would constantly adapt myself, eager, above all, not to stand out. In consequence, in early adulthood I found it extremely difficult ever to contradict others, to offer opposition, to be my true self. Even today, people often praise me for being the perfect guest. To be a perfect guest one always intuits the wishes of one's hosts and unostentatiously falls in with them.

It was unjust that I should prefer my King relatives, whom I then saw so seldom and who did so little for me, to my Read relatives, whom I saw so often and who did so much. The two clans were totally different from each other: the Reads middle-class, conventional, conservative, philistine; the Kings aristocratic on their German side, Bohemian, radical, intellectual. It was the Reads who provided me with a succession of homes, who fussed that I took baths and changed my underwear, bought my school uniform at Daniel Neal, saw me off on the school-train and met its return. They were the Marthas in my life. It was the Kings, the Marys in my life, who would suddenly descend, to take me to the London Zoo, the Science Museum or *Peter Pan*; to buy me extravagant presents; to feed me not at an ABC or a Lyons Corner House but at the Majestic in Kensington High Street or at Rules in Covent Garden. The Kings always talked to me as though I were an adult.

Eventually my two elder sisters, Pamela and Aileen (some years later, the latter changed a name which she hated to Anne), arrived in England from Switzerland, where they had been pupils at an international girls school, St George's, in Montreux. Aileen/Anne was an exceptionally gifted girl – fluent in French, accomplished in ballroom dancing, tennis and bridge, witty, alluring. Later, I shall tell the story of her sad final years. Pamela, two years her junior, was then so timid and shy that, when she had to cross a room, she would do so like a mouse, scuttling in jerks close to the walls as though for protection. Already she was characterized by the unselfishness which, in later years, drove her constantly to immolate herself on the altar of other people's needs and demands. Aileen/Anne, who dazzled me as she passed meteor-like through my young life, soon left to join my parents in India, her education finished. Pamela, who became a pupil at Brickwall, a progressive school established in a beautiful Elizabethan mansion in Northiam, became my closest confidante, ally and friend.

Although she was then only in her fifties, my King grandmother – my Read grandmother had long since died prematurely – looked like a little old woman in her long black or grey frocks, low-heeled black court shoes with diamanté buckles on the insteps, and a succession of drab hats, which she often wore indoors as well as out. Round her neck she wore a black watered-silk ribbon, with a gold heart-shaped clasp and a small locket containing a portrait of my grandfather. Hers had been what many might consider at best a sad and at worst a tragic life; but she was always perkily self-sufficient, never demanding sympathy and so, inevitably, rarely receiving it. Her own mother had died when she was still a small child, and her father had then married a Miss Pringle, from a family well-known in Scotland, who had proved not so much an unkind stepmother as a wholly indifferent one. At seventeen my grandmother, who had been hoping to study at Oxford, had been betrothed to my grandfather, then retired (as I have already related) from his judgeship in Madras and the possessor of a substantial fortune, the accumulation of which still puzzles me. This grandfather came from an Anglo-Irish family, descendants of an eighteenth-century Dublin bookseller. One of his brothers, my great-uncle Richard Ashe King, a sweet and unworldly character whom I knew in his still vigorous eighties and early nineties, started his career as the immensely popular vicar of Low Moor, near Bradford; lost his faith and resigned his living; produced a succession of novels which induced the critics to compare him, somewhat recklessly, to Trollope; and, having been a friend of Yeats, A.E. and George Moore, was eventually elected President of the Irish Literary Association. Another of my grandfather's brothers married Geraldine Harmsworth, and fathered the newspaper magnate Cecil King.

When my youthful grandmother married my ageing grandfather – who, according to family rumour, had already had a brood of children by an Indian mistress – the former Miss Pringle had totally omitted to tell her anything of what would be expected of her. On the wedding night, she was therefore appalled by her husband's demands – crying out, as she related to my mother, 'Go away, you horrible old man, leave me alone, don't do that!' He must have soon overcome her scruples, since in the next eleven years she was to produce ten children.

Of these children, more than half were to predecease her: two boys in infancy; her favourite, Willie, in the war; my father, as I have related, from tuberculosis; her lesbian daughter, Evelyn, a talented painter, in effect by suicide, since she starved herself to death in a nursing home for the mentally ill after her lover, a beautiful and wealthy Jewess, had been run over in a Paris street. As I have also related, another of her daughters, Olive, was married to an Indian Army officer, Billy Haycraft – father of the publisher Colin Haycraft and the educationist and writer John Haycraft – who was murdered in tragic error for someone else.

Having returned after her terrible bereavement to Switzerland to be with my grandmother, Olive then had an extended breakdown from which she eventually emerged with so little emotional response to anyone or anything that it was as if, during that long period of twilight, her feelings had atrophied.

In the First World War my grandmother had had an appalling time. At the outbreak of hostilities, already a widow, she was in Germany with her younger children. Cyril, then a sixteen-year-old boy at Winchester, was at once interned at Rühleben, not to be released for four years. When she and the other children, all girls, had eventually managed to travel from Germany to the haven of Switzerland, two of the four, May and Lucille, announced that they wished to return to England in order to do their bit – as they themselves put it. But they had no sooner arrived at Dover, then they were detained as possible German spies. After two days of intensive interrogation, they were freed, to undergo the drudgery of work in the Land Army.

My grandmother herself eventually also made her way to England. She, too, met with the same hostile reception; and when one of Cecil King's brothers was killed in action and another drowned in the Irish Channel after a German torpedo had hit the ship in which, a Winchester schoolboy, he was travelling to spend the holidays with his family in Ireland, that branch of the clan ceased to have anything to do with either her or her offspring. Meanwhile many of her German relatives had come to regard her as a traitor. It is therefore hardly surprising that, the war over, she should have spent so much of her time in neutral Switzerland, now renting chalets and now putting up in hotels.

The Second World War, during which she died, presented her with another agony of divided loyalties. I can clearly remember her anguished face, mouth bunched and eyes half-closed, as we listened to Hitler's yelping, hate-filled voice on the wireless in my mother's flat.

After a stroke, my grandmother was taken to New End Hospital in Hampstead, where my mother found her already dead. She had always worn a number of rings on tiny hands twisted with rheumatism. Not one was on her fingers. The ambulance men accused the nurses, the nurses accused the mortuary attendants, the mortuary attendants accused the ambulance men. None of the rings was ever traced.

As a child this happy, stoical, generous character had played the piano for Brahms, a guest in the family house. How Brahms, a perfectionist, reacted, my grandmother could not tell me when I asked her. 'He was a dear,' was all she said – an opinion which many of those who knew him might have disputed. She was also an accomplished amateur painter. I still possess a pretty collage of a woodland scene constructed out of dried flowers which she herself had picked during a springtime walk soon after my birth in the luxurious Park Hotel in Adelboden in Switzerland. My parents, then on leave, were staying there as her guests. She always preferred to lavish the substantial fortune left to her on her children and their families than to spend anything on herself. Because of this generosity, she left surprisingly little on her death.

*

Uncle Cyril, my father's younger brother, had been deputed to find a suitable preparatory school for me. He was the obvious choice for this task, since he himself was a schoolmaster. But in making his choice of Rosehill in Banstead, he was guided as much by geographical considerations as by educational ones: it would be easy for the relatives to visit me in a village (as it then was) so close to London.

A few years ago, when my friend and lover David Atkin was driving me to Brighton, I persuaded him to turn off the highway so that I could once more see Rosehill. Converted into a municipal office, the house, much of it Queen Anne in period, looked far smaller than I had remembered. Where there had been an extensive garden, bisected by a ha-ha so deep that anyone in it was invisible to anyone outside, there were now ugly modern buildings. The playing fields and the home farm had been similarly covered over. I felt the sadness which usually assails me on such occasions of return.

Contemporaries of mine have told me stories of how, at their preparatory schools, they were frozen in the winter, half starved at all times of year, scarcely educated, bullied, beaten, even sodomized. I have no such complaints. Clearly Uncle Cyril chose well. The standard of teaching was high; food was ample; and the dormitories were well heated in winter and airy in summer. If anything, the staff were too solicitous about our health. Whereas I was accustomed to my Christian Science relatives brushing aside any complaint of headache, stomach-ache or sore throat, Matie (as the Matron was called by staff and boys alike) was constantly saying to some boy or other, 'You're looking rather peaky' or 'You're looking rather flushed' and then whipping out a thermometer to thrust it into his mouth. My hypochondria, derived from my mother's anxiety over my father's health, was now sharpened by Matie's over mine. After breakfast each morning, we would first be obliged to 'do our duty' (as she put it) under her supervision or that of one of her two assistants and then queue up to be dosed with a variety of remedies and prophylactics. For a boy with the then fashionable complaint of 'acidity' there was a drink of glucose; for a boy whose 'duty' had been less than satisfactory a dose of Petrolagar; for a boy with a weak chest a dessertspoon of Angier's Emulsion; for me with no specific ailment a tablespoon of something called Radio Malt, so sweet and sticky that I found it quite as delicious as a Mars bar. After lunch we all had to lie down, not on our beds but on cushions on the floor of the main schoolroom, in order satisfactorily to digest what we had eaten.

The school was owned by two men: one energetic, called Mr Hughes, and one so dozy, Mr Buckley, later to become Lord Wrenbury, that the phrase 'sleeping partner' at once comes to my mind. Buckley was a charming man; Hughes a tough one. I infinitely preferred Buckley; but from Hughes I learned infinitely more.

As I have already written, most of the boys at Rosehill came from rich families. The Jewish parents of one of my closest friends, for example, would, in the absence of any of my relatives, take me out on Parents' Days in a chauffeur-driven

Rolls Royce, the rear of which — marvel of marvels! — could be converted into a lavatory. I myself never had occasion to use it, and so have no idea whether this lavatory consisted of an earth closet or a flush one. It was used by my friend's mother, who suffered from some kind of kidney or bladder complaint. At a signal from her to the chauffeur, he would pull up, we would all tumble out of the vast car, curtains would be drawn. My friend's mother showed no embarrassment. On one occasion I used the pretext of tying a shoelace to peer under the car for a tell-tale trickle of water; but the car must have been equipped with a tank of some kind.

Hughes and his wife — a sister of the theologian Charles Raven, who would descend to preach at the school — tended to favour any boy who came from this kind of inordinately wealthy family. They were often the guests in the Canary Islands of the parents of two boys with the odd name of Staib. One guessed that it was for this hospitality, and not because of their athletic prowess and striking looks, that the Staibs were pre-eminent among the Hughes' favourites. For the younger of the two Staib boys, with his oriental face, brown skin and butter-yellow hair, I developed a passion during my last year at the school. When we were alone, he would, in abstracted indifference, suffer me to move a hand gently under his shirt, over a shoulder smooth and firm to the touch, over his flat belly, over his already muscular chest. The pleasure which I derived from this was aesthetic, not sexual. I was extraordinarily innocent at the advanced age of thirteen, accepting a schoolfellow's revelation that babies were born through their mothers' navels. After all, he was a doctor's son and so surely must know.

Apart from a certain proficiency in running and the long jump, I was never much good at games. But, having been efficiently tutored by a governess in India and having already become an assiduous reader, I was ahead of all my contemporaries and even of many of those older than me in the classroom. About this scholastic ability, I became insufferably conceited, forever holding up my hand and pleading, 'Me, sir! Me, me, *me*!' If the master called on some other pupil who then produced the wrong answer, I would laugh derisively. This bumptiousness dates from a period when, after a term or two, I had grown accustomed to the discipline of the school. Before that, having been endlessly indulged by my parents and our innumerable servants in India, I was profoundly unhappy.

As a defence against boys stronger than myself, I developed a sharp tongue. Passing through the library on a cold winter's day, the hefty captain of football left a door ajar. I shouted after him, 'Were you born in a tent?' He was too dim-witted to appreciate the taunt. But Mrs Hughes, who happened to overhear me, was cross: 'That was a totally unnecessary thing to say. In fact, it was rather horrid.' I am afraid that I was often rather horrid; but then most young boys are.

After Aunt Hetty and Uncle Charlie had bought themselves a house on the outskirts of Bournemouth, it was there that my sister Pamela and I usually spent our holidays. No longer able to work because of the deterioration of his lungs, Uncle Charlie had to support Aunt Hetty and their daughter Rosemary on his Army pension. Rosemary was at Claremont School, situated in what had once been the country mansion of Princess Charlotte, daughter of George IV, and the fees there were high. Pamela and I would often comment on how 'stingy' or 'mingy' he was; but I now realize that he must constantly have had difficulties in making ends meet. It was no doubt because of these difficulties that he wrote to my mother and father to ask them to increase their weekly payments, on the grounds that I ate so much.

Uncle Charlie had a number of women friends, many of them rich and elderly spinsters. Of close men friends he seemed to have none. Often, for want of anything better to occupy him, he would decide to take us for a trip in his car. A day or two before the trip was due to take place, he would say to Aunt Hetty, 'We might aim for Torquay, don't you think? I'll ring Meg and Mary Spicer and ask them if they can rustle up some lunch. Then we could go on to Poole for a cup of tea with Jean McDowell. For supper we could always . . .' These female providers of food seemed to be scattered all over the British Isles. In return for their hospitality, Uncle Charlie would flirt with them, commenting, 'That looks very snazzy, I must say,' about some shapeless cardigan, or remarking, 'You're looking even younger than ever – a female Dorian Gray!' to some shrivelled, bowed spinster. When, many years later, I met Dr Bodkin Adams, after his acquittal on charges of murdering some of his elderly female patients, his appearance reminded me irresistibly of Uncle Charlie's. Both men were far from good-looking; yet both exuded a sexuality which women of a certain age clearly found overwhelming.

Although he was fond of Pamela, Uncle Charlie once played a typically cruel trick on her. Having kept rabbits at Brickwall, she had a horror of eating them. One day Uncle Charlie, who was skilled as a cook, prepared a curry for luncheon. Pamela loved curry. 'Have some more of this chicken curry,' Uncle Charlie urged her. She had some more. Then he told her, 'You say you can't eat rabbit, but you've just eaten two large helpings.' Pamela rushed out of the dining-room in tears.

Just as adults now rely on television to keep their young occupied, so Aunt Hetty and Uncle Charlie relied on the cinema. Scarcely a day passed when we children were not sitting in the ninepennies, sometimes with them but far more often on our own. Bournemouth was then full of cinemas; we knew them all. Rosemary had a wind-up gramophone and on this we used to play the hits of the day. I can, as a result, still remember all the words of innumerable Thirties songs: 'She Wore a Little Jacket of Blue', 'The Isle of Capri', 'Red Sails in the Sunset'.

Oddly, we three children had virtually no friends, spending day after day with no company but our own. Pamela and I would wander round the bookshops, then almost as numerous in Bournemouth as the cinemas. Our purchases of poetry and adult fiction would overawe Aunt Hetty. Uncle Charlie merely thought us batty for wasting our pocket-money.

I was constantly reading; and I was also already writing. The world of my relatives seemed such a drab one in contrast to the earthly paradise of India or even the world inhabited by the parents of my schoolfellows, that I had to escape from it into the imaginings either of others or of myself. To these parents I told whopping fibs when, as often happened, they took me out on Parents' Days or half-term. It is a wonder that I grew up to become merely a novelist and not also a mythomaniac.

Of this fibbing, I can give one example. One holidays I went to stay for a week with a sweet-natured fellow pupil, Tony Inchbald, later to lose his life in the war. A cultivated family, living in a capacious and comfortable house in Chobham, the Inchbalds were constantly talking about concerts and plays. At Victoria Station, on my way down to Chobham, I had seen a poster advertising a concert by Gigli. 'Last holidays my aunt and uncle took me to a concert by Gigli in the Albert Hall,' I announced, eager to keep my end up. 'By *who?*' Mrs Inchbald queried, mystified. Unfortunately I had pronounced Gigli as 'Giggly'.

My closest school friend was one of those boys who, in their gravity, their good sense and their air of responsibility, seem to be premature adults. Ill with quinsy, Cleary was confined to the sickroom. Missing his company, I asked if I might visit him. I was told No; he might be infectious. I then wrote him a letter. Purely in joke – since, unlike the younger Staib boy, he exerted absolutely no physical attraction over me – this letter parodied the kind of 'soppy' love-letter I had read in novels. 'Dearest Heart' it began, and concluded 'With oceans of love.' Matie came across this letter and had no scruples in reading it. She passed it on to Mr Hughes. I knew nothing of this and was therefore mystified when, the next afternoon, I was told not to change for soccer and to wait in the library. Eventually I was summoned from the library to the Hughes's private drawing-room, where I found Uncle Philip seated by the fire and Mr Hughes standing by the french windows. Tea was laid out on a tray on a table.

'Your uncle is here. He'll explain to you why,' Mr Hughes said. Since I had already been greeted by my uncle, the information that he was there might have been regarded as superfluous. 'I'll leave you to it,' Mr Hughes then said to my uncle before quitting the room.

Uncle Philip was clearly embarrassed. He showed me the letter. Had I written it? I acknowledged that I had.

Uncle Philip cleared his throat. It was not the sort of letter that one man, er, one boy wrote to another. It was, well, an unmanly sort of letter. It would be better if I didn't write that sort of letter again.

'But Uncle Philip, I wrote it *as a joke!*'

'As a joke?' He clearly did not believe me. 'Well, if it was a joke, it was a very silly sort of joke.'

I think it greatly to Uncle Philip's credit that he all too clearly felt that Mr Hughes was making far too much fuss about little. Why on earth, he was probably saying to himself, could Hughes not have dealt with something so trivial himself, instead of forcing a man with only one leg and no car to make the troublesome journey from Barons Court to Banstead?

I myself remained bewildered and smarting from a sense of injustice.

Uncle Philip left after he and I had demolished the sandwiches and most of the cake. Neither Mr Hughes nor any master ever referred to the subject of the letter. But I noticed that Cleary was now embarrassed in my company and tended to avoid me. Presumably he had been warned.


One Christmas holidays the relatives were, for some reason never explained to us, unable to have my sister Pamela and myself, and we were therefore despatched to friends of my parents in Eastbourne. Before his retirement, Sir Robert Dodd, kindly and upright, had been my father's superior in the Indian Police, of which he had been Director-General in the United Provinces. Gertie Dodd was equally kindly and even more upright; but she was the first person in my life to teach me the lesson that to be kindly and to be generous are two wholly different things. Although she and her husband lived in a comfortable Edwardian mansion, now demolished to make room for a block of flats, on a comfortable income, she was extremely careful about money. So it was that, in the run-up to Christmas, she made my sister and me trail all over Eastbourne, delivering the Dodds' cards by hand, in order to save postage. The fact that Sir Robert Dodd was President of the local Conservative Association meant that there were a huge number of these. 'Oh, let's just chuck this lot away,' I eventually said, footsore and exhausted, to Pamela. But she was more conscientious than I. 'Oh, we can't possibly do that,' she retorted. 'No one will know,' I argued. 'That's not the point,' she said primly.

Gertie Dodd told us and the other remittance children that all Christmas presents must be bought at Woolworths – where, in those days, nothing cost more than sixpence. We thought that this ordinance applied only to ourselves. But on Christmas morning it was clear that the Christmas presents given to us by the Dodds had also been bought at Woolworths.

Gertie Dodd was proud of her economical housekeeping. A standing joke among us children was her 'stewed breast' – a dish which I had never before encountered and which, I am glad to say, I have never encountered since. She was also religious in the Victorian manner, so that we always dreaded Sundays, being obliged to go twice to church, morning and evening, and being forbidden to play the piano or cards and to read anything other than the Bible.

Food was so scant that Pamela and I used often to slip into a Lyons for a Welsh rabbit, a spaghetti on toast or a cake, when sent on some errand. What we did not realize was that this Lyons, with its plate glass windows through which we were all too visible, was situated opposite the solicitors' office in which the Dodds' only son, John, was employed. One day, as we were getting up from an even more exiguous luncheon than usual, he whispered to Pamela, 'Lucky you and Francis had that large elevenses.' For a moment Pamela was terrified that he was going to report us to his mother. But then he gave her a conspiratorial wink.

During these holidays I suffered from a hacking cough, from time to time bringing up sputum streaked with blood. A doctor friend, to whom many years later I told this, thought that I had probably been suffering briefly from my father's tuberculosis. This would account for scar tissue found in adulthood on my lungs. The Dodds did not notice the cough; and I should not have dreamed of complaining of it to them.

The death of my father coincided, as I have related, with my first term at Shrewbury. With the return of my mother to England, I ceased to be a remittance child. Having for four years been given some harsh, if salutary, lessons in self-reliance, I was now to be over-protected by a woman who can truthfully be said to have lived all her life for others.

# — 3 —

## *Living for Others*

Believing herself to be pregnant in 1890, my maternal grandmother consulted the sole English doctor in Gorakhpore. He told her that she must have an immediate operation: she had a growth in the womb. My grandmother refused to accept this diagnosis and secretly – not even my grandfather was aware of what she was doing – consulted an Indian doctor. At that time, for an Englishwoman to submit to an examination of any kind, let alone one so intimate, at the hands of an Indian doctor was highly unusual. The Indian doctor confirmed that she was indeed pregnant. Despite the English doctor's and my grandfather's warnings and pleadings, my grandmother then adamantly refused the operation. The Indian doctor continued to visit her, unbeknown to anyone in the household except a trusted ayah. When my mother was born prematurely, she was so tiny that she was first placed in one of my father's cigar-boxes, filled with cotton wool. Because her birth had been the result of my grandmother's faith in God and the Indian doctor, Faith became her name.

My mother's hair was blonde, her skin fair, her eyes blue. An Army officer to whom she was for a time engaged before becoming engaged to my father, described her to me, reminiscing sentimentally in his and her old age, as 'a Brunnhilde of a woman'. All her children had a similar colouring, as did her youngest brother, Uncle Philip, and his son, Peter; but her older siblings and their children were all olive-skinned and dark-haired. For this genetic discrepancy, my father had an explanation which outraged my mother. It went as follows.

My Read grandfather's father had been a captain in the Royal Navy. In a moment of rage, he had hurled a rating overboard, and had been cashiered. He had then taken himself off to India, to become a pilot on the Hooghly, a river notoriously perilous to navigate. In Calcutta he met and married a woman reported to have been Portuguese. 'Portuguese' was a euphemism often used in India in those days for a person of mixed race, particularly one from Goa. That so many of my great-grandfather's descendants should have been dark was therefore, according to my father, hardly surprising.

But how was one to explain the blondness of my grandfather's two youngest children and their children? Like my German grandmother, my English one married a man considerably older than herself, who – so family tradition has it –

had previously either married or lived with an Indian woman and had had a number of children by her. Having taken part in the Relief of Lucknow as a boy of seventeen – I possess the medal which he then won – my Read grandfather became a tea-planter. But things went badly for him and he was obliged to declare himself a bankrupt. My grandmother's father, a missionary in Gorakhpore, took pity on him, allowed him to live in a tent in his garden, and virtually provided for him, while he studied for the bar. So it came about that my grandmother married him.

Near the end of my grandfather's life, one of his closest friends was a handsome, blond Englishman, employed in the Opium Department but also involved in business – two of his family's enterprises were the once luxurious but now sadly run-down Savoy Hotel in Simla and Carlton Hotel in Lucknow – called Charles Lincoln. He became my mother's godfather; and after the death of my grandfather, he became her stepfather. That he was also her real father, and the father of my Uncle Philip, was my own father's contention. But if my father ever put forward this theory, my mother would cry out in dismay, as she continued to do, up to the time of her death, whenever I put it forward, 'No, no, no! My mother was a thoroughly *good* woman! She loved my father! She would never have had an affair! Never, never!'

My Read grandmother died prematurely in her forties, unlucky in an Indian doctor as she had once been lucky in one. When she was taken ill on a journey, this second doctor, suspecting that she had had a mild heart-attack, injected her with what he thought was camphor but what was in fact morphia. She went into a coma, from which she never emerged. 'Gotty', as my mother called her stepfather (or father) survived for many years. When, in his old age, he was dying, my parents travelled to Gorakhpore to be with him. To their horror, they discovered that he was sharing his bedroom with the Indian nurse – 'She was absolutely *hideous*,' my mother used to say – engaged to look after him; and it was to her that, after his death, he left what little remained of what had once been a sizeable fortune. That he had often told my parents that he was leaving everything to my oldest sister, Anne, may have had something to do with my mother's untypically harsh verdict on the Indian nurse.

My mother and her siblings were all educated in India, the boys at one of those schools, then common throughout the Empire, which were scrupulously modelled on public schools 'back home', and the girls by a succession of ill-qualified but much-loved governesses. Since my mother and my Aunt Hetty had no marked intellectual gifts, they did not suffer. They learned to read and to write lucidly and grammatically in the bold hand which my mother retained into her hundredth and second year; to keep domestic accounts and to be agile at mental arithmetic; to play the piano, sing, knit, sew, embroider, cook sweets and cakes. It was my Aunt Amie, oldest of the girls, who would have benefited from an education less narrow and more rigorous. She was a woman of masterful intelligence who, born in a different place and at a different time, might well have become a doctor, a don or a businesswoman. To this frustration and the frustration of being married to a sweet-natured, scholarly, withdrawn railway engineer in India, never happier than when hunched over an Everyman volume, I ascribe her seventy or so years of energetic valetudinarianism.

In both senses Aunt Amie had a heart. Like my mother, she was quick to come to the aid of anyone in need or distress; and she was constantly complaining, hand pressed to breast-bone and head on one side as though straining to listen to a beat which she feared might at any moment stop for ever, of the 'agony' (she never used the word pain) that she was suffering. 'Be a dear, run upstairs and fetch my pills,' she would gasp to one or other of us children. When the two sisters were together, my mother was unremitting in her attention to Aunt Amie: she should be careful of the stairs, of draughts, of getting herself excited, of doing too much. For some years, in the immediate aftermath of the war, Aunt Amie and Uncle Billy lived with my mother in her mansion flat in Iverna Court in Kensington. Selflessly my mother exerted herself to spare Aunt Amie's heart any exertion; but there were occasions when my mother's own usually capacious heart shrivelled with a resentment born of utter weariness, and one was then aware of the strain on her.

I adored Aunt Amie for the quickness of her intelligence, her shrewdness and her sense of fairness and of fun. In her prime, when she was known for her courage and skill as a side-saddle horsewoman, she looked like some imperious maharanee. In her old age, heavy-lidded eyes glinting with amused interest in a sallow, lined face, she might have been mistaken for an ancient ayah.

As a young girl, my mother underwent a strange experience. One of her young male cousins, to whom she was greatly attached, would travel over from a neighbouring town on his motor cycle to see her. One day, as she was waiting for him in her ground-floor bedroom, she turned at a sound at the open french windows. The blind blew up at a sudden gust of wind and there her cousin was standing, staring at her. His shirt was drenched in blood, his face was extraordinarily pale – 'waxen' is the word my mother would use, when telling the story. She ran to him, asking him what had happened. He vanished. By then hysterical, she sought out her mother, who consoled her: it must have been a dream. But soon the news came that the boy had been killed in an accident on his journey to the house.

The courage shown by my mother and other women in enduring the horrors and hardships of life in India before the First World War never ceases to amaze me. At a time of plague, orders were given that the stable block of the house in Gorakhpore must be burned down, since it was infested with plague rats. Innumerable rats, their fur blazing, staggered out of the block, to be beaten to death with sticks by the Indian servants. Fascinated, my mother looked on. Often she would accompany my father both on shoots – an excellent shot, he was in frequent demand to deal with man-eating tigers terrifying nearby villages – and on tours of duty which necessitated putting up in dak bungalows or even in tents. On one of these tours, my father had ridden off on his horse to visit some village in which there had been trouble, leaving my mother and my oldest sister, Anne, then a baby, in a tent with the bearer. News arrived that a bull from another, even closer village was on the rampage. It appeared before the tent, with a number of villagers keeping a wary distance behind it. The villagers were Hindus, the bearer was a Muslim. The bearer fetched one of my father's guns, loaded it, and aimed it at the bull. Horrified, angry cries erupted from the villagers. Fortunately, distracted, the bull then raced off in another direction. 'He would have killed the bull to save us,' my mother said. 'And the villagers would then have killed him. He knew that, of course.'

To survive such a life, without the present-day boons of antibiotics, anti-malarial drugs and air-conditioning, required toughness of both physique and spirit. My mother had that toughness, allied to a character of extraordinary sweetness and gentleness. In the manner of memsahibs of that time, she would constantly be attended by servants: planting shrubs in our garden in Naini Tal, she would stand over the gardener, instructing him to dig a hole, here, *here*, not there; bending over a primus stove to make for us children the divinity fudge which we so much loved, she would instruct the cook to beat the egg-whites and, later, grease the dish. But she would never snap or shout, as so many memsahibs did.

Because of constantly worrying about my father's health, anxiety became a habit with my mother. But throughout her life she never worried about herself, always about others, especially her children. Her natural assumption was not that the worst might never happen but that it usually did. Long ago I caught the contagion of this anxiety, at its most acute for me when I wake in the early hours and then, even in the coldest weather, break into a sweat as I review all the possibilities for disaster in the day ahead.

As I have already recounted, after the murder of my uncle, Billy Haycraft, his wife Olive and their two little sons, John then four and Colin then two, came to stay with us in Naini Tal for a few months before embarking for Europe, where they were to make their home with my grandmother. The news of Billy's death was carried to Olive, who was away in a hill station with her children, by the wife of his colonel, Mrs Trevelyan. Mrs Trevelyan was the mother of the writer Raleigh Trevelyan, who, by one of those coincidences so common in my life, eventually became a friend of mine long before we knew that we shared in the tragic story of the Haycrafts. In her old age Mrs Trevelyan once described to me the meeting with my aunt. 'Frankly I dreaded the task, absolutely dreaded it. I knew that she had Italian blood [in fact, of course, the foreign blood was German] and, as we all know, Italians can be so emotional, lacking all self-control, hysterical even. But when I and the wife of one of the other officers arrived, she knew, she *knew* already, before I had even opened my mouth. Quite calmly, she said, "It's Billy, isn't it? He's dead." I said, "Yes, dear. I'm afraid that's the news I've come to give you." And then I added, "Now have a good cry." '

Dazed by the tragedy, Olive spent much of her time lying out on the bed of one of the two rooms which my father and mother had put at her disposal, either completing the crosswords in the weeks-old copies of *The Times* which reached my father by sea, or reading novels. Then, suddenly, she would jump off the bed,

change into tennis clothes and make her way to the tennis club or to some private
tennis-party. A tennis-player good enough to have played at Wimbledon and to
have taken a game off Suzanne Lenglen in a tournament in Nice, she deployed her
strokes with a skill and ferocity which made her unbeatable in Naini. Of the two
children she took scarcely any notice, leaving them to the care of a slovenly and far
from clean bearer whom she had brought with her. Both boys began to look sickly
and emaciated. My mother, reluctant to interfere, would nonetheless sometimes
venture, 'Are the children all right?' Olive would reply that, yes, of course, they
were all right, the bearer was devoted to them.

Eventually my mother could stand aside no longer; and fortunately, when she
took charge, Olive showed no jealousy or resentment. Both boys were suffering
from dysentery – no doubt the result of the bearer constantly stuffing them with
Indian sweets from the bazaar. They were seldom bathed or even washed. The
English doctor told my mother that, by intervening, she had saved their lives.


After the death of my father, relatives and friends all wondered: How was Faith
going to manage? He had been so dominant in their marriage, taking all decisions;
and occasional visits apart, my mother knew little of England. In the event, she
surprised everyone by her capability.

At the time of my father's death in Ratlam, my two older sisters, Anne and
Pamela, were with my mother. Anne, with no wish to set about undergoing a
training or getting a job, opted to stay on in India, clearly with not merely the
hope but also the determination of finding a husband. This she soon did,
marrying an Indian Army officer, George Short, not unlike Errol Flynn in looks,
physique and specious charm. Pamela returned to England with my mother.

At a period when people in London usually rented, not bought, flats and even
houses, and so were far more mobile than now, my mother found a capacious
maisonette at the top of 72 Redcliffe Gardens in Earl's Court. Having furnished
it, she then set about learning how to run it without any domestic help except that
of a charwoman. Since money was short, she became an economical shopper. She
had always been a excellent maker of sweets, biscuits and cakes. Now, without any
instruction other than from books, she became an excellent maker of stews,
curries, pies, puddings. I wrote of this courageous adaptation to a new life in what
I consider to be one of my best novels, *The Widow*. The book was intended as a
tribute to my mother; and so it has appeared to everyone but her. She hated the
book on its publication; she continued to hate it up to the time of her death. Why?
I have decided that, to someone of her generation, any revelations of the privacies
of family life are likely to be abhorrent. The writing of the book was the only
major grudge that she ever held against me.

Soon after the marriage of my sister, we had an unexpected visitor. Jaunty,
moustached, and lacking all but one of his front teeth, he announced that he had
just returned from India, where he had attended my sister's wedding. She had
asked him to look us up. My mother, who had profoundly regretted not having

been able to be at the wedding herself, was eager in her questioning. How had Anne looked? Was George as handsome as everyone reported? Were there many people at the reception? To all such questions, our visitor was disappointingly vague. But he was far from vague about himself. He had had to visit India on business. He was owner of a firm, well, a bank really, which had branches all over the world. He had flown back from India, that was why he had arrived so soon after the wedding. Yes, it *was* a terribly expensive form of travel, but for a man like himself time was all-important. He then went on to explain the absence of all his upper front teeth but one: he had broken his plate and his Harley Street man was unfortunately away on holiday.

After he had drunk a number of cups of tea and eaten a number of sandwiches and cakes, he asked my mother if he could have something a little stronger – he was still exhausted after his journey and needed a pick-me-up before going on to a dinner given by the Lord Mayor at the Mansion House. My mother, who seldom drank alcohol, apologized: 'I'm afraid that all I've got in the house is some sherry.' The sherry was cooking sherry. Our visitor looked far from pleased with it, but he nonetheless drank one glass and then another.

He was in a bit of a fix, he then announced. He had foolishly forgotten to cash a cheque before the banks closed and now he found that he had not got 'the wherewithal' to pay for a taxi to the City and to meet the other expenses of the evening. Could my mother perhaps cash a cheque for him? My mother, gullible right up the close of her life, harboured no suspicions; but she genuinely had no money in the house. I then volunteered ten shillings. 'Well, every little helps,' our visitor said, in what struck me as a rather grudging and ungrateful manner. 'Not worth writing you a cheque for that,' he went on. 'But I'll return it to you tomorrow when, as I hope, you'll all let me drive you in my Rolls down to Brighton for a day by the sea.' None of us speculated as to why he should require a taxi to take him to the Mansion House if he possessed a Rolls; nor as to why he was wearing a check suit and not tails or at least a dinner-jacket at a time when everyone dressed for a formal dinner.

Leaving, he suddenly said 'Oh, I wish I had my camera with me! It's such a beautiful evening and I should love to take some snaps of the Thames, the Mansion House and so forth. I suppose you don't have a camera, do you?' he asked my mother. My mother said that no, she hadn't, but that I had. At that period I had thoughts of a career in photography, and my mother, prone to impulsive fits of extravagance where her children were concerned, had bought me an extremely expensive German camera, a Reflex Korelle. 'Oh, could I borrow it? Could I?' our visitor asked. 'I'll bring it back tomorrow.' 'Of course! I've just put in a new film.' 'Oh, splendid!'

Needless to say, we never saw our visitor again. On the following day we waited for his Rolls to arrive to take us to Brighton; and then we speculated that perhaps he had had an accident. Finally, at the urging of my Uncle John, we went to the police. 'The classic con!' a bored detective told us. 'You were lucky not to lose more than ten shillings and a camera.'

But I did not lose the camera. My cousin, Derek, son of Aunt Amie and Uncle Billy and a naval cadet at Dartmouth, was spending his holidays with us, a remittance child as I once had been. He and I were wandering through the streets of London, as we often did, when, in the window of a second-hand camera store in Knightsbridge, he spotted a Reflex Korelle. The make was an extremely rare one in England. I was sure that it was mine. Boldly, we went in to ask who had sold it to them. The salesman consulted a ledger. 'A Mr Francis King of 72 Redcliffe Gardens.'

Even for a confidence trickster, the trick seemed particularly mean. The police surmised that our visitor must have read the announcement of my sister's wedding in *The Times* and that the fact that she was there described as 'the daughter of the late E.A.C. King' must have emboldened him. After all, a widow was likely to be far more credulous than a man in the Indian Police. He had then thought nothing of robbing a fifteen-year-old boy of his camera and meagre savings.

We were still in Redcliffe Gardens during the Battle of Britain. My two sisters, my cousin Derek and his sister Daphne, and I would climb up on to the roof to watch the planes passing overhead on those sunlit evenings of high summer. 'Oh, look! Look! Look at that fire over there!' With the heedlessness of youth, we never thought that, if there was a fire, people must have died in it, might indeed be dying in it at that very moment. 'Beautiful!' Then my mother's head would appear at the top of the staircase that led up on to the roof. 'Come down! Come down at once! Are you absolutely crazy? Do you want to be killed?' But we never believed for a moment that we could be killed. We believed ourselves immortal.

Because the flat in Redcliffe Gardens was so vulnerable to bombs, my mother eventually moved us to another, with an extensive air-raid shelter in the basement, in Iverna Court, where she was to remain for twenty or so more years. Normally so large a flat in so elegant a block, just off Kensington High Street, would have been beyond her means; but rents were tumbling as people fled the city for the country. Amazingly, at that period when men were being called up and labour was short, the block still had day and night porters.

The war brought out the best in my mother, as it brought out the best in so many people, though not in myself. Her ample figure swathed in widow's black, with a black hat on her head, she would sally forth each morning in the quest for food. In Earl's Court Road there was a fishmonger who would always have something under the counter for her. The only trouble was that, before stooping and handing over the parcel, he would put a hand, stinking of fish, up to my mother's cheek, to stroke it, or up to her chin, to pinch it. 'Well, how is my sweetheart today?' he would ask. My mother, a fastidious woman, would try not to recoil, for fear of endangering the supply of fish. On hearing that there was a consignment of this or that rarity far away from Kensington, she would valorously set forth by bus or tube to join the long queue. We children accepted this ceaseless endeavour on our behalf, in the manner of children. We never ourselves thought to join any queue, unless it was for a National Gallery concert, for pit or gallery theatre seats, or for the ninepennies at the local cinemas.

Scarcely a night passed when there was not some guest – a relative, a friend, a casual acquaintance – sleeping on the couch in the sitting-room, on a folding bed in the hall, on a mattress in the corridor. Often these guests had to rise extremely early to get back to camp. My mother, in dressing-gown and hairnet, would rise even earlier than they, to prepare them breakfast. In later years, she would sometimes speak with bitterness of some of these people: they had totally forgotten her; they never even bothered to send her a Christmas card, let alone look her up.

When the bombing was at its worst, during the summer holidays, my Uncle John persuaded my mother to take us into the country. So began one of the weirdest interludes of my life. Aunt May, one of my father's sisters, a woman as close to being a saint as any person I have ever known, had become patient of the psychiatrist Graham Howe, a man of towering will, who for many years to come was to hold her in submissive thrall, now encouraging her and now humiliating her, and constantly using her as unpaid secretary and servant. Howe had a 'community' at Langley Rise, King's Langley, where his patients, largely housed in wooden huts erected around the main building, sought escape both from the bombs and from their neuroses. Aunt May arranged for us to be accommodated here.

I was fascinated by the other inmates: among them an imperious German Jewish refugee, from a once wealthy family, who keenly felt the humiliation of being obliged to do domestic work in order to earn her keep; an elderly man, Mr Stevenson, with the face of an angel and the mind of a child of five, who would try to scramble into my mother's lap in order to sit there; the manic-depressive wife of a famous economist, who eventually abandoned her, sickened by riding the switchback of her moods; and a horde of elderly, well-to-do women, one of whom, as soon as the air-raid siren sounded, would scream, 'The bom*b*ers are coming! The bom*b*ers are coming!' (the b as explosive as any bomb) before retreating under her bed, her head wedged into a tin chamber-pot for protection.

We shared in the daily lessons in relaxation which, at that time when most of the population of the British Isles were bracing themselves to make an even more strenuous contribution to the war, were a part of Howe's treatment. 'I want you to imagine that your left hand is totally dead,' one of Howe's female assistants would instruct us. 'Totally dead!' She would stoop and lift up my hand. This hand isn't dead,' she would announce contemptuously. 'It's *stiff*.' Throughout my life I have never been able to relax. An elderly woman would emit a loud fart. 'Oh, I'm sorry! I *am* sorry!' 'Nothing to be sorry about, nothing at all, dear. Never hold it in! Let it all out! Much better for you!' Repeated farts would follow this instruction, with repressed giggles making it even more difficult for me to relax.

I noticed how these neurotic and sometimes even demented women would be drawn to my mother, as they would not be drawn to Aunt May, despite all her concern for them. A prey herself to irrational anxiety, of which she never spoke and which she bore with admirable stoicism, Aunt May was too like them for them to look to her for consolation. But my mother, so serene, so sane, so understanding, so kind, always seemed able to calm and reassure them. When bombs fell near, it was interesting to observe how many of them would cluster round her, as though they believed that, in her orbit, nothing bad could befall them. Their behaviour was merely a variant of elderly Mr Stevenson's attempts to clamber into her lap for safety and comfort.

In later years, people who were mortally ill would often ask for my mother to sit with them. Many of these people had never been particularly close to her in their years of health. Merely by holding their hands and saying the most banal things to them, she had the ability to reconcile them to their fate and so to bring them peace.

At no time could my mother have been described as in any way domineering; but her eagerness to submit herself to our wills, to sacrifice herself for us, to do what we wanted and not what she wanted, paradoxically gave her a formidable authority. Submission, I have seen throughout my life, can be as much a source of power as self-assertion; and it can be quite as destructive. One example will suffice. When I was working as a pacifist on the land in the Surrey village of Chelsham, my mother visited me on a particularly raw day. In the tiny room which I inhabited in the lodge cottage of the mother of the remarkable woman who, in the absence of her husband on military service, was running the farm, she shivered. 'This room is *freezing*. Haven't you got a stove?'

I replied that there was a fire in the sitting-room next door and that the heat came through the wall.

'Well, no heat's coming through now!'

When my mother next visited me, two or three weeks later, she brought down with her an oil-stove, which she had bought second-hand through an advertisement in the *Exchange and Mart*. She had lugged it down to Victoria Station; she had lugged it off and on the train to East Croydon; she had lugged it on to the bus to Chelsham; she had lugged it down the muddy lane to the cottage. Other mothers might merely have said, 'Why don't you get yourself an oil-stove?'; or, having bought the stove, have told their sons, 'There's a stove here for you. You could take it back with you when next you come up.' (Almost every weekend I travelled up to London.) That was not my mother's way.

It was good for me to have the oil-stove, as I sat, early in the morning or late in the evening, working at a novel; but the manner in which it had come to me was bad for me. Each such sacrifice was a silken cord to bind me even closer to my mother. It was because of this feeling that her love had the power to emasculate me and even destroy me that, once I had finished at Oxford, I opted to join the British Council and so go abroad. My love for her has been, with one exception, the deepest I have ever experienced; but it has provided me with as much unease as comfort.

During a year of unpaid leave which I had taken from the British Council after winning the Somerset Maugham Award, I was staying with my mother in her flat in Iverna Court. As she took my clothes to the cleaner, mended my socks, booked me theatre seats, bought me the *Spectator*, *New Statesman* and *Times Literary Supplement* when she went out shopping on Friday morning, urged me to inhale if I had a cold or take an aspirin if I had a headache, I suddenly thought, 'I must get away from this!' I went out and at once rented a one-room furnished flat in Campden Street, not far from where I live now. She was deeply hurt: 'Aren't you happy here? Did I do something wrong?' It was impossible to explain to her that she had done nothing wrong, she had merely done far too much that was right.

In similar fashion she constantly sacrificed herself for my sisters. In turn, two of them, Pamela and Elizabeth, have constantly sacrificed themselves for their daughters. Like the abuse of children, the spoiling of children is passed on in families.

Sometimes my mother's excessive protectiveness of her children had its comic side. Once, when she was staying with me in Brighton – I was then in my forties – I was preparing tea in the kitchen for her and the three women friends with whom she was playing afternoon bridge. Through the hatch, I suddenly heard a snatch of conversation.

'Where on earth does Francis get the material for his novels?' one of the women asked in a clearly needling voice. 'Some of it seems so – so *sordid*.'

'From the newspapers, of course,' my mother retorted firmly.

On another occasion, on April Fool's Day – I was then in Japan, working for the British Council – Uncle John, an inveterate practical joker, put his actress daughter Sylvia up to telephoning my mother. In a West Indian accent, Sylvia announced herself as 'the close lady friend of your son Francis'. She then went on to declare that she had that very day been delivered of a child by me – 'a beautiful boy'.

'Out of the question! I refuse to believe it!' My mother was indignant. Then, triumphantly, she declared, 'Francis has been abroad in Japan for the last *ten* months.'

In the absence both of myself, working abroad, and of my sister Pamela, now married, my mother kept her flat constantly filled with people in need of a temporary home. Such people either paid her nothing or far too little. Then, not long after the marriage of my sister Elizabeth to the American writer and television producer John Rosenberg, my mother did an extraordinary thing. First, she gave up the flat. Then she took a post as companion to an elderly Jewish woman.

At the time I was extremely embarrassed that, in her sixties, she should go out to work for the first time in her life. 'I hear your mother's gone into domestic service,' the ophthalmologist Pat Trevor-Roper said to me disapprovingly. 'Surely you have enough money to save her from *that*?' I should have willingly saved her; but she did not want to be saved. To be an employee was an experience which, for some reason, she wanted. The elderly Jewish woman treated her like a friend; the elderly Jewish woman's daughter and son-in-law treated her like a servant. 'Why on earth did you do it?' I often asked her in later years. 'You didn't need the money. You had a horrid time.' 'Well, I felt I had to,' or 'Oh, I don't know,' were the only replies she ever gave. The compulsion was as mysterious to her as to me.

After two years of this work, she made her home now with my sister Elizabeth and her husband in Battersea and now with my sister Anne and her husband in Alderley Edge. When I returned prematurely from the British Council in the mid-Sixties in order to devote myself entirely to writing, she also spent a third of her time with me in Brighton. Her two sons-in-laws were devoted to her and she loved them; but whereas my sister Elizabeth showed her nothing but kindness, Anne, sadly, was sometimes cruel.

Anne might be said to have been singularly fortunate in the hand which fate had dealt to her: she had been born both intelligent and beautiful; she had been educated at a famous international school, where she had made many lifelong friends; she had married a handsome, charming man, who moved on from the Indian Army to ICI and thence to the United Nations, earning higher and higher salaries; she had a sweet-natured and pretty daughter and eventually three no less sweet-natured and pretty granddaughters. But she was one of those people addicted to that most sterile of occupations, blaming. For such people, life is an endless If only. If only she had not been 'abandoned' by our parents with those 'dreadful' relatives; if only my mother had demonstrated her love for her by travelling out to India to be at her bedside when she was 'hovering close to death' (in fact, she had merely had a severe reaction to an anti-tetanus injection); if only her twin boys had not died, one at birth and another a few months after; if only her husband George were more understanding of her; if only ... If only, I used often to think, there could be some end to this self-pity.

In addition to being a constant blamer, she was also an avid grievance-collector. Unfortunately, grievance-collecting, as sterile an occupation as blaming, has been something all too common among the Read members of my family, with even my mother indulging in it. 'It really is quite extraordinary that Aunt Lucille should have forgotten my birthday ...' 'Rosemary has stayed with us for almost ten days and never once has she taken us out to dinner ...' 'The Wrights gave a party to celebrate their Silver Wedding but, to our amazement, we were not invited. When I think of how, when Jennifer Wright was ill, I used to drive those brats of hers to school day after day ...' Anne's letters and conversation were full of such remarks.

Anne had an effulgent charm, so that a Greek homosexual, Thanos Veloudios, who, at a brief meeting in Athens in the Fifties, had complimented her, 'You are even more attractive than your brother,' asked me for news of her forty years later. She could also be extraordinarily kind, if the spirit took her. But she was full of sudden jealousies, resentments, rejections. Constantly she complained that this or that relative or close friend had 'behaved unforgivably'.

What she never saw was that her own behaviour could often be unforgivable. In a fury with my mother because of some trivial remark, she pummelled her so hard, as she was walking ahead of her up the staircase, that the doctor had to be summoned. Loyally, my mother pretended to the doctor that she had had a fall down the stairs; but the bruises were such that the doctor all too plainly disbelieved her. On another occasion, I had invited Aunt Hetty, convalescing from a mastectomy for the cancer which was eventually to kill her, to stay with my mother in my Brighton house while I was abroad on a British Council lecture tour. Anne then invited herself to stay in the house at the same time. Having arrived, she had one of those *crises de nerfs* which were becoming increasingly common in her life. She could not have Aunt Hetty around, she upset her, she made her nerves even worse. My mother must get rid of her. This, with that compliancy which she always showed when her children demanded anything, however unreasonable, of her, my mother did. I could never really forgive Anne for this cruelty to an elderly and sick woman. At Anne's funeral, I suddenly found myself brooding on it.

After his retirement from the United Nations – the job had taken the couple to Mexico, where Anne was probably happier than at any other time in her life – they settled for a time in Bexhill, why I could never conceive. Then, understandably bored, they emigrated to Spain. Anne hated the gin-and-bridge existence of the expatriate community around Alicante; George was content. When he refused to make another move, she threw what were, in effect, the tantrums of a spoiled child, but on such a scale that George reported a breakdown to us. A Spanish doctor put her on tranquillizers, which George – who had started life as a veterinary surgeon – would administer to her, by injection, in increasingly large doses. When she had a premature stroke, the specialist in England thought that it was these massive doses which had precipitated it.

Her last years were spent in a succession of expensive but dreary nursing-homes, which she seemed to have no wish to leave. She never spoke of George unless one mentioned him first; and on the occasions when she did so, it was as though she were talking of a stranger. She who had once been so elegant and taken so much care of her appearance, squandering money on designer clothes, expensive jewellery, Mayfair hairdressers and beauticians, now sat slumped in front of a television set, in the company of the other pathetic inmates of the home, her greying hair straight, a fuzz of down on her face, her once expertly capped front teeth discoloured, her face totally devoid of make-up. When she was taken shopping for clothes, she showed no interest, accepting whatever was chosen for her off a peg in Marks & Spencer's or C. & A. Someone once so worldly had become totally unworldly. Perhaps at another time people would have thought a woman so ascetic a saint. If, as the psychiatrist had told her, she had suffered from guilt, then she must finally have expiated it in those last terrible years.

Anne posed and still poses for me a problem which is often in my mind. Her final mental illness seemed to me to be merely an extension of the self-absorption which she had displayed throughout her life, as though some small growth had swollen to monstrously malignant proportions. If the final mental illness were not her fault, then could one with justice say that the self-absorption had been? Perhaps it had merely been the first symptom of the later illness. But if one were to exonerate her from any blame for that self-absorption, then should one not exonerate, as equally sick, people who were dishonest or violent or cruel?

Aunt May's neuroses never seemed to have their origins in the same pathological self-absorption. She always made light of her irrational terrors; she was even reluctant to talk about them. She was constantly concerned for the happiness of others, never for her own. Her sister Lucille once said of her to me, 'She's a terrible neurotic'; but, so untypical was she of neurotics, trapped in the increasingly restricted universe of self, that I always felt that some other word should be used to describe her.

My mother remained active into her late eighties – washing up and preparing vegetables for my sister, ironing my brother-in-law's shirts, keeping up a voluminous correspondence. As I helped her on to a 49 bus after a visit to me, she remarked loudly of a woman who, rubber-ferruled stick in hand, was struggling to board, 'Poor dear! She shouldn't be travelling on public transport at her age.' The woman must have been at least twenty years her junior.

Until she reached old age, my mother had been subject to sudden darkenings of mood, such as I myself still experience. This kindest of women would suddenly come out with bitter and cruel things. Of someone whom she had appeared to love, she would amaze me by exclaiming for no apparent reason, 'Oh, I'm fed up with him!', or 'She's such a little fool,' or 'No, I do *not* want to see her when she comes round.' It was as though some devil had entered her.

In her later years these moments of demonic possession became rarer and rarer. Then they virtually ceased. She appeared to look out on life, through eyes undimmed by age, with a tolerant, ever kindly stoicism. Even after deafness had incarcerated her in a tower of virtual silence, her serenity remained.

When she was ninety-nine, my mother and I appeared in *The Sunday Times* in their feature 'Relative Values'. My mother spoke to the interviewer, Michael Leech, with extraordinary clarity, her memory undimmed. Later, when the paper sent a young man to photograph us, she instructed him, 'I don't want you to photograph my legs. Please remember that. When I was a girl, I had what people thought very attractive legs. But now they're swollen.'

'Don't worry,' I assured her. 'I'll put a shawl over them.'

'Certainly not!' she protested. 'If you do that, people will think me an old woman.'

She was far vainer at ninety-nine than she had been at half that age.

As I near seventy, my memory is beginning to fail, especially for names. Even in her hundred-and-third year my mother never had that problem. 'Have you remembered to send Cousin Sylvia a birthday card? It's her birthday tomorrow.' I would have totally forgotten.

My mother was devoted to David, as he was to her. I never spoke to her of the exact nature of my relationship with him, any more than I ever spoke to her of my homosexuality. She certainly knew about both; but I felt sure that she would prefer them to remain unstated. It was my sister Elizabeth who broke to her the news of his early death. At once my mother began to wail, rocking her body back and forth in her chair – like an Irish peasant woman, Elizabeth described it. 'Stop that!' Elizabeth commanded. 'You're not helping anyone.'

'Yes, I am. I'm helping myself.'

It was one of the few occasions when my mother opted to help herself, rather than others.


Had my mother died on her hundred-and-first birthday, her life, despite the tragedy of my father's premature death and all her subsequent tribulations, could have been regarded as enviable. Unfortunately, so blind that she could no longer read and so deaf that she could no longer listen to television or wireless, she continued to live on in increasing misery and – worse than misery – boredom.

One day when I visited her in Elizabeth's house in Sydney Street, she told me that she had embarked on the writing of a novel. 'It's to be called *The Bedsitter.*'

'But you've never lived in a bedsitter.'

'What am I doing now? I never leave this room.'

By then she had been all but totally immobilized by a fall. Elizabeth gallantly nursed her, as she had gallantly nursed her husband through his last terrible illness. Then, herself in far from robust health, she was increasingly obliged to rely on nurses. As my mother grew even frailer, these nurses balked at transferring her, single-handed, from bed to chair or commode and then back again. There must be two of them, they insisted. Since, financially, this was out of the question, Elizabeth and I eventually reached the reluctant conclusion – a source of guilt to both of us – that we must put her into a nursing home. This was the one thing that she had begged us never to do.

Fortunately, when we told her of our decision, she took it with resigned fatalism. The matron of the home, St George's in Pimlico, told us that when people so old were transferred there, one of two things happened: either they died in a short space of time or they improved. My mother improved.

Even before she had entered the home, she had got into the habit of telling me at each of my visits, 'I want to die. Why can't I die? I've had enough.' On one occasion she even begged me, 'Please tell the doctor to give me an injection!'

I said that I could not possibly do that.

'Well, ring the vet then!'

When I told a friend of mine, a retired cancer specialist, of this constantly expressed wish for release from a life that had become utterly tedious, he advised me to leave some pills and a bottle of whisky by her bedside. But even if I could have done such a thing without any fear of prosecution, some atavistic scruple would have held me back.

On the day after my mother's admission to St George's, the senior sister told me, 'I'm afraid that her mind must have become disturbed. All last night, she was calling to her father to take her away. She must have reverted to her childhood.'

I explained that my mother, a religious woman, was calling not to her earthly father but to her heavenly one. It surprised me that the sister, Irish and therefore presumably Roman Catholic, had not realized this.

Just as I visited David every day while he was dying in Charing Cross, so now I visited my mother every day at St George's. As at Charing Cross, I was constantly impressed by the efficiency, kindness and cheerfulness of the staff, and yet could never enter the doors without a darkening and deadening of the spirit. My mother's fate struck me as piteously similar to that of the Struldbrugs in *Gulliver's Travels*: people who wish only to die and who are denied that wish.

Seated in the hall on most evenings, there was a still beautiful and elegant octogenarian. When I entered and said good-evening to her, she smiled eagerly at me and sometimes half rose to her feet. This was Margaret Duchess of Argyll. The sister explained to me that her memory was now so faulty that she could not remember whether some friend or relative was coming to take her out to dinner or not; so she waited there each evening, in case that someone should arrive. Whether I was that someone was something which she also could not remember.

There was one satisfaction in visits otherwise so sad. For so many years my mother had lived for us, her children, not herself; and we had made so little return to her, often hardly acknowledging or even noticing all she did for us. Now, she was the child, ailing, bewildered, unhappy, and Elizabeth and I were the parents, coaxing, consoling, cosseting. When, during the rush hour, I fought my way into and off one overcrowded train and then another, on the journeys back and forth between Kensington and Pimlico, I used to remind myself of my mother's far more arduous journey with the oil-stove from Kensington to Chelsham during the war. When I pushed into her mouth the pulp brought to her for her luncheon or supper, cut the nails on fingers twisted with arthritis, or rubbed embrocation into her swollen, aching joints, I felt a sudden satisfaction. Strangely, on rare occasions, this satisfaction even blossomed into an unaccountable joy.

At eight o'clock on Christmas morning in 1992 Elizabeth and I were summoned to the nursing-home. My mother had gone into a coma. For much of that day we sat with her. Then, with her amazing powers of recuperation, she came out of the coma and even began to talk lucidly to us. The following day was a horrendous one. Unable to swallow and barely able to breathe, she kept asking us for water. In turn we placed swabs soaked in water between her parched lips and attempted to bring some peace to her by stroking her hands, her cheeks and her hair. Finally, in the early afternoon, she was at last granted her long-held wish. Even then, despite the rictus of her final struggle, she looked amazingly beautiful: the skin totally smooth, the features as unblurred as they would have been if a Canova or a Rodin had just finished carving them from marble.

I felt a terrible amazement, as well as a terrible anguish: 'How *can* she be dead?' I had imagined her to be immortal.


When I told her that I was writing this autobiography, my mother said, 'I wish to make one thing absolutely clear. I do not want to appear in it *at all*.' But how could

I write an autobiography without mentioning her? Was I to say that I had been a foundling?

She will now never read this book. But, were she able to do so, I hope that what I have written of her, with so much admiration, so much gratitude and so much love, would not upset her.

# — 4 —

## *Shrewsbury*

People often say to me, 'You must have loathed your years at Shrewsbury.' But, although a number of my contemporaries and near-contemporaries did so, I can truthfully answer, 'No, not at all.' In fact, on balance, I was happy. This is surprising, since so many of my immediate recollections of my life there are so grim.

One of these dates from my first term. At high tea, the new boys at School House were all seated together at a long table. When, in a huge, chipped enamel pie-dish, a particularly disgusting cottage pie, all gristle, fat and half-cooked potato and onion, was set down at one end, there were cries of 'Pooh! What a stink!', 'Chuck it away!' and 'I'm not going to eat that muck!' A boy tipped the contents of a salt-cellar into the pie. Other boys then began gleefully to add mustard, pepper, sugar, chunks of bread and, finally, all the water from a carafe.

At the end of the meal, a maid by then having sneaked on us, we were all summoned to the monitors' room, where the dusky, diminutive Head of House, Tony Chenevix-Trench – whose enthusiasm for beating boys was sustained into adult life and even into the not wholly successful period of his headmastership of Eton – was awaiting us. The enamel pie-dish was on the table before him. Fourteen spoons lay beside it. Having reprimanded us for our 'quite disgusting behaviour', he handed each of us a spoon. 'Now you can eat the mess you created. Eat! Eat! Go on, eat!' We ate. Then having selected the five chief miscreants for beating, he dismissed the rest of us. I at once rushed to the lavatories and was sick.

During that year when Chenevix-Trench was Head of House, I hated and dreaded him. He struck me as supercilious, capricious, cruel. But when, the war over, I met him again at Oxford, I came to admire his scholarship, his intelligence and his courage. He and I would often spend an afternoon walking around Christ Church Meadows. As the walk progressed, I noticed that, at first so voluble, he would eventually subside into an increasingly gloomy silence. Was he bored by my chatter? Then one day he said to me, 'I think we'd better find another walk.' He had just realized, he explained, that a circle of Christ Church Meadows was exactly commensurate with a circle of the camp in which he had spent so many hellish years as a prisoner of the Japanese. 'I used to walk round and round that camp, day after day, longing for my freedom and wondering if I'd ever survive.' We then chose other routes.

Another vivid memory of Shrewsbury is of the yelp of 'Doul!', derived from the Greek word *doulos* or slave, resonating down the stone corridors when some monitor wanted a fag to perform some service for him. There would be a clatter of feet as the douls rushed to form a queue. The last boy in the queue was the one to whom the service fell. If one was a private doul – an office for which it was necessary to be bright, pretty or both these things to qualify – then one was exonerated from this frenzied scurry. Eventually I myself was appointed private doul to a monitor called Bagott. Intellectually dim, extrovert, extremely handsome, a fine athlete, he was always kind and considerate to me, and I adored him. On leaving Shrewsbury, he went into the Army. On the eve of his marriage, he shot himself, no one knew why. Even now I often think of him, trying to puzzle out the enigma. With his blond hair, square face, reddish-gold complexion and muscular physique, he became the prototype of so many people who were instantly to attract me in the years to follow.

Other vivid memories are of the extreme cold of the stone passages and the dormitories, every window open, in the winter; of the male stench of the changing-rooms and the female stench of the maids, lumpish girls who seemed to have been chosen for employment on the negative criterion that they would put no temptation in the way of even the randiest schoolboy; and of the total lack of privacy, so that junior boys each morning scurried naked but for a towel round the waist to the showers, there was frequent recourse to chamber-pots during the night, and the privies lacked locks. Once on the door of one of these privies, I read 'King is the house tart.' It was totally untrue; I was far too prudish to have gained that distinction. But as I deciphered the scrawl, my emotions were a strange mixture of indignation and pleasure.

Despite all these discomforts, I was lucky in my house. Its housemaster, Hope-Simpson, a seemingly sexless bachelor interested in rowing, gardening, music and dogs, was more liberal than all but one of his colleagues. Even while I was in his house, he discontinued the tradition of monitors beating younger boys – often for offences no more serious than leaving on the light after quitting a room or failing to take a cold shower on getting out of bed. In many other houses, the beating was ferocious.

Shrewsbury then provided a classical education the equal of any in the country. Any boy who arrived, as I did, on a scholarship, was expected to go on to the classical side, whatever his natural inclination. One of the regrets of my life is that I never became a doctor, a career for which – to judge from my success in diagnosing the illnesses of my friends long before their own doctors have been able to do so – I have, perhaps mistakenly, always thought myself to have been suited. But I loved Greek and Latin, especially the writing of verses, and I was prepared to work assiduously at them, getting up at half-past five or six in the morning, before anyone else, in order to be able to go over the work of the day ahead in total quiet. I was top of each class in which I found myself, and won a variety of prizes – not merely for Classics, but for French, history, essay, poetry.

Looking back, I see that, in many ways, I must have been an insufferable boy:

priggish, prudish, conceited. Since I was physically no match for other boys, I took pains to hone my tongue. That, throughout my four years at Shrewsbury, I was never once beaten, is an indication of how goody-good I was. Until the beating by monitors was abolished, there were boys even in comparatively liberal School House who were repeatedly beaten in the course of a single term.

The great influence on me was a master, not of Classics but of science, called H.J. (Humphrey) Moore. Like so many, perhaps the majority, of truly influential masters, Moore was a pederast. There was never any impropriety in his behaviour to me or, I believe, to any other of his protégés; but he clearly preferred the company of one of his boys to the company of any adult, however attractive, intelligent or entertaining. To help his boys fulfil themselves, he would stint neither effort nor time.

Moore lived with two or three bachelor colleagues in a gloomy Edwardian house, surrounded by spindly evergreens. Along with a few other boys, I was free to go there at any time I wished. We would listen to records of Horowitz, a favourite of his – 'the greatest pianist in the world' – playing a Beethoven sonata on a wind-up EMI gramophone with a vast horn. We would have thrust at us an early volume of Auden's poetry. Moore would read to us some poem of his own. He would scrutinize my own writing, now saying eagerly, 'Yes, yes, that's *good*'; and now frowning, 'No, this is awful, really awful.' That was a period when I had a great love of Charlotte Mew, a poet for whom Moore could feel only scorn. When I wrote a poem very much in her style, about a prostitute praying to the Virgin in the gloom of Westminster Cathedral, he all but reduced me to tears by upbraiding me: 'This ghastly Mewing makes me want to *vomit!*'

If I ran into any of the other masters who occupied the house, I would get a hostile look.

'What are you doing here again?' one of them once asked me pointedly, as I entered at the moment when he was coming out.

'I've come to see Mr Moore, sir.'

'You're not on the science side, are you?'

'No, sir.'

'Well, I really don't see . . .' He did not finish the sentence as he hurried off down the drive.

I knew, innocent though I was then, that he thought that there was something disreputable taking place between Moore and me. But all that was taking place was the transfer of a love for literature, music and art from an adult to an adolescent.

After I had been at Shrewsbury for two years, Moore was called up and vanished. I should guess that, even if there had not been a war, he would have vanished in any case. He had confessed to me, with characteristic lack of discretion, that he thought the headmaster, H.H. Hardy, father of the actor Robert Hardy, 'a shit' and that Hardy in turn disapproved of him and would like to boot him out (his phrase). The war over, Moore did not return to Shrewsbury but went to Clayesmore, a public school not so highly regarded, where politically he swung further and further from the left to the right and where he continued to earn the love of his pupils and the distrust of at least some of his colleagues. To my regret we never again met. Why, I often ask myself, was I so ungrateful as never at least to write to him, to tell him how much my association with him had meant in my life? This is a question which I often ask myself when remembering those who were helpful or hospitable to me in my early years. It makes me excuse the seeming ingratitude of young people now similarly failing to thank me.

Curiously, Hardy had almost as profound an influence on me as Moore, and I admired him almost as much. In his tight-fitting dark suits, the trouser-legs extremely narrow, all three buttons of the jacket fastened, and a gold pince-nez dangling on a chain from a button of the waistcoat which he wore in even the hottest weather, Hardy managed to project two images simultaneously: that of the Army officer which he had been in the First World War (he always liked to be known as Major Hardy), and that of the clergyman which he might have been. Holding himself stiffly erect as though by a conscious effort of the will, so that even as an adult I felt a constant discomfort in looking up at him, he spoke in the clipped manner of someone who not merely demanded but expected to be obeyed. Every morning at seven forty-five he could be seen riding on a high bicycle in cap and gown from the vast house in which he lived across the cricket pitch to the school. As his nickname 'Hitler' will convey, masters and boys were equally frightened of him. But to me, as soon as I had entered the sixth form and so become one of his pupils, he showed a totally unexpected kindness and even gentleness.

I write 'unexpected' since one might have supposed that he would have heartily disapproved of a boy who was not merely such a muff at games but who had refused to join the Officers' Training Corps despite increasingly peremptory urgings. There was the further problem of what Chenevix-Trench had repeatedly derided as my 'girlish' manner. When, during my second year, two boys were caught misbehaving themselves together, they had not merely been praepostored i.e. savagely thrashed by the praepostors or school prefects, each in turn administering a stroke, but been threatened with expulsion. Hardy had then delivered what was in effect a sermon to the school. He did not, he announced, wish to preside over a school consisting of 'hobbledehoys skulking together nefariously in corners'. This phrase occasioned a lot of stifled giggling at the time and of subsequent hilarity. 'Are you a hobbledehoy?' we would ask each other; or 'Have you two been skulking together nefariously in a corner?' Yet Hardy, who might well have decided that I was a hobbledehoy, clearly approved of me.

I think that the reason for this approval was that, though in many ways so different, in some ways we were so alike. I have always been punctual and punctilious: the sort of person who answers letters as soon as he receives them; who submits a commissioned article weeks, and a commissioned book months, before they are due; who is driven to exasperation and even rage by any inefficiency. Friends often tell me that these traits are inherited from my German grandmother. Hardy could be equally Germanic.

Underneath all his stiffness, as under mine, there was also a romantic, yearning sensibility, which made him, like myself, a lover of the Victorian poets, especially Arnold, Tennyson and (to a lesser degree) Browning. I remember a Latin verse translation of 'Now sleeps the crimson petal, now the white' with which I won his particularly energetic approval – 'Well done! You've got it absolutely right! I love that poem!'

I also earned Hardy's approval by my proficiency in what we called Divvers. It was he who taught the Classical Sixth the New Testament in Greek, a subject which I genuinely loved. Because I not merely loved it but was also so successful at it, he came to the wholly erroneous conclusion that I was a staunch believer. This was a conviction not shared by a shrewd master, Frank Macarthy, later to be chaplain of Balliol when I returned there after the war, who once said to me, 'Christian doctrine might be the *Times* crossword for any spiritual involvement you have in it.'

Hardy, for all his forthright manner, was a subtle and sometimes even devious man. Shortly before I arrived at Shrewsbury, an Old Salopian, who had only just left the school, murdered his mother in Dublin. Hardy decided that any publicity would be extremely bad for Shrewsbury. Cajoling some editors and exerting pressure on others, he ensured that the case received virtually no mention at all in the press of the day. If it did receive mention, there was nothing to link the murderer with Shrewsbury.

The most impressive of my contemporaries was a boy from Belfast, called Bruce Williamson. He was a magnificent actor, giving a performance of Macbeth which I still remember in many of its now sombre and now fiery details. (I myself played Lady Macduff in clothes borrowed from my sister Pamela. The production was a modern dress one.) He was also a remarkable poet. He, another boy, Ian Grimble (later Librarian to the House of Lords), and I privately published a collection of poems, *Even for an Hour*, when we were fifteen. My own poems, impeccable in their scansion and rhymes, were precocious merely in their technical skill. Williamson's poems were precocious in the originality of their expression. I was convinced that he would become an actor as great as John Gielgud or a poet as great as Auden. In the event, he became a respected and much-liked journalist on the *Irish Times*, eventually being appointed senior deputy editor. He had decided not to go on the stage for the odd reason that his parents did not wish him to do so; and, as in the case of Peter Quennell, the adolescent flame of his poetic talent had soon guttered out.


During the holidays the war constantly impinged on my life: a bomb exploded noisily near the Lyric Theatre in Hammersmith, causing me to start up from my seat but not for a second interrupting the speech which Pamela Browne was delivering on the stage; when a V1 cut out over Kensington Gardens on a Sunday morning while my sister Elizabeth and I were walking there, we were reduced to derisive laughter by the spectacle of well-dressed church-goers flinging themselves down on to the ground; travelling on the tube in the evening, one picked one's way past humped sleepers, looking like piles of abandoned clothing. But despite stints of fire-watching, despite the deterioration in the already unpalatable food, despite afternoons of thinning sugar-beet on neighbouring farms, despite the reappearance on the staff of men long since retired, and despite the news, solemnly delivered by Hardy in chapel, that this or that old boy had been killed, Shrewsbury, mercifully spared any air-raids, remained a world largely sealed off from the horrors and heroic deeds going on around it.

The happiest hours of my last two years at Shrewsbury were spent in the Sixth Form Library, an attractive room overlooking the Severn. Since very few other people used it, here, mostly alone, I used to write Greek or Latin verses; read voraciously; and compose the poems which, now one of its editors, I used to publish under a variety of pseudonyms in the school magazine, *The Salopian*. When, eyes stinging or hand aching, I felt in need of a break, I used to sit on one of the window-seats and gaze down the green slope to the river far below. On late summer evenings, this slope would be dotted with couples, usually servicemen with their girls, body pressed again body, mouth glued to mouth. Then a feeling of desolation would come over me: an overwhelming melancholy at my own isolation and the isolation of most human beings for most of the time. I was to be possessed by this sense of isolation into middle-age. It is one of the dominant themes of my early novels, *The Dividing Stream* even being prefaced by Matthew Arnold's 'To Marguerite', with its opening lines:

> Yes! in the sea of life enisled,
> With echoing straits between us thrown,
> Dotting the shoreless watery wild,
> We mortal millions live *alone*.

To escape from the prison of this aloneness, work was the key. Whereas so many of my friends at Shrewsbury, even the cleverest, hated work, for me it was a source of comfort, even joy, and so it has remained into old age. At five-thirty in the morning, the house would be silent. Shivering against the winter cold in an unheated study, I would draw out an exercise book and start to revise a poem intended for the next fortnightly issue of *The Salopian*, or take down my copy of the New Testament in Greek in order to be prepared for any question that Hardy might put to us. I was happy then, totally happy, as I am happy, totally happy, however ailing in health, worried about money or discouraged by the reception accorded to a book, even today when, at a similarly early hour, I settle down to write.

# — 5 —

# *Going Up*

When I arrived at Oxford in the third year of the war, the atmosphere was febrile. A few undergraduates, exempted from National Service on medical grounds, knew that, with luck, they would finish their courses. The rest were assured of no more than a year. For these it was difficult to concentrate on lectures and tutorials. Having worked so strenuously at Shrewsbury, I now worked hardly at all. With John Gear, later to be Keeper of Drawings at the British Museum, I frittered away afternoons wandering round the junk shops in search of what we called 'tat'. For a few shillings or even pence an item, I accumulated vast quantities of now valuable Victoriana, which I gave away to my scout on my departure. I particularly regret a vast stuffed carp in a grotto of iridescent sea shells, and a bust of Florence Nightingale which looked as if it had been carved out of Pears soap. In the company of a Harrovian called Ronwald Gunn, plump, placid and lovable, I stayed up late into the night, drinking, talking, and listening to him thunder on the grand piano imported into his rooms. Soon to be killed in the war, Ronwald told me on more than one occasion that he was the son of the painter James Gunn, whose portraits I admired and to whom I wrote a letter of condolence, never answered, when hearing of Ronwald's death. Recently I met the sculptress Chloë Gunn, James Gunn's daughter, who told me that, as far as she knew, her father had never had a son either of that age or with the name of Ronwald. A mystery.

Ivor Novello arrived on tour with his operetta *The Dancing Years*. With the cruel tactlessness of youth I referred to it first as *The Dancing Drears* and then as *The Prancing Queers* when talking to him. The result of this was a justifiably chilly refusal when I invited him to a party in my rooms, attended by other members of the cast. One of these confessed to me gleefully, 'I must be the oldest chorus-boy in the business.' Although during the war there were all too many elderly chorus-boys in the business, I could well believe him. With his camp, self-deprecating wit, he must also have been one of the most amusing.

The literary life of Oxford revolved around a small group of poets, with Sidney Keyes and the formidably erudite and near-blind John Heath-Stubbs at the centre. I knew them but was never really of them. Drummond Allison, a promising poet later to be killed, was an enchanting character, for whom I nursed a profound but unconfessed devotion. In the vacations, he was a visitor to my mother's flat in Iverna Court, sometimes bedding down on a sofa in the sitting-room or, if there was no room there, on a camp-bed in the corridor. He chattered endlessly, endearing himself to my mother by treating her as though she were the same age as himself and shared his interests. Sidney Keyes tended to chill me with his haughty taciturnity. Calling on him once at Queen's, I found him typing away at a poem. I sat down on the chair at which he pointed. He then went on typing, totally ignoring my presence. Eventually he handed the sheet to me. 'What do you think of that?'

I criticized a line.

'Yes, it's not right. But I haven't time to change it.'

'Think about it and change it later.'

'I haven't time!' He snatched the sheet away from me.

I am sure that he already knew that he would soon be killed.

Sidney Keyes, John Heath-Stubbs and I collaborated in producing the Oxford contributions for an inter-varsity magazine, Z, of which John Lehmann had agreed to be the munificent godfather. A contingent of us travelled from Oxford to Cambridge to discuss with our opposite numbers there. The leader of the Cambridge poets, Anthony Brown, informed us that, since there were not enough beds available at his college, King's, John Lehmann had kindly offered to put up one of us in his *pied-à-terre*. This caused consternation among us. Then Drummond Allison hissed at me, 'It must be John, it must be John. No one would dream of making a pass at John.' John Heath-Stubbs it was. The other John, who had no doubt been hoping for someone more attractive, remained sulky for the rest of our visit.

We all exploited John Lehmann's kindness and tried his patience. Although he was then only in his early forties, we regarded him as tottering on the precipitous verge of old age. When he offended the Oxford poets by omitting from the magazine many of what they considered to be the best of their contributions, I sent him the following quatrain on a postcard:

> Pity the Oxford poets whom you scorn:
> Because we failed to take the right precautions
> Not only is our progeny unborn,
> But you, dear John, have bungled the abortions.

We were all constantly being rude, in this manner, to or about our elders and betters.

I shared with many of my Oxford contemporaries a love of practical jokes. Thus on one occasion I invited to a party in my rooms a number of undergraduates with what, at that period, struck me as funny names: Lawrence Lillycrapp, Christopher Tosswell, Audrey Smellie, Ivor Dick, Grizelda Bottome. I arranged some wine bottles and glasses on the table and left a note: 'I've been held up. Do introduce yourselves to each other and help yourselves to booze.'

It astonishes me now that, intellectually so mature, I should have indulged in behaviour so puerile. It also astonishes me that, at that stage of the war, I should have had two rooms at my disposal; that a scout should have made up a coal fire for me every day; and that by travelling out early in the morning to a factory in Cowley I was able to buy excellent chocolate cake for my guests at tea. But at that time I took all these things as a matter of course.

Living above me was the philosopher-to-be Richard Wollheim; and through him I met a number of people from his school, Westminster, all of whom have also achieved distinction. In comparison with the Old Salopians who had come up at the same time as myself, these Old Westminsters seemed enviably urbane, cultured and sophisticated. I regarded them, and still regard them, as the best argument for a day-school education.

Richard Wollheim then had a sense of humour even more cruel than mine. On one occasion he dressed up in some flamboyant clothes inherited from his father, a famous impresario connected with Diaghilev: a Sulka scarf, a coat with a fur collar, a gold-knobbed cane. Thus garbed, he persuaded me to accompany him to the George Street Milk Bar, then a favourite haunt of homosexuals, where by assuming a lisp so sibilant that it could be heard all round the room and by sticking out his little finger as he sipped at a cup of extremely weak coffee, he succeeded in attracting the attention of a muscle-bound RAF sergeant with a North Country accent. Asked his name, Richard simpered, fluttering his eyelids as he did so, and replied that it was 'Alphonse'.

Soon the situation was completely out of hand. The sergeant was growing more and more ardent and persistent; and when Richard, by now beginning to lose his nerve, told him in his normal voice not to be such a bloody fool, he seemed not to hear. Following us at the double up Broad Street, he grabbed Richard's arm, began to exhort him to 'be a sport' and to 'give a bloke a chance', and finally threatened to bash his fucking face in. It was with great difficulty that we managed to slip through the gate into the safety of the college.

This attempt to provoke and then repudiate the attention of a homosexual was a parody of my behaviour to many kind and decent people at that period. I wanted to exert an attraction, and yet I was terrified and ashamed of what might follow once that attraction had been exerted. At about that time John Lehmann, after I had first responded to him and then turned him down, called me 'a silly little cock-teaser'. He was right.

The Master of Balliol was Lord Lindsay of Birker. I have always managed to get on well with idealists; and with cynics I am entirely at home. But the people who, like Lord Lindsay, try to live on two levels at once, now soaring up into an empyrean of abstract ideas and now plunging down into a trough of practical considerations, in the manner of a ship in a storm, invariably induce in me what is almost a physical malaise.

My first encounter with Lindsay, at a viva voce for the scholarship which I was eventually awarded, had hardly been happy. I had confused Hugh Walpole with Horace Walpole, when a question had been put to me about the latter; and whereas Cyril Bailey, the kindly and humane Classics tutor had laughed at my error, the Master had hectored me. There had followed a discussion about 'useless knowledge', during which Lindsay put to me a series of questions beginning, 'You would agree, wouldn't you...?', 'Then it would follow, wouldn't it...?', 'In that case, you'd admit...?', to each of which, though the logic was obscure to me, I uttered a nervous Yes. Finally he burst out, 'Good heavens, boy, can't you see I'm leading you around by the end of your nose?' As he had intimidated me into swallowing link after link of his chain of fallacious reasoning, not unlike the Greek gastroenterologist who, a few years later, was to coax me into swallowing inch after inch of a rubber tube, his contempt for my lack of intellectual independence must have sharpened. It is surprising that he allowed me to win the scholarship.

When, in subsequent years, I used to have to sit and listen to the discourses with which, from time to time, he took pleasure in regaling the assembled college, it was invariably of that first humiliation that I would be put in mind. Surely he could not be leading the whole college around by its collective nose? Yet his logic still seemed to be equally tenuous, his language equally cloudy. I used to be worried about this, suspecting some intellectual deficiency in myself, until two of the sharpest undergraduates at Balliol at that period – Brian McGuinness, later to become Wittgenstein's biographer and exegete, and Peter Heyworth, later to become music critic of the *Observer* – confessed to me that they were equally bewildered by the squalls and gusts of the Master's eloquence.

After that viva voce my only encounters with the Master were at eight o'clock each morning. Still distressingly religiose, I was one of the half-dozen people, the majority of them Wykehamists, who were regular attendants at morning service. The Master would give me an approving nod as we coincided, either entering or leaving the chapel, and grunt, 'Good morning, Kent.' I never had the courage to correct him, particularly since this brief civility could never wholly convince me that he had forgotten my gaffe of connecting Horace Walpole with the *Herries Chronicle*.

Like many other pacifists, I thought at the time that I was a pacifist because I was a Christian; but I now see that my Christian belief, such as it was, had nothing to do with my pacifism. I then had a horror of taking life, which I no longer feel – so that if a mortally sick friend were (in the case of my mother an irrational taboo restrained me) now to ask me to help him out of his pain and misery and I felt that I could do so without being found out, I should at once agree. I also had a horror of the idea of the Services. I used to think that this latter horror was an aberration peculiar to myself; but recently Edward Blishen, also a pacifist in the war, confessed the same feeling to me. Being naturally domineering, a disciplinarian and a stickler for punctuality and efficiency, I should probably, I now realize, have enjoyed life in the Army. But had I not pleaded a conscientious objection, the likelihood is that I should have ended up not in the Army but, along with so many of my Oxford friends, either working on ciphers at Bletchley or studying Japanese at the School of Oriental and African Studies.

When I recently came across a dog-eared copy of the statement I made to my tribunal, I was filled with self-disgust. It struck me as priggish, pompous and self-regarding: I was amazed that the tribunal dealt so mildly with me. Admittedly one of its members, Professor Holdsworth, at that time Vinerian Professor of Law at the University of Oxford, whose son, also an Old Salopian, had recently been killed in action, humphed with desolate petulance that he refused to believe that I had been a pacifist at the age of fourteen, as claimed in my statement – 'No boy was ever a pacifist at fourteen.'

Politely I said, 'Perhaps you'd like to look at that letter from my former headmaster, sir. It confirms what I've told you.'

'The man must be talking through his hat,' Professor Holdsworth retorted.

Then he looked at the letter, saw that the headmaster in question was head-master of the school of which he himself was a governor, and said nothing more.

I got exemption on condition that I took up work on the land. I was disappointed that I had not been directed to work in a hospital. I was also disappointed that I should not now be able to take Classical Mods.

Learning of my imminent departure, Lindsay summoned me to see him. Nervously I waited for him in the Master's Lodgings. All at once, Lady Lindsay – for whom I felt an affection and respect which I knew that I ought, but could not, feel for her husband – scurried into the room.

'Would you like to see the old MG?' she asked.

Bewildered, I thought that she must be talking about a car and half rose to glance out of the window.

Then I noticed the newspaper which, good liberal that she was, she was holding out to me.

Lindsay began a long discourse on the ethics of pacifism, during which I sat mute in my habitual inability to follow him. I remember only a reference to Gibbon, who had pronounced – according to Lindsay; no student of Gibbon has ever been able to find the passage for me – that the Christians were perfectly justified in being Christians and the Romans were perfectly justified in persecuting them. Lindsay, it appeared, felt the same about pacifists. They were entitled to their opinions, and in turn those not sharing those opinions were entitled to make their lives as disagreeable as possible.

Then suddenly came the swooping plunge, as though an eagle were forsaking the lofty heavens to pounce on a minuscule mouse.

'I thought you were supposed to have a bad back. I saw you with a stick last week in chapel.'

Yes, I agreed: the doctor was afraid that I might have slipped a disc.

'And did you ask your doctor whether this injury would disqualify you from military service?'

I shook my head.

'I must say that was rather foolish of you. What was the point of this – this *stand* of yours if, in fact, you would have been exempted unconditionally in any case?' I was silent. 'Well?'

'I don't know.'

He went on to chide me for not having consulted him earlier. It was true that pacifists did not automatically receive deferment like those who would be going into the Services, but he could certainly have arranged it for me. Now, he added with a mixture of annoyance and satisfaction, it was too late, far too late.

I left him realizing that he despised me as much for not being the right kind of practical man of affairs as for being the wrong kind of idealist.

My other vivid memory of Lindsay dates from after the war. When he was about to leave to take up his appointment as Vice-Chancellor of the newly created Keele University, it was suggested to us undergraduates – where the idea originated I have no idea – that we should subscribe to have his portrait painted. Lawrence Gowing, an underestimated painter whom I have always admired, was the choice of artist. When Lindsay was eventually presented with the portrait, he made it clear that he thought little of it. Then he went on to speak, humorously he no doubt thought, of the perils of sitting for Gowing. 'I did the sitting, he did the spitting.' This reference to Gowing's difficulties with his stammer struck many of us as even more maladroit than his frankly expressed dislike of the portrait. Subsequently Lindsay sat to Epstein for a bust – 'Delightful man, delightful, not at all like Gowing,' he told me years later.


Although it could hardly be regarded as newsworthy, an account of my appearance before the tribunal had appeared in the *Oxford Mail*. This brought me a call from an undergraduate, previously unknown to me, from next-door Trinity. Even less demonstrative then than I am now, I was taken aback when this tall, sinuous youth, with a bullet-shaped head and sandy hair, rushed towards me, arms outstretched, and embraced me. 'The moment I read about you I felt that I must, must, must come over to congratulate you.'

This was Desmond Stewart, who, by turns benevolent and malign, was perpetually to rush in and out of my life, now metaphorically to embrace me, as at that first meeting, and now metaphorically to give me a kick in the crotch. He, too, was a pacifist, but for reasons totally different from mine: he was an admirer of Hitler and a follower and friend of Oswald Mosley. When he in turn appeared before a tribunal, there was no longer a pressing need for farm labourers and he was therefore directed to work in a hospital – as I should have liked to have been. Always charming, always bold, even brazen in his sexual behaviour and his political views, and always adroit at looking after himself, however unfavourable the circumstances, he managed to keep his hospital duties to a minimum and therefore had what might be called a 'good' war. Subsequently he wrote some fine novels, which would, I am sure, have received far more attention if his political views had not been so abhorrent to so many people.


Looking back, I see my twenty-year-old self as insufferably cocky, supercilious and precious. Then, overcome with embarrassment and remorse, I reassure myself: 'That wasn't me. That was someone else.' Just as few of the cells of which my body is now composed are the cells of its youth, so little of my present character bears any resemblance to my youthful one. This is why I am disturbed when I read of people now in their seventies or eighties being put on trial for crimes committed during the war. The people who committed those crimes are now merely shadows under the palimpsests of the people they became.

# — 6 —

# *Land Boy*

My first job was on a small-holding a few miles outside Dedham, owned by a blue-stocking widow called Diana Belfield, a friend of a blue-stocking friend of my mother. For the next two years, I rarely saw anyone but her, her son and daughter when they came on leave, and the farming family who lived opposite. This family persisted in the belief, despite everything that Mrs Belfield told them to the contrary, that the real, secret reason for my presence was not pacifism but mental illness. As a consequence they all showed a pitying unease in my presence, clearly thinking that I – and, indeed, they – would have been better off if I had been confined to a bin.

At first I was so much exhausted by the physical labour of the day that, at the end of it, I would enter my room, fling myself on the bed and at once fall into the deepest of sleeps. It was during this period that Mrs Belfield remarked to her daughter, then a Wren, in my presence, 'Francis reminds me irresistibly of Ferdinand.' I was huffy, thinking that she was referring to the Walt Disney cartoon *Ferdinand the Bull,* in which the pacific bull of that name refuses to enter the bullring. In fact, highly literary as she was, she was referring to Ferdinand in *The Tempest.* Once this was explained to me, I was mollified.

Fortunately, after a few weeks, I grew used to an exertion which did wonders for both my physique and my health, took it as a matter of course, and resumed the novel, *To The Dark Tower,* which I had already sketched out at Oxford. All day I would plan what to write as I moved about my tasks; then in the evening I would settle down to the actual writing, by hand at a folding table in my minuscule bedroom. I have never met with more ideal conditions for work.

When this novel was completed, I began to send it out, from my mother's flat – which I was free to visit once a month for the weekend – to a succession of publishers. I would arrive at the flat, to be told, 'I'm afraid it's back.' I did not have to ask what 'it' was. It was not my mother's recent shingles, our dog's intermittent eczema, or our cat – which had a way of slipping out of the flat and away if the door was left ajar. It was that wretched novel. Finally, I sent it to a remarkable agent, Patience Ross of A.M. Heath, a woman who was not merely an excellent judge of the literary value of a book but who – a far rarer gift – could also tell one, within two or three hundred, how many copies it would sell. She eventually disposed of it to the newly founded firm of Home & Van Thal, the three directors of which were the mother of Alec and William Douglas-Home, the schoolmaster father of the novelist David Hughes, and an expert on Victorian fiction called Bertie Van Thal. Bertie, the presiding spirit, was 'hopeless' in both senses of the word. He had no business acumen whatever; and he was totally without hope for any book which he published, so that, lunching or dining a reviewer or literary editor, he would sigh and groan, 'I *love* so-and-so's book, but I'm afraid we'll be lucky if we sell five hundred copies.' In fact, since the then paper shortage ensured that virtually any book which got into print could be sold, *To The Dark Tower* did remarkably well. When it was reissued some years ago in paperback, I reread it and was pleasantly surprised. Home & Van Thal published my two subsequent novels. They then went bust owing me £60: today about a third of the average payment for a review but then a sizeable sum.

When not reading, writing or working out of doors, I used to go for long, solitary walks through what remains some of the most beautiful country in England, the valley of the Stour. Although a person of extreme sociability both before and since, at that period I suddenly developed a morbid shrinking from any human contact. Some of the labourers on the neighbouring farms tried to befriend me, but I always failed to respond. One boy, stocky, with wide sloping shoulders and a thick neck, was particularly importunate, hanging about the lane outside the small-holding so that it would appear that our encounters were accidental. 'How about going into Chelmsford on Saturday?' he would coax. Or 'How about having a drink this evening?'

Invariably I mumbled some excuse.

Many years later, in the Coleherne, a gay pub in Old Brompton Road, I thought that I recognized him in the portly, middle-aged man with the congested face and unnaturally blond hair, who was staring at me, mouth half open, with a mixture of hostility and surprise, while drawing me a glass of beer. But perhaps I was wrong.

From time to time women friends of my employer would appear for weekends. Like my employer, they were intellectually powerful; and like her, they gave the impression of preferring the company of women to that of men. In the absence of such guests, Mrs Belfield and I spent a lot of time together: at meals, working on the small-holding, competing at the *Times* crossword every evening, discussing the books which, in the absence of television, provided our chief recreation.

Suddenly, Mrs Belfield conceived the idea of creating a 'plantation' of rare shrubs, and thenceforward part of almost every working day was spent on this task. This had, of course, nothing to do with producing food or aiding the war-effort, but the plan fired my imagination and I never resented working at it, even though a number of busybodies expressed their disapproval – among them Alfred Munnings, a neighbour, who snorted to me, as I was kneeling to bed in a shrub, 'What the hell does she think she's doing? Doesn't she know there's a war on?' I like to think that perhaps that grove of exotic flowering shrubs still exists, when the Nissen huts, bell-tents and balloon barrages have long since disappeared.

In his 'Doesn't she know there's a war on?', Munnings exemplified the censorious, more-patriotic-than-thou attitude of so many civilians at that period. On a journey to Manningtree Station to pick up some syringa bushes for the plantation, I bumped up over the pavement on my ramshackle bicycle. An elderly man, idly basking in the sunshine on a bench, at once looked up at me and glared. 'You'll wreck those tyres doing that,' he admonished. 'These days tyres are in short supply. Don't you know there's a war on?' Blushing hotly, I muttered, 'Sorry, sorry. I didn't mean to do it.' My present self would have sharply asked why, if there was a war on, he was lounging on a bench outside the station, fag in mouth, instead of himself doing something for the war-effort.

After two years on the small-holding, I suddenly decided that I wanted a change. Mrs Belfield could be excellent company, but she could also be bossy and shrewish; I also felt that I must escape from a stagnant backwater. On one of my monthly weekends off, I went not to London but to a pacifist community near Market Rasen, to see if I liked it and if the community liked me. I was accompanied by two friends, the poet John Hall, also a pacifist, and his then wife, Stella. The community, to my amazement, turned out to be far from democratic. Those who had combined to buy the buildings and land lived together in a handsome house handsomely furnished. The rest were less happily accommodated, the single among them often being crowded half a dozen to a dormitory. While we were there, an icy wind blew across a grey landscape stretching on and on to the horizon.

Since there was no bed available for me in any of the dormitories, I was bedded down on a camp-bed in the dining-room. There one of the girls, round-faced and with yellow plaits down her back, came to me in her pyjamas. First she sat on the edge of the bed, talking to me. Then she shivered and shivered again. 'Christ, it's cold. Shall I get in beside you?' I laughed, as though I thought that she was joking; but she must have been aware of my underlying panic. 'Well, perhaps not,' she said. 'Perhaps I'd better get back to my own bed. Goodnight.'

Had I failed a test in the art of communal living? At all events, two or three days later I received a letter telling me that 'We came to the conclusion that you would not really be happy with us.' Stella and John were accepted – because, Stella thought, there were far fewer women than men and there was a need of more women to act as domestics. But, no more impressed than I by the community, they decided to go elsewhere.

Soon after that a friend of my cousin Sylvia told me of a friend of hers running a farm, in the absence of her husband on service abroad, at Chelsham in Surrey. She wanted someone sympathetic to live on the farm and work for her. This was a wholly remarkable woman called Mrs Hallidie: intelligent, energetic, resourceful, efficient. Never idle, she would simultaneously follow an elaborate Fair Isle pattern, listen to the news on the wireless and read a book, while waiting for one of her excellent cakes to bake in the oven. Her household consisted of two young sons, their Swiss tutor, already mortally ill with tuberculosis of the bones, and a female lodger and her baby daughter. I was accommodated in the minuscule lodge inhabited by her formidable, deaf mother.

Although highly intelligent, Mrs Hallidie was no intellectual. But I got on better with her than with Mrs Belfield. She had a herd of cows, which it was my duty to milk by hand. She also kept pigs, ducks and hens. One of my less popular novels, *A Game of Patience*, written many years later, was based on my life with her. With V1s and then V2s constantly passing overhead and even crashing on to nearby fields, across which a balloon barrage bristled, life here was far more perilous than at Dedham; but I was far more contented. I could now go up for a night each week to London, setting off extremely early, as soon as I had milked the cows, and returning extremely early the following morning, in order again to milk them. Mrs Hallidie would herself milk them on the evening of my absence.

Mrs Hallidie's friends were always kind to me, inviting me to their houses when they invited her and showing no disapproval of my pacifism – in the case of one couple even though they had lost a son at Dunkirk. The farm-labourers with whom I came into contact also showed no disapproval. Indeed, some of them even showed admiration for my cunning (as they saw it) in evading the call-up – 'If I had your brains, I'd be a conchie too, but I wouldn't have the foggiest what to say to get myself off' was a sentiment I often heard. It was the shopkeepers who, unlike those in Dedham, could be pettily nasty. I'd go into some little shop, often on an errand for Mrs Hallidie, and whoever it was behind the counter would pointedly serve someone or even several people who had come in after me. Similarly, in the little restaurant attached to the bus garage, the waitresses always kept me waiting for a very, very long time – even when there was no one else present to be served. In neither case, being young and timid, did I ever make a protest. Now I should do so.

Soon after my arrival in Chelsham I volunteered for Civil Defence duties. After a puzzling interval of several weeks – were not Civil Defence workers supposed to be in critically short supply? – I was summoned for an interview with the commandant, a retired hospital matron, of the local ambulance service. She showed absolutely no interest in any qualifications which I might possess; but instead put me through an interrogation about my pacifist views, far more severe than I had received at my tribunal. At the conclusion, she said, 'I'm afraid that you wouldn't really be suitable for us. We need a total – and *fearless* – commitment.' 'Well, I think I could give you that,' I said, sweating and blushing, and with none of the forcefulness, perhaps even acerbity, with which I should have now argued with her. She smiled ruefully, shaking her head: 'Well, perhaps, perhaps. But ... I think – probably – not.'

At Mrs Hallidie's urging, I wrote a letter to the controller of Civil Defence in the whole district. Were there so many people available for voluntary duty that it was government policy to turn down conscientious objectors? I demanded with the kind of indignation which, at that period, I found so easy to express in a letter and so difficult in any face-to-face confrontation. No doubt, on receipt of my letter, the controller, a pudgy, tallow-faced man in his thirties, whom one might have expected himself to be in the forces, dreaded what every civil servant dreads: a *fuss*. Having invited me to go down to the municipal offices in Caterham to see him, he then treated me as though I were Florence Nightingale offering to take over the running of the local hospital. *Of course* my help was needed, indeed enthusiastically welcomed. There were countless jobs, which the manpower shortage had made it all but impossible to fill. At that very moment he was setting up a decontamination unit, to deal with a possible German recourse to poison gas. Might he enrol me in that? Yes, certainly, I said. 'Good! That's terrific! You're just the sort of person we need. We shall be starting a course of instruction in the, er, procedures very, very soon. May I then get in touch with you?'

He never got in touch with me. Whether the unit was ever set up, I do not know.

Apart from some furtive mutual masturbation with another boy at Shrewsbury, I was, on my arrival at Chelsham Place, still without any sexual experience. How many men – or indeed women – in their twenties could say that now? But at that period my case was in no way exceptional. This situation changed when, one afternoon, Mrs Hallidie asked me to take one of the cows to the bull on a nearby farm. I had no idea what this involved, and was too ashamed to expose my ignorance by asking. I was terrified. Fortunately there was a young land girl, the daughter of a London vicar, working on the farm, who giggled when I confessed to her, 'I haven't a clue about the drill,' grabbed the halter from me, and led the cow, by now mooing plaintively, into the shed in which, through a tiny window misted with cobwebs, I could just make out the vast shape of the bull. 'So quick?' I said when she re-emerged with the cow. Watching through the little window, I had felt a growing excitement. With her straight blonde hair, her stubby hands, the nails bitten, and her strong, boyish figure, the girl struck me as more attractive than any I had ever met. Her name was Evelyn; but like everyone else in the village I soon knew her as Evie.

We chatted for a while, she relaxed and I embarrassed. It was she who eventually suggested a future meeting: 'We might go into Croydon to take in a flick.' I agreed with sudden joy.

I can recapture the excitement which I felt when, after we had said goodnight at the end of that outing, I could smell her healthy sweat on the fingers with which I had nervously stroked the back of her neck in the cinema.

On our third meeting, when I was walking her back from the bus stop to her farm, she suddenly put her arms up around my neck in the dark, deserted lane, kissed me over and over again, and then drew me into a leafy alcove. Suddenly she was on her knees, undoing my trouser buttons. 'No, no! No!' I was at once horrified at what she was doing and in a state of tremendous excitement. Then, disastrously, I was aware that my erection was subsiding.

As we walked on, she kept telling me that it didn't matter, I was nervous, there would be other times. But I knew even then that there would be no other times.

This was the first of many incidents of that kind through my twenties. I was genuinely attracted by women; Evie I even briefly loved. But when it came to that moment of attempted sexual union, I always failed.

We remained friends, but the intimacy had evaporated. Later, I heard that she had married a colonial officer in Africa; and, later still, that she had been killed by a truck when riding a motor bike in the bush.

# — 7 —

## Out of the Refrigerator

I stayed on the farm for almost two years after the end of the war. Then, at
long last, I was free to return to an Oxford wholly changed from the Oxford I
had known. Instead of each having two rooms to themselves, undergraduates
were now obliged to double up; tutorials were shared; and the food was even
worse. I decided that to take first Classical Mods and then Greats would require
far too much effort of me, at a time when I had published two novels and, having
already made for myself a small reputation, was eager to publish more. I therefore
took the easy option of English.

'I envy you,' Peter Heyworth said to me grudgingly, referring to those two
published novels. 'At least you have something to show for all those years, I have
nothing.' But I in turn envied him and my other friends. Emotionally I was still
the teenager who had confused Hugh and Horace Walpole five years before,
however much labour on the land might have changed me physically. All my
coevals now seemed so much older than myself: settled; heavy with experience
and responsibility; sexually knowledgeable; even married and the fathers of
children. Most of them craved nothing but the familiar, the safe, the orderly, the
regular; whereas I was suddenly consumed with the desire to embark on a life of
action and adventure, to get out of England, to meet people, to make up for what
then seemed to be five years wasted in the wilderness. I was like a cat which,
having long been domesticated by confinement in a tiny London flat, suddenly
has the freedom of the countryside. Cautiously and fearfully I went on journeys
abroad: first to Sweden, a land of plenty then wonderfully cheap; then to Italy;
then to Germany. Looking back after years of constant wandering about the
world, I can hardly believe that I am the same person who set off for those trips in
such a state of dithering excitement and dread.


On my visit to Italy, undertaken in a Long Vac in order to write a book, *The
Brownings in Italy*, commissioned by Home & Van Thal but never completed, I
was seduced (there is no other word for it) by a gondolier. As I stepped out of his
gondola – in those days even an impoverished foreign tourist could from time to
time afford one – and began to walk away, he suddenly called out after me, 'Hey!
Hey!' I turned reluctantly, thinking that he must be dissatisfied with his tip. Then

with a series of gestures – hand pointing to his mouth, as he mimed eating, then at me, then at himself, then at a trattoria on the Zattere beside us – he clearly indicated that we should eat together. I looked at my watch, worried that at six thirty I was supposed to be meeting the English friend with whom I was travelling. Then, swept up and away in a whirlwind of excitement, I thought, To hell with him!

I already knew a little Italian. With these rudiments, with recourse to a pocket dictionary, and with a use of gesture so frantic that it soon attracted the amused notice of the other diners, all Italian, in the little trattoria, we managed somehow to converse with each other, with mounting pleasure. He was called Gino, I learned. His father and his grandfather had been gondoliers before him.

From the first, without words, we seemed to apprehend what each of us wanted. Gino led me to the landing stage where we waited for the *vaporetto* to take us to the Lido. Now we did not try to converse. We merely from time to time looked at each other and smiled as though in some conspiracy about to be brought to its triumphant conclusion. At the Lido we walked out along the darkening beach, past other lovers, until we came to a narrow stretch where there was no one at all. I was pitifully maladroit, greedy, precipitate. 'All these years I've lived for this,' I told him. It was only the truth. But of course he did not understand my English, merely shaking his head and laughing.

For the remainder of my week in Venice I spent much of my time with him. From time to time I wondered whether to give him money. Mustn't that be the only reason why he had in the first place picked me up? But I never did so and he never asked for any. Instead, I bought him a tie, a shirt, a pullover – the latter one which I had seen in a shop window and had marked down for myself.

When I left Venice, we exchanged addresses and promised each other a swift reunion. From Oxford I wrote to him, frequently consulting my dictionary to make sure that my Italian would be intelligible, and received a barely literate letter back. I wrote again. To my amazement, the reply on this occasion came not from Venice but from Genoa. He was working there as a stevedore in the port, he explained, in order to earn the money to join me in England. At first I was thrilled by the prospect. But then, as the days passed, I began to be increasingly troubled by doubts. Would he be allowed through immigration? And if he were allowed through, what would he then *do*? I could hardly expect my mother to put him up, and I myself was in no position to support him. I wrote to the address in Genoa which he had given, attempting to express these misgivings in a manner which would not be hurtful. But at the same time I longed to see him once again. Perhaps I could come to Genoa for the Christmas vacation, I suggested. When he next wrote, it was from Marseilles. He was getting nearer and nearer. Then it was Toulon. After that, at once mercifully and devastatingly, I heard nothing more. A letter addressed c/o a shipping company in Toulon was, after many weeks, returned. What became of him? Did he return to Venice, at last realizing that he would not be welcome in England? Did he meet some other lover? Did some disaster befall him?

Three years later – by then I was working in the British Institute in Florence – a sudden impulse sent me on a weekend journey, on my own, to Venice. First I went to the address which he had originally given me. After my repeated knockings at the heavy wooden door, an elderly woman answered, squinting at me from under the cloth tied over her head and low across her seamed forehead, with what seemed to me suspicion, even hostility. '*È partito*,' she said. Where? I asked. Abroad, she replied. '*Lontano, lontano*.' She raised a hand and made a weaving gesture with it, as though his travels had sent him zigzagging on and on and on across the world. Was she his mother? Or merely his landlady? I felt constrained from asking, so clear was it to me that she did not welcome my presence.

After that, I wandered for hours on end along the canals looking for him. At last I saw a gondolier to whom, when we had once been together, Gino had stopped to chat. I asked him, in my faltering Italian, if he knew where I could find Gino Neri. Gino? he queried. Gino was there, over there! He pointed to a nearby gondola. But this was another Gino, grey-haired, stout, bearded. I repeated Gino's surname. The man shook his head, shrugged his shoulders. My Gino might never have existed.

With a mixture of sadness and relief, I then gave up.

Soon after my return from that tumultuously happy week with Gino in Venice, I met Angus Wilson at a party in London. We were friends, but friends still wary of each other. He stared at me. Then he said, 'You look different.'

'Different? Different? How?' I thought that he was about to say something malicious – as he so often did at that period.

He laughed. 'You've come out of your refrigerator!'

With that remarkable perspicacity of his, he had at once realized the change in me.

I had first met Angus during the war, when I was introduced to him by my lifelong friend John Croft. John and he were colleagues at Bletchley. The three of us, sometimes with the addition of such of Angus's British Museum friends and colleagues as Bentley Bridgewater and Audrey Beacham (of whom, when he became briefly engaged to her, Maurice Bowra remarked ungallantly, 'Buggers can't be choosers'), would meet for lunch in the Museum Tavern. At that period, before he became a writer, Angus was difficult: envious, touchy, demanding, given to making hysterical scenes. But he was also already the most entertaining of conversationalists. While at Bletchley, he suffered a nervous breakdown, during which – the story is no doubt apocryphal, since the Bletchley staff included many creative writers and many even more creative talkers – he was reported, among other eccentricities, to have raced naked around the lake and to have bitten a female colleague in the breast. His psychiatrist then suggested – as I and some other of his friends had done already – that writing might help.

Unfortunately, the Bletchley Writers' Circle – of which another friend of mine, the poet Henry Reed, was also a member and about the inept self-importance of which both he and Angus were characteristically funny – failed to provide him with the needed incentive, and it was therefore not until 1946, when he had returned to his job in the British Museum Reading Room and was already thirty-three, that he produced his first story, 'Raspberry Jam'.

As an example of how touchy and hysterical Angus could be in those days, one particular remembrance, among many, now comes back vividly to me. Angus tended to have friends with odd names – Bentley Bridgewater, Perkin Walker, Forrest Fulton. It was the last of these, Forrest Fulton, to whom, for a period, I became close – partly because there was something about his obsessive dottiness which appealed to me, partly because I was fascinated by the medical research, at that time into the common cold, in which he was concerned, and partly because, living at Kensington Close, then a block of service flats and not a hotel, he was a near neighbour of ours. Eventually quitting the Cold Research Unit near Salisbury – after its fifty or so years of existence, now terminated, unfortunately we all still get colds – he announced that he and the young laboratory assistant with whom he had fallen in love were departing to posts in Nigeria. One of his colleagues, an eminent doctor whose name I have forgotten, then gave a farewell party for him, to which both Angus and I were bidden. The majority of the other guests were doctors and scientists and their wives. Angus brought along with him the young man, Ian Calder, with whom he was then having a tempestuous affair. I had never met this young man, who eventually came over to me, glass in hand, and started a conversation about another Forrest, the Northern Irish novelist Forrest Reid, whose influence he had rightly detected in my second novel *Never Again*. Suddenly Angus was thrusting his way through the other guests towards us. When he was about three feet away, he screamed out, 'You bitch! You bitch! I knew you'd do this! I knew you'd make a pass at Francis as soon as you got here!' Everyone turned and stared in amazement as Angus gripped the young man's arm and began to tug him towards the door. 'Oh, stop it, Angus!' the young man said, as though to an obstreperous dog yapping and pulling on its lead. Clearly to him Angus's scene was the most ordinary of occurrences. But, as the two of them disappeared, Forrest Fulton and I were overcome with embarrassment. Forrest, as guest of honour, could not make a get-away. I did so at once.

In later years Forrest, now back from Africa and sundered from his research assistant, became more and more eccentric and more and more prone to cyclical depression. On the last occasion when I ran into him by chance on a Central Line platform at Notting Hill Gate, he shocked me with the lined pallor of his face, the wildness of his gaze, and the dishevelment of his hair and clothes. He began to tell me, with mounting excitement, that he was working on a gigantic painting of 'St Joan of Arc – a masterpiece – a real masterpiece ... I have researched the materials which will ensure that no atomic explosion can possibly destroy it ... It will survive when everything else in this city has vanished ...' As he told me all this, I made such inadequate comments as 'Oh, really? ... How amazing! ... Well, that sounds a wonderful idea.' A train came in. I boarded it. Mysteriously he didn't. Soon after, I heard of his death, by his own hand. I had been fond of him and feel saddened even now by the thought of that once powerful steam-engine of a mind jolting off the rails and crashing.

Contrary to popular belief, people are usually spoiled by failure, not by success. After he had achieved success, Angus made fewer and fewer of such scenes as that which I have here described, becoming calmer, kinder, more considerate, more self-possessed. One of the increasingly rare scenes of his later years occurred when he walked out of a PEN dinner because he had been placed in what he regarded as an insufficiently prominent position. Unfortunately this position was next to a Japanese woman writer, who then assumed, erroneously, that he had walked out because he felt insulted at being obliged to sit next to someone of her race. She burst into tears. Years later, he apologized for what he called 'that silliness'. Later still – as an act of reparation, I should guess – he gave the most brilliant lecture, on Dickens, which I have ever heard at PEN.

Although he could sometimes take himself too seriously, Angus could also mock at himself. When he still had a small flat in Dolphin Square – at that time and, for all I know, still the haunt of minor politicians and spooks – he told me an entertaining story. Going to answer a ring at his bell, he found a small girl, with a hoop in one hand, standing on the doorstep. He recognized her as the daughter of some neighbours, unknown to him, in the flat at the end of the corridor.

'Are you Mr Wilson?' she asked.

'Yes.'

'Mr Angus Wilson?'

'Yes, dear,'

'Mr Angus Wilson, the novelist?'

'Yes, that's right, dear.' Angus was now beaming, convinced that here was his youngest fan.

'Well, my mummy says that you're a silly old queen, so there!'

At that, with excited squeals of mirth, the girl raced off down the corridor, bowling her hoop.

Success was not the only thing which changed both Angus's life and his character for immeasurably the better. Almost at the same time as he embarked on his career as a writer, he was to embark on the relationship with a then employee of the Museum, Tony Garrett, which was to bring him so much happiness and which was to last until the end of his life. It is a common view among heterosexuals that homosexuals are promiscuous, rackety, bitchy and quarrelsome in their personal lives. This has certainly not been my general observation. Angus's remarkably steadfast and happy 'marriage' to Tony is only one of many such known to me. Never once did I hear them indulge in the kind of prolonged bickering with which heterosexual couples can make a dinner-party such an embarrassment or such a bore for everyone present. Never once did I dread, as I often do with my heterosexual friends, that their relationship might be starting to unravel.

Angus's homosexuality was an essential part of his nature and his writing. In his early work, especially in *Hemlock and After*, one feels that it was something which he hated in himself. Then, no doubt largely because of his relationship with Tony, he came to terms with it. With that high voice of his ('Oh, for God's sake, turn off that ghastly female!' J.R. Ackerley once urged me, not realizing that it was Angus to whom I was listening on the wireless) and that appearance which to Rebecca West suggested Jane Eyre and to W.H. Auden Margaret Rutherford, he could never be mistaken for anything other than he was. But he nonetheless showed considerable courage in being one of the first homosexual writers in this country publicly to declare himself.

Having publicly declared himself, he was taken aback when, from time to time, he and, by association, even Tony became victims of intolerance. This was particularly the case after the two of them had agreed to take part in a television documentary about their shared life. The general reaction was favourable to this touching demonstration of how two homosexuals could live contentedly and usefully together. But Angus was upset both by some vicious letters of a kind that anyone in the public eye receives from time to time but which he, with surprising innocence, had never expected, and by the malice of some of his neighbours.

That he should have been so upset is an indication of an insecurity that he was never wholly to lose, and which, on balance, was to be more of a strength than a weakness to him in both his life and his writing. Speaking once of Patrick White's truculence, I said, 'I suppose it's because he's so insecure,' to receive from Angus the answer, 'Aren't all novelists insecure?' I could not agree with him – Greene, Waugh, Forster, Compton-Burnett and Powell struck me as obvious exceptions to this rule – but Angus was certainly insecure. This insecurity made him simultaneously welcome a knighthood, as confirmation of the merit which he sometimes doubted, and question himself and his friends as to whether he ought to accept it. 'I suppose I was right to say yes, wasn't I?' he wrote to me, in answer to my letter of congratulation. I wrote back to say that of course he was right: he deserved the honour both for his writing and for all his services to his fellow writers – at the Society of Authors, at the Arts Council, at PEN, at the Royal Society of Literature.

When Angus quit England for what he intended to be his final home in Saint Rémy in Provence, it seemed to me a grievous error. But if people have already made up their minds to a course of action, then it is both pointless and cruel to tell them that it is wrong. He gave me two reasons for the move. One was that he could not bear to live any longer in Mrs Thatcher's Britain. The other was that he now enjoyed more esteem in France than at home. Both reasons seemed to me insufficient. The Britain in which we were living was, for the most part, not Mrs Thatcher's Britain but *our* Britain; so that, if there were things that he hated about it, then it was more logical to lay the chief blame on his fellow countrymen, not on her. His attitude struck me as similar to that of a woman who once stood beside me one afternoon waiting, on and on, for a 49 bus which never came. 'I shan't vote for Her again,' she told me. 'Not on your life! Not in a hundred years!' 'Do you think that she ought to be in the bus station, telling the drivers to leave their teas and get on the road?' I asked. The woman glowered at me. 'Well, everyone's entitled to a cup of tea,' she said. As far as Angus's reputation was concerned, he should have comforted himself with the knowledge that the reputations of all writers, even those of the stature of Conrad, Woolf and Kipling, go up and down like yo-yos.

My last memory of Angus is a particularly sad one. I was a guest of Victor and Dorothy Pritchett at luncheon in their house in Regent's Park Terrace. Suddenly I looked up from my pudding and saw, outside the dining-room window, an old man shuffling past, head bowed. Somehow he looked vaguely familiar. Then, when I glimpsed Tony behind him, I realized that it was Angus. 'Look, there's Angus!' I cried out. Victor Pritchett, then in his late eighties, jumped up from the table and literally ran to the front door. 'Angus! Angus! Come and join us!' Angus slowly shuffled in. There was a difference of thirteen years between these two fine writers. But it was Pritchett who looked like a man in his early seventies and Angus like one in his late eighties.

Another novelist whom I met at about this same time, and whose reputation slumped in similar fashion, was C.P. Snow. I like to think that it was I, in a letter to J.R. Ackerley, who first referred to him as 'The Abominable Snowman' –'Here is my review of the Abominable Snowman,' I wrote – but it may well be that someone thought of that sobriquet before me. The book which I had reviewed during a six-month stint when I was still up at Oxford – Ackerley wisely never allowed anyone, however proficient, to review novels for more than six months at a stretch for *The Listener*, thus ensuring that no one got stale – was *The Light and the Dark*. There were things that I admired in this novel, but there were other things – above all in the characterization of the hero Roy Calvert – which I found preposterous. Snow wrote to me. He was delighted that, by and large, I had liked his novel. Of course I was right in my criticisms. Were he writing the book now, he would be writing it differently. At all events, he was a great admirer of *my* work. Would I consent to have dinner with him one evening, at the Athenaeum? I accepted; and so began what for a brief period might have been called a literary alliance and for a long period might have been called a literary acquaintance, but what was never a literary friendship, since, try as I might, I could never feel any great affection for a man who so much resembled a Baked Alaska – sweet, warm and gungy on the outside, hard and cold within.

I returned from that first dinner to tell my sister Elizabeth that Snow was just like Maugham's Alroy Kear. Now modestly disclaiming any great merits for his own work and now extravagantly praising the merits of mine, he had, I had felt, been adroitly manipulating me. There were people who were hostile to him, there were people who were supportive of him, he had explained to me more than once. All too blatantly he was wishing to enrol me in the second of these groups.

I genuinely admired – and still admire – Snow's narrative gift; his intellectual curiosity and energy; his ability to create a certain kind of character. But I fretted beneath the conviction that, without ever saying so, he wished me to go further than that. He wanted me to say that he was not merely a good writer but a great one. I suspect that it was in order to coax me into doing so, that he was prepared to go on record that I was 'one of the half-dozen most talented novelists to appear since the war'.

Even then, when he was still in his early forties, Snow looked like an old man. He also moved like one – one could not imagine him running for a bus or hurrying up the stairs of the Athenaeum without a small, white, flipper-like hand resting on the banisters. Yet he was tough. Many years later, during a literary conference in Sofia, he had a haemorrhage of the stomach – presumably from the ulcer which was eventually to kill him – after drinking vast quantities of vodka throughout an evening of the kind of literary and political pontification which he came so much to enjoy. Despite this, he was one of the first down the following morning. Even more remarkably, he ate a huge breakfast.

In later years, we became increasingly distanced from each other. However much one tries to dissemble, writers usually know when one has no great enthusiasm for their work; and with Snow there was the further problem for me that John Davenport, more effective as a bully-boy than as a novel reviewer, passed on to him, no doubt maliciously, my declared preference for the novels of Snow's wife Pamela Hansford-Johnson ('a natural novelist,' I'd said unguardedly to Davenport, whereas Snow, I'd added, had 'become a novelist by a combination of intelligence and an exertion of the will').

My last meeting with Snow, three or four years before his death, was a strange one. At about nine one evening, there was a ring at my bell. Abandoning the review on which I was working, I went down to find Snow, his usually pallid face blotched and his breath heavy with alcohol, on the doorstep. 'Terribly sorry, terribly sorry. Forgive me. The truth is – I've been taken short. On the way back from a party at some friends.' He did not specify who the friends were. Having returned from the lavatory, pulling up his zip as he tottered down the stairs, he showed no eagerness to leave but instead began questioning me about the novel on which I was engaged. Eventually I invited him into the sitting-room and asked him if he would like a cup of coffee or tea. He opted for whisky.

There followed a rambling conversation, interspersed with hiccoughs, of which I remember nothing. Then suddenly he began talking about Pamela Hansford-Johnson – 'I know you have a high opinion of her work – as she has of yours. I know you like and admire each other.' He had behaved badly to her, very badly. It was something on his conscience. I knew about X, didn't I? – his affair with X. I shook my head. The only affair of which I knew, since she herself had told me about it, was with someone called Maureen Gebbie, later Money. 'Oh, I thought you'd known about it.' He had had this affair with X before he and Pamela had met – 'No harm in that. But where I behaved badly was in continuing with the affair after our marriage. And still continuing with it.' There followed a lot of self-laceration. Pamela was a wonderful woman, really wonderful, but a man had a variety of needs and sadly one woman could not always satisfy all of them. As he meandered on and on, I became more and more embarrassed. Next morning he would, I felt sure, regret this frankness. Finally, having again gone up to the lavatory, he left in the taxi which he had asked me to summon for him.

Thinking now of Snow, I feel a certain guilt. I have felt genuine affection for people far less worthy, who did far less for me. Why can I feel, even in retrospect now, no affection for him?

During my Oxford years I also met Dylan Thomas and his wife Caitlin intermittently. It was soon after I arrived at Oxford from Shrewsbury that someone – could it have been Tambimuttu, a beautiful and giddy Sinhalese who at that period from time to time included me in his *Poetry Today* – asked a group of us literary undergraduates to 'show Dylan round'. Showing him round meant, in effect, taking him on a pub crawl. Looking like the sort of cherubic but depraved choir-boy who might have figured in the wet dreams of Firbank's Cardinal Pirelli, Thomas then had, even more potently than in his later years, a voluble, dangerous charm. I was fascinated by him. When we finally ended up for yet more drinking in the rooms of one of us, I decided to make my excuses and leave. By then Thomas and many of the others were drunk, and drunks always bore me. After I had left the room, Thomas asked morosely who the fucking hell that was. Having been told, he said, 'He's been watching me, he's been listening to me all evening. He has eyes and ears in his bloody arse.'

For part of my second period at Oxford the Thomases were living in a house lent to them by the then wife of A.J.P. Taylor. About someone who had for so long been their generous patron, both Thomas and Caitlin said some singularly disobliging things. Thomas once referred to her in my presence as 'that stupid cunt', and on another occasion he told me, 'She's desperate for me to poke her, but who wants to poke a bowl of cold porridge?'

I was present at a party given by an eccentric aristocrat, Anthony de Hoghton, in his Beaumont Street house, when David Carritt, whose brilliant career as an art expert was prematurely cut short by his death from cancer, became the victim of a mock rape by Caitlin. Having wrestled him to the floor – she was physically strong, he feeble – she glued her mouth to his lips and placed a hand on his crotch. As he struggled to free himself, the couple rolled over and over. Whereas the other guests crowded round to cheer Caitlin on, David's twin sister Christian, now a doctor, began screaming, 'Leave my brother alone, you horrible woman! Leave him alone!' Eventually Christian tried to pull Caitlin off, and David then succeeded in wriggling away from under her.

It was David who, with camp wit, nicknamed me both 'Francesca da Nimini Pimini' and, in admiration or disapproval of my punctiliousness, 'the Clockwork Queen'. It was also he who nicknamed Desmond Stewart, because of his love of the Arab world, 'Florence of Arabia'.

At that period David was noted for his tactlessness. On one occasion Lily Lancaster (Gardiner), a delightful woman but an indifferent artist, had been explaining to us how she had acquired a superb painting by Sickert, whose pupil she had been: 'He very much liked something I had done. So I decided to give it to him. He then said that I must have something in return, went over to the wall, and took down that picture of his.'

David gasped. 'Heavens! What a *bargain*!'


I first began writing for *The Listener* while still on the land. During that period Ackerley, the best editor for whom I have ever worked, accepted some of my poems and rejected even more. He never returned work without jotting down some comment on the rejection slip – 'Sorry, dear, this just doesn't reach your usual standard,' 'I wish I could like this but I don't,' 'There's an air of tiredness about this one – perhaps you've been overdoing things?' When he had published about a dozen of my poems, he asked me if I should like to review poetry for him. In the capacity of poetry-reviewer, I was responsible for a rift, fortunately only temporary, between him and Edith Sitwell. I had given a patronizingly unenthusiastic review to a volume of her poems and, like many another writer in such circumstances, she decided to blame not merely the author of the review but also the literary editor who had commissioned it.

From reviewing poetry, I passed on to reviewing novels. My novel reviews for Ackerley at that period were often both brutal and silly. Of a novel by Storm Jameson, for example, I wrote that it was 'a Storm in a Poole Pottery teacup'; of one by Elizabeth Bowen that she was 'a high-class sob-sister, the intellectual's Godfrey Winn'. Both Jameson and Bowen were friends of Ackerley.

I was eventually to meet Bowen at a party given by Angus Wilson. 'You know Mrs Cameron, don't you?' Angus said, approaching me in the company of a large, handsome woman, with a sly smile. 'No, I don't think so.' Angus left us together; and soon Mrs Cameron was asking me what I did. I was up at Oxford, I told her; but I really liked to think of myself as a writer, a novelist. 'Oh, how nice! How very nice!' she exclaimed, adding that she must look out for one of my novels. How would I describe them? I set about attempting to do so at inordinate length. She listened patiently. When she had left the party, Angus came over to me. 'I'm so glad that you and Elizabeth Bowen got on so well.' Elizabeth Bowen! I was appalled. I had been talking to her as though to some upper middle-class housewife who borrowed her weekly quota of novels from the Times Book Club, Mudie's or Smith's.


It was some time before I met Ackerley, instead of merely corresponding with him. Repeatedly I suggested that I might drop in at his office to pick up the books which he wished me to review; and repeatedly he ignored this suggestion and continued to post them to me. Then, at long last, he invited me to luncheon at the Jardin des Gourmets. It was summer and I therefore decided to wear what I had come to call 'Uncle Archie's suit'. Uncle Archie, an uncle not of myself but of Mrs Hallidie, had been the black sheep of the family. His suit, passed on to me by Mrs

Hallidie after his death, was a pale yellow silk one, which fitted me to perfection –
although it certainly would not do so now. Whenever I wore it, which I did in hot
weather for several years to follow, my social or sexual success was always assured:
people, instead of edging away from me at parties after a brief time, demonstrated
a determination not to let me edge away myself; strangers on trains, buses or even
in the street would try to pick me up; shop assistants smiled ingratiatingly at me
and asked, 'What can I do for you, sir?' I came to the conclusion that when I wore
the suit, Uncle Archie must be somehow looking after me.

In the Jardin des Gourmets the suit worked its usual magic. I was at an age
when I was timorous about entering such places; but the head waiter was
welcoming, even obsequious, beaming as he extended an arm and invited me
'This way, sir! Just over here, sir!', when I told him that I was Mr Ackerley's
guest. To my surprise, Joe was in a pair of grey flannels, an open-necked shirt and
sandals – dress just acceptable in a Lyons Corner House in those days but highly
unusual in a restaurant as smart as that in which we were meeting. A rucksack
rested on the floor at his feet, bulging with the novels which he later, and most
inconveniently, passed on to me. 'Shall I take that for you, sir?' the head waiter
asked, clearly not wishing such an object to be seen by the other diners. But 'No,
no!' Joe said. 'It's no inconvenience to us here.'

Joe and I at once got on well; and so began a friendship which continued till his
death. He did not always approve of my work and I did not always approve of his
behaviour – as each of us had no hesitation in making clear on a number of
occasions; but amazingly this caused no disruption. Joe was born with something
which I acquired only in late middle-age and then in far less potent form: charm.
By virtue of this charm – which had little to do with his remarkable looks,
inherited from his father, the 'Banana King', and shared by his sister, Nancy
West, and his half-sisters, Diana Petre and Sally Duchess of Westminster – he
could, as my mother once put it, 'get away with anything'. But the price of charm
is, almost always, a certain insincerity, since to charm people it is necessary to
present them with the image that is most likely to appeal to them; and so it was
with Joe. Many of his friends imagined that he found them far more lovable,
admirable and entertaining than he did. At least one of them still imagines this.

I suspect that it was because of this charm that Joe was always so reluctant to
bring his friends together. To one he had offered one image of himself, to another
an image subtly different. How were the two images to be reconciled if the friends
were present at one and the same time? For years he resisted my requests to be
introduced to E.M. Forster, Geoffrey Gorer, William Plomer. When he did
finally bring Forster and me together, Forster, then an extremely old man, said to
me, 'Oh, I've wanted to meet you for so long! Why didn't Joe bring us together
sooner?' Why indeed! Gorer I did also finally meet – as I did Plomer, albeit not
through Joe but at a party. When, many years later, Joe was staying with me in
Brighton, I suggested that David should drive us over to Rustington to visit
Plomer. Joe did not welcome the idea. 'Oh no, dear, no. I want to spend this
weekend with you *alone*. I've come here for you. I don't want to waste time on

other people.' All very flattering; but, as so often, I could see the real reason for the refusal behind the ostensible one.

During that period, as throughout his literary editorship of *The Listener*, Joe always preferred to entertain me in some such restaurant as the Jardin des Gourmets, Chez Victor or the White Tower, rather than in the cramped eyrie which he inhabited, often with his sister Nancy or his Aunt Bunny and, in later years, with his truly dreadful Alsatian dog, in Star and Garter Mansions, overlooking the river at Putney. At first I thought that it was he who was paying for these expensive meals and, since he was all too clearly not at all well off, would either offer to pay my whack or would tell him that I'd be just as happy to be entertained by him at home. It was only after a considerable time that he revealed to me that the BBC allowed him to charge up the entertainment of any prospective contributor, and that, as far as the BBC was concerned, it was as a prospective contributor and not as a friend that I was his guest.

In those years, before misanthropy, like some frenziedly proliferating liana, strangled his natural good nature, and before deafness made it harder and harder for him to take in a general conversation, he was a wonderful companion. From time to time, I used to invite him back to my mother's flat; and she and my sisters, like myself, were enchanted by him. Such was that charm that, however outrageous, he never shocked my mother. 'I'm trying to persuade Francis to accompany me to the Gang Show this evening,' he announced on one occasion, 'but for some reason he's resistant to the idea.' 'Oh, Joe, why on earth would you want to see the Gang Show?' my mother asked, puzzled, since Joe for her was a tremendous intellectual. Joe beamed: 'I want to see the Gang Show because I want to see all those pretty Boy Scouts.' On another occasion, during a bus strike, when the public had been asked to give people lifts in their cars, my mother complained that she had 'stood for ages and ages in Hammersmith and not a soul, not a single soul stopped for me.' 'How strange!' Joe said. 'I saw a very beautiful boy waiting for a lift outside Derry and Toms, and *two* cars skidded simultaneously to a halt to offer him one. They all but collided.'


It was through Desmond Stewart that I became interested in the German prisoners held, so long after the war, at a squalid and bleak camp outside Oxford. Whenever I now travel along the dual carriage-way between Oxford and Woodstock, I think of them, since it was they who created it. All of them struck me as decent, companionable, and amazingly cheerful in view of their circumstances. As I entertained them in my rooms or, having illegally lent them clothes of my own (they were not allowed out of uniform), took them to a theatre or a concert, there was a curious conflict of emotions within me: affection, pity and admiration on the one hand, and, on the other, unease and bewilderment, as I thought of all the terrible things which German soldiers just like them had done in occupied Europe.

Many of these Germans were extremely attractive. With one of them, Karl, a sturdy farmhand whose village was now, to his bemusement and sorrow, part of Poland, I even fell half in love, so sweet was his character and so admirable his stoicism, as uncomplainingly he limped around with a leg shattered at the knee by a bullet. It was he who laboriously made for me a ship in a bottle, which I still possess. After his return to Germany, I should like to have kept up with him, but to have others translate my letters into German and his letters into English became too much of a burden.

To my certain knowledge Desmond made love to at least two of these prisoners; but I was inhibited from doing so, feeling that it would be wrong to take advantage of their loneliness and their sense of gratitude for what little one did for them. Many years later, one of them, now a businessman in late middle-age, looked me up at my hotel in Hamburg during a PEN congress, having seen a photograph of me in a newspaper, and invited me out to dinner. As he said goodnight, having driven me back to my hotel, he took my hand in both of his: 'There is so much that could have happened that did not happen,' he said in a low, urgent voice. I was not sure what he meant; and since his wife and daughter were in the car, I was too embarrassed to ask.

I wrote a novel about these prisoners; but John Guest of Longmans, to whom I showed it after the bankruptcy of Home & Van Thal, persuaded me that it was not good enough to publish after the success of my first three books. I wish now that I had not listened to him. Rereading it not so long ago, I thought it had its merits. From it I salvaged a story, 'To the Camp and Back', subsequently made into a mediocre television play.

It was largely my interest in these prisoners and the question which they prompted, 'How could people like these have been guilty of things as terrible as that?', which persuaded me to join a party of students on a trip to Göttingen University during a Long Vacation. Years later this trip became the subject of what I consider to be one of my best novels, *Punishments*. Writing it, I found that things seemingly long forgotten returned to me with a painful, sometimes even excruciating vividness.

During the trip, I shared the bedroom of a young German medical student, Götz Domagk, son of the Domagk who won the Nobel Prize for his discovery of the sulphanomide drugs and today himself well known in the world of German medicine. Unlike the German in *Punishments*, an avenging angel or devil, depending on how one sees him, Götz was an infinitely gentle, infinitely kind, infinitely understanding host. Each morning he would give me an egg for my breakfast, at a time when food was far more scarce even than in England. Eventually I learned from another medical student that anyone who gave a blood transfusion in Göttingen was rewarded with three eggs. I was, in effect, breakfasting off Götz's blood. Subsequently he visited me in London and in Florence.

We English students arrived in Göttingen in a state of self-righteousness: it was our task, we were all convinced, to 're-educate' our German hosts. But the line between the righteous and the wicked began at once to blur. For me there was

Götz, so much more admirable than many of the callow English in the party; there was a German professor of chemistry who, sharing my love of Joseph Conrad, a writer equally influential in my personal life and my writing, spoke to me about Conrad's conception of honour in a way then revelatory to me; there were wonderful performances at the local opera house, for which many of the Germans, then half-starving, turned up in evening-dress. Above all, at the close of our visit, there was a visit to Hildesheim, a once beautiful medieval city wantonly flattened by Allied bombs.

Brian McGuinness, who was one of the party, remarked to me, 'It's disconcerting that people who behaved so badly in the war can behave so admirably in defeat.'

Indeed, it was.


Desmond Stewart invited Oswald Mosley to speak to a group of sympathizers in Oxford and urged me to attend. I half wanted to do so, since I was fascinated by all that I had heard about the man; but then I thought that it would be wrong to accord any encouragement, however small, to someone so vicious. This did not prevent Desmond from giving the *Daily Mail* a story, in which he announced that 'the successful young novelist Francis King' was one of the undergraduates who had welcomed Mosley. I was furious. 'But it was only a joke, only a joke!' Desmond protested, with laughter, as he was so often to do when he annoyed me in the future. I suspect that it was because of this 'joke' that, when I later applied to join the British Council, my security clearance took so long.


For my first two years at Oxford my tutor was John Bryson. A rich, homosexual dilettante of unerring taste, scion of a family of Belfast linen merchants, he shuttled between exquisitely furnished rooms in college and a no less exquisitely furnished house of his own.

Entering those rooms for the first time, I could not restrain myself from commenting, 'What a wonderful portrait that is!'

He replied drily, 'I'm glad you like it. . . . It's by Degas.'

Because the university was then so crowded, with men both straight from school and from the forces, tutorials were shared. My partner at tutorials with Bryson was someone called Lloyd, whom I was later to meet again as a colleague in the British Council. Lloyd took immense pains over his weekly essays, which tended to be prolix. I took few pains over mine. As Lloyd, head bowed, read on interminably from page after page, Bryson would drag with increasing impatience on one of the cigarettes which he chain-smoked. Then he would look over to me, raise an eyebrow, pull a face, and raise a hand to his mouth, as it gaped in an extravagant parody of a yawn. This mockery, always unnoticed by its victim, delighted me. It ranged me on Bryson's side, it made me feel superior to Lloyd.

The desire to please Bryson made me think far more about the subjects which he set me than I might otherwise have done. In consequence I produced for him some essays which, though often based on a perfunctory study of the texts, none the less contained some original assessments and were entertainingly written. Unfortunately, for my last year at Oxford, Bryson was absent on a sabbatical, and my tutor then became someone wholly different. J.C. Maxwell was undoubtedly a better scholar than Bryson; but, awkward, shabby, prickly and unsociable, he made me feel as uncomfortable as I all too clearly made him. He did not care for the glib sparkle of my essays, and took to doggedly interrogating me in order to reveal – no difficult task – the gaps in my knowledge. I became bored with him, I became bored with my work.

One week he told me to write about Shelley's politics. With the assistance of some friends – Brian McGuinness, John Pollock and Patrick Gardiner among them – who were reading philosophy, I concocted a spoof essay, full of nonsensical jargon of a kind then, and indeed still, popular at Oxford. Maxwell had no idea what to make of it. He guessed that I was pulling his leg but could not be certain. Loping up and down the room, as he was apt to do, while I read, he kept emitting strangulated groans, a hand splayed over his mouth and chin. When I had finished there was a long silence. 'Yes,' he said at last. 'Yes. Well yes. . . . That was – interesting.' About the essay he said nothing more, turning at once to Shelley's poetry.

To the switch from Bryson to Maxwell in my crucial third year I in part ascribe my failure to get the First expected of me. In part I also ascribe that failure to a meeting with someone called Richard Rumbold. A few years older than myself, Richard was the nephew of Sir Horace Rumbold, who in the Thirties had served as British Ambassador in Berlin. Richard had written an iconoclastic account, *Innocent Victims*, of his unhappy years at Eton, which had brought him some early fame and – since it included accounts of adolescent sex – even more notoriety. He was rich, handsome, charming, childish, self-indulgent, rarely happy. Attached to him was a middle-aged American widow, Hilda, as rich as himself, who clearly doted on him. Richard was devoted to Hilda, as to a family nanny, but his doting was confined to people, usually tough and rough, of his own sex. He did no job, since he could afford not to do so and in any case regarded himself as a writer, even though he wrote so little. Harold Nicolson was one of the many influential people who, attracted by his tall, muscular good looks, had befriended him. It was through Harold that he entered my life. I, too, was briefly smitten with him.

Richard would often come down to Oxford from London. Sometimes his spirits would be boisterously high; sometimes he spoke of depression and even suicide. As Schools approached, I told him of my anxiety that I should do less well than expected of me. He then offered me 'some pills' which would ensure that I gave of my best. The pills were benzedrine – of which, at that period, I had never heard. On his instructions I took one pill half an hour before each examination, and then wrote in a state of wild exhilaration, ideas scampering through my mind.

'How did you get on?' Richard enquired when we met after each session.

'Wonderfully, wonderfully!'

'I told you that you would.'

But I realize now that, in producing my answers, I showed absolutely no care or self-criticism, dashing down, in the manner of a Jeffrey Archer or Barbara Cartland, the first things that came into my head.

Some years later Richard and I were to have a one-night stand, when, after dinner with a mutual friend, he took me back to the St John's Wood house which he was then sharing with Hilda. As we climbed the wide flight of stairs – it was long past midnight – a voice called out, 'Is that you, Richard?'

'Yes, it's me. Go to sleep,' he answered crossly.

On the first landing, we passed the open door of Hilda's room. Propped up in a four-poster bed with a book, her head cobwebbed with a hairnet, she glared over her reading glasses at me, with angry hurt.

Not surprisingly what followed in the room above hers could not be accounted a success.

'I'm afraid I'm not doing anything for you,' Richard said.

'Well, it's so embarrassing ... with Hilda just below.'

'Hilda doesn't mind. She's used to my bringing people back. She'll be reading her book. She always reads late into the night.'

But I was convinced that Hilda would be listening to every sound above her. I jumped off the bed. 'I think I'd better go.'

Hilda followed Richard to Japan, where, shortly before I myself arrived there, he briefly played at being a Buddhist monk. She stayed in the Miyako Hotel, the best in the city, while he accompanied his fellow monks, a blond giant dressed in saffron robes, on their begging expeditions. Often Hilda would also be present, but in a large hired limousine, crawling along behind him. Needless, to say Richard excited a lot of attention; and, oddly, he was always given far more money and food than any of his Japanese companions.

Hilda was also with Richard, taking down dictation from him at the typewriter, when, on a terrible whim, he suddenly, without any warning, precipitated himself out of a hotel window in Taormina, landing by a swimming-pool surrounded by people, many of them children. He was killed instantly.

Poor fellow, he had always been inconsiderate.

Before my débâcle in Schools, John Bryson, back from his sabbatical, had asked me if I would be interested in a Fellowship. 'Good God, no!' I had replied rather tactlessly.

Whether he would have been able to deliver a Fellowship, I do not know. Since J.R. Tolkien's son Christopher was awarded one after gaining, not a Second like myself, but a Third in English in the same Schools, perhaps he could have done so. At all events, I am glad that I was not tempted. Academics rarely make good novelists.

*Part II*

# — 1 —

## *Florence*

By a curious coincidence, of a kind that was disconcertingly often to recur in my life, I was actually in Florence, holidaying with friends, when I received a letter, redirected by my mother and taking only three days in transit, from the British Council offering me a job at the Institute there. If today such a letter were to be redirected from London to Florence, no doubt the British Council, having waited weeks for an answer, would eventually offer the job to someone else.

When the letter arrived, I was occupying room number 13 in the Pensione Jennings-Riccioli on the Lung'Arno delle Grazie. When I had first been shown up to this room, I had, being superstitious, protested at its number; but the proprietor had laughed at me – 'No, no! In Italy thirteen is fortunate, always fortunate! You will have good fortune! Soon something fortunate will happen to you!' He had been right.

I accepted the British Council offer with alacrity, sending a cable despite the expense. I was already in love with Florence – as I have remained, despite the ever-increasing crowds, din and pollution, up to the present.

It is difficult now to convey the thrill of crossing the Alps or even merely the Channel in the immediate aftermath of the war. Like an athlete who, after the superhuman effort of winning a race against all the odds, lies supine on the ground, incapable of any movement other than an occasional twitch or grimace, England was in a state of total exhaustion. People who had been so full of vigour, cheerfulness and optimism during the years of conflict, now for the first time began to indulge in an occupation which they have never fully abandoned since: moaning. What then made life so dreary was, in large measure, the way in which the English kept moaning about how dreary it was.

Across the Alps, it was not only the light which seemed so much brighter. Although in Italy there was then far more poverty than in England – want turned even adolescents into prostitutes or black-marketeers, peddling their illicit wares in such places in Florence as the Piazza della Repubblica or the Loggia dei Lanzi – there was, at the same time, far more joy. I can remember how, on my first evening in Florence, I wandered through the streets listening, in delighted incredulity, to the sound of people laughing all around me – at the tables of outdoor cafés, under the arches of the Ponte Vecchio, even at tram stops. It was extraordinarily rare to hear public laughing in England, unless in derision.

At first I put up once again at the Jennings-Riccioli. The premises of this pensione once housed the Pensione Simi, in which E.M. Forster and his mother stayed in October 1901, and which then became the prototype for his Pensione Bertolini in *A Room with a View*. I was pleased by this link, albeit tenuous, with a book and an author admired by me far more then than now.

After two or three weeks, I found myself a tiny flat, at the top of a gaunt building in the then working-class Via Parioncino, which was the property of a charming woman, previously lady-in-waiting to the Duchess of Aosta, called Daisy Martinucci. Since Signorina Martinucci's morals were beyond reproach, it was a mystery why her flat, full of elaborate gilt-framed mirrors, pink bows, pink lampshades and pale blue and pink flounces, should so much resemble that of a tart. In one corner of a bedroom dominated by a huge double bed, there was a sitz bath and wash-basin, discreetly concealed behind a screen. Inset into the floor of the lavatory was a rusty iron handle, which visitors always mistook for the flush. In fact, a jerk of it upwards would open the downstairs door, thus obviating a descent of innumerable stairs in near-darkness. When the bell rang, I would pop my head out of the lavatory window and shout down, '*Chi è?*'. Then I would decide if I wished to admit the caller or not. Outside the lavatory window there was a pulley with a basket on a rope, used if I wished to purchase anything from one of the many food vendors who in those days plied their trade from house to house.

Before I moved into this flat, I met at the Jennings-Riccioli a young American novelist, Hilda Osterhout, who had won a lavish prize, given by MGM, for a first novel. Despite my youthful envy – having read the novel, I lay awake one night fretting, 'But my novels are *far* better than that!' – she and I got on well together. I often wonder about her subsequent career. After a brief blaze of publicity, she seemed to pass into the shadows, confirming me in my view that every young novelist at the outset of his or her career should offer up to God the prayer: 'Not too much success, dear Lord – and not too soon!'

The Institute was then, as now, an independent establishment, so that I was employed there on secondment from the British Council, which paid my salary but not those of other members of the staff. Had my colleagues been less agreeable, this could have been a source of unpleasantness between us, since, far younger and far less experienced than they, I was none the less paid far more. Admittedly I had a university degree, which all of them lacked; but I soon realized that, in the teaching of English to foreigners, degrees, diplomas and doctorates are of far less importance than experience and force of personality.

At first my attempts to teach were pitiful. The classes which I enjoyed the most were the literature ones, since they were largely attended by attractive and

The author's father (1913) in Indian Police uniform

The author's mother, 1931

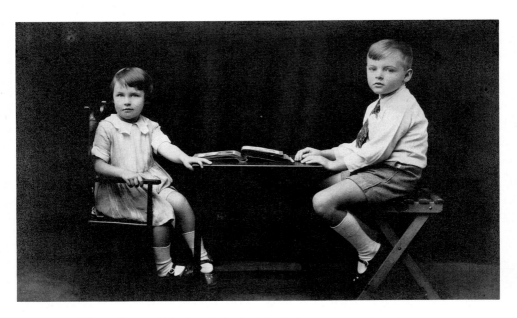

The author and his sister Elizabeth in their schoolroom in Naini Tal

The author in Lucknow, aet. 7

The author in Bournemouth, aet. 10

Fancy-dress dance on ship taking the author from India to England

Colin Haycraft during his
National Service

The author and his mother in Florence in 1949

The author with Harold Nicolson and the Greek society columnist
'Madame Cosmique' (far left) in Salonika

Alethea Hayter, a Greek guide, Brian de Jongh and Maurice Bowra
in Delphi (from left to right)

Elizabeth and John Rosenberg with the author at Vouliagmeni

Dino

Ronald Bottrall

The author and J. R. Ackerley
with students in Kyoto

James Kirkup

'Winifred God' – or Godfrey Winn

vivacious young girls of good family, whiling away their time until marriage claimed them. They teased me, they flirted with me, they giggled a lot, and they did little work. The classes which I enjoyed the least were in what was called Business English. They were largely attended by glum and far from attractive young men, eager to make a success in the shops and offices in which they had taken up, or were about to take up, employment. At the first of these Business English classes, I arrogantly announced that there was no such thing as Business English, there was only good English and bad English. The class over, a deputation of dissatisfied students went to see the Director of Studies, who then put me right. Soon I was instructing my Business English classes to write letters beginning: 'We thank you for your esteemed favour of the sixteenth ult., which has this morning come to hand.'

All the other teachers were women; and with the exception of one, Anita Ryan, all were middle-aged. Anita Ryan soon became a friend and an ally. The others soon became surrogate aunts, sometimes over-eager to instruct or even correct me, but always protective, indulgent and kind. Three of them had stayed on in Italy during the war; and one of these three was said to have been an admirer of Il Duce. Not merely was their Italian fluent, but they would often introduce Italian phrases into their English – 'I'm feeling just a little *giu* this morning,' 'That's not very *amabile* of you, *carina*,' 'How about slipping round to Giacosa for a *bocconcino*?' Totally unaware of my sexual proclivities, they would suggest that I had a 'crush on' or was 'sweet on' this or that of my girl students; or would tip me off that this or that mother 'had her eye' on me or 'had me in her sights' as a possible match.

I did in fact take to one Italian girl, appealingly shy, gawky and vague, who was a daughter of the well-known painter Ottone Rosai. But when, having invited her to the opera with me, I was told by her mother that an aunt would have to accompany us as chaperone, I soon lost interest. I was not planning to do anything of which the aunt would have disapproved; but her regally lowering presence, beringed hands constantly clicking her handbag open and shut in her lap even during an aria, filled me with exasperation, even rage.

The Director of the Institute was a musicologist, Francis Toye. To my surprise, it was almost two weeks after my arrival before I was summoned to the luxurious flat which he inhabited on top of the Palazzo Antinori, then the home of the Institute, for a meeting. He was a crashing snob, and it was all too clear that he regarded me, in common with all the other teachers with the exception of Anita Ryan, as hardly worth his notice. After having perfunctorily enquired whether I had found 'satisfactory digs' and whether I had settled down in my work, he said, 'I suppose you've read my life of Verdi?'

I was taken aback. 'No. No, I'm afraid I haven't.' In fact, I had never even heard of it.

'What! You haven't read the best life of Verdi in existence?' He rushed to the bookshelf behind him and took down a copy from a row of at least a dozen. 'Well, the sooner we remedy that, the better. After you've got through my life of Verdi, you can start on my life of Rossini.' He raised an admonitory forefinger. 'Now be sure to let me have that copy back! I don't want it swiped.' I had absolutely no wish to read it, let alone swipe it. But I attempted to appear grateful for the loan.

Toye, married to an American painter of means, had a crush on Anita Ryan, often inviting her, in the absence of his wife, to intimate suppers in his flat. With a lot of laughter, she would the next day relate to me how he would first try to coax her to drink more than she wished – 'But, my dear, I've opened this bottle of the Widow specially for you, it would be *cruel* to waste it' – and would then, unaware that she was totally unmusical, sit himself down at his grand piano and croon to her the sort of songs which he hoped might bring them closer.

With the war the English community had dwindled; but such as it was, it was extraordinarily kind to both Anita and me. Many of its members still lived in houses far too large for them, looked after by elderly servants whose meagre wages they found it increasingly difficult to pay. Of them at this period in their lives I wrote in my novel *The Ant Colony* – a book which, because it was largely composed in affectionate reminiscence, elicited from some reviewers, habituated to more highly seasoned fare from my literary kitchen, the criticism that it was too 'bland' for their tastes. One of the same reviewers had in the past complained that my novels were too sordid and grim.

As in the nineteenth century, many of these expatriates had an interest in spiritualism. 'Would you like to join our little group?' an otherwise hard-headed Scotswoman, Mrs Dundass, asked me. Out of curiosity, I accepted. The group included a member of the Whittaker family of Marsala exporters, a man generally out of favour with the rest of the English community both because he had energetically espoused Fascism during the war and because he now shared his life and ample fortune with a sinister-looking German, one of whose cheeks was disfigured with a duelling-scar; Una Lady Troubridge, eager to get in touch with her mate Radclyffe Hall on the other side; an American papal count, of Irish origin; and an American woman who was later to be murdered by the jealous Italian lover, a handsome cripple far younger than she was, whom she was keeping in idle luxury at a period when the word 'toy-boy' did not exist. The medium was a vast, Italian woman, her greasy black hair parted in the middle and lipstick smeared over her large, yellow front teeth, who groaned, grunted and sweated a great deal and delivered messages, among them one to me from an 'Auntie Flora' whom I did not possess, in an English so bizarrely accented – had she learned it from a Cockney nanny or in service in some restaurant in London? – that it was virtually unintelligible. In the same accent, she brought the papal count a message from his mother, and Una Troubridge one from her chum. Did she still have the rosary, the rosary bought in Assisi? the author of *The Well of Loneliness* demanded of Una Troubridge. And would she be sure to give Maria – or perhaps it was Margaretta – greetings? She concluded by telling Una

Troubridge that, from the other side, Toby – apparently one of their dachshunds – sent her a loving bark.

Harold Acton, sleek and plump, was one of those who was kind to me – as, over decade after decade, he has been kind to so many other visitors to Florence. This was a time when, his father still alive, he could not command the wealth now at his disposal; but he was always munificent in his entertaining, so that, thanks to him, I dined at many a restaurant which would have been far beyond my means. People said then, as they say now, that he was malicious; but his malice has always been of the tongue, not the heart. Despite his intermittent feuds with such other long-term foreign residents of Florence as Joan Haslip and Violet Trefusis, he is a man of huge kindness and tolerance.

I cared far less for his father Arthur, who had been involved in a scandal before the First World War, when the police were tipped off by a mother dissatisfied with her pay-off that, along with a local politician, he was photographing pubescent girls in a studio rented for that purpose. I do not think that Harold cared for Arthur much more than I did. Certainly he was afraid of him. On one occasion I remember that Harold took me into an upstairs room at La Pietra, where, on a stereoscopic viewer, he began to show me photographs of Florentine Anglo-American society at the turn of the century. We were behaving with total propriety. But all at once Arthur was in the doorway, saying in a sternly disapproving voice, 'Harold, I think it would be better if you showed Mr King the garden.'

Harold at first assumed that, because I saw so much of Anita Ryan, we must be having an affair. So it was that, when I arrived late at a party given by Elneth Capponi, the English widow of an Italian admiral, he greeted me with the words, 'I know *exactly* what you've been doing! You've been *cock*tailing with Miss Ryan.' The emphasis which he gave to the word 'cock', the voice first fluting upwards and then sliding downwards, in the manner of Edith Evans, caused general laughter and made me blush with embarrassment.

It was through Harold that I met Elle Milani-Comparetti – a worldly, vivacious woman, separated from her husband, a well-known psychiatrist. Shortly before my arrival, Elle's son, on whom she had doted with an almost unnatural passion, had committed suicide – to escape from her, some of those hostile to her unkindly suggested. She talked obsessively about him, as though he were still alive; and in me she saw, I suspect, a substitute son. No one, during my period in Florence, did more for me – supervising me, encouraging me, introducing me to innumerable Italian writers, actors, musicians, artists, whom otherwise I should never have met. Tough on herself and therefore often callous to others, highly intelligent, amusing and amusable, she liked to direct the life of anyone sucked into her orbit. Was I going out with Harold? Well, I'd have to cancel that, because she had arranged for me to meet the Director of the Accademia. Had I agreed to take on one of Anita's classes, because she was ill? No, no, it was out of the question! We were going to drive to Rapallo for the weekend, and we must start at midday that Friday. Sometimes I fretted against her domination; but more often I was glad of it, since almost everything which she, a foster mother determined to spoil the child in her care, arranged for me proved to be so interesting and exciting.

It was through Elle that I in turn met Bernard Berenson – or B.B., as she and almost everyone else in Florence called him. Like Harold Acton today, he was the peak which every visitor to Florence at that period craved to boast of having climbed. At my first visit to I Tatti, I was in a state of trepidation. Talk to him of your novels, Elle told me. Or of Oxford, he would like to hear all about Oxford. Or of your recent visit to Siena. But, sick with nerves, I doubted if I could talk about anything.

At first Berenson totally ignored me. He chatted to Elle, who knelt at his feet, chela to his guru. The room was gloomy and damp. A manservant carried round cups of a tea which was the colour, and smelled, of straw. Berenson's redoubtable secretary and lover, Nicky Mariano, was in conversation with a haughty Italian woman who worked in one of the museums. I was left to talk to an elderly French professor, now in my dreadful French and now in his no less dreadful English. Then Elle rose to her feet and summoned me: 'Come over here! B.B. wants to talk to you.'

I went over. I did not sit at his feet but on a stool.

Elle had told him that I was a novelist, he said. What kind of novels did I write?

That question, often put to me, is one which I have the greatest difficulty in answering. But I did my best. Berenson closed his eyes. Was he concentrating on what I was saying? Or had he gone to sleep?

Next, having opened his eyes, he asked me who were the novelists whom I most admired. Without any thought, I answered, 'Proust.'

'Proust? Proust!' He appeared to be astonished. 'But didn't Max Beerbohm do it all so much better before him?'

Was the old boy saying something extraordinarily perceptive? Or was he going gaga? Or was he making fun of me?

I still do not know.

We talked of other things both on that occasion and on others; but sadly, as so often when one has had such privileged conversations, I have little, if any, memory, after so many years, of what he said.

My most deeply etched memory of Berenson is of a luncheon party given by him for the black American dancer Katherine Dunham. She was a woman, sinuous, large and vivid, who exerted a phenomenal attraction, to which Berenson was clearly not impervious. After luncheon we went out into the garden, where she threw herself down on the grass. Berenson, pale and fragile, in a brown tweed cape-coat, stood over her, leaning on a stick. She looked up at him, smiling her wide, wicked smile. He smirked. There was so much life in her. He looked so close to death.


Most days, when we had a break from our teaching, Anita Ryan and I would drink coffee in Giacosa, then, as now, one of the two smartest cafés in the Via

Tornabuoni. Often we would be joined by our friends: American students, on Fulbright grants at the university; young English transients; young Italian writers, painters or teachers. We talked and talked, Anita more volubly and more amusingly than any of us.

At that period she was far from well, with a diseased kidney which often caused her fevers. Later, she had the kidney removed, became more robust, read for the Bar, and eventually emerged as a QC. Resembling a handsome horse, she had a splendidly upper-class manner and voice. To her, even strangers were 'my dear', and it was as 'my dear', not as 'm'lud' that she once inadvertently even addressed the formidable Lord Goddard in court.

I can truthfully say that, during those eighteen months which I spent in Florence, seeing her every day, I loved Anita and even repeatedly thought, with a growing anguish, 'Shall I ask her to marry me?' But I knew that the hurdle of sexual intercourse was one at which I should certainly fall. We continued to be friends until the time of her death. She even became godmother to one of my nieces.


After six months I moved from my tiny flat, already becoming stiflingly hot as the summer approached, into a large and handsomely furnished villa, the property of the Duke of Simoniato, out at Poggio Imperiale. What enabled me to do so was that I could share the rent, about four times that of the flat, with a friend, Michael Swan. Even so I was extraordinarily fortunate to be living in Florence at a time when such a villa, and a live-in manservant to look after it, were within the means of two young men neither of whom had any income other than what they earned.

Michael I had met while I was still an undergraduate at Oxford. As an author, he is now almost wholly forgotten; but at the outset of his career, he attracted the same kind of admiration for his travel writing as Bruce Chatwin did at the outset of his. He was handsome, entertaining and bold – even pushy, in the view of Somerset Maugham, with whom he, in effect, first invited himself to stay and then remained impervious to hints that perhaps the time had come for him to go. During a childhood scrap, his elder brother had inadvertently put out his eye with a knife. How precisely this had happened, I never discovered. Not only did Michael never refer to this disability, but it was only by an accident that, to my amazement, I discovered it when, as my guest, he was once staying at Balliol. I had gone along to his guest-room to take him to breakfast in Hall. He was having a bath and the room was empty. On the dressing-table was a leather box, such as one uses for cuff-links and studs. For want of anything better to do, I opened it. Three glass eyes stared up at me. In horror, I slammed the lid shut. Perhaps it was the lack of an eye, and the consequent need to reassure himself that he could nevertheless still be attractive to women, which made Michael into so frenzied an amorist; and perhaps it was that very frenzy which so often repelled women, instead of attracting them.

As I corrected one composition after another at a desk overlooking the courtyard, I would from time to time glance out and see Michael, nude but for the flimsiest of bathing-slips, sunbathing below me. How much I envied that brown, muscular body, that exuberance, that boldness, that ability to go to bed with a succession of women, evening after evening! How feeble and neurotic I was in contrast to him! But in making this comparison I was, as later events were tragically to show, wrong, wholly wrong.

Harold Acton was reported to have said, at a party, about Michael and me, 'Some say they do, some say they don't. But two such attractive young men . . . all alone in that villa . . . *I* say they do.' He must have been one of the few people to say that we did. Michael was quick to acquire a reputation as a rake in Florentine society.

When he was not in pursuit of any girl at hand, from the daughter of the impoverished aristocrats who were our closest neighbours to the seamstress at the nearby tailor's shop, Michael was excellent company. 'You have an eye,' I once said admiringly to him, when he had pointed out to me an architectural detail, previously unnoticed by me, on top of the Duomo; then I had blushed, realizing that my choise of phrase had hardly been tactful. With that eye, he was constantly seeing things others did not see: something small but important in the background of a picture; some oddity of human behaviour in a café, a railway station or a street; something weird or comic in a newspaper. Years later, in Japan, I found that Raymond Mortimer had the same gift. In both their companies, I saw things long familiar as though for the first time.

Before leaving England, Michael had urged the writer Isabel Strachey to come out and stay with us. He and she had been having an affair. But as the date of her arrival approached, he became more and more anxious, since he had started an affair with someone else. 'What am I going to do with her?' he kept asking me, without doing the obvious thing – putting her off. What he did eventually do was to dump her on to Maurice Cranston, who had arrived at about the same time to stay, and me. She clearly did not feel that the two of us were any sort of compensation for the lack of Michael, and passed most of the visit in a state of despondency.

Isabel had just published another – probably her second – novel, with Jonathan Cape. When she presented me with a copy, she told me the story of how her first novel had come to be accepted. 'He wrote me a letter and told me that he liked my novel but that, before he reached a definite decision, he wished to discuss it with me. Would I have lunch with him at the Ivy? At lunch he told me that I was a beautiful woman, and that, if I wished him to do me the favour of publishing my book, then I must do him a favour in return.' She stopped, gazing at me with those huge eyes of hers, above high cheekbones.

'And did you do him a favour in return?' I eventually prompted.

'Well, the book did get published, didn't it?' At that she burst into laughter. 'And doing the favour was really rather fun.'

Isabel took an unaccountable shine to the manservant who had come on to us from Sinclair Lewis – then an alcoholic resident of Florence, puffing asthmatically at the fag-end of what had once been a resplendent career. That the manservant wore a wig rakishly tipped over an eyebrow which looked as though it had been vigorously plucked, that he too, like Lewis, had all too clearly taken to the bottle, and that he was obviously (in the parlance of the time) as queer as a coot, in no way deterred her. On one occasion she gave me a postcard to post for her. No doubt inexcusably, I could not resist a glance at it. I read: 'There is a manservant here who looks exactly like Jesus Christ. Michael and Francis are beastly to him. They *crucify* him.'

I came to love Isabel both for the toughness under the fragility of her appearance and manner, and for her courage when her only daughter, Charlotte, married first to Anthony Blond and then to Peter Jenkins, was dying slowly of leukaemia. Before Charlotte's second marriage, Isabel invited Peter Jenkins's mother to dinner. Would I come too? Mrs Jenkins was very proper, Isabel had heard – whether erroneously or not, I do not know; and I would make the right impression on her. Bentley Bridgewater was also invited to make the right impression. Isabel had cooked an excellent dinner, Mrs Jenkins was charming. Then suddenly, over the pheasant, Isabel turned to me and drawled in her parody of an upper-class Twenties voice, 'Oh, Francis, you know everything. Do tell me. I keep hearing this word "frigging". What does it *mean*?'

'I've no idea, Isabel.'

'Bentley?'

'I've no idea either.'

Fortunately Isabel did not enquire if Mrs Jenkins had any idea.


Although I often disapproved of Michael's behaviour, thus justifying him in more than once telling me that I was a prig, we quarrelled only once during the months of sharing the villa. This was when, in my absence in Perugia to give a lecture, he and the now forgotten novelist Humphrey Slater picked up two tarts and had an energetic foursome in the largest bed in the villa, the ducal *matrimoniale*, in which I used to sleep. Returning home late at night, exhausted, I found that the pillows smelled of cheap scent, that there were stains on the sheets, and that a used condom was lying on the floor. I stormed into Michael's bedroom and, like Daddy Bear, demanded, 'Who's been sleeping in my bed?' At first Michael denied that anyone had done so. Then he burst into laughter and confessed all. As outraged as myself, Luigi the next morning announced that he was leaving. But when I returned from a day at the Institute, he was still in the villa, his face shiny and flushed with the gin which he swiped from us, his wig askew, and a bruise, hitherto unnoticed by me, on one cheekbone. He had prepared, as always, an excellent dinner.

On the first occasion when I invited two charming, unsophisticated American students, husband and wife, to dinner at the villa, Luigi held open the door for them to enter the dining-room. No doubt awed by his black trousers, white pleated shirt and patent leather pumps, the male American put an arm round his shoulder and propelled him, ahead of himself, into the room with a booming *'Prego, signore! Prego!'*, in the accents of Minnesota. Luigi was even more embarrassed than I was. Michael burst into laughter.

After so brilliant a start, Michael's life plunged into tragedy. Back in England, he had an affair with Margot Walmsley, employed by *Encounter* and already a literary hostess of great kindness and charm. When Margot, like many another woman before her, broke off the affair, Michael succumbed to a suicidal depression. He made one half-hearted, failed attempt to kill himself in the Regent Palace Hotel. Then, with greater resolution, he took a room in a Coventry Street hotel and, one afternoon, cut his throat and his wrists in the bath. By a fortunate or unfortunate accident (depending on how one views it), the maid decided that day to turn down the beds earlier than usual and, her knock having not been answered, blundered into the room. Michael was rushed to hospital and, after a succession of blood-transfusions, survived. But such had been the loss of blood from his brain that he was never subsequently able either to speak or to write coherently.

Being on leave from Greece, where I had been posted after my spell in Florence, I went to the Charing Cross Hospital, then located off the Strand, to visit him. He seemed pleased to see me; but when he attempted to talk to me, all that emerged was gibberish, as though, in a telephone exchange, all the wires had got muddled. 'P-p-please give me that – that p-p-puddle,' I remember him stuttering at one moment. I had no idea what he meant. Then I saw that he was pointing at a handkerchief which had fallen to the floor beside his bed.

On my second visit, I brought him an ant-colony, imprisoned under glass. He was so much fascinated by it, staring down at the teeming life of the ants, that he paid no attention to me, until I got up to go. Then, like a child on the point of being abandoned, he emitted a strange, desolate wail.

Eventually Michael married; and it then seemed to all of his friends – so staunch and capable was Joan Swan – that his life, so terrible to contemplate, might at last take a turn for the better. The documentary film-maker Hugh Gibb generously gave the couple an allowance. Other friends also provided financial assistance. Joan produced a daughter, Anna. She also produced reviews and poems which people, some of them literary editors, who knew nothing of the true circumstances, accepted as being by Michael.

Then Joan, no doubt wearying of life with someone who was really only half alive, fell in love first with a man and then with a woman, the writer Kay Dick, who wrote of their relationship and its tragic end in her fine novella *The Shelf*. Her life in a chaos with which she felt she could not cope, Joan eventually took an overdose of sleeping pills in a hotel. Kay Dick's letters to her were under the pillow of the bed in which her body was found.

Unable to look after the infant Anna, Michael handed her over, seemingly without a moment's hesitation, to the writer 'Gabriel Fielding' (Alan Barnsley) and his wife, to be brought up with their numerous children. After a court action, Anna's maternal grandparents eventually got custody of her.

From then on, Michael became increasingly reclusive, shrinking from any contact with his former friends. When I once ran into him at Chiswick House, he talked for a while, more coherently than in the past, but refused a lift back into central London or even a cup of tea at a nearby café. On a later occasion, seeing me approach at Victoria Station, he raced away into the crowd, a look of panic on his face. If others had not had similar stories, I might have supposed that I had inadvertently done something to frighten or annoy him. Finally, this poor, maimed, distracted man, once so handsome, so vivacious and so brilliant, succeeded in killing himself.

Whenever I see Sebastian Coe on television, I think of Michael, since there is an uncanny resemblance between the athlete and Michael in his youth. Michael's sister married an Indian. Sebastian Coe is her grandson by one of the daughters of that match.


One advantage of working for the British Council was that I met so many interesting people whom, at that period of my life, I should in other circumstances never have done.

Edith Evans arrived to give a reading at the Institute. Francis Toye, already in his sixties, introduced her: 'I am extremely happy to say a few words about Edith Evans, at whose feet I have metaphorically sat since, as a small boy, I first saw her perform.'

He might have been extremely happy to say the few words; she was certainly not extremely happy to hear them.

Later, at a party in her honour, he asked me, 'Are you at all interested in the theatre?'

I replied that yes, I was.

'Well, in that case, I'm going to put Edith Evans in your charge. I'm sorry but there's nothing else for it. I'm correcting proofs and I just can't spare the time to act as her bear-leader. In any case – to be absolutely frank with you – I find her far from *simpatica*. Apart from anything else, I just cannot *stand* large noses in women.'

I forbore to point out that Anita had a large nose.

It is always gratifying to earn a good mark for undertaking what is thought to be a chore by others but is a pleasure for oneself. Edith Evans was clearly flattered by the reverential devotion with which I attended to her every need: first interpreting for her in the shops and then carrying out for her whatever she had bought; opening doors for her with a bow whenever she stepped across a threshold; even waiting for her outside the Ladies in Giacosa. 'Are you what is called my *cicisbeo*?' she once gaily asked me. 'Well, up to a point,' I answered guardedly. Feature by feature, she was an ugly woman; but even then, in her fifties, she could persuade one that she was beautiful. Like most of the actors whom I have met in the course of my life – Gielgud, Ian McKellen and Anna Massey are exceptions – she seemed to lack any central core of personality. Throughout that Florence visit, she was for me not herself, whatever that might be, but a modern, English Ranevskaya. This impression was strongest when I took her out to dinner with an Englishman called Lionel Fielden at his villa in Antella. To an admiring audience of guests she was by turns capricious, coquettish, petulant, witty, pensive. Then, as she and I stood alone on the terrace, looking down at the wide landscape darkening beneath us, she launched into an extraordinary hymn to its beauty. What she said was of the order of 'Look at the purple shadows under those olive trees,' 'Oh, those clouds, those clouds!' and 'I can *smell* that thyme, can't you?'; but the intonations of that extraordinary voice and the changing expressions of that no less extraordinary face turned the banalities into jewels and so made the whole occasion magical.

When the time came for her to leave Florence, Edith Evans told me that she was worried about arriving in Bologna with no one to meet her. Could I perhaps accompany her there?

I longed to do so. But would the British Council pay my fare? (I was, as so often then, totally broke.) And, in any case, I had a class early on the Monday morning. 'I'm sure that someone from the Institute at Bologna will be at the station to meet you,' I said.

That day, when Edith Evans and I were having luncheon with Francis Toye in a restaurant, I told him, 'Miss Evans is worried about not being met in Bologna. But I've told her that I'm sure that someone from the Institute will be there.'

'On a Sunday? Oh, I very much doubt it! No one will want to turn out on a Sunday.'

'What a brute he is!' Edith Evans exclaimed to me afterwards. 'Do be a darling and ring up the Institute yourself.'

With some trepidation, I did so. Of course the Director was only too willing to turn out on a Sunday to meet so great an actress.


The Old Vic Company arrived with a production of *Twelfth Night*. That remarkable actor, Ernest Milton – whose wife, the novelist Naomi Royde-Smith, I had met through a nephew of hers up at Balliol at the same time as myself – played Malvolio with so consummate an artistry that I have never seen the role better performed. One of those actors – like Olivier and Antony Sher – who are prepared to take colossal risks, so that their performances are either demonstrations of genius or the most indigestible *prosciutto crudo*, Milton mistakenly but perhaps not unnaturally assumed that he was leading the company. Sadly for him, this was not the view of the company itself or of the Italians, since the Viola was Celia Johnson, then known all over the world for her performance in *Brief Encounter*. 'She's a *plucky* little actress,' Ernest Milton remarked to me of her, as we ate what he called 'cold cuts' in my cramped little flat. 'And she has a certain sweetness of manner.' He pondered for a while, chewing on some lettuce. 'I have a feeling that she may go far.' Then, in a steely voice, he concluded, 'But she'll have to *work at it*.'

I took one of my classes to a performance, each student armed with an Italian version of the text. Unfortunately, they managed to get ahead of Ernest Milton's Malvolio in the most famous of his scenes, so that laughter constantly preceded, instead of following, his delivery of a line. That night he refused to take a curtain. I never confessed to him that it was I who had brought to the theatre 'those jackanapes' (as he called them).

Another visitor was the dancer Mona Inglesby, who, thanks to the generosity of a patron, had a ballet company of her own. No one in the British Council, other than myself, seemed to be aware that in certain Italian dialects the word *mona* has an indelicate connotation. I finally succeeded in persuading the Rome office of the British Council that it might be better if its publicity should merely refer to the dancer as 'La Inglesby', dropping the 'Mona' – despite a retort from the Representative, the poet Ronald Bottrall, 'But that's precisely what she is!'

Ronald Bottrall was then at the height of his glory in the Council: a fluent speaker of Italian; friend of Moravia, Montale, Bassani and a host of other writers; lodged in a magnificent apartment in the Palazzo Doria. At that time he was married to his first wife, Margaret, a lady-like and scholarly woman of quiet charm. It was not difficult to see that, he so ebullient and she so fastidious, they were likely eventually to separate. At a summer school for Italian teachers in the Dolomites, at which I was a totally inadequate instructor, they were constantly quarrelling. Returning one evening, after one of these quarrels, from a lecture given by Ronald, I remarked to Margaret, 'That was a wonderful lecture.'

She replied acidly, 'I'm glad you liked it. ... I wrote it.'

I had, indeed, thought it above Ronald's usual standard.

Back in the London office of the Council, Ronald eventually married his secretary there. Volubly amusing, sharp, tough, hospitable, Margot was the complete antithesis of her predecessor Margaret – thus providing an exception to my rule that, when people remarry, it is to rejigged models of their previous partners.

Ronald's attractive young secretary in Rome became a friend of mine. I was therefore able to persuade her to show me his annual report on me. Having described me as 'rather callow', 'tactless' and 'indiscreet' – all perfectly justifiable criticisms – he then had a number of flattering things to say, the last being: 'Of all my staff, he is the only one who has bothered to make friends with ordinary Italians.' No doubt he had reached this conclusion after seeing how, in the evening at the summer school, I used often to forsake the company of the Italian teachers to go down to one or other of the village taverns, where my contact with a clientele composed almost entirely of farm labourers was wholly innocent but none the less enjoyable.

It is a common misapprehension among heterosexuals that homosexuals are snobbish. Of course there are homosexual snobs; but in general homosexuality encourages people to leap social barriers – so that a middle-class homosexual writer like J.R. Ackerley shows far more understanding of the working classes than many a middle-class heterosexual one. Ackerley had, of course, acquired that understanding through his guardsmen friends and their families.

Throughout my eighteen months in Florence, I slaved away at my novel of Florentine life, *The Dividing Stream*. Years later, Anita told me how amazed she and the rest of the staff had been at the way in which I used to come out of a class, hurry over to my desk in a corner of the common room and, oblivious of the chatter, laughter and clinking of coffee cups, settle down, in the twenty-minute break, to another paragraph. My years at Shrewsbury, working away in a study shared with other boys, had fortunately trained me in a concentration which has remained with me to the present, so that the interruptions of telephone call, postman, milkman, daily cleaner never leave me gasping for my next sentence, as they leave so many of my writer friends.

# — 2 —

# Bay of Desolation

Posted to Salonika, in the immediate aftermath of the civil war from which even today Greece has still not wholly recovered, so bitter are the memories of it, I stayed for one night in Athens with the Representative, Wilfrid Tatham, and his wife, Rachel.

Wilfrid, a former Olympic athlete and Eton housemaster, was a benevolent, bumbling, philistine but by no means stupid man. His classy, sharp-tongued wife, often said to be the prototype of Osbert Lancaster's Maudie Littlehampton, treated him as though he were the child which, to his regret but not hers, they had never had.

The Tathams had planned a dinner-party for me, to which they had invited some British Council colleagues and some junior officials at the Embassy.

'I expect you'd like to have a bath and to change,' Rachel said.

I did as she instructed, eventually returning downstairs in a brown tweed suit.

Rachel looked me up and down, in pop-eyed horror. (Later, on a visit to Athens, the famous surgeon Sir Arthur Porritt instantly diagnosed, merely from her appearance, that she was suffering from thyrotoxicosis and eventually operated on her.) 'Are you planning to wear that suit?' she demanded.

'Well, yes.'

'But you can't wear a brown suit to a dinner-party! Haven't you got a dark blue or dark grey one?'

I told her that my dark grey suit was in the trunk sent to Salonika ahead of me by sea.

'Oh, my God!' She rushed to the bottom of the stairs and called up them, 'Wilfrid, Wilfrid! He's wearing a *brown* suit!'

Wilfrid appeared, tying his O.E. tie. 'But hasn't he –?'

'No, he hasn't! Can you imagine . . .? What *will* people think?'

When, some six or seven years ago, I last attended a dinner-party given by a British Council Representative in Athens, one of the guests, a young teacher, was wearing grey flannels, an open-necked shirt and espadrilles. No one seemed to think anything of it.

\*

I had been thrilled with Athens; but as I was driven in the Council car from Salonika airport to the hotel in which I was to be accommodated until a flat was ready for me, depression seeped into me. First we jolted over a fissured road, through an immense plain, metallic in its hardness, coldness and bareness. There were hills, resembling huge, unformed lumps of lead, desolate fields where the autumn wheat sprouted like a greenish sheen on copper, and everywhere long, reed-fringed expanses of water, the steely surfaces of which reflected the pale blue sky, the stationary clouds and the almost stationary gulls. Sometimes we would pass a track, leading off into nowhere, and there, in the distance, would be the minute black figure of a man on a donkey, of a woman stumbling over the ruts with a bundle on her head, or of some solitary child, seemingly abandoned and turned to stone against the desolation about it.

On the outskirts of the town, Robin Duke, the Director of the Institute, turned to me after a long silence. 'The refugee quarter. Greeks from Asia Minor.' We were passing down an avenue of corrugated iron sheds. One might have imagined that one was passing through a chicken-farm. 'Is this what you expected?' Robin asked.

'No.'

'I know just how you feel.'

Again we sat in silence.

Then Robin said, 'This is the town's smartest suburb. We live out here. Your flat will be out here, if the Armenians in it finally move out.'

Ancient, mustard-coloured trams swayed and clanged through the dust, as the British Council driver, a White Russian who claimed to have been a colonel in the Tsarist Army, expertly edged the car between them and the cracked pavement. The large villas on either side of us had once been inhabited by the tobacco-merchants who had made Salonika prosperous. Now their gardens, the railings of which had been plugged with bird-nests of rusty barbed wire, looked as if they had been scratched over by generations of hens, their imposing steps were disintegrating into muddy ramps, and cardboard or plywood often covered their windows.

Robin Duke took me into the hotel and, after I had registered, accompanied me up to the frowstily over-heated bedroom. 'Christ!' It was he who exclaimed it, as he surveyed now the cracks in the ceiling and the walls and now the dusty, dilapidated furniture. I had restrained myself from doing so. 'Well, at least it's fairly spacious. And you do have a bath and loo to yourself.' He essayed the flush. Nothing happened. He tried again and again. Water finally trickled down.

I pulled back the curtain and looked out of the window at the dimming harbour. 'What's that ship out there?' I could hear a low rattle and hum throbbing from it.

'Oh, that? That brings the town its electricity. It acts as the power-station, until they build a new one to replace the one that was blown up. That's why the lights everywhere are so dim. From time to time we even have a black-out.'

Robin left me, saying that I'd probably like an hour or two to settle myself in, before he called in his car to fetch me for dinner. But I did not need more than twenty minutes. After that, I sat on the edge of the sagging bed and stared down at the floor. I tried to lift my depression, as though it were some damp, heavy blanket thrown over my head; but I could not do so.

Everyone in Florence had been so friendly. No doubt here the Greeks would have been equally friendly too, but most of them spoke no English, so how could we communicate? The Dukes, who had already been in Salonika for several months, did as I should no doubt have done in similar circumstances: they had me over to two or three meals, they took me on two or three excursions in their car, and then, absorbed in their own affairs, they left me to sink or swim. Harold Davies, the English lecturer at the university, and his wife Dorothy were intelligent and kind; but they had two young children to preoccupy them. There was one locally appointed English teacher, an obese and semi-literate Scotsman married to a Greek, who clearly decided that he did not like me when, having invited me to a taverna, he realized that I was far more interested in talking to his wife, an attractive and cultivated woman, than to him. A further black mark was that I did not at all take either to ouzo, with its disagreeable flavour of aniseed, or to the pine disinfectant which goes under the name of retsina.

Another Englishman married to a Greek worked for the Institute as its administrative officer. A former Army corporal, he was up to all sorts of dodges to eke out a salary totally inadequate to satisfy his attractive, if over-plump and over-dressed, wife. For some reason he made me into his confidant, revealing how one Greek had given him 'a sweetener' for sending the Council vehicles to his garage for repair, and how another Greek had lent him a villa for a family holiday in Kavalla, on the understanding that future contracts for building work to the Institute would be awarded to him. When Christmas came round, this jolly rogue presented me with a volume of Churchill's memoirs, from which I noticed that the fly-leaf had been ripped out. A few days later, the librarian at the American library asked me if we had many thefts from our library. 'Not all that many,' I replied. 'We've had an epidemic of them,' she said. 'Only the other day the new volume of Churchill's memoirs arrived, and within less than a week someone had removed it.'

Some obscure loyalty to my crooked little benefactor prevented me from telling the librarian that the book was in my possession, just as it prevented me from telling Robin Duke about the graft over the repairs to the Council cars, the building work to the Institute and a number of other things.

The Institute premises, formerly the German Consulate, were perched out on a narrow spit of land overlooking the bay. From its balcony, I could each evening watch the most spectacular sunsets, such as I have never seen anywhere else in the world, except in Cochin. In these sunsets, so beautiful when so much else was so ugly, I found an unexpected alleviation of my depression. Leaning on the rusty iron railing, my chin in my hands, I used to feel an almost physical lightening. Then the bell would sound, and reluctanly I would make way back to the classroom. For an hour or two my exhilaration, like the effects of some drug, would remain with me.

My students in Salonika were very different from my students in Florence. After the occupation and the years of civil war, only the wealthiest of the women showed any elegance. Men and women alike often irritated me with that characteristically Greek assumption that everything is simpler and easier than it is. When, to an advanced literature class, I tried to explain, say, the whole spectrum of critical interpretations of a Hamlet soliloquy, a look of fretful boredom would appear on all but a few of their faces. 'Yes, yes, that's obvious, that's clear, get on with it!' they seemed to be chiding me.

Soon after my arrival, I set a composition to one of my classes: 'An Exciting Adventure'. The most arresting composition, though far from the best written, was produced by a muscular, moustached youth, of about seventeen or eighteen, who came from a family of refugees from Asia Minor. It told of how a band of communist guerrillas had descended on the refugee settlement, a few miles outside Salonika, in which his family lived, had killed anyone who had attempted any resistance, and then, as though they were rustling cattle, made off with a number of children and adolescents. Among these victims had been the youth. After months of hardship in the mountains, he had seized an opportunity to escape, and somehow, ragged and half starving, had eventually returned to his home.

When the time came to hand back the compositions, I selected this one for special praise. 'You have the imagination of a potential novelist,' I told him. 'You must write more of these stories. You visualize everything so clearly.'

He stared at me in increasing bewilderment. Then he said, 'But all that I wrote is *true*, Mr King. That is what happened to me.'

There were many people in Salonika, I later discovered, who had had similarly dramatic adventures in either the war or the even crueller civil war which followed it.

While still waiting for my prospective flat to be vacated, I made friends with a medical student, met in the Institute Library. A communist – confessing this to me, he asked me to tell no one else – and, rare in Greece, a passionate and knowledgeable lover of plants and birds, he spoke excellent English, learned, I eventually discovered, from a British Army officer who for several months had been his lover. Curiously, he preferred to make love in the desecrated Jewish cemetery, a waste land strewn with fragments of tombs and dotted with thorn bushes, than in my hotel room or in his own lodgings. It was safer in the cemetery, he would tell me; but in fact it was far more dangerous, since the main road was only some five hundred yards away. He must, I decided, get some kind of thrill either out of the danger of discovery or out of the tragic location itself.

From this youth I contracted gonorrhoea. At first, such was my innocence, I had no idea what the increasingly unpleasant symptoms could mean. Then it struck me. In trepidation I made an appointment with the British Council doctor, a jovial, anglophile septuagenarian, who, in his youth, had trained at Edinburgh University. In advance I prepared an explanation.

'No doubt about it,' Dr Alexandrides told me with a triumphant grin. 'You have a dose of the clap.' He prided himself on his colloquial English, even if – as when he described some girl as 'a stunner' or some man as 'a rotter' – it was already out of date. 'How did you manage to get this?'

I came out with my story. In the bedroom next to mine at the hotel a middle-aged Greek widow was living. We had got into conversation; she had eventually invited me into her room for a drink; one thing had led to another . . .

Dr Alexandrides roared with laughter. 'Just what happened to me in Edinburgh!' he said. 'There was this older woman, an actress, in the room next door to me in my digs. But you are luckier than I was. It took me six months to get rid of my dose. But now, thanks to the discovery of your Dr Fleming . . .'

The next day, at our next meeting – on my insistence, not in the Jewish cemetery but in my hotel room – I told the medical student of what had happened.

He flew into a rage. 'But how do you know that you have caught this disease from me?' he demanded. 'I do not have this disease. I am not ill!'

I explained that I had not had intercourse with anyone else for more than three months.

'You have this disgusting disease and then you try to put the blame on me! No, no! This is enough! This is too much!'

I begged him to consult a doctor; I offered to pay for him to do so.

He stormed out of the room. He never spoke to me again. When, as inevitably happened, I ran into him in the street or at the Institute, he would not even look at me, let alone return my greeting.

As I used to wander alone through the streets of Florence, so now I wandered alone through the streets of Salonika. But whereas my Florentine peregrinations used to fill me with joy, my Salonikan ones filled me with gloom. Any present-day visitor to Salonika will have difficulty in imagining the brutal squalor and abject poverty – such as nowadays, in Europe, can only be encountered in Albania and Romania – to be seen on every side. Barefoot children would shout, 'Amerikano! Amerikano!' or 'Johnny! Johnny!' and patter after me, demanding money, money, money. On the cracked pavements peasant women with dirt-seamed faces would set out their pathetically meagre wares: jars of mountain berries, a basin of potatoes, a few sticks of celery. Emaciated horses would drag creaking carts over the cobbles; no less emaciated donkeys, belaboured with sticks and intimidated with guttural shouts, would stagger under vast loads.

In the centre of the town there was a pastry shop and restaurant, Flocca, to which the richer Greeks and the foreigners would resort. Sitting at a table by its window one evening, in the company of the medical student (this was before our rift), I was suddenly aware of innumerable children gathered outside in the cold brought down from the mountains by the razor-sharp wind known to the Greeks as the Vardari. Many of their faces were pressed against the glass dividing them from us. A plate of cream cakes rested on the table between the student and me. Suddenly, on an impulse, I picked it up and hurried out of the shop with it. I held the plate out to the children. First they stared at me, as though I were either crazy or were making an attempt to poison them. Then, with whoops of delight, hands reached out and grabbed. Those who had been too slow to gain any booty began scuffling with the others.

I returned with the empty plate to the table. All the other customers were staring at me.

'Are you mad?' the student asked.

Suddenly what I had done seemed to me silly, futile, exhibitionistic.

'That's not how to improve things for those children,' he reproved me. I knew that for him the only way to improve things was for the revolution to succeed.

'I know, I know,' I said.

'Now I must ask the waitress to bring some more cakes.'

When the waitress brought them, I was unable to eat.

Eventually I moved into the flat for which I had been waiting. Though extremely small, though decorated a garish blue throughout, and though possessing only a wood-burning stove for the heating of bathwater and a single primus for cooking, it was, by the standards of those days, comfortable, even luxurious. But, situated far out in the suburb in which the Dukes also lived, it made me feel even more isolated. Every morning I used to walk down the road, its paving-stones cracked and broken and its surface corrugated with water-filled ruts, to wait interminably for a crowded tram in which I would then stand pressed between people many of whom had clearly not washed for days, perhaps even weeks. In the evenings I used to make the same journey back. Mine was no great hardship, and I was feeble not to have been more resilient. In the flat below lived an Anglo-Levantine family: father, mother, small son. The son cried endlessly, as though vocalizing my own increasing despair, and the mother would then scream at him and he would cry even louder. The couple made no attempt to befriend me, even though from time to time I used to hand them a present – some sweets, some ill-made toy, some book bought from the international bookshop – for their child. With him I felt an odd solidarity.

Soon I was slipping inexorably into what, I now realize, was a nervous breakdown, such as (I am glad to say) I have never again experienced. First there was depression of a kind to which I am often prone: everything seemed increasingly difficult, I worried about trivialities, I had little appetite, I was reluctant to get out of bed in the morning and, on returning home, I wanted at once to go back to bed. Then, in the middle of the night, I woke up with the terrible conviction: Nothing, nothing at all mattered. It was as though, in the middle of a meal, all food had suddenly ceased to have flavour for me.

Somehow I concealed my condition from everyone. 'Are you all right?' Dorothy Davies asked me, clearly concerned, one Sunday when I was having lunch with her, her husband and their children. Perhaps I had been unusually silent; perhaps she had noticed a strained or haggard look. 'Oh, yes, thank you,' I replied.

Each day I used to consider the possibility of killing myself. At that period there was no difficulty about buying sleeping-pills at any Greek pharmacy. I bought some barbiturates. Lying in bed, I used to pick up the bottle from the table beside me and even, on some occasions, unscrew its cap and shake some pills into my palm. Then I used to tell myself: Wait until tomorrow. Everything may change tomorrow. So it went on, day after day, for more than a month.

What caused this depression? Perhaps the breach with the medical student had something to do with it. I had not been in love with him but in him, so intelligent, entertaining and vivacious, I thought that I had found the congenial friend for whom I had been looking. Perhaps, having been so much spoiled in Florence, I felt unappreciated in Salonika. Perhaps, as the winter approached, I could less and less stand this dimly lit, dilapidated city, with its alien language, its icy winds, and its insistent poverty.

One day I woke up and found myself thinking, as I looked out of the window at the unkempt garden belonging to the couple below me: What a beautiful day! There had been a frost; the grass glittered in the weak, amber sunlight. Wisps of fog clung to the branches of the trees. That was the beginning of my slow climb up out of the pit. When, many years later, Alan Ross came to luncheon with me in such a state of mute depression that he raised knife and fork to his mouth as though they were made of lead, I knew precisely what he was feeling.

Among my students, was a beautiful and elegant Alexandrian Greek, married to the head of the Flocca dynasty which owned both the best cake-shop and restaurant in Salonika and a number of similar establishments in other parts of Greece. No doubt bored with a city so much less exciting than her native one, she attended the advanced literature course which I taught three times a week, always arriving early to claim a seat in the front row. When I wished to wipe out something on the blackboard, she would leap to her feet and cry out, 'Let me do it, Mr King!' Taking the cloth from me, she would work vigorously at the blackboard, her slim, sinuous body swaying from side to side and a charm-bracelet tinkling on one of her fragile wrists.

With her, I fell in love, in the only way in which I have been able to fall in love with any woman: romantically, without any sexual desire whatever. If she did not fall in love with me, she was certainly fond of me.

She and her husband, who was reputed to have affairs with young girls, would often invite me back to their house, where the food was always excellent – it was sent over from their restaurant – and the company, by Salonika standards, smart. From time to time they would also take me on expeditions on their yacht.

Eventually, the British Council officer whom I was replacing quitted Greece for a posting in Africa, and I then moved into his flat, high up in a block on the seafront. This was far more satisfactory for me. I had by then made a number of Greek friends, the majority writers, and in the evenings they took to dropping in – in the Greek manner, without any prior warning – if they happened to be passing. From my predecessor I took over a maid called Poppy – a woman who, for all her defects, had in abundance a quality which I always admire: valour. Wearing slippers, a battledress blouse and an old tweed skirt fastened at one side with large safety-pins, she would break off from her perfunctory cleaning of the flat with a broom or a soft hand-held brush, to tell me about the latest outrage committed by a husband whom, to my novelist's regret, I was never to be allowed to meet. He beat her up; he took her wages and spent it on drink, gambling and women; he lost one job, got a worse-paid one, and then lost that too. Could he really have been such a monster? Or did she only want to make me believe that he was, in a desire to arouse my pity?

I knew that, in shopping for me, she was cheating me; but the sums were so pitifully small and she herself was so impoverished that I never uttered a word. When I threw out some socks with holes in them, she asked if she could take them for her husband. When I abandoned a threadbare jacket, she somehow made herself a waistcoat out of it.

When I fell ill with flu, she crooned over me, 'Poor mister! Poor mister!' as she trickled water from a saturated sponge over my forehead. The water ran down my neck on to my chest, so icily uncomforable that I lost my temper with her. 'Oh, Poppy, do go and clean out the bath! It's filthy!'

One evening when I returned from work I found Poppy, in petticoat and grey woollen stockings, lying out on my bed, the light off.

'Poppy! What are you doing here?' I was far from pleased.

She put a hand to her forehead. 'Headache,' she said. 'Bad headache.' Then she sat up on the bed and gave me an impish smile.

'Oh, get off my bed! I'll give you an aspirin. Then please – go *home*!'

She got off the bed with a sigh. She did not accept the aspirin.

One of my successors, now dead, had an affair with Poppy; she even bore him a daughter. I have often wondered what has happened to the girl. I never dared to ask him.


Robin Duke was transferred to Athens, and was succeeded by John Davison. John and his wife Cynthia are two people to whom the epithet 'good' can be unreservedly applied. Like many good people, they are also unworldly, always believing the best of others and therefore always surprised and sorrowful when the worst is revealed. In the once tidy house inhabited by the Dukes, they lived in a state of total chaos. But if I was depressed, I knew that I had only to go there to experience an immediate raising of my spirits. Whatever he was doing, John would greet me with a smile. Cynthia would put down one of the children from her lap and would rush into the kitchen to make me a cup of tea or coffee.

In the interregnum between the departure of the Dukes and the arrival of the Davisons, I had been in charge of the Institute. It was therefore as Acting Director that I received a call in the office from a goblin-like man, a White Russian called Tsaipi Britnev, who told me that he had arrived in Salonika as representative of a firm of tobacco importers. He was, I subsequently discovered, brother of an actress, Maria Britnevna, whom I had seen perform in London, and who, later, was to marry Lord St Just and to become a friend and the literary executor of Tennessee Williams. I at once took to Tsaipi, as I invariably take to people who give an immediate impression of vigour and incisiveness. I therefore asked him if he would like to come out to dinner with me. He accepted.

We went to a taverna, in which many of the customers were workmen and soldiers and the only women were tarts. There was a small bouzouki band playing. Having thrown back a few glasses of ouzo, Tsaipi got up and performed to it. He had never been in Greece before but, amazingly, merely from having watched the others on the floor, he gave an acceptable version of a Greek dance. Back at the table, he talked vivaciously.

When we left the taverna, we happened to pass a shooting-gallery, which Tsaipi suggested that we should enter. I protested that I was the most appalling shot. 'Well, let me see if I can win anything,' Tsaipi said. Time after time he won something, until the owner of the gallery vigorously shook his head at the request for yet another round and made it clear that enough was enough.

After that I saw a lot of Tsaipi. Unlike myself during my first weeks in Salonika, he seemed to have no difficulty in making friends among the foreign community. Many of these were young men, of various nationalities, who, as United Nations observers in the aftermath of the civil war, had to ensure that there were no breaches of the armistice between the two factions.

Being a novelist, I wanted to learn about the tobacco industry, so important to the economy of Macedonia. I therefore questioned Tsaipi at one of our early meetings. He appeared to be embarrassed; tried to change the subject; and, when I persisted, answered in the vaguest terms. The Davisons – to whom I had introduced him – and I eventually decided that his work as representative of a firm of tobacco importers must be merely a front for some other activity. This seemed to be confirmed when he announced that he was off to Athens to see an uncle of his there on a visit. Who was this uncle? we asked. Tsaipi named one of the leading English merchant bankers of that time. How could an English Jew be related to a gentile White Russian, we wondered. Then Cynthia said, 'Perhaps he's an uncle by marriage.'

On his return from Athens, Tsaipi fell ill with jaundice. This seemed in no way to dampen his irrepressibly high spirits. Now the colour of an unripe orange, he cracked jokes, hooted with laughter at them, and pinched the nurses' bottoms from the hospital bed to which he was confined. The Consulate was solicitous about him; he received many visits from the United Nations observers.

Soon after that, he vanished from Salonika and from our lives. Then, more than a year later, when I was on leave in London, he hailed me in Piccadilly. I'd often wondered what had become of him, I told him. He replied that he had often wondered what had become of me. Would I have lunch with him one day, to talk over old times?

We had luncheon in the Hyde Park Hotel. As always he talked volubly and laughed a lot. Then, over a brandy, he said, 'I think that I must make a confession to you. When I was in Salonika, I wasn't really working for a firm of tobacco importers.'

'Well, of course, I realized that,' I said. 'And so did the Davisons.'

He was stunned. 'You realized that?'

'Of course. You knew absolutely nothing about tobacco.'

He began to recover his composure. He laughed. 'You *are* bright . . . Yes, I was doing some hush-hush work there. That was my cover.'

I wanted to ask what precisely this 'hush-hush work' was; but I refrained from doing so.

He went on, 'You know, before I went to Salonika, I was keeping an eye on a group of people who frequented Soho pubs. Among them, were your sister Pamela and her husband and some friends of theirs. I had to pretend to be one of their set.'

'Really? How extraordinary!'

'Well, the husband is an anarchist, isn't he?'

I laughed. 'Well, not an anarchist in the sense that he wants to blow anyone or anything up! He just doesn't believe in government, that's all.'

'Yes. I see.' But he did not sound convinced.

He went on to tell me that he had now 'left the firm'. He was going to Rhodesia to farm.

'Tobacco farming?' I asked.

Usually so ready to laugh, he did not laugh at that.

When we said goodbye outside the hotel, it was with reassurances to each other that this time we would keep in touch. But I doubted whether there would be any further contact between us; and there has been none.

This was my first experience of the sinister and absurd world of Intelligence. It was not to be my last.

In Salonika I met a man – I shall call him Jones, since after all these years I no longer remember his name – who, shabby, peevish and dreary, might have been mistaken for a commercial traveller down on his luck. His wife, socially and educationally a distinct cut above him, came from a rich Greek family, known to a Greek friend of mine, a lawyer. To the lawyer this family often complained that Jones had merely married his wife for her money, and had then ill-treated and sponged off her. They also told the lawyer that Jones had been working for British Intelligence.

One raw evening, when I was waiting outside the Institute for the bus to take me down into the town and so home, Jones's car screeched to a stop beside me. 'Want a lift?' Usually so torpid, he now seemed agitated.

As I got into the car, I noticed that its rear window had been shattered, as though by a stone.

'What's happened to your rear window?' I asked.

'Oh, that! You know what the roads are like here. I was driving back from Cavalla and a stone must have got thrown up.'

Suddenly, I noticed a small area of splintered wood in the dashboard in front of me. I peered more closely.

Jones noticed that I had noticed the splintered wood. I could tell that from the way that he glanced at me and then shifted in his seat and hunched yet closer over the wheel. I said nothing, he said nothing.

A year or two later, when I was in England, I read of the mysterious killing of Jones in the Bayswater bedsitter in which, now divorced or separated from his wife, he had been living. He had been shot in the head. His murderer was never found.

From time to time the British Embassy would send the Council staff in Salonika a consignment of duty-free booze and fags. When one such consignment arrived for me, the Council driver, the portly, dapper, moustached Russian who claimed to have served as a colonel in the White Russian Army, brought it over to my block of flats in the Council station wagon. Would he mind helping me carry the two crates upstairs? I asked him, planning to give him one of the bottles of Scotch for his pains. He shook his head indignantly. 'I am not a porter,' he replied. He pointed to the caiques moored at the quay which flanked the street in which the block of flats was situated. 'Perhaps you can find a porter over there.'

'Well, I'm not a porter either. But I'm not too proud to carry a crate up some stairs.' Angrily, I heaved up one of the crates and, staggering, started up the stairs with it. So far from being shamed into helping me, as I had imagined, he merely shrugged, got into the station wagon, and drove off.

All at once, half-way up to my flat, I experienced a sudden, sharp pain. I had ruptured myself.

Dr Alexandrides was on holiday. The young locum whom I saw diagnosed the trouble and then gave me a chit to take to a shop, dilapidated and dusty, which sold surgical appliances of a kind that used to be advertised in cheap newspapers and magazines in my youth. There I was fitted up with an extraordinarily cumbersome truss, which might, at a perfunctory glance, have been mistaken for a medieval chastity belt. It made me feel far more uncomforable than the hernia.

When I eventually told the Davisons of my predicament, they insisted that I should go to Athens for an operation. There, I saw the most famous surgeon in Greece, a suave, cultivated man called Manos, and entered the Evangelismos Hospital. When I had sufficiently recovered from the anaesthetic to examine what he had done to me, it struck me that the scar was unusually high. 'Isn't this scar very high?' I said to the sister, a Greek who had spent the war years in the States, when she came round to take my blood-pressure.

She pursed her lips and shook her head impatiently. 'That is the usual place for an appendectomy.'

'But I didn't have an appendectomy. I had a hernia repaired.'

Alarmed, she hastily examined the chart at the bottom of my bed. Then she said briskly, 'You must discuss all this with Dr Manos.'

Later that evening Dr Manos arrived with his usual entourage of young men in white coats, stethoscopes around their necks. 'I'm afraid there was a problem,' he said. 'When I cut you open, I found your appendix in such a terrible state that it was imperative to remove it at once. I had to leave the hernia.'

I had never had any of the symptoms of appendicitis. I am convinced that one of Dr Manos's underlings was told to perform what is, my surgeon friends tell me, a simple operation; and that he performed the wrong one. Two weeks later, I was again trundled down to the operating theatre. This time, the rupture was repaired.

After the second operation, a huge box of chocolates, the largest I have ever seen, was delivered to me. It was in the shape of a heart and was covered in red velvet. It had been manufactured by Flocca, and came from Mrs Flocca.

Inevitably I offered these chocolates to my visitors, since there were far more in the box than even a chocoholic like myself could devour; and no less inevitably my visitors would put the question: 'Who on earth sent you a box as large as that?'

Then Robin Duke came to see me. He and Yvonne had been tirelessly attentive.

I offered him a chocolate. He took one and began to chew on it. 'Delicious.' He continued to chew. Then he said, 'Forgive me for saying this, but – but I wonder if you haven't been just a little bit indiscreet.'

'How do you mean?'

'Well, I don't care a damn what you and Mrs Flocca may have got up to – or may still be getting up to. More power to your, er, elbow, as it were! But I honestly don't think it wise of you to *publicize* the affair.'

'*Publicize* it?'

'Well, by telling everyone that it was she who sent you those chocolates . . .' He was clearly embarrassed. 'You have to think of her reputation – and of her husband's reaction. And of course you have to think of the Council . . .'

'But, Robin, there's *been* no affair! Haven't you realized? I'm not – not interested in women. Not in that way.'

Robin was visibly upset by the euphemism. Clearly he had not guessed at my homosexuality. In those pre-Wolfenden days, people were far more innocent than now – no bad thing for homosexuals.

My confession, although it made absolutely no difference to my friendship with Yvonne and Robin – indeed, it continued up to their deaths, within a few months of each other, some five or six years ago – did, however, have one unfortunate result. For my convalescence they invited me to stay with them in the handsome villa, set in a large, luxuriant garden, which the Council had rented for them in Kifissia. They were unsparing in their attentions to me; but they were also all too clearly worried that I might misbehave with one or other, or indeed both, of their pre-pubescent sons. The boys had taken to me and would frequently, to my exasperation, come out into the garden to interrupt my reading. When, having been told by Dr Manos to walk as little as possible, I used to hire a pony carriage to take me on jaunts around Kifissia, the two boys, understandably enough, wanted to come along too. In consequence from Yvonne there was a lot of: 'Boys! Boys! I want you to lend me a hand!' and from Robin a lot of: 'Boys, come in and get on with your prep!' Like many heterosexuals, the Dukes were clearly unable to grasp that a homosexual is no more likely to molest children than anyone else.

At the end of my convalescence, I made a tour of Delphi, Tyrins, Mycenae and Epidaurus with a colleague, Michael Bagenal, and his wife, Alison. 'I'm afraid that my mother will be with us,' Michael said. But there was no reason for the apologetic tone. His mother was Barbara Bagenal (née Hiles), a run-of-the-mill painter, an associate member of the Bloomsbury Group in her youth, and the companion of Clive Bell in his and her old age. She and I at once got on so well that, during the tour, I spent so much time in her company that I could see that there was a danger of Alison and Michael taking umbrage. Barbara, although well past sixty, was amazingly agile, leaping goat-like up and down mountainsides to secure either some botanical specimen or a photograph with a Box Brownie seemingly even older than herself. She expected me to follow her; and often, despite Dr Manos's warnings that any strenuous activity might undo his repair, I did so. The result was that, after some initial pain, I recovered with astonishing rapidity.

Barbara told me that Harold Nicolson, whom we both knew, was travelling round the Peloponnese with the then Ambassador, Charles Peake, and his wife, Catherine. 'Won't it be fun if we run into them?' she said.

A few months before, in the course of a Council lecture-tour, Harold had been my guest in my Salonika flat. Would he not prefer me to book him into the one luxury hotel? I had asked him. But he had replied that no, certainly not, he wished to stay with me. People often now speak of his snobbery; but I can honestly say I never saw him show any. With its stone floors, broken-down furniture, and tiny guest-room overlooking an open-air cinema, my flat must have been even less appealing to an inhabitant of Albany and Sissinghurst than it was to me. But nothing – not even the long wait in his dressing-gown, as I struggled to get a wood-burning stove to produce hot water for his bath – clouded his *bonhomie*. He even put on a show of enjoying Poppy's barely comprehensible chatter and ghastly cooking.

Because of a puncture, the Bagenals and I arrived late at night at Delphi. Next morning, at about five, I was woken by the industrious tap-tap-tap of a portable typewriter in the room next to mine. At first I was furious. Then I realized that it must be Harold, writing yet another of those *causeries* for the *Spectator* which, in my memory at least, seem so much more cultivated and entertaining than those, by people like Taki and Jeffrey Bernard, which have appeared there in recent years.

The ambassadorial party was already breakfasting when I entered the dining-room. Harold, beaming, plump hands outstretched, jumped to his feet when he saw me. 'Francis! *Francis!* Tell me, tell me – how is the *hernia?*' Harold shared my intense interest in anything medical.

Everyone in the dining-room turned to stare at me. Lady Peake's mouth fell open over the slice of bread she had raised to it.

After that trip, I spent a night as a guest of the Tathams before returning to

Salonika. On this occasion I wore my dark grey suit, a shirt with a stiff collar, a Balliol tie and black shoes for the dinner which they gave for me.

Over drinks before dinner, Rachel talked about a visit which she and Wilfrid had paid to Salonika while I had been in Athens. They had stayed with the Davisons. 'The squalor in which that couple live!' she exclaimed. 'Unbelievable! Cats and children everywhere! There was a long black hair right across my fried egg at breakfast – whether from a cat or a child, I have no way of knowing. And this you will not believe! In the cupboard of the guest bedroom – I found a *truss*.'

I could believe it all too easily, since on my way to Athens for my operation I had stayed with the Davisons and had there thrown away the truss. Presumably one of the children or the maid had rescued it from the dustbin.

Later, in bed, in what was Wilfrid's dressing-room, I found that I could hear every word that Rachel was saying to him in the room next door. What he said I could rarely hear.

Rachel began by speaking of Arthur Sewell, then Byron Professor at Athens University – such a squalid little man, why did Wilfrid do nothing about getting rid of him? Next, she spoke of Louis and Hedli MacNeice, who had been among the dinner guests – Louis never had a single word to say, and Hedli never stopped talking, they were both impossible at any social occasion. She went on to speak of a junior colleague: he was just not up to Athens, it was not the place for him, couldn't he be posted to Crete or Patras or somewhere like that? I dreaded the moment when she would begin, 'And as for Francis King...'

But when she did mention my name it was to say that Wilfrid should swap me for the junior colleague whom she thought 'not up to Athens'.

So it came about that, some four months later, it was to Athens that I was posted.

On my return to Salonika I found that David Thomson, who had been teaching my classes in my absence, was not merely still sleeping in my bedroom but had also managed to reduce the whole flat to a state of total squalor. 'What can I do? What can I do?' Poppy asked, as she trailed behind me from room to room. Then, at the sight of some dirty khaki underpants on the sofa – I later learned that they had been abandoned by a soldier guest, who had gone off in a pair of David's – she began to giggle. I could see that she was really on his side. This made me even angrier.

David and I had a row. I told him that he had turned the place into a sty, and he retorted, 'Oh, don't be such an old maid! Don't be so prissy!' Anyway, he would have to move out, I said; I wasn't prepared to share the flat with him. To that he replied that he had been taken on by the Council until the end of that month; that he could not afford to pay to live anywhere else; and that the understanding was that he could make use of the flat until his departure.

Eventually John Davison had to arbitrate between us. 'I have a feeling that you two are going to get on extremely well. Just try it for two or three days and then we'll see. All right?' Like many saintly people, John Davison could also be extremely shrewd.

We tried it for two or three days; then the two or three days extended for a month. By then we had become close friends, remaining so until David's death, in his fifties, from cancer.

Even though David had, like me, been a conscientious objector, going to prison for his beliefs, no two people could have been more totally unlike. He owned a pawnbroking establishment in Hammersmith, so that he was obliged constantly to shuttle between Greece and London. This establishment earned him both a lot of snobbish derision from Embassy and British Council officers in Greece, and the money to be such a generous host – frequently inviting not merely me but my whole family to the third row of the stalls in the theatre, and then treating us all to a slap-up dinner at the White Tower or Quo Vadis. For these occasions, he would sport on brawny hands the flashiest rings to be found in his shop. Unlike myself, at that period so fearful of offending or shocking others, David did not care a fart (as he would put it) for what anyone thought. A former Rugby player, he had a muscular, hairy physique and an aggressive manner which totally belied his sexual preferences. In any situation, I felt safe with him. When a bouncer once tried to debar us from entrance to a gay club because we were not members, David merely said, in a good-humoured way, 'Oh, do me a favour, piss off' and pushed his way past. The bouncer said and did nothing more. Perhaps he thought that David was a copper. David was, indeed, often mistaken for one. This mistake was a source of inconvenience: his entry into a cottage – he was an inveterate cottager – would often precipitate a general exodus of men hurriedly adjusting their dress.

I remember with particular vividness one story which David told me, when he was having luncheon with me at the Chanterelle. It was about his life as a teacher of English in Egypt, in the immediate aftermath of the war. He had a servant, Abdul, who cleaned and cooked for him. Meat then being scarce, Abdul asked David if he would like some from the black market. David, having no scruples in the matter, readily agreed. From then on Abdul would bring him delicious joints – until, one day, he failed to turn up for work. It then transpired that he had been arrested. He had been moonlighting at the local hospital as a porter, and the blackmarket meat consisted of limbs and other organs of which he had been instructed to dispose.

The difference in David's and my characters was piquantly illustrated by our behaviour at the close of this tale. I at once spat out the delicious piece of kidney which I had just popped into my mouth and wondered for a moment if I was about to be sick in public. David roared with laughter. Then he said, 'I never told Eddy Gathorne-Hardy that he had once committed cannibalism at my flat.' He roared with laughter again.

One of David's lovers was an Army marathon champion. On the day when this boy won his race, David and I were present both to cheer him on and to stand on the dais when a portly general, resplendent in his uniform, handed him his trophy. All the other victors had passed on their cups to their mothers, wives or girl-friends. The boy looked around, saw David, and then, beaming, passed on his cup to him. No one seemed to find this odd. David also beamed. The general and the brass on the dais beamed back. There was clapping from all sides.

David's battle with cancer was a protracted one; and throughout he behaved with exemplary courage. But my experience is that most people behave with exemplary courage when confronted with a terminal illness. Indeed, I can think of none of my friends or relatives who showed cowardice in such a situation.

Not long before he died, David said to me, 'You know, the greatest mistake of our lives was that we never became lovers.'

Despite our many quarrels, I think that he may have been right.


All the time that I was living there, I had an overwhelming desire to escape from Salonika. But now, so many years later, I have a no less overwhelming desire to return, not to the modern city of high-rise apartment blocks, well-paved streets and luxury hotels, restaurants and cafés, but to the city, half-Turkish and half-Greek, impoverished, dilapidated, riven by political dissension, which I once knew and which, like so much else in Greece that was unlike anything else in Europe, has now vanished for ever.

# — 3 —

# The Gulf of Pleasure

My flat in Athens was a vast improvement on my flat in Salonika. Situated in Kolonaki, then as now the Mayfair of the city, it belonged to an Admiral Lappas, uncle of the actress Melina Mercouri. The Admiral, owner of the whole house, had let the flat to an elderly Greek diplomatist and his wife, who, being abroad, had then sublet it to me. Mercouri's mother, Mrs Eliopoulou, also inhabited one of the flats, as did a camp Greek antique dealer, whose activities in the basement *garçonnière*, furtively gnawing away at the foundations of propriety, led to the Admiral referring to him, with lofty disdain, as 'the termite'.

My flat was sparsely but elegantly furnished with antiques from the Ionian Islands. There was a long, low-ceilinged sitting-room, with a dining area at one end, a handsome bedroom with bath and lavatory off it, a tiny kitchen and an even tinier maid's room, in which I used to put up guests. I soon found a maid, Irene, who came from the island of Mytilene. Rachel Tatham would invariably refer to her as 'your Lesbian', thus bewildering English visitors, unaware firstly that Mytilene and Lesbos were names for the same island and secondly that it was Irene's birthplace. Irene, a superb cook, was totally illiterate. But such was her intelligence, she was able to conceal this fact from me for several months. Scrupulously honest (unlike Poppy), she would hold a piece of paper in her hand and appear to read out from it her shopping list for that day. Potatoes had cost so much, beans so much, olives so much. At the end, she would come up with a total. Similarly, if anyone left a telephone message with her, she would again hold up a piece of paper and put on the same act of reading. I only realized her disability after I had shown her an article in a Greek newspaper about a scandal involving the Bishop of Mytilene. Once again she pretended to read; but when I began to talk about the story, it was all too clear that she had taken nothing in. When Irene married, I was the sponsor. I feel guilty now that I took my duties so lightly, soon losing touch with the couple after I had quit Athens.

Admiral Lappas had decreed that the four maids in the house took it in turns, week by week, to clean the staircase and landings. Although Irene was – as I knew from her work in my flat – a scrupulous cleaner, she rarely put in her stint without either Mrs Eliopoulou or Melina Mercouri emerging from the downstairs flat, to criticize and give instructions. Mrs Eliopoulou did this in a comparatively lady-like manner. Melina Mercouri might have been the captain of a Greek caique bawling out a sailor ordered to wash down the decks. 'Look at this! Look, look, *look*!' I used to hear her scolding. 'There's dust here. Look at this dust on my fingers!' Such scoldings were liberally peppered with expletives of a kind more often heard in Piraeus than in Kolanaki. Could this be the same woman whom, in the house of her brother-in-law, the extremely rich Spiro Harocopus, I had heard speaking so vehemently about the need for the peasants of Greece to be 'respected as equals' under a socialist government?

One day, Irene burst into tears at this treatment, after she had returned to the flat. I then stormed downstairs to speak to Melina Mercouri. Would she please tell me if she had any instructions or criticisms for Irene, instead of scolding her herself? Like almost every Greek, Melina welcomed a quarrel. I was a man, what did I know about cleaning? she demanded, legs apart and hands on hips. If the cleaning wasn't done properly, then she had every right to tell Irene. And while she was about it, she'd like to mention that my party the previous night had gone on until long after midnight and had been extremely noisy. Her mother hadn't slept a wink.

Eventually I crept back upstairs, feeling that I, not she, was the guilty one.

When I next saw her a few days later – I was entering the house, she leaving it – I avoided her gaze. But she greeted me with the utmost *bonhomie*. '*Yassoo*! Where have you been? I haven't seen you for ages.'

I always liked this Greek way of having a blazing row and then, immediately afterwards, forgetting all about it. For a Greek, revenge is a dish best eaten hot. If the dish has grown cold, then one chucks it into the dustbin of oblivion.

Melina Mercouri went on to ask me if I could spare the time to attend a dress rehearsal of *The Second Mrs Tanqueray*, in which she was appearing. She wanted to ensure that her performance was 'a properly English' one. Stage-struck as I was, I at once agreed.

The performance was powerful; but so far from being a properly English one, it was all too often an improperly Greek one. I tried to hint at this: Paula's laugh should be rather more subdued; her voice should be rather less strident; she should not put her shod feet up on a drawing-room chair opposite to the one in which she was slouched. But it was all to no avail. 'Yes, darling, yes, I see, I see,' Melina repeated over and over again. But when I went to the first night, she was playing the role as she had all along been determined to play it.


At first my duties were to teach English language and literature at the British Institute. I think that I was efficient; and I think that I was also popular with my students. But it was a far from exacting job, and my free time was ample. Having previously read a book every two or three days, I am ashamed to say that during this period of my life I read virtually nothing. Nor did I write all that much. There was a dangerously seductive atmosphere of *dolce fa niente*, which, during the hours of the day when I was not teaching, would lure me out of my flat to one of the cafés in Kolonaki Square, to Zonar's just by the Grande Bretagne Hotel, or to a bar called Apotsos. There I would be certain of meeting people, both foreign and Greek, as idle as myself, with whom I would drink and talk for hours, literally, on end. Many of these people were writers; and their talk was usually far more interesting than anything they had ever published, or were to publish. In the evening, I would often go to some working-class taverna, where both the food and the wine were vile, but where I would see some spectacular dancing and where, with luck, I would pick up some sailor, soldier, airman or manual worker eager both to enjoy himself and to make some money. On the page it sounds squalid; but there was friendship, joy and, yes, a kind of innocence in those encounters on some deserted beach below the noisy taverna or in some woodland behind it.

At this first period of a stay which was to last for almost seven years, Louis MacNeice was on secondment from the BBC to the British Council in Athens. He had even less to do than I had; and unlike myself, he could not be bothered to do it. His title then was 'Fun. O.' (Functional Officer) but, unless he was drunk, no one could have been less fun. Hedli, his wife, was fun; but she was also pushy both for herself and for him, so that it was inevitable that she and Rachel, each a stately galleon under full sail in that crowded little backwater, would soon ram into each other. My problem was that, having always liked difficult women, I liked the pair of them equally. Neither was disposed to accept this. 'You haven't been to that dreadful woman's party, have you?' Hedli greeted me, when I arrived at her house for dinner; and when, a few days later, I arrived at Rachel's house, she told me, 'I gather you've been at Hedli's. I'm not at all sure I want to see you after you've been there.' Rachel was, of course, the First Lady of the Council; but many Greek intellectuals, because of their admiration for Louis, behaved to Hedli as though it were she who occupied that position.

When, after a year, Louis quit Athens to return to the BBC, I took over from him his negligible duties as Fun. O., while continuing my teaching at the Institute. As soon as I had settled into his office, his former secretary, who had now become mine, threw open the doors of a cupboard. 'Mr MacNeice never dealt with these.' 'These' were innumerable playscripts submitted to him, in his role of BBC producer, which he had not bothered to return, let alone read. The secretary and I spent two whole days packing them up and posting them off.

That was a time when it was common for the British Council to recruit distinguished writers or scholars for limited periods of service. Such people often either knew nothing of administration or, if they did, could not be bothered with it. This was irritating to the administrators of the London office, so that gradually a 'career structure' came to be created, with Council staff all too often being recruited from the sort of people who were either too undistinguished to become diplomatists or too adventurous to become civil servants. These bureaucrats were dab hands at submitting estimates and writing reports; unlike so many of the amateurs before them, they were hard-working, punctilious and efficient. But whereas, in Greece, a whole succession of these bureaucrats have been instantly forgotten on their departure from the country, it was a long time before people forgot such 'characters' as Steven Runciman, Rex Warner, Louis MacNeice and, after my own day, Peter Levi.

A representative distinguished in his own right was Wilfrid Tatham's successor, Roger Hinks. It was often said in criticism of me during my British Council career that I was incapable of delegating. Hinks was so adroit at delegating that he did very little work at all. According to Angus Wilson, a colleague of his at the time – other colleagues vigorously dispute his version – this gift for delegating was the cause of Hinks's downfall at the British Museum, where, in the period immediately before the war, he had been Deputy Keeper of Greek and Roman antiquities. One day, sauntering through one of the galleries under his command, he noticed (as Angus told it) that the Elgin Marbles looked a little off colour. 'Those could do with a clean,' he said to an underling. The underling set about cleaning them as he might have set about cleaning the tiles in one of the museum's public conveniences, with the then equivalent of Harpic. The surface of the marbles emerged cruelly abraded; and since one, indeed the chief, argument for British retention of these national treasures was that we would care for them far more scrupulously than the Greeks, there followed what Angus called 'an unholy stink'. In that stink, Hinks vanished, to re-emerge in the British Council in Sweden in the war. There, too, he was all but asphyxiated by an unholy stink, this time of a wholly different sort; but an adroit and energetic intervention from Ronald Bottrall, then Representative in Sweden, saved him – for which, to his credit, Hinks was always grateful. Ronald, so intolerant of stupidity or inefficiency, was always tolerant of homosexual behaviour. Discussing homosexuality with me on one occasion, he remarked, 'I once thought of becoming a homosexual myself when I was at Cambridge, but then I decided that I was far too big for it.' I do not know whether he was alluding to his height, of considerably more than six feet, or, boastfully, to something different.

On form, Hinks was one of the wittiest men I have known. When he deployed this wit, he was totally reckless as to its consequences. One evening, soon after his arrival in Athens – how bizarre and how typical, I have often thought, of the British Council to have awarded such a coveted posting to the despoiler of the Marbles! – he gave a dinner-party in his beautifully furnished flat on a slope of Mount Lycabettus for all the most distinguished Greek archaeologists available. I was also asked to come along. We had barely started on the first course, when Hinks began to talk about the Acropolis: 'I went up there some years ago. I'm not sure if I'm going to bother to go up again. What is the *point* of the Parthenon, I keep asking myself. It's – it's just a marble table with too many legs.' All the Greeks present looked either stunned or furious. To have provoked this response had clearly made Hinks's evening.

Hinks's judgements of people were always shrewd. Soon after he met me, he told me, 'You know, you suffer from a Mary Pickford complex. You want to be the World's Sweetheart.' He could also inspire intense affection and loyalty from women. One of these was Alethea Hayter, who was Assistant Representative to

Hinks's Representative and, in my view, a far more considerable scholar and writer than he. At that period the British Council had a department called Aids and Displays. I used to say that Alethea was the perfect Aid and Roger the perfect Display. It was he who kept attenders of Council parties in a state of shocked amusement. It was she who kept the administration of the office perfectly functioning.

Hinks was an excellent lecturer; but, because of his innate laziness, he would often recycle a lecture, however inappropriate for the occasion, rather than compose a new one. So it was that his inaugural lecture at the Council in Athens was about Newport, Rhode Island. He was extremely witty at the expense of the insularity, vulgarity and philistinism of the millionaire denizens of the place. But looking round the hall, I could see a lot of puzzled Greek faces and a lot of affronted American ones. Why someone who was supposed to be instructing Greeks in what, in those days, used to be called 'the British Way of Life', should instead be instructing them in the Way of Life of a small American minority, was a question not worth asking him. 'Who cares? Who cares?' would have been his lordly answer.

All through his time in Athens, Hinks laboured at his journal. He wrote it, he rewrote it, and he rewrote it yet again. 'But, Roger, a diary should be spontaneous!' I once protested. 'Oh, I hate spontaneity! When people are being spontaneous, they say and do such silly things!' he retorted. I think that he genuinely believed that he was producing something on a par with the Goncourt Journals. But when, under the title *The Gymnasium of the Mind*, a selection was published in a single volume, it caused little stir. Perhaps a more generous and less discreet selection may eventually bring him the posthumous fame which he so clearly expected.


It was thanks to Roger Hinks's laziness that I became a friend of Anthony Blunt. The British Council had dispatched Blunt to Greece on a lecture-tour, in the immediate aftermath – though I did not then know this and presumably neither did the Council – of his first interrogation over the defection of Burgess and Maclean. 'Would you be willing to accompany Blunt to Delphi?' Hinks asked. 'I don't really want to go there again – and I really ought to spend the weekend answering some letters. He's not all that jolly, I'm afraid. But of course you can use one of the Council cars and all expenses will be paid.'

I was delighted.

When I picked up Blunt at the Grande Bretagne Hotel, I noticed that one half of his face was frozen and assumed that he must have had a stroke. He kept laying the palm of a hand on the frozen area, not so much to conceal it, it seemed to me, as to check if any sensation were returning. Eventually, he said to me, 'You must be wondering what has happened to my face?'

I had indeed been wondering; but I pretended not to understand him. 'Your face? What do you mean?'

'It's something called Bell's Palsy. It tends to afflict one after some shock or strain. I've been through a lot of shock and strain recently.'

I longed to ask him the nature of this shock and strain but felt that I could hardly do so. After all, we had only just met. He volunteered no more.

Having mentioned the paralysis to me, he seemed at last able to relax. He began to ask me about my work for the Council; about my novels ('I'm ashamed to say I've yet to read one'); and about Roger Hinks, about whose recently published book on Caravaggio he spoke with a grudging admiration. Then, all at once, he asked a question about the 'queer' life of Athens – presumably Hinks or someone else had told him of my proclivities. I indicated the driver in front of me, frowned and put a finger to my lips. Blunt nodded. Since the driver had spoken to him in English, I was surprised by this lack of discretion.

As we clambered over the totally deserted hillside of Delphi – nowadays, of course, there are tourists everywhere, whatever the hour – Blunt reverted to the subject. Was it easy to find sex? And what was the going rate?

The upshot was that, during the course of a walk after dinner, I found myself coping, not altogether willingly, with the task of finding someone 'big, butch, good teeth' (his specification) for him. A young man was driving a donkey laden with brushwood down the road. He smiled at us, I said something in Greek about the warmth of the evening. It was all far easier than finding a taxi in Athens.

Afterwards, Blunt looked far more happy and relaxed. 'Marvellous!' He went into some details. 'Oh, I am grateful to you. That was just what I needed. I feel much, *much* better now.'

But the improvement was to be only temporary. In the middle of the night I was woken by two screams, one immediately after the other, from the room next to mine. I jumped out of bed. Had some burglar woken Blunt and attacked him?

An ominous silence had followed the screams. I banged on his door. There was no answer. Fearfully I went in. 'Anthony, are you all right?'

He sat up in bed, palm of hand to the frozen side of his face. 'What is it? What?' He seemed to be confused.

'You were screaming. I was worried.'

'Oh . . . Oh, yes . . . A dream . . . A nightmare . . . I'm apt to have nightmares.'

'Well, provided you're all right . . .'

'Yes, I'm fine now. Fine . . .'

Next morning he made no allusion to the nightmare, and I thought it better not to make any allusion myself.

When we returned to Athens, I saw a lot of Blunt during the remaining days of his visit. Twice I took him to dinner in tavernas in the company of groups of friends. He picked at the food (who could blame him?), gazed furtively around him, and would then lean over to whisper into my ear, 'That one's rather jolly' or 'I rather like that one over there.' On the second occasion he brought a dock-worker back to my flat. For some reason, the transaction completed, he did not himself wish to hand over the sum already agreed. 'You pay him, you pay him,' he hissed. 'I'll settle with you later.' Once the youth had gone, he reimbursed me.

When we said goodbye, he told me, with unusual warmth, 'You really made my visit.'

In view of this, what happened a few months later was disconcerting. Having returned to England on leave, I was having dinner with John Guest in the Travellers' Club. Blunt was also in the dining-room, with three other men. Repeatedly I tried to catch his eye, but could somehow never do so. When the time came for the other party to leave the dining-room, they walked past our table. Again, I tried to catch Blunt's eye. This time it was clear to me that he was deliberately avoiding looking at me.

'Anthony!' I called out.

'Oh ... Oh! Fancy seeing you here ...' He turned, to give me a glacial smile. 'Aren't you in Athens?'

'I'm over here on leave.' In Athens I had told him that I should soon be in London.

'On leave! ... Oh ... oh, good. Well, do get in touch. ... I'm in the book.'

With that, he turned away from me and left the dining-room.

I did not get in touch. It was all too clear that, were I to do so, I should embarrass him yet further.

A few years later I met him at a publisher's party; and a few years after that at a dinner given by two of his close friends, the historian James Joll and the painter John Golding. On both occasions he was charming to me; and on both occasions I found myself greatly preferring his ex-guardsman friend, John Gaster.

When, finally, Blunt was revealed to the public as a traitor, I felt sorry for him, as I tend to feel sorry for anyone who, however unforgivable his or her past behaviour, has been kicked into the gutter. My friend Elsie Crombie, sharing my feelings, asked me to a dinner-party which she was giving for Blunt, to console him, in some small measure, for his fall. I should have accepted, had I been free. Later, she reported to me that another guest, finding Blunt in her drawing-room, had asked if he might have a word with her in the hall. He then explained that he could not possibly sit down to a table with Blunt and went on to chide her for inviting him to dinner without revealing that a guest so controversial would be of the party. Elsie thought that this complaint was 'unreasonable'; but I could not agree with her.


Another eminent visitor whom I conducted to Delphi – with Alethea Hayter and the Anglo-Levantine writer Brian de Jongh also in the party – was Maurice Bowra. 'Do you know him well?' Ivy Compton-Burnett once asked me; to which, to her astonishment, I replied, 'Well, I did once take down his trousers.'

It was Bowra's hosts, the British Ambassador and his wife, who decided that, after a week of giving lectures and talking volubly at parties, 'Maurice could do with a rest'; but I suspect that it was not he but the Peakes for whom the rest was needed. People who are themselves indefatigable have a way of first stimulating but then fatiguing others.

In the car returning from Delphi, I was woken by what I at first took to be a violent punch on the nose. A lorry, hurtling round a hairpin bend on the wrong side of the road, had ploughed into our car. I had been flung forward at the impact and what had, in fact, struck me was not a fist but the back of Bowra's seat. The driver appeared to be unconscious. Bowra emitted a series of hollow groans, like an elephant in rut, and then also passed out. I staggered out of the car, looked down at my shirt and, seeing that it was saturated with blood, assumed that I had been seriously injured. Overcome by faintness – I have never been good at blood, even once passing out when it was my mother who had cut her hand – I lay down in a ditch.

Within seconds an elderly woman, swathed from head to toe in black – the mother, it later transpired, of the lorry driver – was screeching abuse at me in Greek, to which I was in no condition to retaliate. Foreign drivers were all the same: they drove too fast, strayed on to the wrong side of the road, never paid attention, were often drunk. Greek friends later explained to me that this shrill tirade was motivated not by heartlessness but by the paramount need to establish her son's innocence in the affair as soon as possible. She had assumed – rightly, as it turned out – that the police would take the side of some seemingly wealthy and influential foreigners rather than that of a semi-literate peasant transporting from one village to another some timber and the womenfolk who had no doubt played a major part in its collection. She had also assumed, wrongly, that it was I, and not the Council driver, who had been at the wheel.

Unhurt, Alethea and Brian behaved with impeccable coolness and resource, and in no time at all they had flagged down a huge American station wagon. By then I was able not merely to climb into its rear but to help to heave Bowra aboard. The Council driver – ashen, clutching his side (we learned later that he had broken a number of ribs), but stoically uncomplaining – also joined us. Alethea and Brian decided to wait with the lorry driver, his lamenting and upbraiding womenfolk and the group of gesticulating and shouting peasants who had materialized from nowhere, until the police arrived.

'You all right?' the American owners of the station wagon would from time to time peer round to ask us. Middle-aged husband and wife, what was really worrying them, I am sure, was not whether we were all right but whether the upholstery of their car was all right. They had already spread sheets of *Athens News* and the *New York Herald Tribune* for us to bleed on to. Bowra, conscious now but dazed, was for once silent even when asked a question, his head lolling from side to side as we lurched round one hairpin bend after another. It was left to me to answer; and suddenly – no doubt as a result of the excess of adrenalin that the shock of the accident must have sent pumping through my system – I experienced an extraordinary euphoria that made me talk and talk and talk, like one of those bomb-victims of the last war who would emerge Lazarus-like from the rubble not merely smiling but chattering their heads off to the mingled admiration and boredom of their rescuers.

Neither of the Americans, who turned out to be missionaries – what on earth were missionaries doing in a Christian country like Greece? – could speak a word of Greek, and it was I who had to ask a villager in Mandra the way to the nearest doctor. After having first ascertained what nationality we were, where we had come from and what had happened to us, he eventually directed us to a 'polyclinic'.

'I hope you'll forgive us if we don't stay with you,' the wife said as we were helped out of the car. 'But you seem to be in excellent hands.'

I never saw them again; I never learned their names. Today, in similar circumstances, I should certainly have discovered their names and addresses and sent them some flowers. But at that period I was far less punctilious.

The Greek doctor, young and handsome, in a short-sleeved white tunic that revealed arms covered in dark fur, placed the fingers of each hand on either side of my nose and clicked it painfully from side to side, so that a few drops of blood trickled out of it. He shook his head, seemingly disappointed. 'Not broken,' he said in Greek.

Bowra, dazed and still silent, was now half-coaxed and half-hoisted on to a couch by two giggling peasant-girls in the uniforms of nurses, after they had first removed his jacket, shirt and tie. The Greek pressed and tapped his supine torso; took out his stethoscope and listened intently, while the two girls continued to giggle behind him; felt his pulse. Then he ordered the two girls to remove Bowra's trousers. They shook their heads vehemently; backed away as though from something contaminated and contaminating; covered their faces with this hands, the cheeks behind them crimson. The doctor shouted angrily at them and, themselves angry now, they shouted back at him.

I resolved the altercation by myself undoing the buttons of the trousers strained tight across the ample belly. Then I began to tug at the trouser-ends. What was eventually revealed, after considerable effort, in the centre of a swelling mass of blubber, was a Delphi in microcosm. The girls averted their eyes, the doctor once more palpated and tapped. With the same disappointment with which he had told me that my nose was not broken, he finally announced that there were no internal injuries. He would merely have to stitch up a cut above an eyebrow. What neither of us realized was that the driver, seated unbloodied and stoical on a straight-backed kitchen-type chair while awaiting his turn (my guess would be that the doctor had left him to the last out of a sense of social precedence), was the only one of us seriously hurt.

The next day, when I called in at the Embassy to see how Bowra was getting on, he said to me, 'Yes, it was a nasty moment – a distinctly nasty moment. When I saw that bloody great juggernaut coming straight at us, I remember my last thought was "My God, what a loss to English culture!" ' My vain (in both senses) hope that Alethea, Brian and I might perhaps have been included in that envisaged loss was dispelled when he went on, 'But I don't know really. Let's face it, my best work – the work by which I'll be remembered – has probably all been done by now.'

Later I said, 'Didn't Alethea behave magnificently? Tearing up all that underwear and using up all those handkerchiefs and never for a moment showing any sign of panic.'

Charles Peake, who was in the room, put in, 'I always think that it was women like that who won the war for us.'

Bowra grunted. 'And made it such hell for everyone else.'

Charles Peake and I laughed; and now, though I have forgotten many Bowra sallies that made me laugh more at the time of their utterance, that particular one has stuck with me, partly because it still strikes me as funny but chiefly because it seems to me to epitomize one of the dominant traits of his character, as of Roger Hinks's. I don't think that either of them would ever have sacrificed a friend for a material advantage; but if it was a question of sacrificing one for a witticism, then that was a different matter. He shared, I knew, my affection and admiration for Alethea, and now we both owed her a debt of gratitude; but that did not preclude a quip at her expense.

Similarly, during our Delphi visit, he had sacrificed his friend Evelyn Waugh to a quip. I had remarked that I thought Waugh's *Men at Arms* trilogy his best thing to date; at which Bowra had expostulated, 'Oh, but you can't believe that! I always call it "The Waugh to end Waugh".'

After our Delphi adventure, I used to see Bowra intermittently during my visits to England, although we were never again to achieve that same intimacy as when I removed his trousers. On one occasion I recommended for acceptance at Wadham College a young, intelligent, cosmopolitan, extremely handsome Greek, Constantine Nicoloudis, who liked to think of himself as a member of the Royal Family on the slender grounds that his Aunt Aspasia had briefly been the morganatic wife of King Alexander before his bizarre death from a monkey bite. Constantine's father, now dead, had been a minister in the government of General Metaxas. His mother was one of the most formidable dowagers in the Athens of that time. Bowra was enthusiastic about Constantine, whose suave good looks clearly appealed to him more than to me. But when Constantine got himself into a number of scrapes, both sexual and financial, Bowra blamed me – 'I wish you'd take more care with your recommendations,' he chided. 'It is extremely embarrassing to have a *crook* in the college.'

Unfortunately, my next recommendation was scarcely more successful. When I was Regional Director of the British Council in Kyoto, a distinguished Japanese professor asked me for a favour. He did this while I was giving him a lift in my car from some function which both of us had been attending. Unfortunately, his English was so bad that I found it all but impossible to make out the nature of his request. On an impulse, I said to my then driver, one of the professor's own students, who was working part-time for me to pay his way through college, 'Could you please translate for the professor?' With great embarrassment, he did so. In my stupidity and impatience, I had caused the professor a terrible loss of face; and I had caused his student one no less terrible.

What the professor wanted, prior to his departure for England on a sabbatical, was an introduction to 'Sir Bowra' – whom, it transpired, he admired more than any other English scholar. Since I could hardly tell a man who was head of the English faculty of one of the most prestigious universities in Japan that his English was not good enough for me to help him, I wrote him the requested letter. Some weeks later a letter arrived from Wadham – 'Thank you so much for sending me your Professor X. We had a long and interesting silence together, for which he eventually rewarded me with a doll ...'

I think that, even if our days together in Greece had not had as their climax that disaster on the road back from Delphi, they would none the less have remained vivid in my mind. Whatever his virtues or defects as a scholar, Bowra was a wonderful communicator. A constant source of tribulation to me during my Council days was the acute boredom, almost a physical agony, which I experienced when I had to listen to a lecture. But I could hear Bowra deliver the same lecture twice or even three times with no diminution of pleasure at the bravura of his performance. His day-to-day conversation was similarly enthralling. Often what he pointed out in Delphi was trivial – the beauty of some olive tree against crumbling masonry, the early morning sunlight on the roof of our hotel, the fact that the main gate to the sanctuary of Pythian Apollo was preceded by five steps to make it impossible for anyone to drive up to the temple in a chariot; but it is all still clear in my memory and uncannily, whenever I return to Delphi, he seems to be close beside me.


Joyce Cary was so lacklustre a lecturer that there was a general feeling of disappointment that a novelist of such originality should have so little that was original to impart. What none of us realized was that he was already suffering the first symptoms of the insidious illness against which he was to battle for so long with so much heroism.

With him I travelled on a tour of the Peloponnese. He put up a courageous show of boundless energy and enthusiasm, but I was throughout aware both of his fatigue and of his bewilderment at being overcome by it. He would talk with an appearance of vivacity for a while and then would fall silent, even closing his eyes.

At one point he questioned me about my own work. I then complained to him of the difficulty of simultaneously doing a full-time job and getting on with writing novels. 'Yes, I know exactly what you mean. Why don't you do what I did – marry a rich wife, who is able to keep you?' At the time I was shocked by the cynicism of this. Now I wonder whether he was merely indulging in his often sardonic humour.

On our return, the British Council librarian, Myfanwy Hammond, gave a party for Cary in her flat. Half-way through it, he disappeared for a long time into the lavatory and then suddenly reappeared from her terrace. Apparently he had found that, on wishing to leave the lavatory, he could not unlock the door. Instead of then banging on the door and shouting, as most of us would have done, he had climbed out of the lavatory window, somehow clambered across to the ledge of another window, and from there had jumped down on to the terrace. It was a feat which, at almost half his age, I should never have attempted.

For that feat, I expressed my admiration to him – an admiration later intensified by the knowledge that he had performed it when already a sick man. But I have often wished that I had also expressed to him my admiration for his novels.

Cary's method of composition, as he explained it to me, filled me with astonishment. Apparently he worked simultaneously on a number of different novels, switching from one to another. He also hopped about within each novel, writing now this scene and now that. My own view of a novel is that, to be successful, it must have the same kind of organic life as a tree. The tree must grow beneath one's hands; one cannot stick on now a leaf or a branch here and now a leaf or a branch there. If the tree begins to die, then it is pointless to attempt to resuscitate it; it is better to abandon it and concentrate on the cultivation of another. Patently this was not Cary's view. 'I have a number of pigeon-holes in my desk, each representing a different novel. I think, "I'll do that African scene now" or "I feel in the mood for that scene in Soho", and I write it and then stuff it into the appropriate pigeon-hole.'

What writers tell one about their methods of work is not always, of course, the truth. On two separate occasions, for example, Beryl Bainbridge has told me totally different things about hers. But, if Cary was being truthful with me, it seems to me miraculous that each of his novels should be so much a living entity when put together (there is no other phrase for it) in a manner so odd.


Another writer whom I met during these years was Daphne du Maurier, who arrived in Athens as the guest of a tough and valiant old bird called Gladys Stewart-Richardson. Gladys, a spinster, lived in what could only be called a cottage, in the heart of Athens, with the Ilissos a mere stone's throw away. The cottage has long since been razed to the ground, to make way for a hideous apartment block; and the Ilissos, like the Fleet before it in London, has long since been covered over to make way for a noisy and noisome highway.

Gladys showed a slightly derisive affection for the queers (as she would robustly call them) who, then as now, were so prominent in the foreign community in Athens. On one occasion, when Brian de Jongh and I were having an argument about Sibelius – I admired the Finnish composer, he did not – behind her during the interval at a concert, she turned round to reprimand us: 'Girls, girls! Please, please! Why don't you just kiss and make up?' When I had a meal with her, she would, when we arose from the table, invariably make a point of asking me if I wished to powder my nose.

It was in Gladys's cottage that Daphne du Maurier stayed; and it was there that I met her on two occasions, a cocktail party and a luncheon party. She was courteous to all the people invited; but I sensed an unease – as though she feared that Gladys's guests, most of them taking pride in being intellectuals and most of them still young, might at any moment make fun of her and her work. When I was trying to talk to her, she had a disconcerting habit of looking not at me but at some object – the ashtray on the occasional table beside her, the bellows propped up beside the fireplace – as though she had never before seen anything of that sort. She licked her lips a great deal. When people are themselves uneasy, they tend to infect others with their unease. This is what occurred on these occasions. The conversation was stiff and faltering, despite all Gladys's attempts to jolly things along.

After these two meetings, I was eating a solitary luncheon in Zonar's, when Gladys arrived with a party consisting of five or six Greek women and Daphne du Maurier. The Greek women were of a kind one often met with Gladys: middle-aged; members of the Athenian 'aristocracy' or, at least, plutocracy; often married to powerful men, known for their philandering; themselves often powerful in cultural or charitable organizations; beautifully but severely dressed in tailor-mades; self-possessed, gracious and grand. Having nothing better to do, I watched Daphne du Maurier with this group. She was wholly at her ease; she looked extraordinarily handsome; she talked volubly and kept throwing back her head and laughing, like some young girl.

A totally different sort of visitor was Felicity Mason, then married to the best-selling novelist Richard Mason, author of *The Wind Cannot Read* and *The World of Suzie Wong*. She was an exhilarating companion, totally uninhibited in her talk and her behaviour. Because of this behaviour, there were a number of people, male and female, who used the word 'nymphomaniac' of her, in sour disapproval. The same people would have shown none of the same disapproval of a man, heterosexual or homosexual, who similarly enjoyed himself.

Felicity would come with me to the tavernas which I so much loved; she would look over the eager sailors, soldiers and airmen, just as I did, and she would, like myself, often disappear with one. Seated one afternoon at a café table in the far more fashionable ambience of Kolonaki Square, she watched the passing world. Then, with a squeal of excitement, she noticed a young naval officer, in white ducks. 'Just take a look at that packet! Have you ever seen anything as large as that?' Everyone turned round to stare at us.

When I took Felicity to the bathing resort of Batis in Phaleron, she picked up a young man of seventeen or eighteen, one of a group who seemed to spend every day of summer there, displaying their well-muscled, sunburnt bodies. He and she eventually clambered aboard a rowing boat. I lay out on the sand, eyes shut.

Then I realized that I was virtually alone on the beach. Almost everyone else was on the terrace of the bathing establishment, looking out to sea. Far in the distance was the boat; from the terrace, it was possible to make out precisely what was happening in it. The Greeks were delighted with the spectacle, making ribald comments, hooting with laughter, and beckoning to people on the road to join them. What a contrast to those English tourists who, a few years later, were to spot, through binoculars, a young English diplomatist similarly misbehaving himself with a young man in the Bay of Naples, and were at once to summon the police, thus precipitating the diplomatist's resignation from the Foreign Office!

Eventually the young Greek rowed the boat back to shore. There were ironic cries of 'Bravo! Bravo!' and a lot of clapping. Felicity, beautiful and startlingly blonde, drooped as she stepped ashore. She put a hand to her forehead. 'I feel absolutely worn out!' she wailed.

Felicity has retained her power to shock into old age. Under the name Anne Cumming, she has published two books of sexual reminiscences. Since her first marriage was to a cousin of the Queen Mother, the second of these books produced in the *Sun* (or was it the *Star*?) the headline: RANDY GRANDMOTHER SHOCKS QUEEN MUM. I am sure that the Queen Mother does not know of the existence of Felicity, let alone her books. In each case, she has missed something.


In 1952, I was awarded the Somerset Maugham Award for my novel of Florentine life *The Dividing Stream*. Maugham, who had made it a condition that any winner of the prize had to spend three months out of England, remarked with justifiable acidity that, in my case, it would have been better if I had had to spend three months *in* England – in, say, Bolton or Wigan. On hearing that I was the winner for that year, I had at once written off to thank him and to tell him that I was proposing to use the money – then £500 – on a stay in Corfu. He wrote back: 'You may be interested to hear that you are the first winner of the Prize ever to have bothered to send me a word of thanks.' Unbeknown to me until, many years later, Maugham himself told me, my mother also wrote him a letter. That she kept it secret must have been because she knew how embarrassed and annoyed I should have been. But Maugham told me how much it had touched him. Usually so hard-boiled, he was sentimental about mothers.

Winter was approaching when, having taken a year's unpaid leave from the Council, I arrived in Corfu. Apart from the Consul and his family, I was one of only three English people on the island during the months which followed. The others were an attractive young woman married to a Greek, and the governess to the Consul's children.

There was then only one hotel, the Pension Suisse on the main square, which offered any sort of comfort. Another hotel, the Astir down on the harbour, was in process of being built. I had a large room, with an open fire, for which one of the domestics, an elderly man, groaning and wheezing his precipitous way up the narrow staircase, would each day bring me a plentiful and inexpensive supply of wood. When I tried to persuade him to let me carry the wood up myself, he was indignant. That was his job and he was determined to do it. In this room, sitting before the fire, I worked away for six, seven, or eight hours each day, on a novel about life in Salonika. Even while I was writing it with so much fluency, I sensed that it was worthless; with the result that soon after it had been completed, I jettisoned it. I then set to work on my *roman-à-clef* of Greek life, *The Firewalkers*. This I knew, from the first, to be all right. When it was ready for publication, I followed the rule of the British Council at that period and submitted it for approval. To my horror, I was told – so scandalous and so potentially libellous did its subject matter appear to Enid Macleod, the officer deputed to read it – that on no account could it appear unless I either used a pseudonym or resigned from the service. In the event I used the pseudonym 'Frank Cauldwell'. The book was generally described in reviews as 'a highly promising first novel'. Some critics also described it as 'risqué', 'outspoken', even (in agreement with the verdict of the Council) 'shocking' – all things which it certainly was not by modern standards. With its piquant cover by Osbert Lancaster, it sold gratifyingly well.

Many people recognized themselves in *The Firewalkers*. Others, perhaps fortunately, failed to do so. Of the prototype of its central character, 'Colonel Grecos', I shall write later. The prototypes of one of its minor characters were both Rachel Tatham and Hedli MacNeice, of whom I made what I hoped was a convincing amalgamation. Rachel told me, 'I just loved that character – you caught Hedli to a T!' Hedli told me, 'What a wicked portrait of Rachel!'

Back in London, after leaving Corfu, I wrote a short novel, *The Dark Glasses*, about the island. My Maugham year was a singularly fertile one. My books tend to receive either more or less praise than they deserve. *The Dark Glasses* received less.

I was fortunate that, during my stay in Corfu, I was treated like a favoured nephew by a remarkable woman, Marie Aspioti, who was then running the British Council Institute there. She loved England; she gave her whole life to the Institute. Her family belonged to the aristocracy of the island; but their fortunes were now diminished, so that they had difficulty in keeping up their large house – in which they often entertained me. In many ways, Marie was like another remarkable woman, Josephine Pullein-Thompson, whom I was to get to know and love in later years, when I was President of English PEN and she was its capable and hard-working General Secretary. Both Marie and Josephine treated the organizations of which they were in charge as though they were extensions of their families. Marie cared about her students and Josephine cared about her members as one cares about a younger brother, younger sister, nephew, niece or cousin. The Institute had its own literary magazine, to which I contributed poetry, stories and reviews.

On my second day in Corfu, I was seated at a café table in the main square, when a handome, blond young man, in the uniform of a captain, sauntered over, smiled at me, and asked in English, 'Excuse me – are you a foreigner?'

'Yes.' I was glad of his appearance, since at that moment I was feeling lonely. 'I'm English.'

'Oh, that makes me happy. May I sit with you? I wish to practise my English and on this island there is no one with whom to do so.'

Kostas came from Athens; he was doing his military service.

From then on, I saw him almost every day – for a drink, for an excursion into the countryside, for a visit to the cinema, for dinner in a restaurant. He never seemed to be short of money; it was often difficult for me to pay for myself. Of course I took him to the Institute and introduced him to Marie and my other Greek frends; but I sensed – I could not understand why – that they did not take to him.

The English governess, departing for England on leave, left her motor bicycle with me. This enabled me to chug off to remote places not served by any bus. Kostas would ask me about these expeditions. Sometimes, if I had told him of one in advance, he would surprise me by arriving there in the Army jeep which seemed to be always at his disposal but in which he never offered me a lift, even when we were once caught in a heavy downpour. I used to take photographs with a Minolta bought off a Greek sailor in a taverna in Salonika, and Kostas would often have these developed and printed for me, free of charge, up at the barracks. 'Why do you want to go to that place?' he would ask me. Or: 'What did you find there?' Or: 'Did you meet anyone?' Greeks have little love of scenery, and I guessed that he was puzzled that for scenery I should be prepared to sacrifice half a day or even a day of my time.

The relationship between Kostas and me was one of close friendship, not sex – although I certainly found him attractive. In Athens, he told me, he had a fiancée. She was beautiful, she would bring him a large dowry. He seemed prouder of the second of these facts than of the first.

When the time came for me to quit Corfu for Athens, Kostas came on board the ship to see me off. Sitting across from me at a table in the bar, he suddenly leaned over: 'Now I must tell you something, Francis. I tell you because I have begun to like you so much, because you are my friend.'

What he had to tell me – the confession was curiously similar to that made to me by Tsaipi Britnev – was that, during all the weeks when we had spent so much time in each other's company, he had been acting on orders to keep an eye on me.

But why, why? I asked.

He explained that it was strange for a foreigner to decide to spend a winter in Corfu, when he could be in Athens. Who would want to endure the cold and rain of Corfu at such a season? Then there were my excursions about the island. At such a time of year, one could not swim or sunbathe. He laughed: he, too, had at first been suspicious of me, then he had realized that I was just an eccentric.

But if I were, indeed, a spy, what could I have hoped to discover? I asked him.

'Many things,' he replied. Even today Greeks believe that most of their ills are due to the machinations of foreign intelligence services. At that period it was the English or the Russians who carried most of the blame; now it is the Americans. 'Albania,' he added. 'Albania is very near to Corfu.'

'But the British don't even have any diplomatic relations with Albania!'

It was useless to go on arguing. He thought it quite reasonable that the authorities had decided that I was up to no good, even though he himself had reached the conclusion that their suspicions were groundless.

Once or twice he called on me in Athens. Subsequently, he invited me to his wedding. I sent a modest present but did not attend. Friendships are sometimes hardy perennials, sometimes annuals. My friendship with him fell into the second category. We really had absolutely nothing in common; but more important there was my feeling that he had betrayed something sacred to me, friendship. That Tsaipi Britnev should have behaved like a friend to my sister, her husband and their friends while secretly spying on them, and that Kostas should have behaved like a friend to me while performing a similar duty, still disgusts me.

My friendship with Marie, once so close, also declined. But in its case, I did not wish it to decline or even acquiesce in its declining. She had been a fervent anglophile; but now she had become an even more fervent advocate of Cyprus for the Greeks. When, on a visit to Athens, she defended the acts of terrorism which were then as horrible and as common on the island as they are now in Northern Ireland, I became angry with her. Subsequently, she returned her MBE to the Palace and resigned from the directorship of the Institute, which for so long had been her whole life. She was reluctant to see any English, even old friends like myself, so that on a subsequent visit which I made, one summer, to Corfu, she met me only once for a drink, never invited me to the house in which, in the past, I had enjoyed so much hospitality, and made excuses for not seeing me again. When some sort of solution was eventually found to the Cyprus problem, long after I had quit Greece, I made a half-hearted effort to re-establish contact. But by then our friendship had died from a lack of sustenance over so many years.

Marie's behaviour was certainly not typical of my Greek friends. I admired the way in which, even at the bitterest period of the struggle for Cypriot independence, they were able to differentiate between individuals and a cause. Apart from Marie and a Greek diplomatist who, no doubt for career reasons, abruptly dropped me, I can truthfully say that I never lost a single Greek friend because of the political troubles. On one occasion, I gave a New Year party for my students, soon after a bomb had exploded at the Institute (planted over the Christmas holiday, it killed no one but caused extensive damage). Two of these students arrived very late.

'What became of you?' I asked as Irene showed them into the room. 'I was beginning to think you weren't coming.'

'We were taking part in the demonstration at the British Embassy,' one of them replied; and the other then took up, in an aggrieved voice: 'The police wouldn't allow us near enough to throw any stones.'

I continued to go to tavernas, frequented by soldiers, sailors and airmen, in the poorer suburbs of Athens. Learning that I was English, people would often come over to my table to argue with me, without any acrimony, in the friendliest manner: Cyprus was Greek, the English had stolen it, it was a scandal, a disgrace.

I used to answer, 'If I had Cyprus, I'd give it to you. Like this.' Then I would take a cigarette out of the pack lying on the table before me and hand it to my interlocutor. There would be a lot of laughter, as the cigarette was lit. In Greece at that period the offering and accepting of a cigarette were symbolic of the offering and accepting of friendship. In this way, I was constantly exchanging cigarettes, English for Greek. Through this exchange, I first came to smoke pot, long before anyone was doing so in England. A Greek sailor offered me a reefer after I had offered him a Camel; it seemed only polite to smoke it. I am glad that I did so. It became the first of many, none of which did me any more harm than a glass of ouzo or a carafe of retsina.

Everyone in Athens knew Colonel Veloudios, the prototype of my Colonel Grecos in *The Firewalkers*. He looked ancient even then, more than forty years ago; but he could always outwalk me and outswim me. He was also a fearless diver, as I certainly was not. First having removed his false teeth and wrapped them in a handkerchief, with the exhortation to me, 'Please look after those for me,' he would launch himself off some pinnacle of rock into the boiling sea around it. Although he owned a whole house in Kolonaki – many years later sold for a huge sum, so that he was at last relieved of financial worries – he could enjoy the kind of life that he craved only by constantly being the guest of foreigners. Since he was such excellent company, I never in the least minded paying for his meals or even his fare and hotel when he accompanied me on some expedition. But there were many who did so – saying things like 'Oh, I'm fed up with his cadging!' or 'He took me for a ride yet again!'

One of his tricks was to return hospitality by taking his present host along with him to the next meal to which he had been bidden. If he thus turned up at my house or in a restaurant with someone like Paddy Leigh-Fermor, Patrick Kinross, Christopher Tower, Peggy Guggenheim or Caresse Crosby (all friends of his), I was, of course, delighted. But I have dire memories of such occasions as when Thanos arrived at Zonar's with a couple from Nebraska and their three tongue-tied children. 'These are my very dear friends the Olsens,' he said. 'I told them how much you wanted to meet them.' I made a valiant effort to be amiable. After all, they were not to blame. At the end of the meal – all three children had guzzled ferociously – when I had settled a bill far larger than I had bargained for, Olsen told me, 'It was so very kind of you to invite us along too – particularly as you'd never met us,' and his wife then put in, 'If you should ever find yourself in Nebraska ...'

Thanos claimed, with what truth I do not know, to have been the first man to have used an aeroplane in war. According to his story, he had flown a biplane into Bulgaria, during the Balkan War, had landed at some military camp, had shot up everyone in sight, and had then flown off again. He would have been perfectly capable of such a reckless act of gallantry. Sadly, after so brilliant a start, his military career suffered a series of checks. 'I haven't the ability to get on well with fools,' he would give as an explanation of his fall from grace. But a Greek general who had served with Thanos in his youth once told me that the real problem was not that Thanos could not get on well with fools but that he got on far too well with his men. Eventually, he was invited to retire on a minuscule pension.

Thanos was passionately interested in folklore. When he discussed the subject, there were constant references to 'rites of passage', 'the sacred phallus' and 'the stuff of life'. He was also the inventor of what he called 'fantasiometry'. This meant the creation of symbolic 'portraits' out of *objets trouvés* – so that, for example, the one labelled 'Paddy' resting on the lid of the upright piano on which he would hammer out such of his musical compositions as his ten-minute 'Plaka Symphony', consisted of two superimposed photographs, cut from magazines, of Paddy Leigh-Fermor and of one of the Landseer lions in Trafalgar Square, to which he had stuck such things as the label of an ouzo bottle, a map of Crete and a Nazi swastika with a chain wound about it.

Another of Thanos's hobbies was to make a plaster cast of any particularly large cock which he encountered. Teasing him, Patrick Kinross had told him that I was 'particularly well endowed' (a phrase often used by Thanos). This was not true, I am afraid; but the result was that he was constantly begging me to allow him to take a cast. 'Why are you English so prudish? Why, why? If you are well endowed, you should be *proud* of it. It is a blessing from God.' Stacked in a cupboard he had innumerable such casts, each with a dusty label attached – 'Shoemaker Nanos in Pankrati', 'Waiter Andrea in Yerophoinika', 'Sailor (name forgotten) from Mytilene'.

Having heard of this collection, a friend of mine, Patricia Murphy, lover of one poet, Philip Larkin, and wife of another, Richard Murphy, begged me to take her along to see it.

'Are you interested in cocks?' Thanos asked her abruptly, as soon as I had made the introductions.

Since she was a doctor, she could truthfully answer, 'Only from a biological point of view.'

Thanos went to the cupboard and returned holding aloft a vast monstrosity as though it were the Holy Grail. He handed it to Patricia. 'You may hold it,' he said.

Patricia accepted delivery of the phallus. She was clearly embarrassed. 'Stroke it, if you wish,' Thanos told her. She did not comply. Instead, she began to blush. Then she stammered, 'One would have thought that such – such an *object* could not possibly exist.'

Thanos cast his eyes to the ceiling; a look of gleeful enchantment spread over his ill-shaved face. 'And yet it *did* exist – marvellous to relate.'

People who disliked Thanos – often those whose parties he had gate-crashed – tended to say that he was 'shameless' or 'wicked'. That he was the first of these things, no one could deny; but his shamelessness was, for me, part of his lurid charm. At a cocktail party at the British Embassy, he would proposition or even grope a waiter with little or no attempt at concealment. Standing outside a cinema or café, he would peremptorily summon some young serviceman over to him. I never met any Greek who disliked or even disapproved of him; but I met many foreigners who did.

One such foreigner was Richard Westbury who, after a period of friendship, used to describe Thanos as 'a filthy old man'. Inadvertently, at a time when I did not know of this aversion, I mentioned to Thanos that I was going to Richard's birthday party – 'I suppose I'll see you there.' In fact, no invitation had been sent to him.

In the middle of the party, a messenger arrived with a packet. He refused to hand it over to the manservant of Richard's host, Spiro Harocopus, saying that it was a birthday present and that he had been instructed by the giver that it must be handed over to Lord Westbury himself.

Surrounded by guests, Richard undid the beautifully wrapped parcel. Inside, was a roll of harsh, grey toilet paper with Thanos's card pinned to it.

The next day Richard sent a note to Thanos: 'Thank you so much for that charming present. I shall think of you whenever I use it.'

It was through Thanos that I met Dino, the young Greek who was to give me so much happiness during my Athens years. When I first met him, Dino was doing his military service in the Navy; later he was to go into the merchant marine. Coming from a village near Thebes, the inhabitants of which were Albanian in origin, he looked, with his fair hair, blue eyes and pale skin, nothing like the conventional notion of a Greek. He was exuberant, scatty, mischievous, naturally intelligent but only semi-literate. Thanos had become a stern father to him, he Thanos's cheeky and wayward son.

My first meeting with Dino was, in Thanos's words, 'a cash transaction'. But I have learned, both from my own experience and from the experiences of my friends, that a cash transaction can often become the foundation-stone of a valuable and lasting relationship. Dino was in no way mercenary; but, inevitably, since his family were so poor, I used to give him and them gifts. So it was that, when his father had the opportunity but not the means to buy a strip of land adjoining his, I gave him the tiny sum required; and so it was that, when Dino wanted a decent suit to attend the wedding of his brother, I paid for it.

Unlike many of my friends in Athens in similar situations, I made no attempt to educate Dino. Remorselessly, one of those friends would take his working-class boy-friend to the National Theatre, to the opera, to art-shows, to museums. Inevitably, the relationship could not survive such a cultural bombardment. If we were travelling together, Dino would enter museums or would explore archaeological sites in my company; but when we met in Athens, it was usually to go to the beach, to a taverna or to a cinema, to watch the kind of film which he, not I, enjoyed.

One of my closest friends during my years in Athens was the novelist and critic Robert Liddell, nicknamed 'The Dame'. Making his home first in Egypt during the war and its immediate aftermath and then in Greece, he refused to visit England for more than forty years. This prolonged absence was detrimental to his literary reputation, which deserves to be far higher. His was all too often a case of 'Out of sight, out of mind.'

There was something both demure and steely about Robert, as about his books. 'Old-fashioned' was a word often used about both; but that must not be taken as a synonym for bland or unwordly. Once one had penetrated the elaborate courtesy of Robert's manner and the formal style of his books, there were always surprises, even shocks.

As he has recounted in what is probably the best of his novels, *Stepsons*, Robert had a bruising childhood, in the charge of a stepmother whom he hated. His beloved brother was killed in the war. These two experiences made him wary of any close attachments; they also developed in him, despite his early conversion to the Roman Catholic faith, a fatalistic stoicism, a mood, in the face of life's batterings and burdens, of 'Bear them we can, and if we can, we must.'

Robert took little part in the giddy life of myself and so many other of his friends, rarely visiting beaches, cafés and tavernas with us. Instead he spent most of his leisure at home, reading and writing. At that period he had one particular Greek friend, who perhaps may also have been his lover. That I cannot be sure of the precise nature of the relationship, even though I was one of the people closest to him at that time, is an indication of the extent of his discretion. He, in effect, adopted both this friend and his family, eventually becoming godfather to the first of the friend's children.

Robert was one of those people who form for themselves very definite ideas of their friends. Often the idea and the reality are widely different. No matter. No adjustment is made to the idea. Curiously, so strong was Robert's personality that people tended, against their wills, to live up to Robert's idea of them, so that they would, in his company, behave in a totally uncharacterstic manner. Thus, Robert having decided that I was 'wicked' (i.e. mischievous), extravagant and impetuous, I found myself being all these things when I was with him. I would tease him or anyone else present; I would give the waiter a tip so large that, if he were honest, he would say to me that he thought that I must have made a mistake; I would recklessly commit myself to doing things that I had no wish to do.

In his personal relationships, Robert was always a Calvinist. Certain people were saved, certain people were damned. The saved could do no wrong, the damned could do no right. No one who was damned could achieve salvation – or vice versa.

When people (and I was one of them) called Robert 'old-fashioned', they were thinking not merely of the formality of his manners but also of his moral rectitude. In his company, I used to feel ashamed of the kind of small dishonesties which most of us commit from time to time: appropriating other people's witticisms or ideas; pretending to have read books or seen plays or films of which, in fact, one knows only what one has read in reviews; boasting of friendships with people who are merely acquaintances. Robert was scrupulous about such things.

His rectitude also made him incapable of telling a comfortable lie about a friend's work. What he would do, if such a work fell short of his expectations, was very much what Henry James used to do in similar circumstances. There were endless periphrases, qualifications and ambiguities, the final impression of which was all too often one of feline malice. To me: 'I am about to reread your *The Ant Colony*. I cannot believe that a second reading will give me more pleasure than my first.' To Olivia Manning: 'How lucky you are to have had such an eventful life that you can constantly draw on it for your fiction and are so absolved from the tiresome need to *invent*.'

Robert had an aversion to making a fuss – regardless of the fact that, in Greece, to make a fuss is often the only way to get anything done. On one of our travels together, we arrived in Navplion to discover that, instead of the two single rooms which we had reserved, we were being given one single room. Even a honeymoon couple would have objected to the propinquity caused by the introduction of a second bed into so small a space. I began to raise hell. Robert cowered. 'Oh, oh, oh, don't make a fuss! We can manage perfectly well! I can go into the corridor when you are dressing and undressing.' If I argued about a bill, claimed a theatre seat usurped by someone else, or pointed out that the bread sold to us was stale, there would be the same exhortation not to make a fuss. For Robert it was always better to endure in dignified silence than to shout in undignified protest. Unfortunately silence, however dignified, does not impress Greeks.

In contrast with my robust and inaccurate demotic, Robert spoke an exquisite *katherovousa*, such as even elderly professors at the university could seldom emulate. Riding with him in a taxi, its radio blaring out a bouzouki song, I put my hands to my ears. He leaned forward to the driver and said (I translate literally), 'Many excuses, dear sir! May I dare to be intrusive enough to ask you if you would have the goodness to turn off your radio or at least diminish its volume?' The driver looked flabbergasted. It might have been some Greek coeval of Lord Byron who had spoken.

Robert, who had been a friend of Elizabeth David in Egypt, was hardly less skilled than her as a cook. It was a foible of his often to practise a culinary version of Thanos's fantasiometry, planning a meal to illustrate the salient facts known to him about the guest of honour's character and life. Thus, on one of my birthdays, he prepared a banquet which consisted of: *oeufs à l'indienne* (my childhood in India), *coq Toscane* (my Italian period) with Swiss chard (my Swiss birthplace), a *macédoine de fruits rafraichis* (Salonika), and a variety of Swiss and Italian cheeses. The wine, which was retsina and certainly not worthy of the food, came from near Dino's village.

Robert was the friend of four of the best women novelists of our times: Ivy Compton-Burnett, Elizabeth Taylor, Barbara Pym and Olivia Manning. When I once asked him in what order he would rate them, he gave me the order in which I have placed them here. Ivy Compton-Burnett had a not wholly beneficial influence on his writing. He himself had a wholly beneficial effect on Barbara Pym's – which justified his annoyance when a critic, reviewing the reissue of his

Oxford novel *The Last Enchantments*, described him as a 'disciple of Barbara Pym'. The truth, as so often in reviews, was the exact opposite.

Robert's relationship with Elizabeth Taylor was a strange one. For a long time they knew each other merely through correspondence. Then, finally, when she was on a Swann's Hellenic Cruise, they met. On both sides, there was considerable trepidation – as there no doubt would have been if Tchaikovsky and Madame von Maeck had ever come together. However, against all my expectations, the encounter proved a success. Subsequently, when she knew that she was dying of cancer, Elizabeth asked Robert to destroy all her many letters to him. Faced with what for me would have been a terrible dilemma – Elizabeth was a wonderful correspondent – Robert, with his old-fashioned rectitude, was in no doubt. The letters, of which there were a vast number, were destroyed.

One winter, when Gladys Stewart-Richardson had gone to her native Scotland, I persuaded her to rent her cottage to a Texan, Joe Baker, who had arrived in Athens with his Mexican lover, Augustine Airola. Both were to weave in and out of my life in the years to follow. Joe, rich, by no means unintelligent, and looking, with his shaved head, extraordinarily like Yul Brynner, was a genuine eccentric. Augustine, no less handsome, had an angelic disposition, usually putting up with his partner's vagaries with no more than a smile and a shrug.

Neither showed any great interest in Greece or even in Athens. Roger Hinks had at least climbed up to the Acropolis once. Joe and Augustine – or Tex and Mex, as we used to call them – never did so. 'Honey, I can look at photographs,' Joe said to me, on one occasion when I had yet again urged him to make the ascent with me.

What the pair most enjoyed doing was to give parties in the cottage, for a variety of guests from a retired Greek ambassador and a first secretary at the American Embassy to Thanos Veloudios and a host of servicemen. Food usually consisted of *chilli con carne* and the cheapest of Greek wines. Tex and Mex were both naturally accomplished hosts. They were also naturally accomplished dancers, which I never was. A lot of dancing, men with women or men with men, took place.

When Gladys reclaimed her house, she remarked to me, in obvious reproof, 'The oddest people keep turning up at the cottage and asking for your friends.'

Tex and Mex continued to wander about the world, eventually making their base in Barcelona but bobbing up now in Amsterdam, now in London, now in Beirut. When I was with the British Council in Helsinki, they suddenly turned up there in midwinter, Mex to study potting – he was an accomplished potter – at the Arabia factory and Tex, as usual, to do little but feed people *chilli con carne*. After this visit, which lasted three or four months, Finnish friends of theirs and mine told me that they had been visited by the security services. What exactly had the couple been doing in Finland? the investigators had asked.

The truth was that, as usual, they had been doing virtually nothing. But to the security services it was clear that they must be involved either in espionage or in drug-smuggling. The suspicion of espionage may have originated in a confusion between Joe Baker and another American friend of mine, Don Baker, who was certainly an agent of the CIA.

The story of Tex and Mex had a denouement worthy of Maugham. When the couple had settled in Marbella, an immensely rich German industrialist, Werner Jaeger, arrived there. Having met the pair, he fell for Mex, and invited him to accompany him on a trip, no expenses spared, round the world. Tex finally said yes to Jaeger's 'May I borrow your friend?', feeling that he should not stand in Mex's path to possible advancement. Half-way round the world Jaeger died, leaving most of his fortune to Mex, who thus achieved a belated independence. Mex was now at least as rich as Tex.

On his visits to England, I always invite Tex around for dinner or luncheon, since I am devoted to him. Invariably he arrives clutching a plastic bag – 'A little present for you, honey.' Inside are innumerable small cakes of soap, picked up in the bathrooms of luxury hotels.

I spent more than seven years in Athens. This was at least three more than the usual British Council period of duty. The Alliance Française takes the view that the longer one of its officers is resident in a country, the greater his usefulness. The British Council, on the other hand, is convinced that any officer who stays more than a few years in a country will inevitably go native – thus coming to represent not Great Britain but the country of his adoption. In this argument, I side with the Alliance Française. I remember the occasion when, during my third year in Athens, I was attempting to see the Greek Minister of Culture about some matter and was constantly being fobbed off with a junior official. 'But the Director of the French Institute tells me that he saw the Minister *twice* last week!' I eventually protested. The junior official smiled: 'The Minister was once the Director's student at the French Institute,' he explained.

That I was able to hang on for so long in Athens was merely because, unlike most of the other English members of the Council staff, I was fluent in Greek. 'We must have at least one person who can talk the language,' was the line taken.

But this was a line that Roger Hinks was not prepared to take. He decided that – for my sake, not the Council's – it was essential that he should engineer a move. 'Francis has been here too long,' he told all and sundry. 'He's got stuck in a groove. It'll do his writing a world of good if he finds himself in a totally strange environment.' There he may have been right. To some people he went on to say, 'In any case, the relationship with Dino needs to be terminated. That boy is a pest and a drag on him.' There he was wrong. But for Dino, so uncomplicated, so generous-hearted and so affectionate, my life would have been far less happy.

My new posting was to the British Institute in Alexandria. The year was 1956 – the year of Suez.

# — 4 —

# *House Arrest*

On my arrival by ship in Alexandria, I found that Richard Simcox, the Director of the British Institute, had booked me a large room with bath in the Pension Leroy. 'I thought it best to leave you to find a flat for yourself,' he told me. But since I so much liked the French proprietors, husband and wife, of the pension and their largely Sudanese staff, since the food was so good, since the charges were so modest, and since it would be so easy to entertain guests in the restaurant and the bar, I decided to make my home there. 'Why not?' Richard said, when I told him. I had thought that he might have objections; but he was the most easy-going of bosses.

I had two friends already resident in the city. One was John Heath-Stubbs, a lecturer in the English department of the university; the other Anthony Robinson, a colleague at the Institute.

I had been looking forward to seeing John, after a period of some years. I still admired his Olympian intelligence, even if my admiration for his Parnassian verse had already begun to wane. Tall, gaunt and grey, with thick glasses covering his already near-blind eyes, he was led by his English amanuensis into the café, next door to the Institute, where I was waiting for him. As so often, he was more interested in delivering a soliloquy than in conducting a conversation; but since the soliloquy ranged so widely and was so erudite and eloquent, I had no complaint. Some of his students did have complaints, one of them, a by no means unintelligent girl, telling me that she could understand little of what he said in the course of his lectures.

Anthony was a totally different sort of character. Intelligent but not intellectual, he drank too much and gossiped too much; but, unlike John, he was naturally avuncular and at once took me under his wing, introducing me, within the space of less than a week, to a host of people, to some of whom I took and to others of whom I certainly did not.

It was while I was at a dinner-party in Anthony's squalid flat – his servant must have been one of the most slovenly in the whole of Egypt – that we learned on the wireless of the English and French 'intervention' in Egypt, in the aftermath of the Israeli invasion. Among the guests was Anthony's boy-friend, son of an English mother and an Egyptian father, who was then doing his military service as an officer in a tank regiment and who the next morning was about to leave for the front. 'Oh, God, let's hope that this bloody war can be *stopped*!' Anthony wailed. 'I couldn't bear to lose you!' Already drunk, he clutched the embarrassed boy protectively to him, even though most of the other people present were heterosexuals.

Soon after I had returned to the pension, I began to feel extremely ill, and assumed that some of the disgusting food which I had eaten had, not surprisingly, poisoned me. When I began to vomit blood, I was so alarmed that I was barely aware that bombs were dropping on the city. I could hear an uproar from the corridor outside my room. I later learned that all the other guests, with the exception of one old Frenchman, resident of many years, had descended from the pension, on the top floor of the building, to the basement.

Early the next morning I rang Anthony and asked for the name of a doctor. He then gave me that of an Englishman who had spent most of his life in Egypt and who was doctor not merely to the Council but to most of the foreign missions. Understandably, Anthony was far more concerned about his boy-friend, already on his way to the front, than about me.

Although bombs were still falling, the doctor insisted that he would come round at once. I tried to dissuade him – it was too dangerous, I was feeling better already – but he would not listen. I was full of admiration for his sense of duty and courage. He told me that I ought to have an X-ray but that, for the moment, it would be best for me to stay in the hotel. His surmise was that I had been bleeding from an ulcer.

That afternoon, I felt well enough to venture out, although I had been forbidden by the doctor to do so. I went round to Anthony's flat, to find him even drunker than on the evening before. He repeatedly tried to ply me with whisky, and seemed unable to grasp that, in my present condition, to drink alcohol would at best be unwise and might at worst prove fatal.

Soon after that, both Anthony and I were placed under house arrest, unable to communicate with each other except by telephone. Richard went underground, setting off on a perilous journey to Cairo, in search of instructions from the Embassy. Outside my room two somnolent, portly, middle-aged guards now sat on canvas folding chairs, smoking incessantly. They showed absolutely no hostility to me. Indeed, one of them, who had once been a student at the Institute, would relieve his boredom, though not mine, by repeatedly irrupting into my room first to cadge a cigarette off me and then to carry on a conversation which consisted largely of questions about the wife and children whom I did not possess. I amused myself by inventing answers as lurid as I could make them: my wife had run off with my closest friend but, even as the war had broken out, had been planning to rejoin me; one of my children had only recently been kidnapped and held to ransom, to be rescued by a heroic bobby; another of my children was a mathematical prodigy. It was this guard who, tut-tutting that the Egyptians and the English should find themselves at war, blamed it all on our ambassador, Humphrey Trevelyan (he pronounced the name 'Trevel-i-an'). But then what else could you expect from an Armenian? he demanded. When I remonstrated that the Trevelyans were Cornish not Armenian, he would hear nothing of it: names with that ending were always Armenian, he insisted.

On the second day of my capitivity, I was taken from my room by a detachment of soldiers so youthful that they might have been a Boy Scout troup. As I was marched through the streets, my hands above my head, I was terrified that one of the two Boy Scouts behind me, each with a rifle at the ready, would trip and shoot me by accident. Inevitably, people stared at me; but with amazement or amusement, never with hatred. Since their city was being bombed at the time, I thought this admirable of them. Equally admirable was the way in which they treated John Heath-Stubbs, permitting him, since he was not an employee of the British, to go on lecturing and moving about the city freely, on the arm of his amanuensis.

In the police station I was asked why, an employee of the British Government, I had arrived in Alexandria less than a week before the Suez invasion. I had known nothing about the imminent invasion, I replied, and nor had the British Council. It was clear that my interrogator did not believe me. A cup of sludgy coffee and a teaspoon of over-sweet jam were set down before me. Then the question was repeated. I was no more able to answer it satisfactorily this time than the last. Eventually, I was escorted back to my hotel.

The next day and the day after that I was again escorted in the same manner to the police station. On the third occasion, I decided, with irrational terror, that now the rough stuff would begin. I would be shouted at, beaten up, perhaps even tortured. But my interrogator, a handsome young man with lacquered finger-nails and a number of heavy rings, remained as courteous as ever. When he still could not get out of me the information which he wanted, he shrugged, smiled and, having shown me some photographs of his wife and three children, sent me once more back to the hotel. That was the end of that ordeal.

I had a Greek friend, first met in Athens, who lived in Alexandria. I rang him up to tell him that I was under house arrest in the hotel. The telephone clicked and went dead. I thought that our connection had been accidentally broken and rang him again. As soon as I spoke, the telephone once again clicked and went dead. Later he excused himself: he had been thinking not of himself but of his mother and sister, he had had to protect them, the police might have been tapping my telephone. Another Greek, met for the first time at Anthony's dinner-party, behaved in a less craven fashion. Hearing that I was under house arrest, he at once himself telephoned, to enquire if there was anything he could do for me. I asked if perhaps he could leave some reading matter for me at the desk of the hotel, adding that I had been forbidden any visitors. Less than an hour later, he arrived in my room. He had, he explained, entered the hotel, outside which a guard had been posted, on the pretext of having a drink in the bar. He had then bribed the barman to lead him to my room and my two guards to let him enter. Married, with young children, he had far more to lose than the other Greek, a bachelor.

When German bombs had rained down indiscriminately on London during the war, I had felt no fear at all; but as English bombs were pinpointed on to selected targets in Alexandria, I was almost as terrified as my guards, who were torn between staying at their posts and scurrying to the basement. Then followed a period of several days when the fear of being bombed was superseded by the boredom of having nothing to do but read, chat to my guards, or speak to Anthony on the telephone. The last of these occupations had by now become painful. Almost as soon as he had reached the front, Anthony's boy-friend had been killed in his tank, in the course of a battle with the Israelis. Over the telephone Anthony would give way to his grief; and, not being with him, I found it difficult to offer comfort. He had always been such a good friend to me that I now wanted to be an equally good friend to him. The boy, handsome and sweet-natured, had clearly been fond of Anthony, who never wholly got over his loss, drinking more and more and becoming rasher and rasher in his sexual behaviour in the years ahead.

At last Anthony and I were both told that we could leave the country. By now, British, French and Israeli troops having been withdrawn from their country, the Egyptians were claiming a glorious victory. But the true victory, an inglorious one, belonged not to them but to John Foster Dulles, Eisenhower and Macmillan.

During the protracted formalities at the docks which preceded our departure, I found myself in a long queue behind a French banker. My cases were opened and the contents scattered everywhere. My Minolta camera was removed and never returned. It was the only occasion on which the Egyptians behaved other than impeccably to me. I suffered all this without any protest. But the Frenchman behind me, more spirited than I, exclaimed loudly to me in French, 'This is disgraceful! A scandal! And to think that, but for the French and the English, the Egyptians would still be walking barefoot!'

Unfortunately the customs official who had been going through my luggage had a knowledge of French; and it was in French that he told the banker and me that we would have to submit to a body-search. Again, I was docile; and again there were angry protests from the Frenchman. We were taken into a room by two grinning officers and ordered to remove all our clothes. I removed mine at once; the Frenchman removed his with extreme reluctance. The body-search was made as humiliating as possible, with the Frenchman crying out, '*Non, non, non! Pas là! Pas là!*' when it became particularly intimate.

Finally we were told to dress again. When I had done so, I became aware that the Frenchman was searching the room. 'What is it?' I asked. He then announced that he could not find his shoes or socks.

It was barefoot that he walked up the gangway on to the Greek ship with me. Awaiting him on the deck were both socks and shoes.

I liked the joke. He, not unnaturally, didn't. '*Quels cons!*' he exclaimed as he all but toppled over while pulling on a sock.


It was a relief to arrive in Athens, after an absence of some six weeks; but it was also embarrassing. Numerous people had given farewell parties for me; and there had also been a clamorous farewell party at the docks, enjoyed more by Dino and the other friends, mostly Greek, who had come to see me off, than by myself. 'So here you are, back again!' Roger Hinks greeted me, with a notable lack of enthusiasm. Having worked so hard to get me posted, he was not unnaturally annoyed that political events had now annulled this achievement. 'I don't know what I'm going to do with you, until another posting has been found,' he went on. 'We're overstaffed already.' Because of this overstaffing, I spent the next few months in a limbo of doing virtually nothing at all. I was able to return to my flat, but all my household effects were stranded in Egypt, never to be recovered. Touchingly, Irene, my former maid, came to my rescue, supplying me with beautiful hand-embroidered sheets and towels from her dowry.

When I consulted a well-known gastroenterologist about my haemorrhage in Egypt, he at once had me admitted to the Evangelismos Hospital for tests. Unfortunately, there were no private rooms available, and I was therefore told that I should have to enter a ward. Since, like an animal, I must be by myself when I am ill, I protested that, if I could not have a private room, then I would wait for one. Finally, a lumber-room next to the ward was emptied of its contents: a rusty, broken-down refrigerator, some cane chairs with perforated seats, cartons of lavatory paper, buckets, brooms, cloths. A narrow iron bedstead was then wheeled in. I was far more uncomfortable there, with only a minuscule skylight for window, than I should have been in the ward; but I was happy. This irrational craving to be left to myself when I am ill made me, when I returned to live in England, pay out increasingly exorbitant subscriptions to BUPA, which I could ill afford, not in order to get quicker or better treatment but merely to procure a room to myself. Sometimes, when privately hospitalized, I have felt a pang of guilt at having bought this privilege; and that pang has been sharpened by the remarks of people, usually far better off than myself, about the scandal of private medicine. What these people do not seem to have realized is that the health of a nation depends far more on diet, sanitation and housing than it does on the provision of first-rate doctors and hospitals. But, when shopping for food without a care for expense, or when exchanging one comfortable, well-heated house or flat for one even more comfortable and well-heated, such people mysteriously never seem to feel a comparable guilt about life's inequalities.

Roger Hinks was soon succeeded as Representative by Ronald Bottrall, who – blustery, ebullient, matey and given to making noisy scenes – was far more to the taste of the Greeks. But by then my departure for Finland, where I had been appointed Assistant Representative, was fast approaching.

# — 5 —

# *Steamed Puddings*

I t was autumn and already chilly when I arrived in Helsinki. Briefly I put up in a boarding house, at which neither the landlady nor any of the other lodgers spoke any English, so that conversation was restricted to signs and a lot of giggling. Then I moved into a house, vacated by my predecessor, in a pretty but inconveniently distant suburb of the city.

The Finns on the British Council staff were so capable and industrious that, had I so wished, I could have done as little work as the charming, intelligent but indolent Representative, Raymond Butlin. With the exception of the administrative officer and the driver, these Finns were women; and, since Raymond had an eye for such things, all were extremely attractive. My chief duty was to tour the thirty or so Finnish-British Societies dotted about the country, to make sure that their English teacher-secretaries were happy and doing all that was expected of them, to give a lecture or two, and to discover what was needed in the way of books, films and recordings.

As soon as I stepped off a plane – an efficient network of air routes meant that I rarely travelled by train or by coach – in some remote town an hour or two after breakfast, whoever had been deputed to meet me would say, 'It's so cold, Mr King. The first thing that you need is a drink.' Useless to demur. Throughout the day, I used to be told the same thing: It was so cold. The first thing that I needed was a drink. It was a miracle that I was able to deliver my lecture. After the lecture, there was a party and more drinking. At these parties, no doubt because Finns have little taste for conversation, there would always be dancing. I loathed this, since I have always danced badly. If I was slow to ask the wife of the chairman of the society for a dance, someone would prompt me: 'Aren't you going to dance, Mr King?' With a sigh, I would then get up and do my duty.

As much as the dancing, I loathed the statutory visit to the sauna. To tell my hosts that I did not enjoy the sauna would have been as insulting as to say that I did not enjoy dancing with the wife of the chairman. Like steamed puddings, the Finns would sweat away in an abstracted but in no way discontented silence, occasionally broken by a few mumbled words. They would then miraculously liven up, whooping and guffawing, as they rushed out to roll in the snow or plunge into an icy lake. I did not join them in either of these activities, despite assurances that it would do wonders for my health.

The next morning, crippled with a hangover, I would struggle on to the plane to my next destination. As, head thumping and gorge rising, I stepped off it, it was to be greeted by a voice saying, 'It's so cold, Mr King. The first thing that you need is a drink.' Once again, I would feebly give in; and so the sequence would be repeated over and again until, pallid, sweating and nauseous, I finally returned to Helsinki, home and abstinence.

The amount drunk by the Finns never ceased to amaze me. Soon after my arrival I invited some of the staff of the English department of the university round to my house for drinks. On a table, I had set out the various bottles of liquor which I had queued at my local Alkoholiike (the sale of alcohol was a state monopoly) to purchase. Being a foreigner, I was not rationed. 'What would you like to drink?' I asked one elderly professor. 'Let us begin with the sherry,' he replied. The bottle of sherry having been emptied, my guests then went on to the vermouth. From the vermouth they went on to the gin, from the gin to the whisky, from the whisky to the vodka, from the vodka to the brandy. They only left when there was nothing more to drink.

Drink often had the effect of making people usually so courteous and mild extremely aggressive. Thus, on another occasion, when two of my male guests, both doctors, got into an argument, one of them suddenly picked up a soda siphon and, with a bellow of 'Satana!' (about the worst swear-word in the Finnish vocabulary), crashed it down on the table before him, so that it exploded like a bomb. I got to my feet and said prissily, 'I'm afraid you'll have to go! I can't have that sort of behaviour here.' This eminent gynaecologist then advanced on me, squinting malevolently, with clenched fists raised. Fortunately, drink, which usually goes to the heads of the English, to the faces of the Japanese, to the livers of the French, to the stomachs of the Greeks and to the sexual organs of the Americans, goes to the knees of the Finns. With what was either an extravagant belch or a strangled cry of fury, the man then collapsed on to the floor at my feet, to be dragged out by two of his colleagues, one of them a brawny woman.

At that period – and perhaps also today – the Finnish attitude to alcohol was similar to the English attitude to sex. Alcohol was supremely important in the lives of the Finns, so that they spent a lot of time thinking about it and talking about it when they were not actually enjoying it. It also filled them with guilt; so that just as English legislation has been directed to making sexual gratification as difficult as possible to procure, so Finnish legislation has pursued the same aim with regard to alcoholic gratification. On the first occasion when I met a Finnish friend for a drink, a large plate of sandwiches curling at the edges was set down before us. Absent-mindedly I picked one up and was about to bite into it, when he warned me, 'Don't eat that!' At that period, drinks in Finland could not be legally served without food, just as in England sex could not respectably be served without marriage; so that a token plate of sandwiches, days, even weeks old, was set down at each table with a drinks order, just as in England a token wedding-ring would be placed on the hand of any woman intending to indulge in a weekend of adultery. Like sex in England, drink in Finland was a constant source of innuendoes and jokes.

After Greece, a country in which, as in Ireland, people tend to tell you what you want to hear rather than the truth, I was sometimes disconcerted by the candour of the Finns. Soon after my arrival, I gave a lecture at the university. It was clearly a success. A few weeks later, the professor concerned asked me to give another. On this occasion, having been extremely busy with looking after both Sir Malcolm Sargent and the pianist Harriet Cohen on simultaneous visits – a task complicated by the fact that they could not stand each other and had therefore to be kept apart – I prepared no lecture but decided to talk impromptu on the subject requested, 'The Modern English Novel'. When I had finished, the professor rose to his feet and said in his excellent English, 'I am sure that we are all very grateful to Mr King for coming here to lecture to us when he has so many other demands on his time. You will remember his excellent lecture on 'The Art of the Short Story'. Unfortunately, this lecture cannot be said to have reached the same level. But it contained one or two interesting observations and one or two items of information not previously known to me, so that our time was not wholly wasted. Thank you, Mr King.'

Raymond Butlin tended to delegate to me much of the work of looking after visitors from England. Being at an age when I still enjoyed meeting celebrities, I in no way objected to this. Indeed, my happiest memories of Finland are of being driven out to the airport in the Council car after dinner on some summer evening – the BEA plane arrived at 11 p.m. – and of then watching the belated setting of the sun while waiting for my visitor. As we drove back to Helsinki, the sky would suddenly redden once again. By the time we had reached the hotel and settled to a drink, the sun would actually be rising. Returning home at two or three o'clock – by then it was daylight – I would find it impossible to sleep and would often take myself off for a walk through the city. In the cold, limpid light, the deserted streets always looked bewitching.

Harriet Cohen – her once beautiful face, which had attracted a host of musicians, now alarmingly haggard and predatory in expression – had an exaggerated sense of her importance. This or that composer, performer, professor, must see her today, at once, *now*. Sadly, the people with whom she demanded these meetings had often never even heard of her. 'She was the, er, girl-friend of Arnold Bax,' I used to explain to them. But often they had never even heard of Arnold Bax. When I had failed to organize some meeting, she would say something like, 'Well, I must say you don't seem to have been very efficient.' But, as well as my exasperation, she also evoked my pity and the tenderness which pity so often produces in me. It was terrible that a woman who, by all accounts, had once been so attractive should now be so repellent; and even more terrible that a previously brilliant executant should be prevented from delighting audiences because of an accident in which a broken glass had severed a tendon in her right wrist. (This was how she explained the disability to me. But her character seemed so typical of the manic-depressive that I wondered whether, at some moment of despair, she might not have deliberately cut the wrist herself.)

Sargent, then at the height of his powers both as a conductor and as a conversationalist, had more reason to be so demanding. He delighted me with his anecdotes, as he delighted everyone else. My favourite of these concerned a previous visit to Finland. Having conducted a concert, he had returned exhausted to his hotel, to be kept awake by a particularly noisy party in the room above. Eventually he had stormed upstairs and battered on the door. When someone, clearly drunk, opened it, he told Sargent that the party was in celebration of Sibelius's birthday. Sibelius himself then staggered over, having recognized the conductor, whom he had met on other occasions. 'Come in, come in, dear fellow!' he urged. 'You must drink to my health.' Realizing that it would be impossible to sleep that night, Sargent remained at the party until, early the next morning, he set off to catch a plane to St Petersburg, where he was also scheduled to conduct. Having returned late on the evening of the following day, he fell totally exhausted on to his bed. Once again he heard the din of a party. Once again he stormed upstairs to make his protest. The person who opened the door on this occasion was Sibelius himself. 'My dear fellow!' he cried out. 'I was wondering what had happened to you! Where have you been all this time?'

I was present at a dinner given in Sargent's honour, after he had conducted a concert which had included my favourite of Sibelius's symphonies, the Fifth. Suddenly, a woman rushed into the room and whispered something to the host, beside whom Sargent was sitting. The host was about to get to his feet to make an announcement but Sargent forestalled him. 'Ladies and gentlemen ... I have a tragic announcement ...' The voice throbbed with emotion. 'We have just received news ... the Master has died.' (The master was of course Sibelius.) The guests, most of whom were connected with music in some way, gasped in shock. Then the well-known Finnish music critic sitting next to me whispered to me, in his near-perfect English, 'The Master' – he put the word into inverted commas – 'must have been finished off by listening on the radio to that terrible performance of the Fifth.'


My chief friend in Finland was a schoolmaster called Vilho Huttunen – Willy, to his English friends. As a graduate student, he had proposed to his supervisor that he should write a thesis on my novels. The supervisor had replied – it was typically Finnish of Willy to relate this to me, with no malicious intention whatever – 'Oh, very well – if you really like that sort of rubbish.' Willy – huge, muscular, the colour of lard – suffered from a disease of which I had never heard before, narcolepsy. This meant that, suddenly, disconcertingly over a plate of food, in a theatre or concert, in one's house even while one was conversing with him, he would sink into a deep sleep. He would also become similarly unconscious if suffering any extreme of emotion. Thus, if anyone said anything funny, he would literally be tickled to death – albeit, mercifully, a death that was only temporary. When a youthful drunk, armed with a knife, once tried to get some money off us in a deserted street at night, my resistance collapsed when Willy, overcome by rage, himself collapsed insensible on to a mound of snow beside me.

Through Willy I met a famous designer of jewellery, married and with a young child. Hearing that I wanted to learn to ski, he offered to teach me. On the following Sunday, he came out to my house for this purpose. Small, dark and hirsute – he was more like a Greek than a Finn – he was a lovely companion, as well as an efficient and patient teacher. After several hours of virtually flat skiing, over the countryside around my house and on the frozen sea before it, he said that he would like to use my sauna. I normally used only the bath, but I lit the sauna and we both then used it. The sauna over, he made it clear that he wanted to go to bed with me. I was in no way loath. He was an inventive and eager lover; but, as soon as he had reached an orgasm, he suffered agonies of remorse – How could he do such a thing to his wife? He would never forgive himself! He was a monster, a monster, monster! At that he burst into convulsive tears. After our next skiing lesson, he went through precisely the same routine. I then told him firmly that, if that was how he felt, it would be better if we brought the affair to a close. At that he began to wail, 'No, no, I wish to make love with you, I must make love with you! I must! I must!' I remained adamant. I had by then reached the conclusion that perversely, he derived as much pleasure from his agonies of guilt as from the ecstasies of sex which caused them.

To mark the close of our sexual relationship – fortunately we continued to be friends – he gave me some beautiful silver cuff-links crafted by himself. Years later, when I was on holiday in Athens, Constantine Nicouloudis – whom, as I have already related, I persuaded Maurice Bowra to accept at Wadham and whom Bowra subsequently described as a 'crook' – saw the cuff-links and asked if he could borrow them to wear at a New Year's ball at the Palace. He never returned them, first telling me that he had put them somewhere safe, he could not remember where, and then that he suspected one of his mother's maids of having stolen them. Finally, he gave me some Greek cuff-links – shoddy, not of silver, the kind which tourists buy in the Plaka – in their place. After I had left Greece, a mutual friend told me that he had seen Constantine wearing the Finnish cuff-links on a number of occasions.

Willy introduced me to a handsome Finn, who was my lover for my last months in Finland. Once a boxer, he had had to give up this profession, just when he seemed to be about to make a lot of money at it, after his left leg had been smashed in a motor-accident. He was sadly self-conscious about the leg, even insisting on undressing in the dark. But for me this one physical flaw made someone otherwise physically perfect even more attractive. Now marooned in a humdrum and ill-paid job, he enjoyed coming to my parties even though, both shy and unable to speak any English, he was usually silent at them. The language difficulty meant that our relationship could never really develop and that, when I finally left Finland, any communication between us was restricted to picture postcards. Eventually this sweet-natured, affectionate man married.

As the days shortened and shortened and I went to work in darkness and returned from work in darkness, I had formed the habit of spending any free Saturday or Sunday on a visit to the ramshackle hothouse in the Botanical Gardens. Few people ever went there; perhaps few people knew about it. I myself had discovered it by accident on one of my long solitary walks through the three-hour twilight which was all we had of day.

I have never experienced so painful a nostalgia as during those visits. Thickly muffled against the outside cold, I would now unbutton my overcoat, remove my fleece-lined gloves and throw my scarf away from my mouth; and, as though these articles of clothing were bandages, I would feel with their removal a terrible rawness that was almost a physical smart. The atmosphere was steamy and opaque as on a late Mediterranean evening before a summer storm. In shadowy recesses there stood tanks in which swam tropical fish often grotesquely shaped or with their skins peeling away from them like blistered paint. I used to spend minutes on end, my warm forehead against the warmer glass, watching them swish endlessly round in circles. The attendant must have got used to my presence; but though, when I passed him, I would smile and nod and even venture a 'Good morning' or 'Good afternoon' in Finnish, he merely stared back at me. Sometimes, stripped to the waist and with his trousers rolled up to his knees, he would train a hose on to the banked tangles of green; and then – perhaps I imagined it – I used to think that he was playing a pointless game with himself and also with me: seeing how close he could bring the jet to my legs without actually splashing me. He was a boy of seventeen or eighteen with a square head on a square torso and a fluffy down on his upper lip and chin.

How far away they were – the places to which I had grown accustomed, the people I loved; and this simulacrum of that lost paradise, though it might temporarily console, in the end only intensified my depression. Worst of all was the moment when, inevitably, my eye would travel out through the thickly knotted fronds and flowers and see the snow gently, implacably falling; grey beyond the steaming green and scarlet, grey before the flat, white trees and the whiter frozen lake beneath them.

Then there came a day when I was having luncheon in the country with a famous woman potter and her family. Suddenly, everyone stopped talking, cutlery poised over their food, heads cocked. 'Listen!' she said. I listened. At first I could hear nothing. Then I could hear a distant sound, as of a tap dripping. At last, in April, the thaw had come. The water was dripping from the eaves.

The potter jumped up. With a squeal of delight she raced round the table and threw her arms round her husband. They kissed and kissed again. All her guests now began to laugh and talk excitedly. It was as though they had awoken from a long, deep sleep. It was as though they were hostages at last released, after many years, from their prison. I myself felt the same.

During my eighteen months in Finland, I had far more free time than ever in Japan; but I wrote nothing but a single poem which, to my amazement, was published in the *New Yorker*, and a far from satisfactory short story. Since I am a naturally prolific writer, I am puzzled by this. Perhaps life in Finland, the nearest I have ever come to a true democracy, was too easy; perhaps that well-ordered office in that well-ordered country made too few demands on me; perhaps the people were just too kind, decent and fair-minded to stimulate me.

At all events, I was ready, in every sense, to move on to Japan.

# — 6 —

# The Rising Sun

The official designation of my Kyoto post was 'Regional Director, Kansai'
– Kansai being the region which takes in Kyoto, Osaka and Kobe.
Although I was the first such Regional Director, there had for some time
been a British Library in Kyoto, with the poet D.J. Enright overseeing it, while at
the same time lecturing at the private university of Kohnan. A dear man, benign,
perceptive and humorous, Enright would often justifiably complain that, whereas
his Council career had been beset with usually undeserved disasters, I (as he put
it) 'got away with murder time after time'. He had already left Japan when I
arrived there; but a number of people, English and Japanese, were only too eager
to tell me of the latest disaster which had precipitated yet another move for him.
At a club for the foreign community in Kobe, some drunken American had
suggested, totally erroneously, that Enright – whose manner might indeed be
thought slightly camp – was a 'faggot'. There had followed an altercation, after
which Enright, who had been asked to leave the club, returned to smash the glass
panel of its front door. Although, because of this incident, Enright spent only a
year in Japan, he wrote one of the best books about the country that I have ever
read (*The Year of the Monkey*).

From Tokyo I travelled to Kyoto in the company of the then Representative,
Leslie Phillips, a man who, devoid of any outstanding qualities of mind, managed
to get surprisingly far in the Council on a combination of kindliness and
craftiness. During the interminable train journey – this was before the
introduction of the bullet express – Phillips from time to time read out to me some
passage of Daphne du Maurier's *Rebecca*, to which, he told me, he was returning
for the fourth – or was it the fifth? – time. He thought it one of the finest novels of
the twentieth century, on a par with *Jane Eyre*.

Phillips had two reasons for accompanying me to Kyoto. One was, as it were,
to officiate at my coronation. The other was to attend the Osaka Festival, which
was about to begin. On our arrival in Osaka – it was in a hotel there and not
in Kyoto that we were putting up – he announced that I must hurry up and
change, since he was going to take me to a performance of *Don Giovanni* by the
Vienna State Opera, to be followed by a 'highly select dinner' (his phrase) given
by Mrs Maruyama, owner of the newspaper *Asahi Shimbun*, which was
sponsoring the Festival. I naturally assumed that Mrs Maruyama had either

herself invited me or been asked if I might come and given her consent.

When we arrived at the 'highly select dinner', attended by ambassadors, university rectors, members of parliament, principals of the opera company and people similarly distinguished, Phillips walked over to greet Mrs Maruyama, a dumpily porcine woman dressed in a kimono and what looked like a black horse-hair wig: 'Mrs Maruyama, dear Mrs Maruyama ... Do you remember me? We met with Princess Chichibu, in Tokyo, I think ... Leslie Phillips, British Council, British Council Representative ... Now I want you to meet Mrs Phillips ...' He drew me forward, chuckling at his joke. 'Mrs Phillips,' he repeated, pushing me towards her, with some more chuckling. Mrs Maruyama did not even smile. For her it was no joke at all. I was all too clearly a gate-crasher. Without even acknowledging my presence, she pointed to some distant, still unoccupied chairs. 'You may sit there,' she said. 'Waiters will bring food.'

'Perhaps I ought not to have come,' I ventured, when we had sat down.

'Oh, nonsense, nonsense! I'm sure she was delighted to see you. She's a sweet woman *au fond*. That's just her manner, just her manner.'

In the years ahead I was often present at social occasions with Mrs Maruyama. I was never able to unchill her *froideur*. If she was in a position unobtrusively to harm or hinder the work of the Council, she could be relied on to do so.

To introduce me to the people of Kyoto, Phillips arranged a party at one of the leading hotels. To this came Quentin Crewe and his enchanting American wife, Martha, both then resident in Kyoto. Crewe was already severely disabled by the muscular dystrophy which was eventually to confine him to a wheelchair; but he insisted on standing for several minutes on end throughout our first conversation, his back against a pillar. Wouldn't he like to sit? I asked him more than once. But he would have nothing of it – no, no, he was fine, fine. I have always admired courage. I was full of admiration for his.

Quentin and Martha were extremely kind to me; and it was into their rambling house, part Japanese and part Western in style, that I eventually moved after their departure. By then it was clear to me that Martha had fallen in love with a young Englishman whom I often met in their company; but Quentin, surprisingly and sadly, seemed unaware of what was going on. It was only (as he relates in his entertaining autobiography, *Well, I Forget the Rest*) as they settled down in their cabin on the ship which was to take them from Kobe to England that Martha confessed to him.

In a review of Crewe's autobiography Auberon Waugh implied that he made crafty use of his disability. But my own impression was precisely the reverse. Quentin behaved, as far as possible, as though the disability did not exist; and he expected similar behaviour from others. In a book which he wrote about his Japanese experiences, he never once revealed that all his strenuous travelling had been in a wheelchair.

The Crewes gone, I endured some lonely weeks in a house far too large for me. Its elderly owner, Mrs Kazama – her doctor son, who had lived in it, had been killed in the war – was a Japanese Christian of extraordinary kindness, toughness and rectitude; but with her, as with so many other Japanese whom I encountered, it was difficult to establish the kind of easy-going, informal friendship which I had enjoyed with Italians, Finns and Greeks. I should never, for example, have called on her, in the house next door, without prior warning; and when we met in the street, as we often did, her elaborate greeting somehow inhibited casual talk such as neighbours enjoy in the West.

The library was sited in a quarter largely inhabited by *hinin* or outcasts. These were originally people involved in such 'unclean' pursuits as the slaughter of animals, the curing of leather and the removal of nightsoil. The British Council officials who had chosen the building had thought merely of its cheapness and its convenience, so near to the four major universities. They had never thought that the presence of a *hinin* community would act as a deterrent to visitors. Why should they have done so? Not merely had the distinction between *hinin* and the rest of Japanese society been legally abolished, but it was forbidden even to refer to it.

Unfortunately, many things can exist in Japan even if they have been 'abolished' and even if no one ever refers to them except in private conversation. Even today, a shadow line sets the *hinin* apart from the rest of the population, so that only recently my Japanese translator asked if he could remove a reference to them in one of my short stories since, as he put it, 'it might embarrass some of your Japanese readers.' In private, many Japanese would claim to me that they could always recognize a *hinin*, just as many people in the West claim that they can always recognize a Jew. Bewildered I would ask, But how? *How?* I would then be told that it was something to do with a sallowness of the skin, a discoloration of the eyeballs, a quality of the finger-nails. I myself could never observe these distinctions. On occasions, when I was seated in a restaurant, café or bar with a Japanese friend, he would nudge me as someone walked past. Then he would extend a hand towards me under the table, thumb tucked in, four fingers sticking out. This indicated: Fourth class. Fourth class meant *hinin*.

At Kyoto University I met a student, in no way different in appearance from any other student, who once in a bar – perhaps drink had loosened his tongue – confessed to me, in the strictest confidence, that he came from a *hinin* family. Subsequently, having graduated, he told me that his attempt to marry a former fellow student had come to nothing, because her family, employing a private detective, had discovered his origins.

I first realized the disadvantage of the situation of the library when a middle-aged woman who attended the conversation classes which I held, not in the library, but in my house, excused herself from a lecture. 'I wish to come, Mr King, I am very, very interested in novels of C.P. Snow. But sadly I am frightened to visit that quarter.' 'Frightened, Mrs Nakajima? Why are you frightened? Embarrassed, she hesitated. Then she said, 'It is not good quarter. It is not good place for British Council.'

The staff at the library consisted of a capable and strong-willed librarian, Mrs Yamaguchi, and an elderly, amiable, far from capable secretary, Mr Otani. Mr

Otani was hopeless as a typist. I would correct all the mistakes in a letter; he would then retype it and return it with a lot of fresh mistakes; I would then correct all those mistakes; he would then yet again retype it and return it to me with . . . and so on, *ad infinitum*. The result, in the long run immensely beneficial to me but a nuisance at the time, was that I set about teaching myself to touch-type. After that, I typed all my letters, and Mr Otani had little to do. When I came to leave Kyoto, my successor, Peter Martin – who has since written a number of good Japanese detective stories under the pseudonym James Melville – sacked Mr Otani. This was bold of him, since in Japan it is rare to sack anyone except for dishonesty or gross insubordination. Curiously, having disposed of Mr Otani, Peter then gave the name Otani not to one of his murder victims but to his detective.

One day each week I used to travel over to Kohnan University, in a suburb of Kobe called Ashiya, to give two lectures. Before I acquired a car, I used to go there by train; later I drove there. I had already been told that one of my two classes would consist of graduate students who would require a course on Shakespeare and the other of beginners who would require a course in 'conversation'. On my first day, the professor in charge of me said that the beginners' class would come first, the Shakespeare class second. I went into the first class. 'Good morning,' I enunciated very clearly. I turned to a student in the front row: 'How are you?' 'I am very well, thank you,' he answered. I turned to another student: 'And how are you?' 'Very well, thank you.' 'And how old are you?' I asked another student. So it went on. I was pleased that beginners should prove so responsive.

To the second class I gave a lecture on Shakespearian tragedy, which owed a lot to a lecture which I had once heard David Cecil deliver in Oxford. The students were admirably attentive. They kept their eyes on me. No one spoke. No one even stirred.

As I left the lecture hall I ran into a Canadian who was also teaching at Kohnan. 'How did you get on with those beginners?' he asked.

'Oh, I had the beginners for my first period. Those are the graduate students.'

'No, they're not! They certainly are not!'

He was right. It amazed me that not one of those graduates had protested, 'But, Mr King, you are supposed to be lecturing to us on Shakespeare,' and that all those beginners had given such whole-hearted attention to a lecture that must have been totally incomprehensible to them.

I cannot pretend that teaching at Kohnan was anything other than a bore. Designed for such children of the Kansai rich who proved incapable of passing entrance examinations into public universities, it had an abysmally low academic standard; and the fact that the students were, by and large, attractive, courteous and charming was hardly compensation. But I soon had a reason for looking forward to my day on the campus. This was the presence, in a house nearby, of an eccentric American, David Kidd.

Blond and willowy – a Japanese professor once said to me admiringly,

'Kidd-sensei is very like Grace Kelly' – David had begun his career as a colleague of William Empson in Beijing. He had soon become a close friend of Empson and his strong, capable, erratic wife Hetta. The Empsons had clearly exerted a profound influence on David; they were almost the only people about whom he talked with unreserved admiration and affection. To the surprise of the Empsons, David had married the daughter of a rich and aristocratic Chinese family. Later, he was to write a book, *All the Emperor's Horses*, about life in the family mansion, until it was abruptly and brutally terminated by the arrival of the communists. Sections were serialized in the *New Yorker*. Since both its quality and its success were indisputable, it is a mystery to me why David never produced a successor to this book. Expelled from China but having fallen in love with the Orient, he settled in Japan. His wife, having fallen in love with the West, settled in the States.

David did some desultory teaching; he also began to deal, with increasing success, in Oriental antiques, of which he is now a world-renowned expert. While I was in Japan, he moved from his Western-style house on the fringe of Kohnan campus to a Japanese farmhouse of extraordinary beauty but scant comfort and convenience, not all that far from it. On my weekly visits to Kohnan I would bring a picnic luncheon with me and eat it with David. What was luncheon for me was breakfast for him. Terrified of the dark, he would sit up most of the night and then sleep on until noon. In consequence, he would greet me in silk pyjamas, the bottoms of the trousers abnormally wide, over which he would wear a flowered kimono. On first seeing this kimono, a student friend who was acting as my driver, could not control his giggles. 'What are you laughing at?' David demanded. 'Kidd-sensei – forgive me for saying this . . .' Again the boy began to giggle. He pointed: 'That kimono . . . It is woman's kimono, Kidd-sensei.' 'Of course it's a woman's kimono,' David retorted. 'That's why I'm wearing it.' To my embarrassment, David would be wearing this kimono on those occasions when he decided to walk with me back to the university for what he called 'a breath of stale air'. Like my driver, students would stare and giggle at this tall, sinuous American in a garishly flowered kimono, one hand agitating a fan before his extraordinarily pale face.

But David's appearance was wholly deceptive. He was both physically and mentally strong; as brilliant a businessman as linguist, connoisseur and writer.

It was through David, who possessed a Cadillac, that I myself came to acquire one, even though I could not drive. Someone in my position ought to have a car, he repeatedly told me. It was disgraceful that the Council hadn't provided one for me. And it must be the sort of car that would impress the Japanese. They judged people by such things. Eventually he persuaded me to inspect a Cadillac which an American colonel, returning home to Virginia, was selling. I had a bargain there, David kept telling me. The car had been beautifully maintained, not a scratch on it, in perfect running order, air-conditioned.

Certainly the car looked superb; and certainly the price was not much higher than that of one of the larger 'Austins' which the Japanese, their car industry still then only nascent, were turning out under licence. In a moment of folly, which I have never regretted – I, too, have been a Cadillac-owner, I am able to boast – I told the colonel that I would buy it. He looked amazed by the speed of my decision. That I did not haggle over the price – 'You should have tried to beat him down by at least a hundred dollars,' David later reproved me – may have added to that amazement.

For the remainder of my stay in Japan, the car was a constant drain on my resources. It guzzled petrol; its air-conditioning system, automatic transmission and power-assisted steering all in turn broke. Once, when its brakes failed at a busy intersection, it was only Yoshihiro's nerve and skill, as he steered the car up and over a steep embankment and into a field, which saved me from death. Once, when Yoshihiro was driving me in the company of a visiting Foreign Office Minister, Lord Lansdowne, the engine suddenly conked out; and the three of us, eventually assisted by two passing Japanese peasants, then joined in sweltering heat to push its vast, weighty carcass on to the verge. I admired Lord Lansdowne's spirit. The low opinion which I had formed of him after hearing him start a speech to the Chamber of Commerce of Osaka with the words, 'I am delighted to be in your beautiful city of Kobe' – Osaka and Kobe were, and probably still are, ferocious commercial rivals – was now at once upgraded.


At first I was totally foxed by Japan; I could not understand it. This puzzlement produced in me irritation, exasperation, even anger. It also produced in me the urge to write a novel about the place, since I knew, from previous experience, that the act of writing about something which baffled me usually brought an end to the bafflement. So it was that I started on one of the three best of my novels, *The Custom House*. Like my *The Woman Who Was God* and *Act of Darkness*, and unlike any other of my novels, it was a book which seemed to be written by someone other than myself, a disembodied entity for whom I was no more than willing amanuensis, so that, rereading a page just completed, I would find myself asking myself, 'Where on earth did this come from?' I am now amazed by the frenzy with which, despite a long day of work for the Council, I raced through chapter after chapter. I managed to do this by getting up at five o'clock each morning and working for two or three hours before dressing, having breakfast and setting off for the office. The manuscript – in those days I wrote by hand – was an extraordinarily clean one.

Without David's assistance, the book would have been far less convincing. Reading a first draft, he at once saw what was wrong with it. 'These people don't talk like Japanese. They might be English.' Patiently, he went through all the dialogue with me, substituting Japanese idioms (in translation, of course) for English ones; introducing actual Japanese words; adapting similes and metaphors to give them the necessary 'foreignness'. He was a master of the language, whereas I could scarcely speak it.

The book presents a sombre, even hostile picture, since it was completed within the first year of my stay there, when I had still to fall in love with both

Japan and its people. 'Do you think that they're going to hate the book? Do you think they'll kick up a fuss?' I asked David. 'Of course they're going to hate it,' he replied. 'But they won't kick up a fuss. As with most other things that are disagreeable to them, they will just pretend it does not exist.' He was absolutely right, as he usually was where Japan and the Japanese were concerned. Even five years ago, when I was lecturing in Japan, the chairman's detailed résumé of my literary career contained no reference to *The Custom House*, even though he spoke admiringly of my other Japanese novel, *The Waves Behind the Boat*, and of my collection of Japanese short stories, *The Japanese Umbrella*. I thought that to ignore the book in this manner was far more civilized than to attack me for it. In a similar situation, the Greeks might well have hounded me out of Greece.

Two things changed my hatred of Japan into a love which has now lasted for almost thirty years. The first of these was that, having drifted for so long at sea, I suddenly felt firm land under my feet. 'I've got it, I've got it!' I could almost have cried out. I had found the key, deciphered the code. I was now able to understand precisely why, in a certain situation, the Japanese behaved in a certain way, and I could myself behave in a similar way in a similar situation. In a society in which there is so little spontaneity and in which people tend to behave according to rigid rules, it is only necessary to learn the rules to find that life becomes extraordinarily easy. One small example will suffice. In the West, when I was young, I was always in an agony of indecision about when I should leave a dinner or luncheon party. In Japan, at a certain hour, the host himself rises from the table and thanks his guests for their attendance. They then all leave together.

The second reason for my hatred of Japan all at once changing into love was the arrival into my life of a young man whom I shall call Noboru. Ebullient, impetuous, constantly laughing, constantly teasing, constantly speaking his mind, he was totally untypical of his race. What first brought us together was an advertisement which I had inserted in a student English language magazine for a live-in driver for my Cadillac. I had had a host of applicants, since students received no government grants, since accommodation was extremely difficult to find in the centre of the city, and since every student was eager to improve his English. Sadly, most of these applicants – this was a period when the possession of private cars was rare – had never once driven a car. Repeatedly I was told that there was no problem, it was only a matter of taking the test, a licence was the easiest thing in the world to procure. Sadly, too, many of these applicants spoke not a word of English, although they assured me, through Mr Otani, who sat in on the interviews, that they had no difficulty in reading or writing it.

I liked the way that Noburu swaggered into the room, grinning at me, instead of creeping in, like most of the other applicants, with a succession of bows, each one lower than its predecessor, at both Mr Otani and me. I liked his strong, square frame, and his jolly, open, round face. I liked the way that, unusual for a Japanese, he put out a hand to shake mine. In his native island of Shikoku he had worked briefly as a truck driver; and in the event he turned out to be one of those people who have an instinctive knowledge of cars. Would he be nervous of driving a car as large as a Cadillac? I asked him. He guffawed. It was his dream. The truck in Shikoku had been *huge*.

I was in no doubt at all that here was the candidate I wanted. But Mr Otani urged caution, hinting that Noboru was insufficiently deferential, was rough, was cocksure. I did not listen. I am glad that I did not do so, since Noboru turned out to be one of the most admirable people – cheerful, honest, affectionate, kind – ever to have played a major part in my life. His looks were unremarkable; but he had a superb physique, acquired in the playing of American football for his university.

Eventually his work for me during the day and his studies at the university in the evening, made him decide to give up the football. 'I am afraid that they will be very angry with me,' he told me, of the coach and the other members of the team. 'I am best player,' he added truthfully – assuming none of the falsy modesty of most Japanese. When he returned from telling the others, his left eye was almost closed from a blow, there was a gash on his right cheek, and his body was covered in bruises. I thought at first that he must have had an accident in the Cadillac, which I had told him to borrow; but he said, 'They beat me.' Apparently, when he had informed the coach and the other players that he wanted to quit, they had at once all set on him, knocked him to the ground, and kicked and pummelled him. I was outraged, and said that I should report the matter to the Rector of the university, who was a friend of mine. 'No, no, no! Impossible!' he told me. He then explained that this was the usual punishment for someone who let a team down. They were within their rights. He deserved what had happened to him.

The submissiveness of the Japanese at that period – never arguing, never rebelling – used to get on my nerves. Often, it also had the effect of making my behaviour even more demanding and unreasonable. Noboru, now laughing amiably at me and now quietly chiding me, was excellent for my character. My two and a half years with him as my constant companion – I had never before lived with anyone else in that way – convinced me that such a relationship was essential for my happiness.


The Japanese are no more concerned with one's sexual orientation than with whether one has tea or coffee for breakfast, or whether one enjoys Noh or Kabuki the more. Their interest in sex is the same as a gourmet's interest in food; whereas the interest of the English in sex is all too often that of a sufferer from bulimia – now indiscriminately overeating and now vomiting in remorse. Sexual gossip, of the kind so common in England, is extraordinarily rare in Japan. I was always careful to be discreet about my sexual tastes; but if anyone guessed at them, they aroused little interest, and absolutely no disapproval.

In this context, I remember taking a Home Office official, called Stephen Gwynn, to see his Japanese counterpart in Osaka. In the course of a wide-ranging conversation, Gwynn, an intelligent and liberal man, asked, 'Now what about the problem of homosexuality?'

'In Japan there is no problem of homosexuality,' his interlocutor replied.
Gwynn was amazed. 'What? Do you mean there is no homosexuality in Japan?'
The Japanese smiled. 'Of course there is homosexuality in Japan. But there are
no laws about homosexuality in Japan. Therefore there is no problem.'

As we left the building, Gwynn remarked to me that this was the most
interesting thing that he had heard in the course of his visit to the country.

I received many visitors, both official and private, in Japan; and, since my house
contained five bedrooms, these visitors often stayed with me. The visitor who
stayed longest, my Man Who Came to Dinner, was Joe Ackerley. From England
he had written to tell me that Morgan Forster had agreed to 'stump up' the price
of a return ticket to Japan and that he would be awfully grateful if I could put him
up for a time. He did not then tell me, as he was to tell me later, that his chief
reason for quitting England was a terror of being sued for libel by the working-
class family depicted so unflatteringly in his autobiographical novella, then about
to be published, *We Think the World of You*. It struck me as highly unlikely that
such people would read the book or even learn of its existence; but there was some
truth in Joe's reply to me, when I gave him this reassurance: 'People have an
uncanny knack of learning of things of which you don't want them to learn.'

I was delighted at the prospect of seeing Joe, so stimulating and amusing a
companion. But I had not really bargained for a stay which protracted itself,
without any reference to myself, for weeks and weeks on end. In general, we got
on extremely well, with Joe joining in my conversation classes, much to the
delight of my students, exercising my five dogs, three of them huge Akitas, and
working in the garden. But inevitably, cheek-by-jowl for so long a period, there
were times when we also got on each other's nerves.

One cause of trouble was the dogs. Like Alsatians and Rottweilers, Akitas (as
anyone who has kept one will know) are wonderful pets if strictly disciplined. I
had strictly disciplined mine. They sat when told to sit; they were quiet when told
to be quiet. They did not beg for food, climb on to chairs, sofas or beds, or urinate
or defecate in the house. To Joe – whose own Alsatian Queenie was an example of
a dog not merely spoiled but ruined by its owner – such discipline was cruelty.
'Come along, darling, come and sit beside me,' he would encourage one of the
Akitas, patting an empty space on the sofa beside him. 'Here you are, darling,
here's a lovely mouthful for you,' he would tell another, proffering a chunk of
extremely expensive Kobe steak or the best part of a slice of cake. During his
afternoon siesta, he would encourage at least one of the dogs to clamber on to the
bed beside him. Useless for me to protest.

A second cause of trouble was booze. Whereas Joe, although not yet an
alcoholic, drank heavily, I drank – and still drink – little. Coming home from the
office, all I wanted was a single gin and tonic before dinner. Joe wanted several –
'Sweetheart, might I just have another gin before eating?' he would wheedle
when, aware that my cook-housekeeper was waiting impatiently for us, I rose yet

again to my feet. Had she been a boy, Joe would not doubt have been more considerate. But she was a woman, and it was a woman's business to put up with inconvenience. If she missed her last bus home, well, that was just too bad.

Gordon's or Beefeater gin was then obtainable only in foreign-goods stores in Kobe. It was far from cheap. In the course of a single day Joe would consume at least half a bottle; but he never once offered to contribute. 'Do you know what Wystan [Auden] did in Ischia?' he once said to me. 'He really is a mean old bugger. He would make me mark the gin bottle each time that I poured from it, with a red-ink pen. He himself would mark it with a blue-ink pen. Then, when the bottle was empty, he would measure how many inches each of us had drunk and divide up the cost. Can you imagine!' I thought it an admirable idea.

In turn, I irritated Joe with my excessive punctuality and tidiness. Although I can truthfully say that I have never hunted out someone else's letter to read, I can never resist reading a letter exposed to my attention. So it was that I came to read a half-written letter to William Plomer, left out by Joe on the writing-table not in his own room but in my sitting-room. 'I don't know how much longer I can take Francis's fussiness. If I smoke a cigarette, he at once gets up to empty the ashtray. If I drop the newspaper to the floor, he at once stoops to pick it up, fold it and place it on the table.'

Like all charmers – and of all charmers, he was the most potent I have ever met – Joe would play off one friend against another. So he played off James Kirkup, then a lecturer in Sendai, and me. Staying with Kirkup, he would write to me of his boredom: dear James was such a pet, but he was a recluse, rarely going out and even more rarely having anyone round; his friends seemed to consist entirely of the dreariest of students and two or three equally dreary professors. From my house in Kyoto, he would in turn write to Kirkup: dear Francis was such a pet, the soul of kindness, but oh dear, he led such a rackety life, there was never a moment's peace, either one was dashing out to some party or some party was afoot at home. To all and sundry Joe complained that I 'insisted' on dragging him out to bars and clubs. But I had no more taste for bars and clubs than for hard drinking, and it was myself whom I was constantly obliged to drag out in the hope of keeping Joe amused.

Joe taught me one valuable lesson. All through a life devoid of any truly satisfactory and lasting relationship, he was in search of 'the ideal friend'. Such a friend must not be his social, intellectual or financial equal; and, even more important, he must not be homosexual or even bisexual. Because of the strictness of these criteria, such relationships as he formed in Japan – with a young student met in the YMCA hostel in Tokyo, with a monk met in a Buddhist monastery on Mount Koya – were merely transitory. It was, I am convinced, because they were transitory that he eventually decided to return to England. Had he demanded less of life, he would have received so much more. His example taught me that to be happy in a relationship one must be prepared to settle for the possible.

That Joe should have seriously thought of making his home in Japan always amazed me. What about 'my three women' or 'my womenfolk' (as he used to call them): his neurotic sister Nancy, his jolly Aunt Bunny, his appalling Queenie? That he should have considered abandoning the first two was no surprise at all. But the beloved bitch! I eventually came to the conclusion that Joe, perhaps prompted by Morgan Forster whose judgement he trusted, had realized that, if he were to survive both as an individual and as a writer, he must get away from the two women and the dog. His trip to Japan was a desperate last attempt to do so. It failed. There followed the years of increasing idleness, self-laceration and drinking.

Joe never returned to Japan, although he often declared that he was about to do so and although he was constantly prodded by Kirkup and me. Forster even gave him the money for another ticket; which Joe then spent on drink. This annoyed Forster, who was something of a puritan for all his advocacy of sexual freedom. 'That wretched Joe!' he protested to me. 'Fancy giving up the chance of another trip to Japan merely in order to booze in Putney!'


Like David Kidd, James Kirkup was a genuine eccentric. He was also a bolter, abandoning a job, a place or a relationship as soon as it became oppressive or unrewarding. When I arrived in Japan, he was teaching for the British Council in Kuala Lumpur. Then I received a telegram from the Representative there: KIRKUP VANISHED STOP GRATEFUL FOR ANY POINTERS. I did not have to point far. Kirkup had called on me only two or three days before, and was still in Kyoto. There had been some disagreement in Kuala Lumpur and, without any warning to anyone, he had abandoned his post.

Joe described to me how, one morning, while staying with Kirkup in Sendai, he had looked out of his bedroom window to see his host, dressed only in his underwear, leaping through a paper-covered hoop dangling from the branch of a tree. 'What are you doing, James dear?' Joe called out. Kirkup then explained that he found that the act of leaping through the hoop facilitated his passage from one plane of reality to another, before he settled down to write a poem.

When, in Kyoto, Kirkup and I were preparing to cross a busy thoroughfare, he suddenly produced a huge fan, painted with the imperial chrysanthemum, out of the voluminous sleeve of his kimono, flicked it open and held it up in front of the oncoming traffic. All the cars squealed to a halt. He then swayed gracefully across.

On leave in England, I received a letter from him asking me to bring back for him a jar of Helena Rubinstein's anti-wrinkle cream – 'It does wonders for my scrotum.'

While taking part as a lecturer in a British Council summer school, Kirkup did another bolt. His students loved his classes, since he had grasped the essential truth about education that to instruct people you must also interest them. But his methods were far from orthodox. On this occasion, the British Council had sent out some dreary expert in the teaching of English as a foreign language, who, having sat in on one of Kirkup's entertainingly unorthodox lessons, was horrified to discover not merely that he knew nothing of phonetics but that his idea of instruction was, at least on this occasion, to read to his students from his own poems. The expert hurried to report this to Ronald Bottrall, who, having by now succeeded Phillips, was in charge of the summer school. Having summoned Kirkup, Bottrall told him that, first thing the next morning, the visiting expert would be giving him some instruction in how to conduct his classes. That evening Kirkup failed to turn up at dinner, and a student was despatched to his room to find him. The student returned to announce, in an echo of a famous sentence in Conrad's *Heart of Darkness*, 'Mr Kirkup – he gone.' Three weeks later, at the close of the summer school, Ronald Bottrall was surprised to receive from Kirkup an invoice for his fee as a lecturer. No doubt it was because of the ensuing argument about this fee that Kirkup thenceforth always referred to the British Council as the Brutish Cuntsall.

After I had left Japan, Kirkup gave a lecture about English writers who had written about the country. He can never have imagined that its contents would be reported back to me; but, confirming Joe's dictum which I have already quoted, they soon were, not by one but by no fewer than three persons, all Japanese, who had attended the lecture. Kirkup had referred to my *The Custom House*. He had then gone on to say that the only Japanese I had ever bothered to get to know were rich, fashionable or powerful. I wrote to protest: he had visited my house, he had seen how it was always full of students. He replied that he had only been joking.

He was such a gifted, such an amusing and such an unusual character that I did not hold this naughtiness against him, any more than I held against him his naughtiness in writing in the *London Magazine* that, when Joe Ackerley was found dead in his Putney flat, hypodermic syringes were scattered around him. But on that occasion I did point out that the doctor who had certified that Joe had died of natural causes might well have grounds for libel.

Many years later, John Mortimer, a friend of Oxford days, asked me, as the then Chairman of the Society of Authors, if I would be willing to give evidence of literary merit in the famous case in which *Gay Times* and its editor Dennis Lemon were being prosecuted for having published a blasphemous poem by James Kirkup on the subject of the Crucifixion. Since Dennis Lemon was a friend of mine, since I felt sorry for him, cruelly isolated by Kirkup's refusal to return to England to defend his own poem, and since, in any case, it seemed to me that a matter of principle was involved, I agreed to do so. It was a great relief when the judge ruled that literary merit was irrelevant in the case and John therefore could not call me. The poem was not one of Kirkup's best.

When he came to write the second volume of his outrageously entertaining autobiography, Kirkup asked me, as Ackerley's literary executor, for permission to quote from some of Ackerley's letters to him. I gladly gave the permission but added the proviso, 'Now be a good boy and don't write any of them yourself.' When I eventually read the volume, I could not be entirely sure that he had obeyed my injunction.

Kirkup's autobiography provides an excellent illustration of what I call 'creative memory'. No doubt parts of this autobiography provide, without my realizing it, a similar illustration.

Curiously, since he was so proficient in other languages, Kirkup appeared to know no Japanese, at least while I was resident in the country. He explained this by telling me on one occasion while we were walking down a street, 'All these signs around us are so *exquisite*, real works of art. But if I knew that that one was an advertisement for cigarettes and *that* one an advertisement for an ointment for piles, it would quite destroy my aesthetic appreciation.' For my own inadequacy in the language, David Kidd provided a different excuse. This was that the Japanese had far greater respect for someone who was both so busy that he did not have time properly to learn their language, and rich enough to afford the services of an interpreter.

Ronald Bottrall was so unsuited to Japan, both physically and temperamentally, that it is unlikely that any organization other than the British Council would have ever thought of despatching him there. I have already recorded how he once told me that he had considered being a homosexual while up at Cambridge but had then decided that he was 'too big for it'. Similarly, he was too big for Japan. When we were invited to a Japanese tea-house, restaurant or home, I would invariably hear a crack, followed by an 'Ouch!' or even 'Fuck!' Yet again he had managed to bang his head on a low beam. Whether the increasingly slurred speech which followed was caused by this injury or by the enthusiasm with which he threw back cup after cup of saké, I could never be certain. Having lowered himself to the floor, with a succession of groans and grunts and, as often as not, an aside to me of 'Why the hell can't they provide a proper table and chairs?', he would then stretch out his immensely long legs and so inadvertently kick the shins of whoever was seated opposite to him. On one occasion, making an extravagant gesture, chopsticks in hand, he managed to put an elbow through a fragile paper screen. On another occasion, he broke the backrest provided for him. No slippers were ever large enough – 'These would only fit a dwarf Chinese tart whose feet had been bound!' he protested on one occasion.

Just as the Japanese physical world was too narrow and delicate to accommodate him, so was the whole Japanese code of behaviour. The candour, directness and domineering vigour which had served him so well in Italy and Greece were here appalling handicaps. I had learned that if I wished to ask, say, the Rector of Kyoto University to dinner, I must not issue a direct invitation but must first ask some intermediary, his PA or the Dean of the Faculty of English, whether such an invitation would be welcome. But 'Oh, I haven't time for all that nonsense!' Ronald would exclaim. 'If he doesn't want to come, he's only got to refuse.' If one is given a present in Japan, etiquette demands that one should not immediately open it in front of the giver. Ronald, however, would at once tear off the wrapping paper and then make it abundantly clear whether he approved of the gift or not. 'Splendid, splendid, very decent of you!' he would exclaim; or 'Well, well, well! What on earth is the purpose of *this*?'

The fact that the Japanese were so submissive brought out the worst in him, as it did in me. He would storm about the Tokyo office – something which I can truthfully say that I never did in the Kyoto one, preferring the weapons of silence or sarcasm – like one of those Japanese typhoons which, in a few perilous moments, can create so much havoc. Then he would disappear into his office, leaving behind him a number of men ashen-faced over their ledgers and a number of women sobbing into their typewriters. Half an hour later, he would re-emerge, a benevolent sun shining over his little empire. He had totally forgotten both his rage and the reason for it. The Japanese, however, never forgot.

Ronald and his tough, amusing and kindly second wife, Margot, would from time to time invite themselves to stay with me in Kyoto. From the Council I received no allowance for either the Cadillac or Noboru's pay as its driver. But Ronald invariably treated both as though I did. 'I'll be wanting the car at nine tomorrow to take me to see the Mayor,' he would say to me; or to Noboru, without consulting either his or my convenience, 'Pick me up from the Noh Theatre as soon as the performance is over.'

The most memorable clash between Ronald and the Japanese way of life took place when, once again staying with me, he gave a lecture at Kobe University, where the Dean of the Faculty of English, Professor Kozu, was an old and valued friend of mine – later becoming the prototype of the Japanese professor in my short story, 'A Corner of a Foreign Field'. Ronald's subject was 'Twentieth-Century English Poetry'. His was a masterly essay but a poor lecture, since he read it out – such was his custom – in a monotonous voice, head lowered over text. The students, like all Japanese students in such tedious circumstances, sat absolutely still, their eyes fixed on him. At the close, he looked up and demanded, 'Well, now, how about some questions?'

There was a silence, which prolonged itself. I was just about to intervene, when Professor Kozu rose to his feet:

'Er – Mr – Professor Bottrall, sir – I have a, er, question.'

'Yes?'

'Whom do you consider the greatest poet – Yeats, Eliot or Auden?'

'Oh, my God!' Ronald slapped what little forehead he had with the palm of a hand. (Roger Hinks, asked by a Greek woman whether Ronald was handsome, replied, 'Well, that all depends on whether you're attracted by men with eyes on the tops of their heads.') 'What a stupid question! What an incredibly stupid question! It's *unbelievable*! No, I absolutely refuse to answer that!' Professor Kozu at once sat down; his students all began to giggle in embarrassment, hands over mouths. I tried to save the situation by myself asking a question about the influence of Yeats on Auden.

The lecture was followed by a dinner, given by Professor Kozu, in one of the most expensive Japanese restaurants in Kobe. The professor was, as always, the most solicitous of hosts, sitting, not merely literally but metaphorically, at Ronald's feet throughout the evening. As we walked towards my car – which Ronald had pre-empted, to drive him on to the Consul General, who had invited him in for an after-dinner drink – he turned to me: 'Well, I think that went off very well, very well indeed! Delightful chap, your professor. I can understand why you've made such a friend of him.'

The car drove off. I waved. Professor Kozu bowed deeply.

Then, when the car had vanished, Professor Kozu turned to me: 'Mr Bottrall will never again lecture in Kobe University,' he said in a quiet, steely voice.

Nor did he. Repeatedly he asked me to set up another lecture for him there – 'I so much enjoyed my last visit.' Repeatedly I went through the motions of doing so. Repeatedly I relayed back to him some excuse or other from Professor Kozu – the most usual being that the students either were preparing for, or were already in the throes of, examinations.

On three consecutive Christmases the Bottralls invited me to stay with them in Tokyo. If they were extremely demanding guests, they were also extremely generous hosts; and I enjoyed gossiping to Margot or listening to Ronald either holding forth about literature, music and art from an immense fund of knowledge, or playing on the Steinway grand which accompanied him about the world (he was an excellent pianist). However, the third of these Christmas stays proved something of an ordeal. Ronald had just received a letter from Sir Paul Sinker, the then Director-General of the British Council, informing him that, as soon as he had reached the minimum retiring age of fifty-five (i.e. in a few weeks' time), the Council would be dispensing with his services. Not unnaturally this news had plunged both Bottralls into a mood which alternated between morose gloom and blazing anger. 'But at fifty-five one is still *young*!' Ronald would wail at one moment. Then at the next he would be raging: 'That bloody, bloody Stinker!' He and Margot helped themselves liberally from the whisky bottle; I, in sympathy, from the gin one. I returned to Kyoto with a terrible hangover.

Ronald's mistake had been to make himself unpopular with many of his colleagues by his manifest disdain for them. 'Stinker', seconded from the Civil Service, was a highly efficient bureaucrat, who succeeded in repeatedly upping the Council's budget; but Ronald, possessor of an alpha-plus mind, was right in saying of him, 'One would have to give him alpha plus for efficiency and effort, but it would only be beta minus for anything else.' Although Ronald can never have actually conveyed this judgement to 'Stinker' in words, he frequently did so by an attitude of condescension or contempt.

Ronald appealed against his enforced retirement to the Chairman of the British Council, Lord Bridges. Since Bridges, son of the poet, was, unlike 'Stinker', a man of great intellectual distinction, Ronald was optimistic that he would soon put things right – 'He's one of our own sort,' he told me more than once. Bridges did, in fact, decide that the matter should be investigated by a Civil Service committee. He then asked Ronald to nominate two referees, Council employees who had served under him. Ronald first nominated Roger Hinks, who had served under him twice, and myself, who had served under him three times. But after a few weeks, he changed his mind, switching from Roger Hinks to an expert in the teaching of English as a foreign language, Arthur King. When I asked him the reason for the change, he replied, 'Well, I thought that two Kings might carry more weight than two queens.' In my written submission I did my best for Ronald, suppressing any mention of his faults and expatiating on his virtues – his intellect and wit; the speed with which he could master a file or a financial statement; the width and depth of his knowledge of literature, music and art; his talents as linguist and poet. I could also affirm, with no deviation from truth, that, although Ronald was frequently criticized for being 'difficult' with colleagues, I had never had a single row with him. I did not add that the sole reason for this miracle was the fact that I was a writer. Ronald had a touching respect for writers, not shared by myself, and therefore allowed them, as D. J. Enright would put it, to get away with murder.

I am sure that Arthur King also did his best for Ronald. But sadly the committee confirmed the enforced retirement.

Before catching their ship home at Kobe – in those days there were a number of regular services between Japan and European ports – the Bottralls invited themselves to stay with me for the last time. In the course of this visit they met two students of mine, one tall and one short, one called Fukushima and one called Fukuda. They were plain, spotty, intelligent, decent youths; and like many plain, spotty, intelligent, decent youths, I should guess that neither had ever received a pass in his life. To differentiate between them, I used to call them (not to their faces, of course) 'The Big Fuck' and 'The Little Fuck'. Ronald overheard me doing this in the course of a telephone chat with David Kidd. As a consequence, on his arrival in England, he would respond to any query about how I was getting on with the answer: 'Francis? Francis? Oh, he's very satisfactorily set up. *Very* satisfactorily. He's got not one boy-friend, but two. One he calls "The Big Fuck" and the other "The Little Fuck".' He would then burst into peals of laughter. He had, as I have already indicated, absolutely no disapproval of homosexuals. Even James Kirkup, whom he nicknamed 'The Lily of Laguna', he viewed with affectionate tolerance.

On that last visit, Ronald was drinking even more than usual. After one particularly bibulous luncheon, I staggered into my sitting-room, where a conversation class of beginners was awaiting me. Ronald had said that he was going to 'have a snooze'. The Council insisted that all teaching of English must be by the direct method; and so – much though I hated it – this is what I now used. I held up a bottle of gin. 'This is a bottle,' I said. I shook it. 'This is a full bottle.' I retrieved from the waste-paper basket a gin bottle, its contents drunk chiefly by Ronald, which I had thrown there. 'This is an empty bottle.' I repeated, 'This is a full bottle . . . This is an empty bottle.' Suddenly a flushed face appeared round the door. 'This is a Bottrall,' Ronald announced. He hiccoughed. 'This is a full Bottrall.' He then disappeared. The students were astounded. To distract them, I again held up one of the bottles on the table before me. 'What is this?' I asked. 'That is a Bottrall,' the dimmest student, a girl, replied. 'That is a full Bottrall,' she added.

Ronald was succeeded by a philosopher, friend of T.S. Eliot and Wyndham

Lewis, called E.W.F. (Freddie) Tomlin. Unlike Ronald, he was a most effective lecturer. During the course of a lecture by him on some extremely abtruse philosophical subject, I used to think with amazement, 'But I *understand* all this!' Sadly, the following day, I would have absolutely no idea of what the lecture had been about.

Perhaps because of his own lack of any small talk and a similar lack in most of his Japanese guests, Tomlin would play music throughout his dinner-parties. As the noisy gulping of soup (to slurp is not bad manners in Japan) vied with the strains of the Elgar cello concerto, for which Tomlin had an inordinate affection, I often used to find myself wishing that I were somewhere else.

Divorced, Tomlin, like at least one Representative who succeeded him, started an affair with a girl in the office. When he finally decided to terminate the affair, the girl stole the manuscript, the only one in existence, of a novel on which he had been working, and refused to return it. Since Tomlin's talent for fiction certainly did not equal his talent for lecturing on philosophy, perhaps one should be grateful to her. With a reversal of nationalities, so that it was an English girl who stole a manuscript from a Japanese professor when similarly given the brush-off in Brighton, I based a short story, 'Loss', on this incident.

Tomlin came to the beautiful resort of Amanano-Hashidate to attend the closing ceremony of a summer school which I had directed. The students all gone, he and I found ourselves having dinner alone together in a now totally deserted Japanese inn. Tomlin began talking about the women students. Although he had only been in their company for a day, I was amazed by how much he had noticed about them. 'That was a pretty little girl with the cast in her left eye . . . That Miss Ishiyama is really very attractive, even though she must be well over forty . . . I was awfully taken by that teacher from Okayama – do you know the one that I mean?'

After dinner, a long evening stretched ahead of us. How was I to entertain him? 'Would you like to go to a strip-show?' I asked.

'A strip-show? *Here?*'

Even the smallest and most remote towns in Japan can usually provide at least one strip-show.

'Yes, it's not far from the hotel. Five minutes' walk.'

'I've never been to a strip-show.' He pondered. 'Well, why not?'

For a while he stared intently at the girl in no more than black G-string and a rosette covering each nipple. He shifted uneasily in his seat. He coughed. Eventually, she pulled off one rosette and then the other. She grinned around the half-empty auditorium and advanced to the footlights, peering out at the audience. She ripped off the G-string and whirled it round and round over her head, while opening her legs wide. Then she threw the G-string towards Tomlin. To a guffaw from the audience it landed in his lap.

He jumped up, pushing the G-string away as though it were a dead bat which had fallen on him. 'Come along! Come!'

He stormed out of the hall. I followed. There was a lot of giggling from the all-male audience.

'How could you have inflicted an exhibition like that on me? How *could* you?'

Things were never quite the same between us after that.


It was during my Japanese years that I formed a friendship which has provided me with constant support and entertainment ever since. I had first met John Haylock in Florence, when he and Desmond Stewart, travelling back to England together by car from Iraq, where they were teaching, stayed for two nights at my villa. John was suffering from a kidney infection and I therefore took him to a urologist, who prescribed him some pills. In the interval at the Teatro Verdi that evening, those of our fellow opera-goers who were relieving themselves beside us were amazed to see that John was peeing what appeared to be Reckitt's Blue. But whatever the unorthodox treatment, it worked.

John, who was now teaching in Tokyo, had a flat spacious by Japanese standards but minute by European ones. He would put me up there, and I would put him up in my house in Kyoto. Sometimes during holidays we would make an exchange of dwellings; but more often we would go off on some trip together. Always jolly, always resourceful, always stoical, John is the ideal travelling companion. We soon found that his knowledge and my knowledge of Japanese perfectly complemented each other: he could say virtually anything but could understand virtually nothing, whereas the exact opposite was true of me. Thus, between us, we could conduct a satisfactory conversation with any Japanese with whom we came into contact.

I cannot say that there are all that many people in the world whom I should rather be than myself. How dreadful, for all their distinction and success, to be John Osborne, or Richard Ingrams, or Dirk Bogarde, or Kingsley Amis, or Salman Rushdie! But to be John Haylock would be perfect. He has robust health and private means ample enough to allow him to travel about the world in comfort. He is naturally kind without being in the least sentimental. He has an eighteenth-century horror of excess, so that he is free from all those passions – love, hate, jealousy, envy, ambition – which can make such a hell of so many people's lives, my own among them.

When he stayed with me in Kyoto, John would suddenly announce, 'Now I must do some more knitting.' What he meant was that he must write another paragraph or two of the novel in hand. Priggishly, I used to be shocked: to produce a novel was surely something different from knitting a pullover? In the event, two of John's pullovers, novels entitled *One Hot Summer in Kyoto* and *Uneasy Relations*, turned out to be first-rate. Had there been more *Sturm und Drang* in his life, perhaps he would have written other novels equally outstanding. But in that case he would have been less happy and produced less happiness in others.

With John, with Noboru, with other friends, Japanese or foreign, I was constantly travelling about the country, sometimes by rail but more often in the Cadillac. In those days £1 was worth 1000 yen, and for that sum it was possible to put up in a country inn, with breakfast, dinner and a Japanese bath included. Sometimes I used to complain about the inconveniences and discomforts: the earth-closet, so malodorous that one's nose would guide one to it; the noise from adjoining rooms, often separated from one's own by the flimsiest of partitions; the inquisitiveness of the maids, peeping through holes in the paper screens in order to see what a Westerner looked like in the nude; the unpalatable diet. But now, in retrospect, those stays in small, dark, ramshackle inns in towns tucked away in remote corners of Japan are among the happiest memories of my life.

In addition to travelling about Japan whenever I had the free time to do so, I explored the then ravishing countryside around Kyoto. On these excursions my companion was often a university lecturer, Mihiko Shimada, who first demonstrated to me the falsity of the common Western view of Japanese women. With a voice so soft that often I had difficulty in hearing what she was saying and a manner so tentative that she put me in mind of a bird too nervous to descend from a tree to peck at the crumbs one had thrown for it, she none the less possessed a formidable strength of character. We would arrive at some monastery to find that it was closed. Never mind, we would drive on to another, I would say. But she would ring repeatedly at the door and bang on it; she would demand to see the abbot; she would then coax and cajole him, explaining that I worked for the British Council, that I was a 'famous' writer, and that I had travelled all this way with the express intention of seeing this particular monastery. Eventually the abbot would relent. On one memorable occasion she had a sex museum, near Osaka, similarly opened up for me. Although it was she, not I, who had suggested that we go there, I was embarrassed that someone so refined should be subjected to exhibits often so gross; but she showed no unease whatever, even asking the curator the sort of questions which I myself hesitated to ask. After our tour of the museum, the curator sat us both down and showed us some pornographic films over cups of Japanese tea. He might have been showing us the family photograph album. At the time I was disconcerted; then I thought – How sensible! If such a museum existed in England, one could imagine the shocked comments ('Ooh! Look at that! Disgusting! They ought to forbid it!'), the innuendoes and the gigglings.

Miss Shimada was only one of a number of Japanese women, self-effacing on the one hand and tremendously tough and efficient on the other, to whom I got into the habit of turning whenever I had a problem. There was always at least one such woman behind every successful man in Japan; so that if I wanted something – from the Dean of the English Department of this or that university, from the Mayor, from the Municipal Librarian – it was not to him that I initially addressed myself but to her.

I often travelled not merely to visit temples and gardens but to be present at festivals. Many of these, particularly the fire festivals and the naked festivals, took place in winter. Shivering despite overcoat, gloves, scarf and hat, I would endure hours, literally, of monotonous chanting in some near-dark, refrigerator-like temple on a hillside or in the heart of a forest. Then, in a thrice, there would be light and movement all around me. Naked bodies would jostle each other. Flames would flash and roar skywards from huge pyres. I have never been so bored as in Japan; and I have never been so excited. Whether at these festivals, at Sumo tournaments or in the Noh and Kabuki Theatre, the boredom is the price of the excitement – the preceding silence and stillness making, by contrast, the noise and movement all that more thrilling when at long last they erupt.

I met some extraordinarily silly Westerners, students of Zen, while I was in Japan; and I often feared that in my love for the country, its customs and its way of life, I might become equally silly myself. The silliest of all were usually American; some of them college boys, some of them former GIs. There was an element of cool sadism in the way in which the Japanese Zen 'masters' would exploit and bully these muzzy neophytes.

During my first year in Kyoto, when I so often felt bewildered and therefore exasperated and when I had still not found someone to share my life, I began to collect animals and antiques. On the departure of Leslie Phillips and his wife, I had taken over their mongrel dog Arabella. A racist, Arabella could by smell unerringly differentiate between a Western and a Japanese caller. If the former rang the bell, she would wag her tail as she waited for the housekeeper, Noboru or me to open the door. If the latter, she would hurl herself at it in a frenzy of barking and growling. After Arabella, I acquired three Akitas and then a little Pomeranian. One of the Akitas, a bitch, and Arabella hated each other, so that I had to keep them separate. When I was walking them on New Year's Eve in the country, the Akita bitch slipped her lead and flew at Arabella. I intervened to separate them and the Akita then bit me in the leg, causing a long and deep wound, from which I still have a scar. That she did not intend to bite me was evidenced by her remorse, as she stood over me, whimpering and trying to lick the wound, while one of my students, who had been walking with me, raced off to fetch the car.

New Year is the great holiday in Japan. In consequence, I could find no doctor willing to see me. Finally the student drove me to the American Baptist Hospital where a young intern, no more than a boy, gasped, 'Oh, my! Oh, my!' as he inspected the bite. Then he announced that he would have to sew it up. 'I'm not a surgeon,' he explained. 'I hope I do this right.' He might have been a young girl starting on her first needlework lesson. As I lay on my stomach I could not see what he was doing. But the student, who had insisted on staying with me, could see. Suddenly, there was a crash as he fainted.

The stitching over, the intern took a test to see if I would be allergic to a tetanus shot. I was. 'This is very unfortunate,' he told me. 'Now I want you to be very careful. If, at any time during the next ten days, you feel any stiffness or twitching of the muscles, I want you to come up here at once. *At once*. Do you understand?' I said that, yes, I understood. For the next ten days, I used to wake up two or three times each night. Oh, God! My neck was stiff, my right leg was stiff, and, yes, my little finger was twitching. Fortunately, on each occasion I decided to wait until the morning before taking myself off to the hospital; and by the morning the symptoms had mysteriously vanished.

Antiques were amazingly cheap at that period, since few Japanese were interested in them. I used to wander from shop to shop, eventually ingratiating myself sufficiently with their owners for them to invite me into the concealed interiors where all their real treasures were stored. Only dealers were allowed to attend auction sales; so, with his usual resourcefulness, Noboru acquired a licence as a dealer, and from then onwards would bid on my behalf. Some of the dealers soon realized what was going on and, quite naturally, resented it.

One of these dealers was an American called Robin Curtis, cool, suave and impeccable in his taste, who for the most part sold to his fellow countrymen. Sometimes, visiting his shop, I would listen with admiration as he pushed some mulish tourist into making a purchase. 'That? That Ming chair? . . . Yes, it really *is* Ming, a particularly beautiful example . . . Oh, I don't know that I really want to sell it, I've come to *adore* it . . . No . . . In any case, I'm afraid it would be *terribly* expensive, it would just *have* to be. You see . . .' There would then follow an elaborate account of its provenance.

Robin had always coveted a vast chest, with the Tokugawa crest on it, which stood in my hall. A few days before my final departure from Japan, he called on me, ostensibly to say goodbye. As he was leaving, he then stroked the chest, as though it were a beloved dog or cat. 'Oh, I love this chest, just love it, love it!' I had been wondering whether it would be worth spending a huge sum of money on shipping the chest back to England and whether, once it was there, I should have anywhere to accommodate it. On an impulse I therefore said, 'You can have it if you like. I'll give it to you.'

'Oh, no!' he cried out. But there was a note of exultation in his voice. Immediately afterwards he was on my telephone, arranging for someone to transport the chest back to his house.

The next day his assistant arrived with a little parcel for me. 'A goodbye present from Curtis-san,' the assistant said. The present was a Sung figurine of a woman, which I still possess.

Soon after I left Kyoto, Robin Curtis was murdered. Since he was a homosexual, the police systematically interrogated all the people whose names appeared in a 'special' address-book. This inevitably caused embarrassment to a number of men, many of them married. But when the police finally caught the murderer, he proved to be an anonymous pick-up from a cinema, whom Curtis had apparently refused to pay the full sum previously agreed between them. Peter Martin based the plot of his first detective novel on this tragedy.


The most interesting of all my visitors was Somerset Maugham. Although, after my winning of the Award given by him, we had from time to time corresponded with each other, usually after I had sent him one of my books, we had never met. That we had so far failed to do so had been largely due to my shyness and, yes, fear. More than once he had urged me to stay with him at Cap Ferrat on my journeys to or from England, and each time I had made some excuse. Our not meeting was also, on one occasion, due to my upbringing. I was on leave, staying with my sister and brother-in-law in their Battersea flat, when Alan Searle, Maugham's 'secretary', had telephoned. He and Maugham were staying at Claridge's for that week. Could I have dinner with them the following evening?

'May I just look in my book?' I said. Then, having done so, I told him that, sadly, I was engaged.

'Oh. I see.' It was rather as if I had refused an invitation to Buckingham Palace.

'I'd love to see Mr Maugham some other time.'

'I'm afraid that won't be possible.' The voice was icy.

My prior engagement had been to have dinner with the parents of John Croft. When they eventually heard from my sister Elizabeth that I had refused to have dinner with Somerset Maugham in order to keep my engagement with them, the Crofts were astounded. They could easily have fixed another night, they told me. Fancy missing the opportunity to meet so famous a writer!

'Even as children we were told by my mother that we must never give up one engagement because something else had come along,' I explained.

The Crofts clearly thought that my mother had been extremely foolish in promulgating such a rule.

So many people have written so many unpleasant things about Maugham. But in all truthfulness, I have little but good to report of him. He was in Kyoto for more than a week and, during that week, I saw him every day, often for hours on end. Such continuous proximity is an excellent test of character. He was then extremely old and frail and tired easily; but never once did he show any anger or even irritability towards me, Alan Searle or anyone else.

Maugham's reputation at that period was far higher in Japan than in England – a fact on which he commented to me, with the sardonic ruefulness of so much of his conversation. 'University professors queue up each morning in my hotel to get me to sign copies of my books. But when I stay in London, no one cares a damn that I'm there.'

Maugham put up some pretence of wishing to be free of the crowds, many of them students, who gathered around him in any temple, garden or museum which we visited; but it was easy to see that all this clamorous attention, as to some pop star, secretly delighted him. On one occasion, he told me how he had taken Johnny Ray, then at the height of his fame as a singer, from Cap Ferrat into Toulon. The American fleet was in. 'Not one s-s-sailor recognized m-m-e of course. But they all recognized J-J-Johnny. "J-J-Johnny, J-J-Johnny, J-J-Johnny!" the kept c-c-crying out, as they b-b-brandished bits of p-p-paper for him to s-s-sign!'

'How ghastly!'

'G-g-ghastly? Not at all! Things will really b-b-become g-g-ghastly when sailors stop shouting "J-J-Johnny, J-J-Johnny, J-J-Johnny!"'

Similarly, things would really have become ghastly for Maugham if, with their identifying cries of 'Mom! Mom! Mom!', excited students had ceased to throng round him.

It was I who took Maugham to the Noh Theatre for the first time. Later he told me that it had been one of the most remarkable experiences of his whole life. Wrinkled and bowed, the great writer had sat watching while the great actor had prepared himself for his role: being sewn into his robes; applying wet white with infinite care; then taking a hand-mirror and staring into it for minutes on end, as though by doing so he could leave his own body and enter an alien one. Although we had to sit on the floor during the long performance, Maugham betrayed no sign of weariness or discomfort.

Unlike Ronald and some other of my visitors, Maugham was extraordinarily considerate of Noboru – whom he described more than once as 'a treasure' and to whom he talked as to an equal. One evening, at dinner at my house, Maugham began to look at though he would at any moment crumble to dust. The meal over, he told me, in a voice so faint that I could hardly hear it, that he must go home. Would I excuse him? He felt 'absolutely done in'. Of course, I said; I'd call Noboru to drive him back.

'You can't possibly ask that boy to drive the car at this hour.' He was indignant. 'I wouldn't dream of it. Please get a taxi for me.'

This I then did.

The only occasion on which I saw another, less admirable side to his character was when John Haylock and I had dinner with him and Alan Searle in the Miyako Hotel. In Maugham's absence, Alan whispered to us, 'I want you to show me the queer bars and clubs. Willy will trot up to bed as soon as dinner is over.'

Willy did indeed trot up to bed as soon as dinner was over. But, when he heard that Alan, John and I were going out for a drink (that was how Alan put it to him), he at once objected: 'No, Alan, I'm not f-f-feeling at all well tonight! I'd like to have you n-n-near at hand in case I need a d-d-doctor.'

Seeing us out, Alan exclaimed, 'Oh, how I long to be *free!*'

But when at long last Alan was free, he did not enjoy his freedom. Maugham's old friends could seldom be bothered to see him. Robbed of his main function in life, Alan drifted aimless, bored and unhappy. Twice he invited me to a meal with him at Claridge's, when he was on a visit to London from his home in Monte Carlo. His once handsome face bloated and his body swollen, he insisted on eating course after course. 'Do have an hors-d'oeuvre before your soup . . . Do have some sole before your duck . . . You must have a savoury . . . Do have a brandy . . .' He was as eager to stuff me as he was to stuff himself. Each time that I refused an offer, it was as though I had slapped him across the face.

Our last conversation was on the telephone when he rang from Monte Carlo to thank me for a review of Ted Morgan's disgraceful biography of Maugham. 'Thank you for saying those nice things about Willy. Even Robin [Maugham's nephew] now seems determined to make out that he was an utter shit. But he wasn't, you know.'

Soon after that, Alan was dead.


Another literary visitor was Edmund Blunden. Although of course he did not receive the same universal adulation as Maugham, he received immeasurably more attention than he would have done on a visit to any English city. The reason for this was that, during his previous stays in Japan, first before and then in the immediate aftermath of the war, he had made a profound impression with his courteousness, his humility and his devotion to his students. Even his lectures, which stuck me as singularly devoid of any substance, aroused enthusiasm among the Japanese.

Blunden had one enviable gift: he could write verses, impeccable in scansion and rhyme, on any subject, at any time of the day or night, within literally minutes. When a foreign writer visits a famous temple or garden or even a school or university, his Japanese hosts have a way of producing a book and asking him to 'compose' something. On such occasions I used to be totally nonplussed. Should I write, as tourists do in visitors' books in England, 'A truly memorable experience' or 'It was worth coming all this way to see this'? James Kirkup would always resort to an English haiku. But, perhaps unduly fastidious, I shrank from producing something like:

> In the Moss Temple a crane cries;
> Evening falls and my home is far.

Asked by the Mayor of Kyoto, at a reception in his honour, to 'compose' something 'about our beautiful city', Blunden at once sat down in a corner and, to my amazement, produced a Shakespearian sonnet, of which he later presented me with a copy in his elegant Italic script. In it he referred to 'Kyoto, with all her tinted leaves' (it was then autumn). When the English language *Japan News* published this poem, the leaves had somehow become 'tainted'. Blunden was vexed; but in view of the pollution that was, even then, affecting the city; I approved of the emendation.


Soon after the visit of this vague, unworldly, sweet-natured man, I gave a cocktail party for the Royal Ballet, then on an exhausting and highly successful tour of the country. So large was the company that the Japanese impresario hired a bus to bring them from Osaka to Kyoto. Each time that this bus bounced over a rut in the unmade road up to my house, many of the male dancers emitted shrill squeals and squawks. John Field, in charge, eventually jumped to his feet. 'Oh, for God's sake. Pull yourselves together. What will Mr King think if you camp it up like this?' The incident was relayed to me by two of the offenders in a gay bar after the party.

A year or so later, a small contingent of the Royal Ballet, led by Margot Fonteyn and Rudolf Nureyev and with Robert Helpmann in charge, arrived in the area. Travelling with them, I was present in Nagoya at one of the frequent arguments between Nureyev and Helpmann.

'Tonight I dance *Corsair*!' Nureyev announced.

'No, I'm sorry. Tonight is the night for *Swan Lake*.'

'No, no! Tonight – *Corsair*!'

Eventually, his patience exhausted, Helpmann hissed, 'Dance what you like, ducky! The orchestra will be playing *Swan Lake*.'

It was on this visit that Helpmann asked me if I could find for him a theme, from myth or folk-tale, for a 'Japanese' ballet which he wanted to choreograph. I suggested *Sumigawa*, later to provide the basis of William Plomer's libretto for Britten's *Curlew River*. Helpmann expressed delight at the suggestion; but, as so often in the world of show business, nothing further happened.


I came to feel so much at home in Japan that I often used to say that I was sure that, in some previous existence, I must have been Japanese. I intended this remark as a joke; but many of my Japanese friends, believing or half-believing in reincarnation, would take it seriously. 'Yes, King-sensei,' they would tell me, 'you feel like us, you think like us, you understand us. You are one of us.' David Kidd's comment was more cynical: 'If you really were a Japanese in a previous incarnation, it's a pity you haven't remembered more of the language.'

Many of the common attributes of the Japanese, both admirable and unattractive, I found that I shared. Like them, I believe in self-discipline and hard work; feel devotion to family and an inner circle of friends and colleagues, but have little generalized compassion; shrink from kissing or even touching anyone but an intimate; insist that the demonstration of an emotion should never be on a larger scale than the emotion itself; and tend to pass aesthetic, rather than moral, judgements.

It was natural therefore that when, after four and a half years, the Council announced that it was planning to move me from Kyoto, I should have wondered how I could bear to quit a country in which, even more than in England, I so much felt that I belonged. I told Japanese friends of this reluctance of mine to go; and in consequence I received a number of offers of jobs at universities. Had I taken one, I should have been extremely well paid for extraordinarily little work.

Throughout my life, I have been haunted by what I call 'The Other Path'. To decide to do something means that one has to decide not to do something else; there are two paths and only one can be followed. Just as I could have opted for an academic career instead of one in the British Council, and for a domestic life, with children and grandchildren, instead of a sexually unorthodox one, so now I could have passed the rest of my years in Japan, instead of at home. In retrospect, the path not taken often seems more attractive than the one taken: an intermittent source of regret.

Having decided, after much agonizing, that I should return to England, I asked the Council for an unpaid sabbatical of a year, such as I had been given when I had won the Somerset Maugham Award. My plan was to see, during that sabbatical, if I could survive as a freelance writer. When I had first joined the Council, my work had been sufficiently undemanding for me to find ample time to write my novels. But as I had risen in the hierarchy, so the calls on my time had become increasingly exigent. In Kyoto, since there was no British Consul there, I was often invited to events which had little or nothing to do with culture or education. I was constantly obliged to entertain and be entertained. On occasion, I even had, in effect, to act as Consul, when some British tourist in distress, unable to find a Consulate, turned up at the Council offices instead. In consequence, I could only write, as I have indicated, by getting up at four or five each morning. I wanted to change that situation.

Having at last decided against taking up residence in Japan, I was now faced with a problem even more agonizing. What was I to do about Noboru? My first impulse was to urge him to travel to England with me. But I had seen what had happened to other Japanese youths who had taken this option. In most cases they had been unable to get work-permits and had therefore been obliged to live off their English friends, doing a little housework and playing a lot of golf. I did not want that sort of demoralizing existence for him, full as he was of energy, resourcefulness and independence of spirit. I therefore told him that I thought that it would be a mistake for him to attempt to make a life with me in England; and reluctantly he agreed. With some assistance from me, he then managed to get an excellent job with a well-known international firm, in which he immediately prospered.

Inevitably there were times, after my return to England, when, lonely and disconsolate without him, I used to tell myself, 'You bloody fool! He *wanted* to come to England.' But I stopped feeling any regret when, some years later, I returned to Japan on a British Council lecture tour and saw him, with his beautiful wife and two children, a boy and a girl, in a flat capacious by Japanese standards in a suburb of Kobe. He was so obviously fulfilled, he was so obviously happy. I had no doubt at all that I had made the right decision, however painful for each of us at the time.


The Japanese believe in good beginnings and good ends. When someone arrives in a place, people turn out to meet him; and they turn out to bid him goodbye. So, when I boarded my ship in Kobe, there must have been at least a hundred people on the quay: colleagues, offficials, students, friends. Even an elderly American teacher, who had had a row with me over his boy-friend – he had imagined that I had been trying to seduce the boy at a party, when in fact, seeing that everyone was ignoring him, I had merely tried to engage him in conversation – was there. Many of the people had brought presents with them. All this touched me; but at the same time I wanted to be alone with Noboru.

When the ship was about to leave, the passengers crowded the decks. In accordance with Japanese custom, paper streamers were then handed to them, which they hurled down to their friends below. I hurled streamer after streamer at the upturned faces and eagerly clutching hands. The ship began to move. One by one, the streamers joining me to all those people below me snapped and fluttered away from me. But Noboru, clutching his streamer, was now running along the quay, endeavouring to keep up and so to ensure that this one fragile thread between us was not severed.

Suddenly I thought of my mother running along beside the train which was taking me away from India and her.

Noboru reached the end of the quay. The streamer pulled taut, snapped, fluttered away like all the rest. But I went on staring at his slowly diminishing figure and he went on staring back at me.

Finally, when I could no longer see him, I went down to my cabin, sat on the corner of my bunk, and burst into tears.

It was the first time that I had cried since my father's death. Like any Japanese in a similar situation, I was glad that no one could see me.

*Part III*

# — 1 —

# *The Pleasure Gardens*

I was forty-three when, in 1966, I returned from Japan to England. At first, as I had already done during recent leaves, I stayed with my sister Elizabeth and my brother-in-law John Rosenberg in the seven-roomed flat which they rented in Prince of Wales Drive in Battersea. By then my mother, having given up her flat in Iverna Court, was also living there. She adored John, who, an expatriate American, clearly looked on her as a surrogate for the mother whom he so rarely saw and with whom his relationship had constantly oscillated between exasperation and love. At that period John and I got on far better than, sadly, we were to do in the last years of his life.

It was I who had initially brought John and Elizabeth together. Staying in my mother's flat when on leave from Greece, I had taken myself off for an afternoon walk in Kensington Gardens. Finding myself without raincoat or umbrella during a cloudburst, I raced for a shelter, where I was soon joined by a heavily moustached, dark-skinned, dark-haired and extremely handsome young man in his early twenties. Standing side by side in silence, we gazed out at the rain. Then I said to him, 'Are you Greek?' In his corduroy trousers, open-necked check shirt and gym-shoes, he might have been a labourer from an Athens building-site. He laughed. 'No, I'm not Greek. In fact, I've never been to Greece. I'm an American.' Since that was long before the emergence of the American hippy, I was astonished. We began to chat. He was Jewish, he told me, the son of a New York lawyer (well known, I later learned); he had graduated at Columbia University, and had then decided to make his home in England, at least for a few months. When the rain finally stopped, I suggested that he might like to accompany me back to my mother's flat, for a cup of tea. Or coffee, I added. 'Tea would be fine. I really love your English tea.' He was to come to prefer anything English to anything American, soon even adopting a wholly English accent and returning only once to the United States, on the death of his mother. Elizabeth was at home. She and John at once fell in love with each other.

Initially, their married live was tough. John taught at a prep school in the Midlands, while she continued to work as a valued editor, such as one now rarely finds in publishing, at Longmans. Among the books which she edited, spending literally weeks on it, was David Storey's first novel, *This Sporting Life*. At a Longmans party, John Guest, for many years senior editor of the general list, was introducing her to a group of people. 'This is Elizabeth King, sister of Francis King. She's a wonderful editor, absolutely wonderful. Without her, David Storey would be *nothing*.' At that point Elizabeth heard a quiet voice behind her: 'Congratulations, Elizabeth!' It was David Storey himself.

Eventually John became a reader of scripts for MGM. Such were his natural efficiency, intelligence and knowledge of what would appeal to the general public that he received rapid promotion, first at MGM, then at Romulus Films, and finally at Anglia Television. Simultaneously, he also wrote novels, the first three or four of which showed an impressively strong and individual talent.

Sadly, under the unremitting pressure of his work for Anglia – he was responsible for the production of the highly successful *Tales of the Unexpected*, the first and best of which were based on stories by Roald Dahl, and for some no less successful adaptations of novels by P.D. James – he found that he could concentrate less and less on his writing and, as a consequence, the creative fire that had once blazed so brightly guttered and died. Something also died within him. Admirably he wanted to do all in his power for his two beautiful and talented daughters; but, slaving so hard to give them the best of everything, he had little time not merely for his writing but for the quiet pleasures which he had so much enjoyed – gardening, carpentry, painting, walking. As a young man he would often burst into singing – some Mozart aria, some American or even English folk-song – from sheer *joie de vivre* as we all walked together down a street. People would look round and smile or even laugh, not in derision but catching the infection of his mood, since he was clearly so happy. In later years nothing of that kind ever happened. In the street, he would often walk beside one silent, his mind no doubt on the getting and spending which preoccupy every successful man of business. At parties he would increasingly tend to sit similarly silent, a look of worried abstraction on his face, until he would rouse himself to what seemed to be a willed *bonhomie*.

I think that the comparative lack of success of his later books had something to do with the gradual freezing-over of our relationship; and that my closeness to my sister Elizabeth before her marriage had even more to do with it. Just as, when he married Elizabeth, I had felt a certain jealousy, and just as, when he had published his first, extraordinary novel, *The Desperate Art*, I had felt a certain envy, so now it was he who felt these emotions. Near the premature end of his life, when he was already ill with the cancer against which he battled with such stoicism, he wrote to me, after some seemingly trivial tiff, to tell me that he had come to the conclusion that he and I just had to accept that we would never get on – we were too unlike each other. It was now too late to do anything about the situation, he added, we must put up with it as best we could. As I read that letter it was as though cold steel were passing through my entrails. I had never supposed that our friendship – I was still genuinely fond of him, still admired him for his intelligence, his kindness and his ability to sacrifice himself to his family in a way that I never could or would – was irrevocably dead. After that, whenever I saw him – which was not often, since the terrible inroads of his illness made it more and more of a strain for him to carry on even an everyday conversation – it was as though we were strangers. Wearily he would put a few questions to me about my life and work; and no less wearily – what was the point of this empty simulacrum of interest? – I used to answer him.

He was, of course, in part right in saying that we were too unlike each other. John was extremely shrewd about money and interested in making it; uncommonly secretive, he would never talk of his plans or activities, never complain that he was feeling ill or that things were going badly for him, never ask for advice; he was unremittingly kind to people in trouble. I, on the other hand, have always been feckless about money, squandering it and hating to argue about it; I can rarely keep anything to myself, confiding even in strangers; and my kindness to people in trouble is often erratic, depending on how much I am involved in my own concerns. There were, however, three things which John and I did have in common: a capacity for hard work, an impatience with humbug, and an uncomfortably nagging sense of duty.

During that period when I first returned from Japan I was close enough not merely to Elizabeth but to John to wish also to live close to them, when seeking for a flat. So it was that I found one some ten minutes' walk away from Prince of Wales Drive, in Albert Bridge Road. Situated on the top floor of Albany Mansions – a block in which my friend the novelist Patrick Gale was later to live – the four-roomed flat would have been ideal but for the drabness of that whole neighbourhood at that period. For restaurants or good shops it was necessary to cross over Albert Bridge into Chelsea. Buses were few. By then, although my earnings were scanty, I had told the British Council that I wished to retire – even though they had come up with the offer of a job in France which most of my colleagues would have envied.

Soon after I had moved into the flat, I received a letter from one of the two younger brothers of Noboru. Toshi was eager to come to England to improve his English for a year or two. He was prepared to do *anything* for me (he underlined the word in his letter) if I would advance him his fare, pay his school fees and give him a home. I had little money; but I was still aware of the huge debt which I owed to Noboru, but for whom I should have been far less happy in Japan and should have learned far less about the country. I sent Toshi his air-fare; and, on his arrival, registered him at the first of the many schools which my cousin John Haycraft was to open, first in London and then all over the world, for the teaching of English to foreigners. Toshi had none of Noboru's boisterous energy and little of his intelligence; but he had his sly, deadpan sense of humour, unusual in a Japanese and a constant source of pleasure to me. He stayed with me for almost two years, to be followed by his younger brother for a similar period.

Although Toshi had promised that he would do '*anything*' for me, his natural laziness soon persuaded me that I also needed a cleaner. In those days in

Battersea, still predominantly a working-class district, would-be cleaners constantly rang at the doors of the few people thought able to afford such a luxury. After all, it was far more convenient for a housewife to have a part-time job near home than one across the river. So it was that I acquired Mrs Boole. A large, lugubrious woman, with a deep lugubrious voice, she told that what she most enjoyed doing in her free time was to visit Brompton Cemetery in the company of her little grandson. She pushed him around for a time in his chair, she told me; then, if the sun was out, she would find 'a nice tombstone on which to bask'. I liked to think of Mrs Boole basking like a seal on one of those ornate Victorian tombs, while the gnome-like little grandson snoozed beside her.

Because of her dismal air, as of someone who is just about to go to the funeral of a loved one, I was astonished by an incident which occurred after she had been with me for some months. Having returned to the flat, I was blasted by the sound of Elvis Presley being played excessively loud on the wireless. I opened the sitting-room door. Her back to me, not hearing me because of the racket, Mrs Boole was pushing the vacuum-cleaner backwards and forwards. As she did so, she was singing, in a parody of an old-fashioned operatic contralto, a Battersea Clara Butt, along with Presley. 'One o'clock – two o'clock – three o'clock – *rock*! Four o'clock – five o'clock – six o'clock – *rock*!' At each '*rock*!', she gave the vacuum-cleaner a violent shove away from her and then shook her vast, shapeless body in the manner of a dog when it has emerged from a swim. I retreated, never letting on that I had witnessed this solitary orgy.

It was at about this time that the novelist Clifford Kitchin, a man who had become extremely rich not through the sales of his books but through his gambling on the Stock Exchange, asked me if I would like to have a dog. Yes, I said, I'd been planning to get one. Having at one time had six dogs simultaneously in Japan, I now constantly regretted not having even one. 'Well, I'm going to give you one,' he said. What breed? I asked. 'That I'm not going to tell you. It's to be a surprise.'

It was indeed a surprise, and not a welcome one. I had been planning to go along to the Battersea Dogs' Home to find the kind of stocky, short-haired dog which I love. Never mind if it were a mongrel. Clifford, however, had been to one of the leading breeders of Pekineses, to spend an enormous sum on the pop-eyed, silky-haired scion of innumerable champions. As we left the breeder's kennels in a hired car for which, of course, Clifford paid, he asked me, 'What are you going to call him?' 'Well, I'm certainly not going to call him Petal,' I said. This was his name at the kennels. On an impulse I added, 'I'm going to call him Wang.' Wang is the Chinese for 'King'.

Years later, in Brighton, I was to have a dog, a bull-terrier, called Joe after Joe Ackerley. Whenever one of my female neighbours met me out with Joe, she would stoop over him and say, 'You must be Joe King.' Then, delighted with her pun, she would whinny with laughter. With difficulty I restrained myself from saying, 'It's lucky you never knew me in the days when I had a dog called Wang.'

In no time at all Wang had completely conquered me. Just as the war soon proved the fallacy of the common belief that all homosexuals were craven effeminates, so Wang's walks in Battersea Park soon proved the fallacy of the common belief that all Pekineses are pampered, yapping lap-dogs. Tirelessly, he would race after a ball, a squirrel or some other dog. Fearlessly he would bark at Alsatians, Rottweilers, Dobermanns, causing them to slink off, their tails between their legs. This fearlessness was eventually to be the cause of his death. Out for a walk on the lead in Brighton with my mother, he barked at a huge, shaggy, emaciated mongrel belonging to some builders at work on a house not far from mine. The mongrel attacked him. My mother did not have the strength either to yank Wang up on his lead or to fend off the mongrel. The mongrel killed Wang. Devoted to Wang, my mother had what was, in effect, a nervous breakdown, taking to her bed, crying incessantly and refusing all food for two days.

Overgrown, empty and forlorn, Battersea Park in those days was the only part of Battersea in which I took any pleasure. Soon after my return from Japan, the idea for a novel had come to me when I had read in the *Daily Telegraph* a brief account of the conviction of a university lecturer in Australia for the murder of his autistic son. How, I had wondered, could an intelligent and presumably decent man have been driven to perform so horrific an act? When I tried to answer that question, I set my story in Battersea, much of it in Battersea Park. I called it *The Last of the Pleasure Gardens*. Like most of my novels, it had a warm critical reception; and, like most of my novels, it sold only modestly. In the two or three years which followed its publication, I was often to receive letters from anguished parents of autistic children, who always made the assumption that I myself must have an autistic child. Some of these, it became clear to me from our further correspondence, felt cheated when I wrote to tell them not merely that I did not have an autistic child but that I had no child at all.

The theatrical producer Michael Codron, whom I had known as a precociously worldly undergraduate at Oxford, read the book and was sufficiently impressed to decide that he would like to put on a dramatization of it. Would I be prepared to attempt the dramatization myself? I replied that no, having cast the story as a novel, I did not feel that I could successfully recast it as a play. In that case, would I mind if he showed it to a promising dramatist, who was himself the father of an autistic child? Of course not, I said. The promising dramatist was Peter Nichols. Sorrowfully, Michael later rang up to tell me that, having read the novel, Nichols had said that he did not feel that the subject of the relationship between an autistic child and its parents was one that would be acceptable to an audience. Codron then abandoned the idea. Not long after, Nichols produced what was probably the best of his plays, *A Day in the Death of Joe Egg*. It was about the relationship between an autistic child and its parents.


It was Clifford Kitchin who eventually persuaded me to quit Battersea for the more bracing air of Brighton. Increasingly plagued by heart-trouble, he was himself planning to give up his two interconnecting London houses in

Montpelier Square and make Brighton his base. 'I am going to get myself a little London *pied-à-terre* in Kingston House,' he told me. The 'little London *pied-à-terre*' proved to be even larger and more luxurious than the flat inhabited by Rebecca West in the same block, facing Hyde Park. Unfortunately, the two of them did not get on and resented it when I combined visits to both of them. Rebecca told me that she found Clifford 'artificial', 'snobbish', 'trivial'. In turn, Clifford once described Rebecca to me as 'a vicious old Wellington boot'. He also once greeted me at the door with the words, 'Rebecca's just told me she thinks the night porter's gone mad. She keeps sacking secretaries, housekeepers and dailies because she says they've gone mad. But she's totally mad herself and, if all the people around her go mad, then it can only be because she's infected them.'

Determined to have me close at hand when he had taken up residence in his new 'base', Clifford instructed me to look for a Brighton house – 'I'll put down half the price and you can get a mortage for the rest.' This was the most generous of a number of benefactions not merely to me but to Elizabeth and John (to the latter he had all too clearly taken a shine) and to one of my two older sisters, Pamela.

Clifford and I came to know each other through a miracle of synchronicity of a kind that has disconcertingly often occurred in my life. While in Finland, I happened to come across a novel of his, *Ten Pollitt Place*, in the British Council library. I so much enjoyed it that I did something which I rarely do and wrote him a fan-letter, addressed c/o his publishers. A week or so later I received a letter from him, addressed c/o my publishers, telling me how much he had enjoyed a novel of mine, *The Man on the Rock*. My first thought was that the posts had been remarkably efficient in conveying my letter to him and then his answer to me in so brief a space of time. Then I noticed firstly that he made no reference to my letter in his and secondly that the date on his letter was precisely the same as the date on which I had written to him.

On my return to England on leave, he invited me to luncheon. 'I never drink anything but whisky,' he told me. 'Wine gives me heartburn, gin makes me pee, and vodka might be surgical spirit for all the taste that it has. But you must drink champagne to celebrate our meeting for both us.' I did not have the courage to tell him that champagne gave me heartburn; and so, whenever we ate out, he would insist that I must yet again have champagne.

Clifford was intensely interested in money, in a way in which I have never been. Each morning he would read the stock prices in the *Financial Times* before telephoning his broker and on some occasions, God knows why, then telephoning me. 'I think I'm going to get rid of those Jokai shares,' he on one occasion confided in me. 'I don't think there's much future in tea. What do you think?' I had no idea whether there was a future in tea or not. Unlike many people intensely interested in money, Clifford was extremely generous with it. He was also always aware of the power of money, both for bad and for good. The central character of the last and least successful of his novels, *A Short Walk in Williams Park*, is a man who uses his wealth to dominate and direct other people's lives. This was an occupation in which Kitchin himself delighted. When he gave money to people, they must use it as he, not they, willed. Thus, it was in Brighton that I must find the house which he supplemented my meagre savings to enable me to buy, since it was there that he was now spending more and more of his time; and since he had decided, I do not know why, that, whereas it was permissible for him to live in a modern block of flats, 'the only style for you is Regency', it was a Regency house that I must purchase.

In his later years, Kitchin gave me the impression of constantly striving to bend the twig of his character in a direction opposite to that in which it had naturally grown in his youth and middle-age. At the beginning of his first novel, *Streamers Waving*, his heroine Lydia Clame – 'people dubbed her a dear pert little thing' – is asked if she is a member of the Bloomsbury set. Lydia replies, Well, no, not really – 'We're just the tiniest bit west, both spiritually and geographically.' The same might be said of Clifford, even though his first books were published by Virginia and Leonard Woolf at the Hogarth Press and even though one of his lifelong friends was Roger Senhouse, once Lytton Strachey's lover. With his resplendent chauffeur driven limousines (at one time he owned a sky-blue Rolls Royce), his visits to the tables at Monte Carlo, le Touquet and Marienbad, and his friends in the City and at the Bar (briefly he had practised as a barrister), he was far richer, ritzier and more cosmopolitan than any Bloomsbery. Furthermore, many of his actions, jokey and prankish, might have struck them, as they struck Rebecca West, as altogether too frivolous – although, of course, the Bloomsberries themselves were not above jokes and pranks.

Clifford had also, for a brief period, been a friend of T.S. Eliot, he and two other homosexual men – Ken Ritchie, later Chairman of the Stock Exchange, and the well-known bibliophile Richard Jennings – providing Eliot with sanctuary in the Great Ormond Street flat which they were sharing, when he and his first wife Vivienne split up. Had Eliot shown any signs of homosexuality? I asked Clifford. 'Well, he would hardly have spent that period living with us if he had not had *some* leanings, now would he? After all, all three of us liked to bring back trade.' He then told me of how Eliot would often, as he put it, 'apply a bit of slap' before venturing out of an evening. Since Clifford, unlike most novelists, was not a fantasist, I had no problem in believing all this. But when I passed on the information to my friend Peter Ackroyd when he was working on his fine life of T.S. Eliot, he brushed it aside. Biographers soon form ideas of their subjects and from then on are reluctant to accept any evidence that might force them to modify them.

Anyone who had known Clifford in youth and middle-age – and, among those, were the Asquiths, with whom he used to play bridge – would have been amazed by some of the things he got up to in his old age when I knew him. He enthusiastically took up photography, buying the most expensive cameras then on the market, a Leica and a Bronica, and even developing and enlarging his work in a dark-room of his own. He bought greyhounds ('I think that racehorses might be just a little ostentatious, don't you?' he remarked to me on one occasion) with which he would proudly parade at White City. While confined to bed during his last illness, he suddenly began to study algebra, from time to time asking me to check some quadratic equation – a task long since beyond my competence. Even his final choice of sexual partner suggested the action of a man determined to do precisely the opposite of what everyone expected of him. When I first came to know him, he would constantly refer to 'my friend George' – telling me that he could not have dinner with me on Tuesday because that was the evening when George would be visiting him, or saying of some story of mine, 'Oh, I must tell George that. That'll tickle him, I know.' Since I was never allowed to meet George, since Clifford never told me anything about him, and since he was not the kind of man whom I felt that I could interrogate until I came to know him far better, I used to try to imagine what George would be like. Yes, he would be a rough, North Country guardsman, of the kind that appealed to my friend Joe Ackerley. Or perhaps a policeman, like E.M. Forster's chum? One day, without warning, I rang the bell of the Montpelier Square two-houses-in-one, in order to leave off a book that I had promised to lend Clifford. The door was opened by an elderly, working-class man in slippers, whom I immediately assumed to be standing in for Clifford's manservant Sidney. I asked for 'Mr Kitchin' and the old buffer then preceded me up the stairs to the first-floor sitting-room, panting heavily. When Clifford had greeted me, he said, more gleeful than embarrassed, 'Francis, I don't believe you've met George.' George, now dead, was married and even older than Clifford. For him and his family Clifford bought a small villa in Hove.

Sidney, who during the war had served in the Catering Corps, had been with Clifford for many years. Sadly, by the time that I got to know Clifford, a relationship which had, according to both L.P. Hartley and Neville Coghill, been ideal, was rapidly degenerating. This was because of Sidney's increasing alcoholism and dishonesty – things apparent to Clifford's friends long before they became apparent to him. On one occasion, as Sidney was pouring me out a gin and tonic, I was amazed, when I happened to glance across at him, to see him rapidly lift the Beefeater bottle to his lips and take a gulp from it. On another occasion, taking my coat and umbrella from me in the hall, he muttered, his speech slurred and his breath heavy with the fumes of Clifford's brandy, 'The old bugger's been playing up all day. God help you if he gets as stroppy with you as he's been with me.'

One evening, a few months before his death, Clifford asked me to look at an account book kept by Sidney. The items in it were barely decipherable and grossly misspelled – 'letice', 'vinaga', 'veel'. 'Can asparagus for two have cost as much as seven pounds?' I had to admit that it couldn't. 'And two fillet steaks – eleven pounds?'

Eventually Clifford sacked Sidney. I tried to dissuade him, but he was implacable. 'He's behaved very foolishly,' he said. 'And now he must take the consequence. It's sad really,' he added. 'There's a legacy for him in my will – but only on condition that he's still in my service when I pop it.'

I often wonder what happened to Sidney when he left. By then he was all too clearly umemployable. For all his peccadilloes and grumblings, he was genuinely devoted to Clifford, I am certain.

By now confined either to his bedroom in the Brighton flat or to its balcony – a shareholder in the now sadly derelict West Pier, he derived pleasure from watching the crowds pour through its turnstiles – Clifford asked me to find him a replacement for Sidney. Fortunately an advertisement in the *Brighton Argus* soon brought me two paragons – a former hospital nurse and her retired policeman husband – who looked after him impeccably up to the time of his death.

L.P. Hartley had been one of Clifford's oldest and closest friends; so, when he was dying, it was natural enough that he should constantly urge me to get Leslie Hartley to visit him. But although Neville Coghill, Lord David Cecil and Lord (Ken) Ritchie all came from farther away, and although Hartley had a comfortable car, with a chauffeur, in which to travel, there was always some excuse – Christabel Aberconway had invited him for the weekend, he himself was far from well, his chauffeur was 'not all that keen' on long drives.

On Clifford's death I was telephoned by a reporter from the *Brighton Argus*, clearly in a state of high excitement. I was C.H.B. Kitchin's literary executor, was I not? I replied Yes. Then did I know that he had left three-quarters of a million? (This was when a million was worth at least twice what it is worth now.) Again I replied Yes. 'But none of us had any idea that such a famous writer was living in this town! That's almost as much money as Somerset Maugham left.' I had to explain that Clifford's money had come not from his books but from the wily investment of a number of inheritances.

Yet, in a sense, Brighton – like the rest of the world – had been in default. Contemporaries of far flimsier talent had attracted far more notice. The gods had showered both possessions and gifts on Clifford Kitchin – did not Leslie Hartley describe him as the most talented man he had ever known? – but they had withheld from him the one thing he most wanted: popularity.

I owe more to Clifford Kitchin than to anyone in my whole life apart from David and my family. There was the financial debt, of course; but more than that there were the delights of his erudite, witty, erratic, eccentric company and the encouragement which I derived, at a time of frequent discouragement, from his over-generous admiration for my work. I wish that his detective story *Death of My Aunt* ('that wretched book', he used to call it) was not now the only one of his works known to the public at large. His was a narrow, highly idiosyncratic talent, but one well worth exploring.


The relationship between Clifford and Leslie Hartley was ambivalent in the warring emotions of which it was compounded. Clifford, whose *The Book of Life* is both similar in theme to Leslie's *The Go-Between* and in no way its inferior, could not understand why it had not enjoyed a comparable success; and in a manner surprisingly illogical for someone otherwise so logical, he somehow held this against Leslie. Leslie, in turn, seemed to suffer from an envy of Clifford. 'I think you approve more of Clifford than of me,' he told me on one occasion. 'As a writer do you mean?' I asked, embarrassed that he should have perceived what was the truth. 'As a writer and as a person,' he said. 'Am I right?' 'Oh, I don't grade my friends in degrees of approval,' I hedged. I think that Leslie also had an uneasy suspicion that, behind his back, Clifford mocked at his taste, shared with Evelyn Waugh, for titled women of a certain age.

On Clifford's death, his couple asked me if I could find them a job with another 'bachelor gentleman'. 'Somehow we've been spoiled for a married couple,' the wife said; and the husband took up: 'And we couldn't abide the thought of a family with young children.'

Leslie had just been obliged to sack a manservant who, like many of his predecessors, had constantly bullied, cheeked and cheated him. Here, I thought, was the ideal solution. When, a few days later, I was having luncheon with him in his eyrie in Rutland Gate, I told him of the couple: former hospital nurse and former policeman, she an excellent plain cook, he an extremely careful driver and skilled handyman and gardener, both totally honest, both utterly respectful and respectable. As I enumerated each of their virtues, Leslie looked glummer and glummer. Then he said, 'Well, I'll think about it.' I realized that what he really wanted was the dangerous excitement of yet another manservant just out of nick.

One such manservant was extremely handsome and also extremely sinister. He and Leslie would have constant rows, at the close of one of which, when I myself was present, the manservant told Leslie, 'Oh, do me a favour, will you? Just fuck off!' When the manservant had stormed out of the room, Leslie looked across at me, his eyes twinkling, clearly delighted: 'What a *very* odd thing to say!'

On another occasion I arrived early for a luncheon party, to realize at once that all was far from peaceful in the Rutland Gate flat. The manservant jerked open the front door when I had rung three or four times and then, not greeting me or even looking at me, strode off into the kitchen. It was with a similar abruptness that he admitted Christabel Aberconway, Lady Glenconner, Lady Roxburghe and the eminent German scholar August Closs. Since, despite being summoned more than once by Leslie, the manservant put in no appearance, I obeyed Leslie's injunction to 'be a dear and see to the drinks'. By two o'clock lunch had still not appeared. Finally Leslie got up and ambled off to the kitchen. Christabel Aberconway and I exchanged glances as we heard voices being raised in the kitchen. Then Leslie reappeared: 'Luncheon will be ready any moment now.' The any moment prolonged itself to at least a quarter of an hour.

Finally, his handsome but brutal face congested with rage, the manservant marched into the sitting-room, one corner of which was used as a dining area, carrying a large tray. He banged down plates containing smoked salmon at each place at the table. 'All right!' he then shouted in a crude, furious Cockney. 'Grub's up!' 'Thank you, thank you, Jack,' Leslie said. He rose demurely to his feet. 'Would you like to lead the way, Christabel?'

Like H.G. Wells, whom he so much resembled in appearance, Leslie clearly exerted a fascination over women. This both delighted and alarmed him. I doubt whether he had actually ever gone to bed with a woman, even though some women – among them a novelist friend of mine, Anne Wignall, married in turn to a Hoare and so briefly mistress of Stourhead, to a Grosvenor and, less grandly, to 'Boy' Wignall and to Tony Marecco – claimed to have succeeded in persuading him to do so. In each such case I think that the relationship was no more than an *amitié amoureuse*.

Certainly, if any woman could have got Leslie to bed, Anne would have done so. She once made a determined assault on me, sadly with only giggles on both sides as its climax. It was she who ended for ever my friendship with Mary Wellesley, another of the aristocratic women who doted on Leslie. Bidden to dinner with me at Mary's palatial flat in Hanover Terrace, Anne Wignall first came to my house for 'a drinkie to relax me'. The drinkie became many drinkies, so that Anne was so relaxed that she had difficulty in negotiating her way into Mary's sitting-room. Over dinner, she began to reminisce about her various marriages. Her first husband, Hoare, had suffered from *ejaculatio precox*. Ebury had not been too bad at it but his member was about *this* size – she held up a little finger. 'Boy' Wignall was fine in every respect, extremely well-endowed and often wanting it two or even three times a day; that was why she had eventually opted for his name. Tony Marecco was also fine, but he rarely wanted it, preferring boys instead. Mary and the only other guest, a clergyman nephew of hers, were far from amused; and somehow, it was obvious, Mary blamed me as much as Anne for the débâcle, so that I never saw her again.

Leslie was a man of wonderful courtesy, demonstrated by his behaviour on one of the last times that I had luncheon with him. Despite innumerable ailments – within a month or two he would be dead – he insisted, in dressing-gown and bedroom slippers, on accompanying me downstairs from his flat in order to see me into a taxi. 'Oh, Leslie, do go back to your flat! Please!' He would not listen. Outside it was raining. He walked out with me into the rain. He then stood on the kerb waving to me in the rain, as the taxi drove off.

I was constantly amazed that this gentle man should have so much savagery in him. On one occasion, when one of his other guests said something about an increase in crime, he began to expound his remedy: branding. A mugger should have an M branded on his forehead, a pickpocket a P, a burglar a B. 'But Leslie, aren't you afraid that, if your plan was adopted, you might have a Q branded on your own forehead?' 'Me? Why? Why me? Why a Q?' 'For queer,' I said. To his credit he laughed. On another occasion, when he had had a sniffy review from John Braine, he said, with real passion, 'I'd like to *whip* that common brute! I'd really like to whip him! And kick him – *hard*,' he added. On many occasions in conversation with me, he would refer to 'the WC'. On the first occasion I was puzzled, since a water-closet had no relevance to our conversation. On the second occasion I realized that he was referring to the working class.

For PEN I conducted one of their 'Explorations' of Leslie, interviewing him about his life and work. About the former, he was, as I had expected, extremely cagey. When I asked him about the Freudian symbols, the belladonna plant for example in *The Go-Between*, he became flustered and tetchy – 'Oh, I know nothing about Freud, I know nothing at all about him, I don't believe in him', even though, in the privacy of his flat, he had talked most knowledgeably and intelligently about Freud to me only a few weeks before. At another point, on the subject of *The Boat*, one of my favourite of his novels, I asked him about an incident in which the hero, rowing on the Avon as Hartley himself liked to row, is threatened by two swans. Yes, that was taken from real life, he answered. In fact, the swans, one male and one female, had become such a nuisance that he had eventually decided to kill them. 'I told my then manservant to do away with them in some way, but he refused, I can't think why. I suppose it was because of that sentimentality which the working class have about animals – they constantly beat up their children but are horrified if someone so much as smacks a puppy for misbehaving on the carpet. So I had to take some action myself. I ground up some Soneryl tablets – prescribed for me by my doctor at a time when I was sleeping badly – and mixed them into pellets with bread. I really only wanted to kill the cob – the male swan – since he was far and away the more aggressive of the two. But I had no sooner scattered the pellets than the pen raced ahead of him and gobbled up most of them. You know how greedy females can be. Later, that afternoon, the swans floated past the house. Both were dead. They were floating upside down, their feet in the air. Most extraordinary! Why do you think they were floating like that?' The audience were appalled. The meeting over, Hartley said to me, 'I feel that I did myself no good with that story about the swans.' I replied, 'No, Leslie, I don't think you did.'

Shortly before his death, Leslie told me that he was making a new will and wondered if I would consent to be his literary executor. I said that Yes, of course I would. A few days later he rang to tell me that he had made the will, adding that, next time that I was in London, he would like to discuss some of its details with me. He died before I could see him again. I then heard that the only will to be found was one made several years before, with Walter Allen – whom Leslie had not seen for a long time and who had been incapacitated by a stroke – named as literary executor. I at once assumed either that Leslie had never made a new will or else that, having made it, he had then thought better of it.

Later, Neville Coghill told me a strange thing, confirmed by two other of Leslie's friends. A woman was claiming to have had, during his last years, a sexual relationship with Leslie, which had resulted in a daughter. She would, she declared, come up from the country at regular intervals – once a week or once a fortnight, I cannot remember which – and go with him to Claridge's, where he would take a room for the night. She also maintained that he had told her, shortly before his death, that he had made a new will, leaving money to her. She was now threatening a lawsuit. Later, I heard that Leslie's sister Norah had paid off this claimant. Norah, elderly and rich in her own right, had no need of the million or so left to her, as sole legatee, by her brother. There was some surprise at PEN that Leslie, a former President, had left that organization not a penny. There was also some regret among Leslie's friends that he had left not a penny to the doctor, Patrick Woodcock, who had tended him so devotedly, often without remuneration, during his last months. I believe that generously Norah made up for the second of these omissions.

The story of the affair carried on in Claridge's strikes me as highly improbable – particularly since Leslie was then in such a poor state of health. But, if one believes it, then here is confirmation that, near the end of his life, Leslie made another will. Perhaps, as in one of his novels, that other will will eventually be found.

I had been an admirer of Leslie's novels long before I met him; but some of those which he wrote when he was both ailing and drinking far too much tried to the full such powers of diplomacy as I possess. 'What did you think of it?' he would ask me of his latest production. 'Now be truthful with me!' But I could not be truthful, since I knew how sensitive he was to any sort of hostile criticism.

One of his last novels, *Poor Clare*, I rewrote for him. 'I've got into a terrible muddle,' he told me. 'Do you think you could possibly sort it out?' When I said that I would do what I could, he handed me a vast pile of typescript, much of it overscored with corrections in a near-illegible hand. There were two or three versions of every chapter. When I had ploughed through all this, I asked Leslie, 'What exactly is it that you're trying to say?' He looked at me in panic. 'Oh dear! Oh dear, oh dear! I don't *know*, you see. I just don't know.' I then decided that I myself must decide what it was that he was trying to say. Was it not that the best way to destroy people was by giving them gifts? Yes, that was it! So that was how I then put the book together. Leslie was delighted: 'Oh, you are a dear, you are a dear!' Then he said, 'This is all rather delicate. Has, has, er, Jamie Hamilton given you anything for your, er, trouble?' I said that he hadn't. 'Oh, in that case . . .' He got up, went over to his desk, and pulled a cheque book out of the drawer. 'No, Leslie, no!' I protested. 'Any help I've given you was as an act of friendship.' But he insisted on writing me a cheque for £50. At that time I needed the money.

I told no one about my work on the book. But with extraordinary generosity Leslie revealed it in the course of an interview in the *Daily Mail*. But for me, he said, the book could never have been published. Perhaps it would have been better if it had not been.

I often used to ponder: If Leslie had not been so nervous about his homosexuality and so desperate to conceal it, would his novels have been better or worse? I suspect that they would have been worse, since it was precisely the damming of all the strongest and deepest emotions in his life behind a barrage of conventional propriety that gave those novels much of their force.

After his death I thought of writing a biography of him. Unfortunately it soon became clear to me that neither Norah nor Lord David Cecil – apart from Clifford, Leslie's closest friend and now Norah's adviser – wished for a biography; and without Norah's approval, it struck me that it would be both wrong and difficult (since she might forbid the use of copyright material) to proceed. I have often since wondered why David Cecil should have been so hostile to the idea. In the Twenties, before he had married, he and Leslie had shared a *palazzo* in Leslie's beloved Venice. Could Cecil have been nervous of what a biography might reveal of their life there together? It is possible. After all, Leslie once described Cecil to me as 'the love of my life.'

Cecil dead, Penelope Fitzgerald embarked on a biography, with Norah's approval. Since Leslie shared my admiration for her intelligence, her integrity, her perspicacity and her humanity, she would have been the ideal person for the task. But, sadly, she has now abandoned it.

Leslie was both a far finer novelist than is now generally acknowledged and a far shrewder and kinder character than these memories of him may imply. 'I get impatient with his sort of gracious living,' Joe Ackerley once remarked to me about him. But graciousness was one of his most attractive qualities.

# — 2 —

# The Brighton Belle

The house which, after much searching, I found in Montpelier Road in Brighton turned out, by a coincidence, to belong to the sister of a then friend of mine, Tom Skeffington-Lodge, and her husband. My reason for writing 'then friend' will become apparent later in this narrative.

With its wide first-floor balcony, enclosed in elegant wrought iron, it elicited from Clifford Kitchin a delighted 'You've made the perfect choice!' But from the first I was never really happy with it. It was tall, narrow and dark; and like so many houses of that period it was so shoddily built that, as soon as I had hammered a nail into one of its walls to hang a picture, I heard a rattle of plaster behind the wallpaper and the nail fell out. Half of what had once been its garden had been sold to the owners of the house behind; almost all of the other half had been sacrificed to the construction of a low-ceilinged extension. It was from this extension that, I decided, there emanated, like a clammy fog, a sense of unease and even fear. That this impression was not wholly a subjective one was demonstrated by two things. That my Aunt Hetty, having slept there for a night, should have asked if she could move into another guest-room, placed inconveniently at the top of the house, might have been ascribed to her having heard me saying something about the 'atmosphere' of the extension; but what of the two robust male Finnish university students who, after a stay, told me that the only thing that they had not enjoyed was sleeping in that guest-room? They had not actually seen a ghost, they said; but they had repeatedly woken to the consciousness of 'someone there'. Then there was the visit which I paid with the American novelist Alison Lurie to Brighton years after I had moved back to London. 'I once stayed in a haunted house here,' she said. 'Really? Where was it?' I asked. It turned out to have been my former house, at a period when an American professor, Leslie Fiedler, had rented it from my friend Gerard Irvine, to whom eventually I had sold it. I had of course told Gerard, before the purchase, about the disquieting feelings aroused in so many people by the extension; but he had no misgivings – 'I don't think any ghost will trouble a clergyman,' he said. So it has proved. Able to spend on the house the money which I wish that I had been able to spend, he totally transformed it into a thing of beauty. The extension is now his study; and when I enter it, I feel none of my former anxiety and even dread.

Tom Skeffington-Lodge's aristocratic-looking sister was, improbably, a keeper of greyhounds. Her plebeian-looking husband was, far from improbably, a keeper of racing pigeons. These pigeons resided in one of the bedrooms, from which the window frame had been removed to provide them with access. The husband asked me to leave the window as it was, until a valuable pigeon, unreturned at the time of their move to a modern house on the outskirts of Brighton, had come home. This reluctantly I consented to do. After a week or two he informed that, miraculously, the missing pigeon had returned not to its former home but to its new one. One could only suppose that it had joined up with some of the other pigeons in flight and had then followed them. Before decorating the room, it took the builders a long time to scrape a coagulated mess of bird-shit and feathers off the floor and the walls.

My sister Elizabeth had suggested to me that I should give a home to a German girl who, before her marriage to an Indian, had worked as an au pair for her. Now separated from the Indian – who, she claimed, had physically abused her – she was looking for a haven for herself and their baby. In return for accommodation, food and pocket-money, she was prepared to do the cleaning but not to cook. At first the arrangement seemed ideal. All too clearly Else had an obsession with cleaning, so that often, late in the evening, when I went down into the basement for a bedtime drink, I would find her on her hands and knees scrubbing the kitchen floor with a violence which suggested that she wanted actually to destroy it. In similar fashion she was constantly scrubbing the floors of the two lavatories, so that they reeked of Jeyes. When I gave a party, she insisted on serving at it, but refused my urgings that she should sit down and eat with us. The baby held in the crook of one arm, while the other was extended to offer a dish, she prompted from Clifford the enquiry, 'Am I supposed to help myself to the child or the chicken?'

Then suddenly, after three or four weeks, the Indian appeared. Somehow he had discovered Else's whereabouts, I never learned how. When I climbed up to the attic to tell her that he was awaiting her downstairs, she was clearly terrified: 'Oh, tell him to go away! Tell him to go away! I don't wish to see him.' I argued with her: it was better to see him, if only for a brief discussion of the future not only of the two of them but also of the child. Eventually she descended, baby held in its usual position in the crook of her arm, to the sitting-room, where I left them together. After about half an hour, she called out to tell me that he, she and the baby were going out for a little walk. From my bedroom window I watched them descending the hill to the sea in scowling silence. She was pushing the pram; he was walking several feet apart from her.

When they returned, they were pushing the pram together up the hill. Both of them were smiling. Once they were in the house, the Indian said that they wanted to talk to me. 'Yes, of course,' I said, 'Let's go down to the kitchen and all have some tea together.' Else, with her usual efficiency, set out the tea-things, prepared fingers of toast covered in Patum Peperium, cut slices of a chocolate cake. While she did this, the Indian talked to me about India.

When we were all sipping our tea, the Indian told me that the two of them had decided to give their marriage another chance. I said that that seemed to me a very good idea. Then he asked me if I would be very upset if Else and the baby returned with him to London that very evening. I said, No, of course not, though secretly I was irked at being abandoned so abruptly. Else, who had been frowning down at her shoes, raised her head at that. She was clearly relieved. Soon after, she rushed upstairs to do her packing. Rejoining us, she asked me if I had any objection to her leaving some of her things – an ironing-board, an iron, an electric kettle, some shoes and so on – in the boxroom. She would come for them later – or arrange for someone to come for them. That was fine, I said. I then helped the Indian and her to transport the things into the boxroom.

For the first time, she kissed me when we said goodbye. As she put her lips to my cheek, I happened to glance at the Indian. He looked so furious that I thought for a moment that he might hit either her or me. Then he was smiling. 'I cannot thank you enough, Mr King. You have been so kind to my wife. She has told me how kind you have been.'

I asked what their address would be. 'We will go to a boarding-house until we have found somewhere permanent,' he replied. 'As soon as we have somewhere permanent we will inform you and come for the things.'

That was the last I ever heard of them. When, some two years later, I moved out of the house, I gave the things to Oxfam. Sometimes – perhaps because I am a novelist – I try to construct a scenario to explain what happened to the couple. At its least melodramatic this postulates that either he persuaded her to go to India or she persuaded him to go to Germany; at its most melodramatic, that in a sudden access of jealousy or rage he carried the former physical abuse to some terrible extreme. One or two friends have told me that I should have gone to the police. But what could I have reported? A woman had been reconciled with her husband and, seemingly happy, had gone off with him. That was all.


My years in Brighton were financially and emotionally difficult ones. I had some meagre savings from my service with the British Council; and I had cashed in my contributory pension. But I had had to buy furniture for the Battersea flat and now, since it had so many more rooms, I had to buy more furniture for the house. There were also essential repairs and decoration to be done. Had Clifford not insisted on a Regency house, I might have bought a small flat and so avoided a mortgage. As it was, the mortgage was a constant drain on my bank balance. In those days there were no credit cards; and, having all my life had a horror of debt, I shrank from ever approaching my bank for an overdraft. In consequence, I was from time to time obliged to sell Japanese pieces which I had brought back with me. Incapable of haggling, I often let these go for far less than their true value – until my friend David, who was skilled at haggling, came into my life and haggled on my behalf.

Since the house was a large one, the obvious solution to my problems was to become, in effect, a Brighton landlady. A language school, directed by a former

British Council colleague, usually provided me with my lodgers. 'Since you're a bachelor, I don't think we can really send you any girls,' warned the middle-aged woman responsible. She clearly did not realize that girls would be at far less risk than boys in my household. Some of those boys were charming; so that my one regret now is that, busy as I was in scratching some kind of living, I had little time to give them the practice in conversation which, it was obvious, so many of them wanted. One, a Lebanese, was terribly lonely and homesick. Each evening he would wait up for me if I had gone out to dinner, the theatre or the cinema. Then, as wearily I mounted the stairs to my bedroom, his bedroom door would open. 'Did you have a nice evening, Mr King?' 'Yes, very nice, thank you.' I would continue on my way up the stairs. 'I watched something so strange on television. Perhaps you can explain it to me.' Reluctantly I would halt.

One lodger, not a boy but a middle-aged man, a doctor from Peru, was clearly distressed to see me cooking and serving breakfast and the evening meal. 'Mr King, I do not like to see you doing these things for me,' he at last protested.

'Why not?'

'You are a distinguished writer. I read one of your books in Peru before I ever met you. It is not right that you should wait on me.'

'Don't be silly! Why shouldn't I wait on you?'

Another lodger was a huge Arab from one of the Gulf States. He wolfed enormous quantities of food at breakfast and dinner – mercifully the lodgers would eat lunch out – and, while doing so, would talk of his unhappiness at being separated from his wife. Eventually, the wife arrived for a stay of a week, before the two of them returned home together. Could she lodge with him in his double room on the ground floor? he asked. Of course, I said. The wife turned out to be even huger than the husband. On the evening of her arrival, she, he, my mother and I sat down to dinner in the basement dining-room. My mother and I watched in amazement as the two Arabs demolished a whole large loaf of bread, held out their plates eagerly for second helpings of chicken and summer pudding, left the cheese-platter bare. Neither spoke a word but from time to time one or other belched. 'Would you like some coffee?' I asked at the end of this meal, to receive from the husband the answer, 'No, thank you, Mr King. Now we go upstairs.' Soon, from the bedroom above, my mother and I, settled to our coffee, heard tremendous thuds. The ceiling began to shake. My mother, in her innocence, looked alarmed. 'Do you think they're having a fight? Don't you think you should go up and see what's going on?'

'I think everything is all right.'

For the rest of the week, the couple would first devour an enormous dinner and then once again retreat to their bedroom. 'What on earth do you think they're doing?' my mother would ask. 'It's *weird*!'

To do the cleaning (Toshi had by now returned to Japan and his brother was yet to come) I had a succession of au pair boys in addition to the lodgers. These were sometimes students from the same school, who were unable to pay for their lodging, and sometimes Japanese who got in touch with me, at a time, so far away now, when there were severe restrictions on the export of money from their country.

One of these au pairs was a Finn who exerted a fierce attraction on me. He was a conscientious worker; then, his work done, he would leave the house, often not returning until long after I had gone to bed. Once I saw him swimming, muscular and sunburned, with a group of other foreign students near Black Rock; once queuing, again with a group of other foreign students, outside a disco. Unlike his predecessors, he was all too clearly disinclined to waste time on conversing with me.

Then, suddenly, he announced, 'I am afraid I must leave you, Mr King.'

'Oh!' I was disconcerted. 'When?'

'Today, if you do not mind.'

I knew that, even if I minded, he would not postpone his departure. 'Oh very well. If you want to go, you must go. But may I ask – why? Haven't you been happy here?'

'Yes, I have been happy, thank you. But now I can go somewhere where it is not necessary for me to work. I have an invitation – as guest.' He smiled. 'To be frank with you, Mr King, I have never before done any housework. In my home, my mother and my two sisters do all the housework. I am not used to it. I do not really like housework.'

'Yes, I understand.'

The next morning he left. It was several days before I learned that he had gone to stay with a friend of mine, a retired naval commander even richer than Clifford Kitchin. The naval commander – who of course had not known that the Finn was working for me – had picked him up in a cottage above the beach in Kemp Town. Later the naval commander told me, 'He was the fuck of a lifetime.'

The Finn was succeeded by a plump Greek of lazy charm. The extent of his cleaning for me was dreamily to push the vacuum-cleaner back and forth over a carpet or no less dreamily to dry the dishes as I washed them. On the one occasion when I entered his attic room to summon him to the telephone, I was overwhelmed by its smell and its squalor. I had paid for him to enrol at my friend's school, since he clearly could not afford to pay for this himself; but my friend told me that he rarely turned up and, when he did so, disturbed the class by attempting to carry on a whispered conversation with any girl who happened to be in his vicinity.

Next to me lived a friendly businessman and his disagreeable and far from prepossessing wife – who, I suspected, made his life hell. On one occasion this wife complained because, in watering the roses in my front garden, I had sprayed some water on to her roses on the other side of the wrought-iron railings. On another occasion she asked me, with a pretence of sweetness, whether I should like her to wash the net curtains in the windows of my basement – 'They look so terribly grimy, really squalid, and, as a bachelor, you probably don't have time to see to them.'

One day, when the Greek was still with me, the businessman called at the house, plainly embarrassed. He was afraid that he had to make a complaint about the, er, foreign gentleman living in my house. What had he done? I asked. Well, it was all rather embarrassing. The businessman hesitated. Then he steeled himself to tell me. His wife had been looking at a window display in Plummer Roddis, when she had been aware of someone standing close beside her. It was the foreign gentleman. Suddenly he had put a hand on, well, on, on . . . The businessman broke off. Then he said, 'Perhaps you would have a word with the foreign gentleman. I know that abroad these things are not thought . . .' Again he broke off.

I had a word with the Greek, who made no denial but merely looked sulky. I felt sorry for him, obliged, in his loneliness, to make a pass at such an old bag.

When the Greek had returned to Athens, I found that he had removed whatever was portable from his room: a chipped ashtray, a pleated lampshade, a tooth-mug, a cushion cover. These petty thefts struck me as quite as sad as the pass made to my neighbour.


On my return from Japan, I had at once attempted to get as much reviewing as possible. Since I loathe asking, much less badgering, people for favours, my efforts to this end were often half-hearted and perfunctory. I had known Jack Lambert, then literary editor of *The Sunday Times*, for some years and so he was one of the first people to whom I despatched a letter. In return he sent me a volume of essays by Maurice Bowra – 450 or so words, he instructed. Well, it was a start. I spent far more time on the review than I should do now, even going to the London Library to bone up on some of the topics with which Bowra dealt. I eventually got a cheque, but the review was never published. Jack sent me no further books and I was too proud to ask for any. It seemed to me that, in sending me the Bowra, his action was similar to that of the prosperous man who sees a former schoolfellow begging, a drunken vagrant, on a park bench and hurriedly slips him a pound before hurrying on with averted eyes. That Terry Kilmartin, of the *Observer*, whom I had met through Peter Heyworth, a close friend of his, should never have bothered even to answer my letter with a negative did not then surprise me and does not surprise me now. Unlike Peter Heyworth and most other people, I found him neither particularly warm nor particularly bright. He was, I have decided, the Terry Wogan of literature. It is surprising how far Irish charm can take one in the media.

Fortunately Tony Curtis, then literary editor of the *Sunday Telegraph*, was characteristically helpful and generous. I became novel reviewer for that paper, continuing to work happily for it, first as book reviewer and then as drama critic, for more than twenty years.

Soon after Tony Curtis had taken me on, I also began to work as literary adviser at Weidenfeld and Nicolson – a job procured through my cousin Colin Haycraft, then himself employed there, before he became the proprietor, often in stormy circumstances in later years, of Duckworth. My job at Weidenfeld involved going into the office one day each week, firstly to attend the weekly editorial meeting and then to sift through all the fiction which had come in and to take home with me any that looked promising. Books other than fiction were also passed on to me, for a second opinion.

I soon surmised that I had been employed by George Weidenfeld not because he wanted to get me in but because he wanted to get someone else out. This someone else was Barley Allison, who had on at least one occasion come to his financial rescue but who had then begun to seem increasingly expendable. By ostentatiously treating me as though I were her superior, whose judgement he must back on any occasion when it collided with hers, he seemed to be set on forcing her into the resignation which, indeed, eventually came about. However, in this resignation, I played little part, since I got on far better with her than I ever managed to get on with him.

Barley was an extremely able and kind woman; but she had one terrible defect – she could not stop talking. Seated in her office at the end of my day at Weidenfeld, I would glance surreptitiously at my watch and realize that I had missed yet another train back to Brighton. Since, long after we had ceased to have any professional relationship, she often used to invite me to her huge and glittering parties in her Harley Gardens flat, I used to reciprocate by from time to time asking her to my small and dim ones at my Gordon Place house. Then I had to stop doing so. Smoking incessantly and repeatedly holding out her glass for another drink, she would sit on and on and talk on and on, long after every other guest had left. More than once she departed after five. Once I actually fell asleep, to wake to hear that voice still droning on in a cloud of cigarette smoke. 'Barley, I really must go to bed.' She ignored that. 'Barley, I'm worn out. I've had a heavy day. I must go to bed.' 'All right. But first just let me have one for the road.' The one for the road became many for the road. On the doorstep – at least the air there was fresh – she would start up again: 'Oh, I know what I wanted to tell you . . .'

Others of her friends suffered in the same way. On one occasion, she was a fellow guest at dinner with my agent Mark Hamilton and his doctor wife. By half-past eleven all the other guests had gone, and I myself had risen to my feet. Quickly Mark said, 'Oh, Francis, are you going home by taxi?' 'Yes,' I said. 'Oh, good!' His face and that of his wife lit up with relief. 'Then perhaps you could give Barley a lift home.' 'Of course.' But the difficulty was first to get her out of their flat and then to get her out of the taxi outside her own flat. There was something panicky about this undammable flow of hers, as though, like Scheherazade, she was talking away literally for dear life. Yet, although she never listened, she seemed, miraculously, to accumulate a great deal of information. 'I hear that you've been on a visit to Greece,' she would say; or 'I hear you have a new book completed'; or 'I hear you've been ill.' How had someone who never listened heard these things? I could only suppose that she had absorbed the facts by some process of osmosis.

No doubt to curry favour with her authors, Barley had a way of telling them that, whereas I had been reluctant or unwilling to recommend their books, she herself had fought for them tooth and nail (her phrase). She did this to Piers Paul Read, when he had submitted his first novel *Game in Heaven With Tussie Marx*. In that case, she was telling the truth: I greatly admire much of Read's *oeuvre* but that particular novel was a jejune confection. In the case of other novelists, some of them friends of mine, she was not telling the truth and a bewildering, albeit mercifully temporary, coldness followed between them and me. It was only after I had left Weidenfeld that I began to learn of this trick of hers.

Like many, perhaps nowadays most, publishers, George seldom read anything written by his authors. But at least in those days he had an uncanny faculty for knowing what would sell and what wouldn't. I had been particularly impressed by one novel, the best that I read during my year with the firm, called *I Want What I Want* by Geoff Brown. It was the story of a transvestite, so authentic-seeming that I decided that, though presented as fiction, it could only have been based on personal experience. At the next editorial meeting, I spoke at length about it in the most flattering terms, while George listened with growing impatience. Then he cut me off: 'How many transvestites do you think there are in England?' I had no idea at all; but I replied boldly, 'Far more than you imagine, George.' 'Right! Well, in that case what are we waiting for? Let's take it.' Whether because there were more transvestites in England than George imagined or whether because the novel showed a genuine artistry, it proved a success. Unfortunately the film based on it proved less of one – not because of any deficiency in Gillian Freeman's script but because, perversely, the producers cast a woman, Anne Heywood, in the role of the transvestite man. Later, I was to invite the author down to Brighton for the day. I wondered whether he would appear in his female persona; in any case I imagined someone small, delicate, girlish. In the event, he was wearing a shaggy tweed suit, heavy brogues and a brightly checked shirt. Most of his face was invisible because of a beard. Despite my initial disappointment, we got on well, and have since kept in touch.

After I had been a year or so with the firm, George asked Colin, 'Why does Francis dislike me?' 'Oh, I don't think he dislikes you,' Colin said. 'Yes, he dislikes me and despises me.' I had never thought that I had given George any reason for coming to this conclusion. But I felt so embarrassed that I decided that, as soon as I had found some other part-time job, I had better tender my resignation. Before I could do so, however, George wrote me a letter to tell me that, because of a reorganization in the firm, of a kind that was all too often to take place in the years ahead, he would, 'most reluctantly', have to ask me to go. From time to time I have met him since then, and have always relished his company. Like L.P. Hartley's, the sexual attraction which he exerts on women continues to bewilder me; but I know no one who can talk more interestingly about history and politics.

Fortunately, almost as soon as I had departed from Weidenfeld, my friend Herman Schrijver (about whom I shall write later) introduced me to James MacGibbon, then in charge at Macdonald. We instantly got on and continued to do so when I began to work at his firm. My immediate superior was Penny Hoare, whom I came first to admire as a discriminating editor and then to love as a friend. She has always realized, as many editors fail to do, that authors are like dogs: unless they are constantly patted and stroked, they cannot be happy.

While reading four or five novels in a week for my *Sunday Telegraph* review (in those days such block reviews were common, each novel being accorded no more than a paragraph or two), reading the same number of novels for first Weidenfeld and then Macdonald, writing a three-weekly television column for *The Listener*, cooking meals for my lodgers and frequent guests, and attempting also to find time to work on the stories which eventually composed the collection *The Brighton Belle*, I would often give way to regret, even despair. By resigning from the British Council, all I had done was to exchange one treadmill for another even more gruelling.

There was also regret, even despair over my decision to leave Japan and Noboru. Writer friends like Frank Tuohy and John Haylock earned lavish salaries for six or seven hours per week of university teaching of English literature at what was no more than sixth-form standard. Had I accepted one of the many offers of similar jobs which had come my way during my last weeks in Japan, I could be doing the same, with Noboru still as my companion.

Having been so happy with Noboru, I now needed a relationship of the same kind. But where was I to find one? In the pubs and clubs one-night stands such as I had so much enjoyed during my years in Greece were sometimes available; but they now seemed to be dead-sea fruit, attractive to the first sight and touch but eventually leaving a dry and bitter taste of dust and ashes in the mouth.

I have already expressed the view that, contrary to popular belief, what usually spoils people is not success but failure. If I had not precisely failed at that period, I had the feeling that I had wandered off the highway of my life into a bog. Unhappy, I was all too often the cause of unhappiness in others. I was irritable and demanding with the succession of au pairs; offhand and unhelpful to the lodgers, many of whom would have been willing, I am sure, to have sacrificed comfort and good food (both of which I certainly provided) for my friendly interest in their doings; and whereas nowadays I seldom write a totally destructive review (if a book is worthless, I prefer not to review it at all), I then often did so, either with praise pockmarked with innumerable grudging qualifications or with outright malice.

After I had been in the Montpelier Road house for some two years, Clifford Kitchin died, leaving me a small legacy and the copyrights in his books. Had I had any prudence, I should have used this legacy to pay off my mortgage, sold the house, bought myself a flat, and then invested any surplus. But financial prudence is something in which I have always been singularly lacking. Soon after Clifford's death, my friends Peter Rose and Albert Gallichen (I think that it was I who first nicknamed them Victoria and Albert) rang up to tell me of the death of the old widower who had lived for many years in the house opposite their own resplendent one, crammed with artistic treasures, in Montpelier Villas. His niece, who had inherited the house, had no intention of living there; and, if I made an immediate offer, they thought that I should therefore probably get it at a bargain price. I had always wanted to live in Montpelier Villas – or the Village, as its residents call it – both because of the beauty of its large semi-detached houses, each with a canopied bow window of curving glass, and because of having so many other friends living there in addition to Peter and Albert. I at once entered into negotiations; and the result was that I did indeed get the house for a bargain price.

For many years little had been done to it; and so, having burdened myself with a mortgage even larger than my previous one, I then had to finance the installation of central heating, repairs to the roof, repairs to the cracked and peeling exterior, redecoration. There were carpets and curtains to be bought and yet more furniture, since the house contained a basement flat, which I was planning to let. It was madness; but a madness which, like the madness of buying a Cadillac in Japan, I have never regretted. I once owned a Cadillac; I once lived in one of the most beautiful houses in Brighton. However absurd it may seem to others, I find it satisfying to be able to tell myself that.

Soon after I had bought the house, my life suffered a jolting disruption, the eventual effects of which were to be momentous for me. I have already mentioned my 'then friend', Tom Skeffington-Lodge. A former Labour MP, he shared a house, not far from Montpelier Road and Montpelier Villas, with John Haylock. John was rarely in Brighton, for the most part living in Japan, where he both taught and wrote. Tom had been kind and hospitable to me on my arrival in Brighton. Having little to do, other than be a Brighton landlady (like myself), write verbose letters, usually to the local *Brighton Argus*, about the political issues of the day (he took the somewhat eccentric view that Harold Wilson was the greatest Prime Minister since Gladstone), and chat up stall-holders in the market, antique dealers in the Lanes and fellow customers in the betting-shop, he often used to make my house a port of call at about eleven in the morning, when he was returning, up the hill, from shopping at Waitrose. I enjoyed his *bonhomie*, even though I should have preferred to have been left in peace to get on with my work. My mother enjoyed his flattery – 'How's my best girl?' would be his greeting to her, to be followed by something like 'Oh, Faith, I *do* like that dress! You look not a day over forty in it. *Doesn't* that dress suit her, Francis? She looks really gorgeous. You always have such wonderful taste, my dear. I wish you could give some advice to poor, dear Mary Wilson. When she came to the Fabian garden party, she had clearly made an effort, but I can't tell you how *dowdy* she looked ...'

One day, when I called on Tom for some plants which he had promised me for my garden, he was giving tea to one of his lodgers, an Italian economist called Giorgio Balloni. Tom had already complained to me about this lodger, as he had often done about others – he was untidy and noisy, he tended to come home late, he had to be reminded when his rent came due. 'I think I'll have to ask him to look for somewhere else,' he now whispered to me, as I followed him into the kitchen where he had gone to fetch a cup for me. 'You know, he *never* cleans out the bath after he has used it.' Instantly I thought, 'If Tom doesn't want him, I'll take him on!' Untidiness, noise, lateness, failure to pay the rent or clean out the bath: none of those things mattered. At first glance, I had felt a sexual attraction stronger than any I had ever experienced in my life. Indeed, I had felt faint with it – ludicrous though that sounds – and had had to sit down.

When I left the house, Giorgio walked down the hill with me, on his way to the university, where he was doing postgraduate research. He began to complain about Tom: chiefly that he was so fussy and stingy – 'I feel like a bad child,' he said at one moment, and at another, 'He has only one wish, to make out of me as much money as possible.'

When I suggested to Tom that I might take over Giorgio, he was greatly relieved: 'You're welcome to him, my dear! Good luck to you!'

So began a period of my life when I really think that, in a sense, I was mad. As I have described in what I consider one of the three best of my novels, *A Domestic Animal*, I became totally obsessed with someone who, although he clearly liked and admired me and although he was no less clearly flattered by my devotion, was totally incapable of the sort of reciprocation for which I yearned. Although married and the father of two children, he had a girl-friend, with whom he spent most of his evenings. Each evening, after he had called out to me, 'Ciao, Francesco, I go now!', I used to suffer a terrible desolation. I would try to settle to some writing, a book, television. But I could not stop thinking of him. What was he doing now? Where was he? Was he making love to that slut? (It was part of my madness thus to degrade a nice, decent girl.) When he at last returned, I used to go into the hall to greet him: 'Oh, you're back, you're back!' It was as though I had dreaded that some terrible, perhaps even fatal accident might have befallen him. I used to look into his handsome face, trying to read whether he had slept with the girl or not.

I was tireless in the tasks which I performed for him. Was he about to take a parcel to the post office? I took it for him. Did he need some out-of-print work on economics? I scoured the bookshops. Did he like *prosciutto crudo*, smoked salmon, peaches? I bought them for him, whatever the cost. He believed that no one who was not Italian could prepare a dish of pasta. While he himself prepared one, I would act as his kitchen-maid, dashing about to fetch him what he wanted. The results were often dire. But I used to say, 'Delicious, Giorgio, really delicious!'

Before becoming an economist, he had been a professional footballer. I had always hated watching football almost as much as watching cricket. But now, when he played in a university match, I used to stand out on the touchline, often in biting cold, watching him, only him.

A feature of such obsessions is not merely that one can think of no one else, one can also talk of no one else. Constantly I would find some pretext to mention him to family and friends, to lodgers and au pairs, to the people in the neighbouring shops. Thus, fetching his shoes after I had left them to be repaired, I had to say, as though it would be of any interest to the grumpily taciturn cobbler, 'These are Italian shoes. They belong not to me but to an Italian friend of mine. Aren't they beautifully made?' Thus, buying some prawns at the fishmongers, I had to say, as though it would be of any interest to the over-burdened assistant darting about to serve a long line of customers, 'An Italian friend needs these for a risotto. He's a really terrific cook.'

When Giorgio finally left (he was later to return with his wife and two children, to occupy my basement flat), I felt both a desolation and relief. It was then that I started to work on *A Domestic Animal*. No book I have written has been a closer transcription of my own experience. In an eerie way, all the events of the past months seemed to have an internal artistic logic, demanding none superimposed from without. I wrote with amazing speed. It had all been a blissful agony to live. Now it was an equally blissful agony to write. What followed after that was an agony with no bliss at all.

Inevitably Tom Skeffington-Lodge's part in the story had to be told. But in his case, I juggled with reality, changing him from a male politician to a female one, called Dame Winifred Harcourt, and altering many other of his circumstances. He had never read any of my books and it was highly improbable that he would read this one; but I wanted to guard against even the remotest possibility of a libel action. What I did not then realize is something that I realize all too well now: if there is ever something hurtful that someone does not know, a 'friend' can always be relied on to draw it to his (or her) attention. 'I'm so sorry about that beastly review you got in the *Sunday Express*.' 'What have you done to make X take so much against you?' 'After all you did for Y, I was disgusted by the way she was talking about you the other day.' We have all had things similar to this said to us by 'friends'.

When the advance copies of the novel reached me, I gave one to John Haylock, who was now back from Japan, in the house which he shared with Tom. John left it out on the sitting-room table (our mutual friend Desmond Stewart remarked to me, 'Freud would have had something to say about that'); and that same evening, the evening paper having not been delivered and the television set being out of order, Tom, at a loss how to occupy himself, picked it up. He was as hurt and outraged as Hugh Walpole when he read of Alroy Kear in Maugham's *Cakes and Ale*.

I am told that one incident in the book, above all others, persuaded him that he and Dame Winifred Harcourt were one and the same person. Some months before, Tom had confided in me his hope of getting a peerage. This struck me as unlikely, firstly because his career in the House had been so brief and secondly because it had been so totally undistinguished. 'I think I'll approach Clem [Lord] Attlee and Frank Longford to have a word with Harold. I had thought of approaching Mary Wilson, but I don't think that would be quite the thing, do you?' Would it even be quite the thing for a socialist to approach Attlee and Frank Longford? But I said nothing. Eventually, at a dinner-party at which I was present, Tom boomed, 'It would be premature to say that the peerage is in the bag, but things look promising, I'm sure you'd all agree.' He then produced two letters, the first from Longford and the second from Attlee, which he passed round the table. With his usual kindness, Longford wrote that he thought the honour in question was long overdue; that he would certainly see what he could do to expedite it; that, in fact, he would mention the matter to Harold when, next week, he saw him. Attlee's note (one could not call it a letter) merely read:

Dear Skeff

Thank you for your letter. I hope that you get what you deserve.

Yours, Attlee.

'With Frank Longford and Clem on my side like that, I can't see how I can fail. Can you?

I could see all too easily.

This incident I used precisely as it occurred.

I can now fully understand Tom's indignation and, indeed, sympathize with it. We writers are all too often cannibals, in devouring family and friends, and cads, in betraying the secrets entrusted to us. People who are not writers find it difficult to appreciate that even in a biography there is no simple equation: a (the real-life person) = b (the person on the page); and that in fact the equation goes $a = b + c + d - x - y - z$. Tom proclaimed, in effect, 'Dame Winifred Harcourt — c'est moi'; and he proclaimed this not merely in a letter to me but in conversation with anyone with whom he came into contact, so that the identification was certain all over Brighton, even among the many people who would never have dreamed of reading one of my books and were in any case unable to read this particular one, since it was not yet on sale.

In reply to his letter, I did, according to the lawyers, a fatal thing: I wrote an apology. But, if one has hurt and offended a friend, what is more natural than to say that one is sorry?

Tom showed the letter to Lord Hailsham, with whom he claimed a closer relationship than Hailsham himself might have acknowledged, and wrote back that, on the great lawyer's advice, he was planning to take out an injunction to have the book withdrawn.

My mother then did a thing almost as foolish as mine, but with consequences less dire. She wrote to Tom, begging him not to take legal action. I worked so hard, she wrote, I was terribly pressed for money, I had not really intended to humiliate or hurt him. From the man who had so often called her 'my favourite girl', she received no answer. Instead he asked John Haylock to write on his behalf, to say that 'he regretted that the law must take its course.'

The law proceeded to take its course. Longmans, my then publishers, summoned me to a meeting with Michael Rubinstein, one of the foremost libel lawyers of the day. He sounded sanguine – Skeffington-Lodge's claim was preposterous, any self-respecting jury would laugh it out of court, I had nothing to fear. The next day I received a telephone call from John Guest, my editor at

Longmans. Rubinstein had been giving the matter some thought, and had now come to the conclusion that we were on really rather a sticky wicket (John favoured metaphors from cricket). In fact, he advised a settlement before the matter went to court. I was stunned. What had caused Rubinstein completely to change his view in the course of so few hours? It was only weeks later that I learned the answer to this question from someone who was working in Longmans. Not long before, the firm had been sued for libel for an allegation by one of their authors, Gavin Maxwell, that a certain Sicilian nobleman was a Mafia boss. There were innumerable Sicilians who could vouch for this fact; but there was none prepared to go into a witness box in order to do so. The jury, incapable of believing such ill of a nobleman without any evidence, then awarded him huge damages. Understandably, the directors of Longmans had therefore decided that another libel action must be avoided. They had instructed Rubinstein accordingly.

John now asked me if I was aware of clause six – or was it seven or eight? – of my contract. This stipulated that, in the event of an action for libel, I should fully reimburse Longmans.

I was appalled. The clause was certainly in the contract but I had never read it. However, I told John that I was still determined to fight the matter, whatever it cost me.

I then consulted my family solicitors, only to be told that none of the five partners knew anything about libel. They referred me to a firm, composed of at least fifteen partners, in the City. This firm told me that, before they could act for me, they would need a sum in advance. We eventually agreed on £500, worth considerably more then than now. I had to go and see my bank manager about an overdraft: something I had always resisted doing.

The City firm told me that it would be necessary to seek counsel's opinion. This took me to the chambers of David Hurst, now a highly respected judge, who had a junior, Leon Brittan, in attendance. From what Hurst said, I suspected that he had been far too busy to read the whole book and that Brittan, having read it for him, had marked the relevant passages. After some discussion, Hurst said, 'Now, I'm afraid I must ask you something bluntly. How much money have you got?' I told him. He looked glum. Then he said, 'Well, if that's the case, I'd advise you to settle.'

'Really? To *settle*?' I was amazed.

Hurst explained. 'I think that I could win the case. I can't be sure but I *think* that I could. After all, juries are usually literal-minded and are therefore unlikely to believe a male former MP, who goes into a witness-box and then tells them, 'Call me Dame Winifred Harcourt.' But the problem is your costs. Even if you won the case, you would not get them all back. Far from it.' He then began to explain to me the function of the taxing master – which appeared to be to ensure that no successful defendant in a libel action left the court financially unscathed. Hurst concluded our interview: 'Well, I must say this is a rum case. When writers come to me for advice about possible libel, I always advise them, "Change sex!"

In your case, this clearly hasn't worked. Ah, well! No doubt in due course there'll be a note in the textbooks about a man suing for libel on the grounds that he was a woman in a book.'

As, sick with rage and mortification, I descended the stairs from the chambers, I heard someone racing down behind me. 'Oh, Mr King! Mr King!' It was Leon Brittan. 'No one said it and I want to say it. I think it a terrific novel.'

I have always been grateful to him for that.

Despite Hurst's advice, there were friends who urged me to go on fighting. Olivia Manning offered, as she put it, 'to back me all the way' – I could return the money in due course or, if that proved impossible, forget about it. Giorgio, who had as much or more cause to bring an action than Tom, touched me profoundly by offering me his savings – 'This is a wonderful book, you must fight for it, I will help you to fight!' Desmond Stewart's behaviour was more equivocal. There were no offers of a loan or a gift, but a lot of encouragement, in the manner of a well-bred woman screaming in support of a boxer about to be reduced to pulp in the ring: I must on no account give in, it was a scandal, a shame, this was a battle that I must fight not merely for myself but for my fellow writers . . . At the same time, I learned later, he was urging Tom: he must on no account give in, it was a scandal, a shame, this was a battle that he must fight not merely for himself but for all those people who had suffered at the hands of unscrupulous novelists . . .

Olivia's ferocious partisanship extended to a practical joke. Staying with me in Brighton, she suddenly asked me for Tom's telephone number. Why did she want it? 'You'll see!' When I had given it to her, she crossed over to the telephone. Screeching in stage Cockney, she asked if she was speaking to Mr Skeffington-Lodge, Mr Skeffington-Lodge the former MP. Learning that she was, she went on, 'Now listen to me, you filthy old git! You just leave my husband alone! . . . No, it's no use denyin' it. 'E told me as 'ow 'e was deliverin' vegetables in 'is lorry to Waitrose and you picked 'im up with a lot of smarmy talk and the offer of cash . . . No, don't give me them lies! I don't want no more of that kind of malarkey! . . . If you so much as lay another finger on 'im, I'll get me brothers to carve you up, so 'elp me God!' Apparently Tom blustered – 'Don't speak to me like that! . . . I've no idea what you're talking about . . . This is clearly a matter for the police.' But, according to a gleeful Olivia, he was terrified.

The book having been withdrawn, much to the relief of Longmans, there followed months of rewriting. To minimize costs, it was essential that each new sentence or paragraph should be of precisely the same wordage as the one it replaced. When an alteration had been made, it had to be submitted to Tom for his approval. As letters passed back and forth between solicitors and between solicitors and their clients, an invisible taxi-meter kept ticking up. From time to time I would be asked for yet another advance; from time to time to settle another bill from Tom's solicitors.

On a lecture-tour in Greece in the midddle of all this, I was invited by my old friend Frances Bébis to a dinner-party in her Athens flat. I arrived early and she handed me some letters. 'These have arrived for you, forwarded from England.

Do read them now, if you like. I still have some things to do.' The first letter I opened was a demand from my solicitors for yet another advance. Before leaving England, I had been told by my bank manager that my overdraft had reached its limit.

When the guests had all gone, Frances asked me, sympathetic as always, 'Aren't you feeling well?'

'Oh, I'm fine. Why?'

'Well, it's not at all like you to be so piano at a dinner-party. And you're looking so pale.'

I explained to her the reason.

By now, Tom had started correcting not merely the passages in which Dame Winifred appeared but others which had nothing to do with her. He had ceased to be an aggrieved plaintiff; he had become a literary critic. This or that episode 'needs some clarification'; this or that passage 'strikes me as rather careless'; he 'did not fully understand the motivation' here or there. At this point, my solicitors fortunately decided to call a halt, writing him a letter to inform him that publication would now go ahead and inviting him to sue if he so wished. He did not wish.

Sadly, the reviews were scanty. Because the first version of the book had been withdrawn only three or four days before the date of its publication, many literary editors had been obliged to pull copy at the last moment. They were disinclined now to reinstate that copy, so many months later. One of the few long reviews was in the *Evening Standard*. I had never heard of the reviewer, Richard Lister, and therefore wondered why his review should have been so acridly personal in tone. Some weeks later, a mutual friend told me that Richard Lister was the pseudonym of T.C. (Cuthbert) Worsley, a long-time friend and Brighton resident. Since he himself was not merely homosexual but was openly living with a man, I could only suppose that the disapproval which he expressed for the relationship described in the novel was born out of guilt over his own. I never let on that I knew that he had written the review; when he was cruelly ill with emphysema, I even used to visit him. On one of those visits, not long before he died by his own hand, he began, 'There's something I've always wanted to confess to you, Francis.' Then he broke off, coughing and gasping. 'Oh, what's the point?' he got out at last. I did not press him.

Despite its initial lack of success, the book has been twice issued in paperback and continues to sell. It has brought me more letters than any other of my novels, not merely from homosexuals but from people who have passed through the sadness of a similar obsessive love.

About the whole affair, I eventually wrote a novel called *The Action*. At the Booker dinner of the year in which it appeared, A.J. (Freddie) Ayer, the chairman of the judges, said that he thought that it should have been on the short-list. But none of my books has ever achieved that distinction.

By then debt had forced me to sell the house in Montpelier Villas, to someone called Lady Elizabeth Berwick. She had once commented to me that she had found the taste of my friends and neighbours Peter Rose and Albert Gallichen 'really rather vulgar'. She now made the same comment about my taste to them. Since I never visited her after she had moved into the house, I was never in a position to assess her taste. But it did not prevent her from removing from the kitchen some William de Morgan tiles, which overscrupulously I had left there as part of the fixtures and fittings, and junking them.

Many years later Tom and I achieved some kind of reconciliation, after the funeral of our mutual friend Desmond Stewart, at which Gerard Irvine, another of Desmond's friends, officiated. The service over, the doors of the church (St Matthew's in Westminster) crashed open and there was Tom. 'I see I've arrived too late. That Brighton line is shocking!' he boomed out to the huddle of family mourners before him. Then he saw me. 'Oh, there's Francis King!' He hurried over to me. 'I feel sure', he said in a voice audible to everyone, 'that Desmond must be looking down from heaven and wanting us to be reconciled.' Knowing Desmond's malicious nature, I was sure that he would be wanting nothing of the kind. 'Let's make it up!' He grabbed my hand and shook it. 'No hard feelings.'

I thought of my Montpelier Villas house; of the hours spent on rewriting the novel according to his increasingly bizarre instructions; of those humiliating visits to my bank manager.

'No hard feelings,' I said.

# — 3 —

# *The Ivy League*

It was only after I had returned from Japan, to settle in England, that I became a close friend of Ivy Compton-Burnett. Of all the people I have ever known in the course of my life, she was the most remarkable and admirable.

Our first encounter occurred at the prompting of Robert Liddell, who had become a friend of hers when, still young, he was working at the Bodleian before the war, and when she, still middle-aged, was living with Margaret Jourdain. Robert was to do more than anyone else to bring her to the attention of the world at large, first by constantly enthusing about her and then by writing a book about her work. She knew what debt she owed to him and, unlike many writers who owe debts to fellow writers, never forgot it. On one occasion she spoke to me of what makes a writer famous: 'One has to have the talent of course. And one has to have the perseverance and patience to build up an *oeuvre*. But one also has to have two or three people – people known for their intelligence, discrimination, that sort of thing – to speak up loudly for one.' As so often when she appeared to be speaking in general terms, one sensed that she was really speaking in personal ones. Her 'two or three people' were firstly Robert and then Raymond Mortimer and Elizabeth Taylor.

I was on leave from Greece when I met Olivia Manning and her husband Reggie Smith in a pub opposite Gloucester Road Station, before being led by them to Ivy's flat in Cornwall Gardens. I was in such a state of nerves at the prospect of having luncheon with the great novelist (as I have always believed her to be, the greatest English novelist of the second and third quarters of this century) that I had to rush at once to the pub loo and refused Reggie's suggestion of 'a quick pint', for fear of another rush to the loo at Braemar Mansions. A quick pint was something for which Reggie was always ready.

'You'll find her rather a bore,' Reggie warned. But I can truthfully say that, unlike dear old Reggie, Ivy never bored me.

The square, high-ceilinged drawing-room, chairs pushed back against its dusky walls, with mirrors (not a single picture) above them, was depressing and, despite the summer sunshine on its balcony, dank enough to make me wish I had not worn a light suit. Ivy offered 'a glass of sherry wine'. On a later occasion, she was to protest to me, after his departure from a similar luncheon party, that Ivo Pakenham had spoken of 'a sherry' – 'so vulgar, one would have expected someone from that family to have known better.' Having often myself spoken of 'a sherry', I was thankful never to have done so in her presence.

When the five of us sat down to luncheon in a dining-room that was even drearier than the drawing-room – its ceiling seemed even loftier, its high, narrow window looked out on a well – Ivy continually prompted us, like a nanny: 'Mr King – Mrs Smith has no butter,' 'Reggie, do see that Mr King has some water,' 'Olivia, don't you want some bread?' When the maid carried in the joint, Ivy asked Reggie to carve it. 'Oh, I'm no good at carving,' Reggie said; and then proceeded to demonstrate that he had only spoken the truth. Ivy peered at the chunks of lamb set down before her. She pursed her mouth. 'I can see that I should have asked Mr King to carve.' Olivia could in fact carve far better than either Reggie or I; but Ivy's was a world in which women did not carve unless no man was present.

After luncheon, Ivy asked me for news of Robert Liddell – what was he writing, what were his chances of becoming Byron Professor at Athens University, had he recovered from his sciatica – 'such a wretched affliction'? Then, suddenly, she said, 'Have you met this boy of his?'

I was amazed and nonplussed. Robert was under the impression that she knew nothing of his attachment to a working-class Greek or even of his homosexuality. 'Yes, I have met him. Once or twice,' I replied guardedly. I was later to learn that it was Olivia who had informed Ivy about the importance of the boy in Robert's life.

'I suppose he gives Robert a lot of pleasure.'

'Yes. I suppose he does.'

'But I gather that he's not all that educated. And that he's mercenary, as Greeks so often tend to be.' She went on to discuss the subject with absolutely no disapproval at all – asking at one moment, 'Would one call him good-looking?' and at another, 'Is he the sort of person with whom one could have a conversation – assuming of course that he knew some English or one knew some Greek?' To both these questions I answered Yes.

I left the flat – 'Do please get in touch when next you are in London' – as I was so often to leave it, at once exhilarated, exhausted and relieved. I might have just completed a difficult climb.

Whenever I was on leave in London, I did get in touch with Ivy, to be bidden either to luncheon or, more often, to one of those nursery teas, the table laden with potted shrimps, scones, sandwiches, chocolate cake, fruit cake, Madeira cake ('The Apple Blossom, near your mother's flat, used to make the best Madeira cake but now, sadly, it's been replaced by one of those awful dress shops. Who *goes* to them?'). But it was not until I had actually settled in London that I felt that I was truly a member of what someone – was it Roger Hinks, with his love of puns? – called the Ivy League.

Ivy's male guests were often friends inherited from Margaret Jourdain, and so, like her, distinguished in the world of the visual arts. Many of them were discreet – and in one instance, that of the Dutch interior decorator, Herman Schrijver, about whom I shall write later, not so discreet – homosexuals. With the exception of such writers as Kathleen Farrell, Kay Dick, Olivia Manning, Elizabeth Taylor and Elizabeth Sprigge, the women tended to be everything that Ivy was not: worldly, much-travelled, rich, glamorous. Of these women my favourite was Theodora Benson, always elegant, witty, kind. One December afternoon, she arrived at one of Ivy's tea-parties wearing dark glasses. Peering behind them, I could see that both her eyes had bruises under them. 'Oh, Theodora!' I cried out in dismay. 'What have you done to yourself? Have you had a fall?' 'Yes. I slipped, getting out of the bath.' When all the other guests had gone, Ivy upbraided me: 'That was very tactless of you. Or were you being malicious?' 'What do you mean?' 'Theodora has just had a face-lift. "One or two tucks," she calls it. So silly of her. She's far too beautiful to need that sort of nonsense.'

I always thought that Ivy was half in love with Theodora, as with a less lovable, because far more steely, character, Madge Ashton (Garland). After Ivy's death, I saw a lot of Madge, whom I admired for her dauntlessness (in old age, suffering from innumerable ailments, many of them painful, she took herself off to an ashram), her chic and her impeccable taste. Late in her life, she had made a marriage to Leigh Ashton, then Keeper of the Victoria and Albert Museum. 'I'm amazed,' I commented to Ivy. 'Yes,' Ivy agreed, 'it is a little improbable. But I think that she likes to be a Lady. And of course we all like her to be a Lady too.' One of Madge's chief marital duties, of which she soon wearied, was to prevent Leigh from drinking too much. Many a tumbler of whisky was emptied out of the window of his room into the courtyard of the V & A. By an odd chance, my sister Anne was briefly a fellow patient of Leigh's in the expensive mental hospital in Northampton in which he spent the last years of his life. By then drink had ravaged his memory, so that when Anne mentioned Madge, Ivy, me, he recollected nothing of us. But each evening, when he, Anne and two other patients had settled down to some bridge, he played brilliantly, his memory for the cards totally unimpaired.

It was Robin Darwin, then Principal of the Royal College of Art, who appointed Madge as its Professor of Fashion. It was a totally suitable appointment, since it was fashion, and not more abiding things, about which she was most knowledgeable. That she and Darwin eventually quarrelled – irreconcilably, as it turned out – was something I first realized when, at the picture dealers Abbott and Holder, I saw one of Darwin's water-colours offered for sale. It was inscribed 'To darlingest Madge, From Robin.' I was tempted to buy it, in order to witness the expression on Madge's face when, on her next visit to me, she saw it on one of my walls. But it was not good enough and its price was not low enough.

Madge is the only woman whom I have ever seen literally spit on someone else. As close friends of Ivy, she and Herman had also been close friends of each other. But Herman, in whose kindness there was a streak of cruelty, like a scrap of silver paper embedded in a piece of chocolate, setting one's teeth on edge when one inadvertently bites on it, loved to bait Madge. On one occasion, he went too far on

Somerset Maugham

E. M. Forster at King's College,
Cambridge

Ivy Compton-Burnett with two of the looking-glasses left to her writer friends

L. P. Hartley

Olivia Manning – or 'Olivia Moaning', as
Herman Schrijver called her

Kay Dick, 1967

The author on Brighton beach, 1969

With David, two years
before his death, in the
garden of Gordon Place,
London

With Diana Petre at a reading for the
Hungarian Centre of PEN in Budapest

The author, Mary McCarthy,
Stephen Spender and Nancy Ing
at a PEN conference in Venice

A group of English writers entertained by Soviet writers in Yalta. Front row, from extreme left, the author, Matthew Evans (Faber and Faber), Margaret Drabble. Fourth from the

Tom Wakefield

The author 1991

the subject of her marriage to Leigh – a homosexual, he had married her for respectability, and she, a lesbian, had married him for his title, was the all too clear implication – and she stormed out of his flat. As he opened the lift door for her – I was standing behind him – she suddenly spat in his face. Later, after his death, she was to say to me, 'He was a really horrible man. What did you and Ivy see in him?' 'Oh, he had lots and lots of qualities.' 'Such as?' I knew that it would be idle to enumerate them.

Another of Ivy's close women friends had also been married to a museum curator. This was Viva King, wife of Willie King, of the British Museum. Blowsy and sometimes even grubby, she had none of Madge's unassailable chic; but, unlike Madge, she had been a beautiful woman when young and she retained much of that beauty into old age. Like both Madge and Ivy, she preferred the company of homosexual men to heterosexual ones – in her case to such an extent that she always struck me as not so much a woman as a queen trapped inside a woman's body. Late in life, she formed a series of attachments to what would nowadays be called toy-boys. Ivy described one of these as 'highly unsuitable'; and I then argued with this view – what was unsuitable about a partner, whatever his age, who kept one happy?

'Do you mean happy *in bed*?'

'Yes.'

As always, Ivy showed not the least disapproval – though she certainly showed surprise – at this revelation.

The toy-boy to whom Ivy referred was not always honest. On one occasion I was present with Angus Wilson at a party at which Viva began to bewail her losses – this or that Meissen figure had gone missing, she felt sure that money had been abstracted from her bag, the 'little wretch' was constantly asking for loans which he never returned. Angus was firm: 'If, when you're in your sixties, you have a lover in his twenties, then you just have to expect that kind of treatment.'

'What a cruel thing to say!' Viva wailed.

It seemed to me a very sensible thing.

Viva had had little formal education, despite some years spent in a convent in Belgium. But she was a naturally intelligent woman, who had been quick to learn from a number of distinguished men attracted by her wit and beauty. These had included Cecil Sharp, Augustus John, Peter Warlock, Norman Douglas. From time to time she would visit me in Brighton, when we would invariably take a stroll through the Lanes. Each such stroll was a lesson to me. She would point out this or that object – holding it up, if it was not too bulky, in one of her small, beautifully shaped hands – and then lecture me about it. To my errors of judgement she was always severe: 'That's a made-up piece!' she would cry out in horror; or 'You *can't* like that. It's sheer hell!'

On one of Viva's visits to Brighton, I took her to Preston House, where I introduced her as 'Mrs King' to the then curator. Subsequently, in conversation with her, he referred to me as 'your son'. Viva was outraged. 'He is not, repeat *not*, my son! Let's get that clear once and for all.' Later, she remarked to me, 'If he had mistaken you for my husband I shouldn't have minded so much. . . . Though I shouldn't have liked it,' she added.

Viva struck up a close friendship with April Ashley, the former merchant seaman who had, with some surgical assistance, converted himself into a statuesque, beautiful woman, albeit with extremely large hands. I always thought that Viva was in love with April. One day she said to me, 'I must get April to show you her Casablanca slit.' It was the last thing that I wished to be shown.

Viva behaved badly as Ivy's life drew to its close. She had often been a guest at the luncheons and dinners; but now, as Ivy shrank and her mind seemed to shrink too, Viva would rarely visit her. In the end, she stopped visiting altogether. To be fair to her, she was one of those people who are terrified of death – it is as though they believe death to be contagious. Less commendably, she also now found that Ivy had become – as she once put it to me with the earthy language she favoured – 'such a fucking bore'. The result of this neglect was that Ivy cut her out of her will. Why this had happened, Viva could never comprehend – 'We were so close, I was one of her oldest and closest friends! Why did she leave that brooch and that money to Madge and fuck-all to me?'

Here she showed me a gun-metal facet of a character which was for the most part made of gold. She showed me a similar facet over her always entertaining and often moving memoirs, *The Weeping and the Laughter*. It was I who – to my later regret, since I should like to have used it for this autobiography of mine – gave her her title; strongly recommended to Macdonald that they should publish the book; and eventually spent many hours reassembling its dislocated events, checking its facts, tidying up its syntax, and correcting its spelling – as Angus had done, to certain sections, before me. Since Viva, unlike L.P. Hartley, was an amateur, one might have expected some small acknowledgement. But this, in contrast with his generosity, she was determined not to provide. She barely thanked me personally and offered no thanks in the book. When she gave a launch party, she 'forgot' (her explanation) to invite me; and when Herman Schrijver said to her, 'I gather that Francis gave you a lot of help,' she responded, 'What on earth are you talking about? It's all my own work!' Gertrude Lawrence was more honest. Godfrey Winn told me that, when he commented to her that her autobiography, *A Star Danced*, was 'not really worthy of her blazing talent', she responded with a smile and the explanation: 'Yes, I know. But the young man who ghosted it was so terribly attractive!'

After one of her teas, Ivy would often ask me to stay on for a drink when the other guests had left. Until that moment we would have either gossiped about mutual friends or discussed such trivialities as whether Twinings' Earl Grey tea was superior to Jackson's, the increasing inefficiency of Barker's grocery department, or the behaviour of her Japanese neighbours. Now, sitting close to the fire, she would begin to talk of books. Often these were novels of the Victorian or Edwardian past: *The Real Charlotte* by Somerville and Ross, *Helbeck of Bannisdale* by Mrs Humphry Ward (I have always been grateful for that recommendation), Conrad's *Under Western Eyes*, Edith Wharton's *Madame de*

*Treymes* (a book I have still to read). She would also talk of contemporary novelists, often with sympathy, particularly if they were known to her, sometimes with asperity. Having taken against Pamela Hansford-Johnson, firstly because, at their initial meeting, she had arrived late (a cardinal sin in Ivy's eyes) and secondly because she had written about Ivy a British Council booklet which Ivy contemptuously dismissed as 'footling', she remarked of her to me, 'The poor dear writes so much and thinks so little that one fears that words have lost all meaning for her.' Of Iris Murdoch she remarked on one occasion, 'I do wish that she had not got involved in philosophy. If she had studied domestic science or trained to be a Norland nurse, I'm sure her books would have been much better.' Having read and apparently liked my early novel *Never Again*, she asked me whether I had ever thought of writing a sequel. No, I answered; had she ever thought of writing a sequel to any of her novels? 'No.' She stared for a long time into the fire. Then she turned her head to me: 'But then my novels end with a full stop, as it were.' On another occasion, she accorded me the dubious praise: 'At least you know how to *build*. Now poor Olivia has no idea of *building*. The materials are good but they're all over the place, just all over the place.'

Ivy once told me, as she told others, that what she most valued in a friend was 'availability'. She had not at all liked it when I had taken my flat in Battersea – remarking, with a grim expression, when I announced my imminent move there, 'I once had a maid who came from Battersea' and always refusing any invitation to cross the river to visit me ('No, I'm afraid it's just too far. One would need a taxi and one might not find one to return.'). She had liked it even less when I had moved to Brighton, even though I used to come up at least once a week to see her. 'Brighton is all right for a day trip,' she told me more than once. She herself had, in fact, spent her childhood and adolescence in Hove.

Often, when I was out with her, I would catch her talking to herself, not me, as we walked slowly down the street. As she repeated the same sentence over and over, each time in a slightly different form, I realized that she was trying out some piece of pungent dialogue for the novel in progress. One of these sentences remains with me: 'Why do people talk of a good deed in a naughty world, and never of a naughty deed in a naughty world? After all, there are far more naughty deeds than good ones.' At first I thought that she was addressing me, and all but answered.

One afternoon we were both guests, along with another dear friend of mine, Edith Clay, at tea with George Furlong and his friend Rex Britcher. George was the kindest of men but a far from lavish host, so that Ivy would often remark to me, as we left the house, 'That's not what *I* call a tea.' On this occasion there was nothing to eat but a Madeira cake. When George offered Edith a slice of this, she refused it – 'I'm recovering from jaundice and the doctor tells me that for the present I mustn't eat anything with egg in it.' Ivy bit into the slice of cake which George had already served to her. She munched appraisingly, head on one side. Then she said, 'I think you'll be *quite* safe with *this* cake, Edith dear.'

The Furlong house was packed with valuable antiques. On one occasion, Ivy gazed around the sitting-room and then said, 'I wonder if this room isn't just a little bit underfurnished.' In her will she left George and Rex a set of Chippendale chairs. The bequest was, I am sure, an indication of love and gratitude; but I suspect that it was also a tease.

Ivy also left eight mirrors, collected by Margaret Jourdain, to eight writer friends. Kay Dick and Kathleen Farrell, who had lived together for a number of years but were now estranged – 'So sad, I do wish they'd get together once more' – were left identical mirrors. I was left a Regency one, no doubt because I then owned a Regency house. Olivia Manning was left a grim Jacobean one. After Ivy's cremation, her executor, Hester Marsden-Smedley, invited all those left pieces of furniture to go back to Braemar Mansions to collect them. This did not strike me as an appropriate occasion and to Hester's annoyance – 'Really, this is going to be *most* inconvenient!' – I deferred picking up my mirror till another day.

That same evening Olivia was on the telephone. It was most strange, she was sure that the labels on the mirrors must have got switched. Ivy had always told her that she was to have the Regency mirror, but my name had been on it and Hester had refused to let her take it away. The other mirror was so clearly a *man's* mirror. It must have been that mirror, not the Regency one, that Ivy had intended for me. Might we do a swap?

I declined firmly.

A few days later I heard that Olivia had taken her mirror to be valued at Christie's and had been astounded to learn that it was Jacobean and worth far more than my mirror or, indeed, anyone else's. I then rang her up. 'Oh, Olivia, I have a terrible conscience about the mirrors. I feel sure that there must indeed have been some mistake with the labels. Let's do a swap, as you suggested.'

There was a long silence at the other end of the line. Then Olivia said, 'That's sweet of you, Francis. But, you know, I've really got rather attached to my mirror, hideous though it is. So if you don't mind . . . let's leave things as they are . . .'

We left things as they were. Someone told me that Olivia eventually sold her mirror. Mine hangs in my sitting-room.

Ivy had been furious to learn that Rose Macaulay had left something like £90,000 at a time when that sum was worth far more than today. She had always imagined Rose to be impoverished – 'I have her round so often not merely because she's such an amusing talker but because I really believe that she hasn't the money to feed herself properly.' Now it was as if Ivy herself had played a similar confidence trick on her friends. We had all been worried about how she was 'managing'; and here she was being carved up (as Viva inelegantly but vividly put it) for about the same sum as Rose.

I have often speculated about the nature of the relationship between Ivy and Margaret Jourdain. But since Jourdain had died before I met Ivy and since, in answer to the sort of over-inquisitive probings in which I often mistakenly indulge, Ivy maintained an affronted reticence, I find it difficult to reach a conclusion. Herman had a story of Ivy telephoning him, in extreme agitation, after Margaret's death. He rushed round to the flat. Ivy was kneeling by the gas-fire in the drawing-room, in her dressing-gown, with her hair, assumed by so many to have been a wig, hanging to her shoulders. She raised a tear-stained face. Then in anguish she cried out, 'My man has gone! My man has gone!' But since he gave a different version of this affecting story to others – according to this version Ivy muttered the words to herself while climbing the stairs to his flat – I have a hunch that, as so often, Herman was here revealing the frustrated novelist within him. My own guess is that the two women were indeed wedded; but that, though far more satisfactory than most heterosexual marriages, theirs remained a *mariage blanc*. After Margaret's death, Ivy all too plainly had her crushes, the last of these being on Madge.

I had many postcards and occasional letters from Ivy; but they usually consisted of little more than things like 'Would next Tuesday do for you for tea? Elizabeth and possibly Olivia will be coming.' One letter, however, is often in my mind. She wrote it to me, on 22 June 1969, only a little more than a month before her death. The novel to which she alludes is my *A Domestic Animal*:

Dear Francis

You must be fearing I had left the earth; and its binding forces hardly increase. May I ask one question? Has this double world the same significance as it would have here, or anything approaching it? Just *Yes* or *No*, and we will pass on.

The book is the strongest you have done, and quality seems to break in everywhere, or perhaps rather to break out. You have great gifts, and the present misfortunes will not alter its inevitable end. You may come to say you are glad it all happened. It is better to be drunk with loss and to beat the ground, than to let the deeper things gradually escape.

Do come and see me when you can.

Yours always with love,

Ivy.

To the question posed in the first paragraph, I could give no answering *Yes* or *No*, since I could not understand it. But the advice in the second paragraph often came back to me during a terrible period of my life, later to be described. Ivy herself never 'let the deeper things gradually escape', and, during that terrible period, I tried not to do so, accepting my suffering instead of trying (as I was often tempted to do) to pretend that it did not exist.

There was something sibylline about Ivy. She had an unnerving ability to see into the inmost recesses of one's heart, as into her own; to find there things that were often unworthy and even evil; and yet to feel no shock or outrage. Equally unnerving was her total rectitude. Like Sybille Bedford's, this rectitude always struck me as Roman, not Christian; and as with Sybille Bedford, I always felt that one could go to Ivy in the search of some solution to a moral problem in the certainty that the answer which she gave one would be the right one.

That tough old writer Elizabeth Sprigge, who produced the first biography of

Ivy, once remarked to me (I quote from memory), 'It's terribly difficult to believe that a woman whom one might mistake for an old-fashioned housekeeper could have produced those Sophoclean novels.' But I never found it in the least difficult. Character and books were all of one granite piece.

Of all Ivy's friends, Herman was the one closest to her. At first this surprised me, since the knowledge and impeccable taste which, like Madge and Viva, he brought to the visual arts, certainly did not extend to literature. On one occasion, he tried, in all seriousness, to persuade me that Marie Corelli was a novelist of the stature of Mrs Gaskell and George Eliot. On another occasion, he was full of a no less eccentric enthusiam for the work of Hall Caine. Although he had many writer friends – it was at his flat that I first met Laurens van der Post, Rebecca West, Anna Kavan, Maurice Collis, Rhys Davies – he gave little evidence of ever having read anything that they had written. By his own admission he could not do with the characters in Ivy's novels – 'I hate people who never stop talking' – and had therefore long since decided not to read them.

What then bound him and Ivy so closely together? On his side was his past admiration for Margaret Jourdain and his gratitude to her for advice and help in his early years as a Jewish foreigner attempting to make a career in a then often anti-Semitic England. There was also a pride, which I always found rather touching, in being the confidant and protector of a woman whom many of his friends (myself among them) claimed to be a genius. The nature of that genius was not something he could grasp; but he was prepared to take our word for its existence.

Ivy loved in Herman what she loved (as I have indicated) in Madge, Viva and many other of her friends: the glamour of someone totally at ease in the fashionable world. A friend of Ernest and Wallis Simpson before the break-up of their marriage, Herman had been called in to redecorate Fort Belvedere immediately before the war – 'He [Edward VIII] was an absolute darling, though terribly stingy, she could be a dragon.' After the war, he had frequently crossed the Atlantic to decorate houses and apartments for American millionaires, whose taste – or lack of it – he would subsequently deride with incomparable verve. On a more humble level he would appear, then one of the few males to do so, on 'Woman's Hour', dispensing worldly advice on such topics as buying Christmas presents for your menfolk or how to get on, while not getting off, with your boss. Ivy would consult Herman about any practical problem, from renewing her lease to buying compost for the plants which she so lovingly tended on her sooty balcony. He was the only person whom I ever heard tease her or chide her. Like a young girl, she would respond to the teasing with something like 'Oh, Herman, you *are* naughty!'; and to the chiding with something like 'Yes, that wasn't the thing to do, was it?'

Herman and I became instant friends. He was the best host I have ever known, conspiring with his Italian maid Maria to produce delicious food and coaxing even a guest as recalcitrant as Cyril Connolly to be gracious to the dullest of the other people present. I have no memory of Herman ever giving a cocktail party, although occasionally he would go to one; and I never attended a luncheon or dinner-party at which more than four people sat down to the table. Herman believed in general conversation, and if the numbers were more than four, then there was a danger that that might be forfeited. He also believed in keeping spouses apart, inviting one one week and the other the next. To this some spouses objected; but he would be adamant – 'They know each other's stories by heart and so either sit back, bored stiff, or constantly correct each other.'

As one would expect from one of the leading interior decorators of the time, each of Herman's flats which I visited, the first in Brompton Square and the second in Onslow Square, was a model of artistic contrivance. Neither was big; but, largely through a cunning use of mirrors – mirrors not merely on walls but on doors, on ceilings and acting as surrounds for windows – each appeared to be so.

In contrast to Ivy's flat, full of valuable pieces collected by Margaret Jourdain but none the less oppressing the spirit with its drabness and dreariness, neither of Herman's flats contained anything of the first class and yet each gave an impression of elegance and opulence. There was an unexpected, sometimes even bizarre, yet always successful juxtaposition of objects from different countries and periods. There was also a smell, never strong, never sweet, never cloying, always agreeable, which I could not define, often though I tried. In answer to my query about it, Herman replied evasively, 'Oh, it's something of this and something of that.'

Because of the lavishness of not merely his hospitality but his whole way of life, I assumed that Herman, like Clifford Kitchin, must be extremely rich. In a sense, he was extremely rich, since the whole fabric of his life was an extremely rich one; but on his death he left far less than I or any of his other friends had expected. When he visited Brighton, he would always refuse to stay with me, preferring, as I myself now do when invited to stay, to put up in a hotel and so to be free to follow his own routine. At the Royal Crescent Hotel he always wanted the same room, the best he maintained, which overlooked the sea and yet was not too noisy. He tipped everyone lavishly, telling me, as Somerset Maugham had done before him, that it was a myth that people resented being overtipped. Certainly no one at the Royal Crescent Hotel resented it, quite the reverse. Herman was served with alacrity in the bar, the restaurant, at the porter's desk. The waiter would whisper confidentially to him – at the table by the window to which we had immediately been ushered – 'I shouldn't have the sole, sir. It's not all that fresh this evening' or 'The lamb's a bit tough.'

By then, plump and ailing, he had none of the vigour which Viva, at least ten years older than he, would display on her visits. We would amble a short distance along the front and then seat ourselves in one of the shelters; or we would take a taxi into the town and then pass through one or two rooms of the museum or the Pavilion before Herman would say, 'Let's go and have some tea.' When I suggested that David might drive us over to Sissinghurst or up on the downs, Herman demurred. He was a man of cities, not of the countryside.

In general, he showed great social adroitness; but this, unaccountably, failed him in the case of our mutual friend Elizabeth Taylor. Elizabeth, like Herman a perfectionist in the kitchen, had invited both of us to luncheon in Penn. She had first fixed a date with him and had then telephoned to confirm that the same date would also suit me. Exactly a week before this date, I received a telephone call from Elizabeth at about half-past one. What had happened to us? she asked.

'But Elizabeth, you asked us for next Wednesday!' I protested.

'I certainly did not!' Now she sounded as if she were on the verge of tears. 'The pheasant is all dried up – and the potatoes look black – and ...'

'Shall I come now?' I had in fact already eaten luncheon.

'That's no use! You wouldn't get her until four o'clock at the earliest.'

'Well, would you like us to come to dinner instead?'

'No. Not at all! We're going out to dinner.' Rage had succeeded the tears.

I at once wrote her an abject apology, although I was convinced that the error had been hers. How could I have done such a thing? How could she forgive me? I hated to think of all that superbly cooked food going to waste. Herman reacted quite otherwise. He got his secretary to telephone Elizabeth. Mr Schrijver and Mr King could not possibly have made a mistake. She (the secretary) had entered the date in Mr Schrijver's diary and had then confirmed that date, to make doubly sure, with Mr King.

Elizabeth soon asked me to luncheon on another date. It was many months before she asked Herman. It is sometimes better not to insist that one is right – however right, in fact, one is.

Elizabeth was both an extraordinarily attractive woman and an extraordinarily kind one. When I was in a nursing-home, run by nuns, in Beaconsfield, she would often come to visit me, even though it was there that she had had an operation for the cancer that was eventually to kill her and so the place might have had bad memories for her. (I had first learned of this cancer at a dinner-party given by the painter E. [Edna] Box. We had been talking of astrology and Emlyn Williams, another of the guests, had commented, 'I wish there wasn't a sign called Cancer. The mere mention of it makes me shudder.' Elizabeth then said calmly, 'I don't see any reason why you should shudder. I am an example of someone who has recovered from cancer.' Sadly the recovery was not permanent.) On one of her visits to me, Elizabeth brought a smoked trout, since she knew that the quality of the food did not rise to the quality of nursing. She handed the trout over to one of the nuns, asking that it should be served to me at supper. When the trout arrived that evening, it had been boiled. Accompanying it were boiled potatoes and boiled cabbage.

There was always, for me, something enigmatic about Elizabeth. Outwardly, she appeared to be a typical upper middle-class housewife and mother; but inwardly I guessed that she was someone wholly different. A dedicated communist in her youth, when my sister Pamela had known her, she retained her left-wing stance, albeit modified, up to the end of her life, so that, at the time of the colonels, she refused, when on a cruise, to disembark anywhere in Greece. It was useless for me to point out that the only harm that this kind of boycott caused was not to the regime but to the wretched people whose livelihoods depended on tourism.

Elizabeth once came, seemingly alone, for a week's visit to Brighton. Like Herman, she politely declined my invitation to stay. Unlike him, she would reveal nothing about what she had been doing when she and I were not together – 'Oh, I went out for a little exploration,' 'Oh, I had dinner in a restaurant somewhere on the borders of Brighton and Hove,' 'Oh, I don't know, I just read,' she replied to my probings. I convinced myself from her air of happiness, even joy, that she was having an escapade of some kind. But she was not the sort of person to announce it or confirm it. As Ivy, who was devoted to her, once remarked, 'Elizabeth keeps her own counsel.'

Ivy told me that, when she had first known Herman, he had been 'very good-looking – in a Jewish sort of way'. Overeating and illness between them had destroyed those good looks by the time I came to know him; but he still had an incomparable charm, derived in part from the readiness of his wit and in part from his genuine interest in everything anyone was doing. Like some no longer sexually attractive people, men and women, whom I have known, Herman managed to delude himself into the belief that men, even those outwardly heterosexual, had only to set eyes on him to fall for him. Thus, he once told me a story, pure fantasy I am sure, of an encounter with a taxi-driver. 'He was really stunningly beautiful. He had these wide, wide shoulders and these wonderful high cheekbones. As I got out of his cab at the flat, I gave him a *huge* tip. He examined it in his palm and then he said, "What's this then? Are you queer or something?" "Yes," I replied. "I'm madly queer." So he then jumped out of the cab, saying, "Right! I can spare you half an hour." ' There was another story of a beautiful young American, an exhibitionist, who would expose himself to Herman each morning from a window across the square. Eventually, Herman had run into him in Harrods – 'and of course you can guess the rest.' The trouble with this story is that it is extraordinarily difficult to see across Brompton Square because of the trees.

When I told Herman about Giorgio, he immediately wished to meet him. He then gave his own, entirely characteristic, reason for Giorgio's failure to respond to my overtures. 'He's queer, of course. Well, if not queer, bisexual. Most Italians are. But the problem is that you're just too young for him.'

'Too young?' I was then in my early forties.

'Yes. It's obvious that he's a gerontophile.'

'What makes you think that?'

'Oh, you're so naïve! You've only to see the way he looks at me – eyes lowered, blushing slightly. And the way his voice trembles when he says anything to me. I find all that awfully attractive!' He put a hand over mine. 'But you needn't worry! I never steal friends of friends. I wouldn't dream of it. I wouldn't be at ease with myself if I did.'

Herman also maintained that Simon Blow, whom I introduced to him in the last year of his life, was similarly smitten. 'He's always coming round or ringing up. Well, he had that totally unsatisfactory father and I suppose he's looking for a father-figure. But he's just not for me – far too spindly and fidgety.'

No less preposterously Herman persuaded himself that Edna Box's husband, Marsden Fleming, a Canadian professor at Imperial College, was secretly attracted by him. It was useless for me to protest that Marsden had been married twice and was the father of children. To Edna, dining without her husband at the flat, Herman suddenly confided roguishly, apropos of nothing, 'I have a funny little feeling that Marsden is rather sweet on me.' Edna was furious. She was too much of a lady to spit on him, as Madge had done, but as we descended in the lift, she remarked, 'That's the last time I'll come here.' And so it was.

Edna lived in a beautiful house, once inhabited by the painter Zoffany, on Strand-on-the-Green. After the death of Marsden, she slowly went to pieces: painting less and less, seeing fewer and fewer people, rarely going out except to exercise a beautiful chocolate-coloured Labrador, drinking more and more. It was terrible to see a once brilliant spirit slowly being extinguished. Each Christmas Day Diana Petre and I used to go out at midday to take her lunch, Diana the food and I the wine. But it was virtually impossible to rouse her from a melancholic torpor. She had a series of au pairs and, on one occasion, since the girl was in the house and it was Christmas Day, Diana and I suggested that we should ask her to join us at our picnic in the upstairs sitting-room. But Edna declared, 'Oh, no, she'll be far happier on her own.' When, in order to make some coffee, Diana and I went down to the kitchen – a dark, grimy room, with an old-fashioned refrigerator which was always empty except for milk, butter, eggs, a pot or two of yoghurt – we found the au pair sitting disconsolate by herself, a plate of Heinz sausages and baked beans (we could see the opened tin on the table) before her. Diana chatted to her, having discovered that she was French. Then we heard Edna call fretfully, 'What's happened to you? What's going on?' Grief, like love, can make people extraordinarily self-centred.

Diana and I both imagined that Edna, now impoverished, was having difficulty in keeping up the house. When she died, she left some six million.

Edna's reddish wig was always, for some reason, a source of fascination to Herman. 'Did you notice how she kept absent-mindedly pushing it off her forehead, so that you could see the wisps of grey hair beneath? I wonder if I should invest in a wig,' he mused. I could not be sure if he were joking or not.

It was through Herman that I met a novelist, Anna Kavan, whose work I had admired since, in my late teens, I had read her remarkable account of her stay in a Swiss mental hospital, *Asylum Piece*. My King aunt Evelyn had been a patient there at the same time. Unfortunately Anna struck me as so self-obsessed that my admiration for her books never extended to her. At our first meeting, she sat through most of dinner in total silence. Clearly she did not like me, I decided. Then, at nine o'clock, she jumped to her feet, excused herself hurriedly and left the room. She was gone for several minutes, during which Herman went on talking as though nothing were amiss. When she returned, it was as though a brilliant light had been turned on in a previously darkened room. She began to talk with extreme rapidity, to fascinating effect. After she had gone, I said to Herman, 'Do you think she was feeling ill during the first part of the evening? Perhaps when she was away all that time, she was being sick.' Herman laughed and then explained that, a drug-addict, Anna always gave herself 'a jab' at nine o'clock. I later realized that she was an example of one of those people with sufficient strength of character to turn a potentially fatal habit into a benign one. When she died, after some forty or so years of addiction, it was not from an overdose but from some disease of old age.

When Herman realized that he was fatally ill, he managed his death with the same sort of efficiency and style with which he had managed his life. He spoke freely about it, announcing to me, 'I've booked my seat on the transcendental express – first class of course, back to the engine.' Later, when I told him that a mutual friend, an American woman, had written to me that she was coming to England and that she was dying to see him, he replied, 'Well, tell her that I'm literally dying to see her – so she'd better make it snappy.'

His closest friends were all asked to choose something from the flat to remember him by. This was tricky of course; one did not wish to be mercenary or greedy. I opted for a picture which I had always admired, of a statuesque young woman, in Edwardian dress, watching an old man playing the last hole on a golf-course. Dusk is already closing in. Even then it had for me an eerie quality; and that eerie quality has intensified over the years, as I have long since persuaded myself that it depicts death watching Herman at the last hole of life. Painted by an artist called Pettigrew who, at an early age, was killed in the First World War, the picture has no great commercial value; but it was one of Herman's favourites, as it has now become one of my own. He was delighted that I chose it.

When I told Olivia Manning, also one of Herman's friends, that he had asked me to choose a keepsake, she was indignant: 'Why has he never asked *me*? How very peculiar!' Herman later told me that, when she next visited him, she not merely raised the subject but told him that what she would most like would be a pair of Blue John candlesticks which had been left him by Ivy. They were among the most valuable of his possessions. Herman had apparently smiled sweetly: 'I'm afraid, my dear Olivia, that I have already found a place for them at Christie's.' He did not ask her to choose anything else.

Some days before his death, he had Maria and his other residuary legatee, Charles Burkhart, sit on either side of his bed while his solicitor read out his will.

It was on the day before his death that I called for the last time to see him. He looked even paler than before and there was a terrible weariness in his voice; but we talked for a considerable time, with him saying, 'No, no, don't go yet, don't go,' each time that I attempted to leave him. The next day Dorothy Stroud, who had looked after him with so much devotion during his last weeks, telephoned to tell me that he was dead.

Although I have no evidence, I am convinced that, when life no longer seemed supportable to him, he made a planned exit from it with the same dignity and courage with which he had handled the preliminaries. Some people have the superhuman strength to manage the whole painful, humiliating process of dying, instead of being managed by it. I have known two such people. Herman was one; my friend David the other.

# — 4 —

## *Friendly Fire*

Just as a mountaineer is exhilarated by the challenge of a difficult rock-face, so I am exhilarated by the challenge of a difficult relationship. I have had many such relationships in my life, but none more difficult and none more exhilarating than that with Olivia Manning.

My friend Jonathan Fryer once told me that I liked my friends for their faults, not their virtues; and provided those faults are not cruelty, treacherousness or pusillanimity, that probably is true. But even more than for their faults, I like my friends for their absurdities. Olivia's was an essentially serious view of life; but her behaviour was often so absurd that even now, as I recollect it, I once again smile with all of the old admixture of exasperation, amusement and love.

Much of this absurdity had its origin in envy. For me, as for any male writer, however successful, Olivia felt no envy whatever. But if favourable attention were lavished on another female writer, she behaved like a little girl who finds herself ignored for some other little girl at a party – she, in effect, stamped her foot and shrieked, 'No! No! Me, me, me! Look at me!'

The first example of this that comes to my mind is a telephone call which she made to me, arousing me from sleep, at about eight o'clock on a Sunday morning.

'Have you seen *The Sunday Times*?' she demanded excitedly.

'No. You've woken me up. Why?'

'There's a review in it of Iris's latest.'

'Oh. Is it a rave?

I knew Olivia to share my affection for Iris Murdoch.

'No. It's *horrible!*' she answered with great glee.

When she herself received a horrible review, she would at once telephone to the literary editor of the paper in which it had appeared. Thus, similarly early on a Sunday morning, Terry Kilmartin was awoken at home to be upbraided by her. Why the hell had he allowed such an idiot to get his hands on *The Rain Forest*? When a review of another of her novels, equally insulting because of its tone and its brevity, appeared in the *Spectator* ('last and by all means least we come to Olivia Manning') she blamed Hilary Spurling, then the literary editor, and would thereafter constantly upbraid me for being 'so chummy with that smug little bitch'. It was useless to protest that no literary editor could be held accountable for an unfavourable review. Did she expect Terry or Hilary to suppress a review

237

merely because it was likely to annoy a friend? Her answer to that was Yes, of course.

As more and more women – many of them certainly of far less accomplishment – won the Booker Prize, Olivia became increasingly aggrieved. Eventually she put up her lover Jerry Slattery to write a letter to *The Times* protesting at the short-list. As a shareholder, he thought it a disgrace, he declared. Unfortunately, as someone – was it Martyn Goff, superefficient administrator of the Booker? – pointed out after consulting a list of shareholders, Jerry in fact owned not a single share.

When Edna O'Brien first appeared in London, Olivia would constantly enthuse about her to me: she was so beautiful, so talented, so modest. Then, after Edna O'Brien had had first one success and then one even greater, her books far outselling Olivia's own, everything altered: Edna would never have got where she was but for her youth and looks, she was pushy, she was scheming.

Once, when Oliva wailed to me in despair, 'Why, why, why don't people appreciate me more?', I tried to console her by telling her, as I genuinely believed, 'But, Olivia, eventually it all will come to you.'

'Yes, I know, I know. But I want it *now!*'

As one of her two literary executors, I feel a sadness as well as a pleasure when, as now frequently happens, film rights, television rights or foreign rights are sold. If only she were still alive to bask in this success!

I enjoyed Olivia's parties as much as Herman's; but they were totally different from his. Instead of the food prepared with such painstaking artistry by Herman and Maria, Olivia dished up the products of the local delicatessen. The lettuce was all too often watery and gritty; the tomatoes hacked into chunks and never peeled. Instead of four people, seated decorously round a candle-lit table, there would be forty, some seated, more standing and even more on the floor. Olivia was bold about inviting literary people met at the parties of others; Reggie brought along actors and politicians, Jerry medical colleagues. Through these parties I made many friends whom I still value.

For a host, Reggie's behaviour was odd. For a short while he would be present to welcome everyone with a bear-hug or even a wet kiss (I loathe being kissed in greeting or farewell by men), followed by an offer of cheap wine splashed into the glass. But eventually, as though overcome by an irresistible urge, he would heave across the room to me: 'How about slipping out to the pub?' I invariably declined this invitation, partly because I am not a pub-goer and partly because it struck me as cruel to abandon Olivia. With some cronies, Reggie would then depart. A few minutes later Olivia would come over to me. 'What the hell's happened to Reggie?'

'I think he's gone round to the pub.'

'The bastard! The shit!'

Since he invariably disappeared in this way at their parties, I never understood why each time she demanded what had happened to him and then reacted with such shock when I told her.

The relationship between Olivia and Reggie, delineated so unsparingly in so many of her novels, was decidedly odd. As everyone who has read her engrossing Balkan trilogy will know, they started their married lives in Romania just before the war. On the outbreak of war, Reggie's robustness contrasted admirably with the cravenness of members of the British Council – if we are to believe the trilogy. But are we to believe it? According to English people who were in Bucharest at that time, Olivia was in a blue funk and Reggie not far off it. As one of those people, who had returned from Romania to England and then joined Fighter Command, once pointed out to me, Reggie, being young, able-bodied and not a pacifist, could also have joined up. Instead he ended up as a lecturer at a university in Egypt.

His and Olivia's passage to Egypt was by way of Greece. On the overcrowded boat between Greece and Egypt, they were obliged to share a tiny, hot cabin with two friends of mine – Harold Edwards, also a university lecturer, and his Greek wife Epi. Extremely elegant in the Athenian manner, Epi had with her a crocodile leather hat-box, filled with Parisian hats. Olivia decided, despite her own numerous suitcases, that there was no room for this hat-box in the cabin, so that, each time that the Edwardses were away, she would hump it out on to the deck. Epi, seeing it on the deck, would then haul it back. By the close of the voyage, the two women were no longer on speaking terms.

Having arrived at Shepheard's Hotel, Epi heaved the hat-box up on to one of the beds, preparatory to unpacking it. 'Thank God that woman is no longer around!' She opened the hat-box. On top of her hats, crushing them, was the chamber-pot from the shared cabin. Despite this, the two couples eventually became friends.

While in the Middle East, Olivia suffered a tragedy which, I am convinced, had much to do with her later spikiness and malice. Having learned with delight that she was pregnant, she then learned with horror that the child was dead within her. This horror was aggravated when she was told that she would have to carry the dead child for its full term. She dealt with such an occurrence in one of the best of her novels, *School for Love* (which also contains an acid portrait of Robert Graves's sister, in whose house in Jerusalem she lodged for a time), and *The Rain Forest*. Since she never again became pregnant, I have always assumed that this experience made her either physically or psychologically unfitted for pregnancy.

Olivia was constantly telling me of her dissatisfaction with Reggie as a husband. This dissatisfaction is also made amply plain in both the Balkan and the Levantine trilogies. He was unreliable, unfaithful, unpunctual, slovenly, hopeless about money, she would say. But I think that what aggrieved her most was that a love which she felt should be focused solely on her was instead diffused on everyone. Reggie was in every way a big man: big in size, big of voice, big in self-confidence, above all big of heart. Anyone who appealed to him for help received it. As a producer at the BBC, he was known for giving employment to actors long past their sell-by date. At the outset of his acting career, my friend David had made repeated attempts to get an Equity card. He had only to mention his difficulty to Reggie, whom he hardly knew, for Reggie at once to get him one.

By the time that I knew them, Reggie and Olivia were no longer sexual partners. Reggie was already the lover of the woman whom he married after Olivia's death and, in addition, he was an energetic philanderer. Offered a lift in the car which Olivia always drove (Reggie did not even possess a licence), my sister Pamela was about to get into the seat beside her. But Reggie boomed, 'I'm not going to have an attractive bird like you sitting beside Olivia, instead of beside me. Denis Enright can sit beside Olivia.' As soon as the car moved off, Reggie at once put his hand on my sister's knee. A few seconds later he was attempting to put it between her legs. She was then in a dilemma, not in the least welcoming the overture but not wishing to upset Olivia by making a protest. A silent struggle between her and Reggie continued until the car reached her flat.

In fact, if my sister had audibly protested, Olivia would not have minded. Once, walking with them in Lewes, I suddenly found that Reggie was no longer with us. 'Where's Reggie?' When I said that I had no idea, Olivia turned back, peering through the doors and windows of shops which we had passed. Then she reached the post office. 'He's chatting up some girl in there.' So indeed he was. The girl was behind the counter and a long queue tailed after Reggie.

'Shall I fish him out?' I enquired.

'Oh, leave him. He can find his own way back to Brighton.'

When Reggie eventually turned up at my Brighton house, he put on a show of indignation. 'That was a nice thing to do, making a bunk like that! I had to hang around for ages for a bus.'

'Serve you right for hanging around ages with that girl.'

'What girl?'

'In the post office.'

'Oh, for Christ's sake! I was just checking up with her about making a banker's order for our television licence.'

Olivia laughed derisively.

By her own admission to me, Olivia had affairs with the novelists Henry Green and William Gerhardie. She would also occasionally make a pass at one of the lodgers in the basement flat of their house in Abbey Road. I know that in the case of both Julian Mitchell and Tony Richardson, this proved, not surprisingly, futile. It may be that with some other lodgers she had success. But for the most part she was content with Jerry Slattery, a man extraordinarily like Reggie both in physique and in character. I discovered the extent of Jerry's kindness when I fell ill with a mysterious numbness of the fingers and toes. My own doctor was on holiday and his locum, unable to come up with a diagnosis, told me what doctors usually tell one when they are baffled: 'I don't think it's anything to worry about. But if it continues, come back in six weeks or so.' Being the hypochondriac that I am, I immediately decided that I had either multiple sclerosis or motor neurone disease. Olivia, who was preternaturally sensitive to the feeling of others, however carefully concealed (this was one of the things that made her so good a novelist), asked me at our next meeting if anything was on my mind. I told her. Soon after, Jerry telephoned me. Would I like him to look me over? He than had a NHS practice near Swiss Cottage and gratefully I trekked up there to see him. He at once sent me off for a series of tests, after which he told me that there was nothing seriously amiss and prescribed vitamin B injections. He absolutely refused any payment – 'An act of friendship, old chap.' I sent him a crate of wine.

Jerry would visit Olivia every afternoon, however busy she might be on a book and however busy he might be in his practice. He was clearly devoted to her; but no less clearly he was devoted to his quiet, patient, highly intelligent wife. Of the four people involved in this odd situation, none showed any jealousy or hurt. They would entertain each other, take holidays together, behave to each other with unalloyed affection. I found this civilized and sensible.

When I heard that Jerry had died, I at once telephoned to Olivia, to comfort her as best I could.

'Olivia, I've just heard the news. I *am* sorry. I know how distressed you must be.'

'Yes, it's dreadful, isn't it?' she said. 'I just don't know where I'll ever find another doctor as good.'

People often used to speculate why Reggie and Olivia, living such separate lives (although I saw her at least once every fortnight, months would often pass without my seeing him), did not get a divorce or a legal separation. But they were like semi-detached houses: open on one side, totally bonded on the other. Like Herman with Ivy, Reggie was proud of Olivia's literary distinction. Like Virginia Woolf with Leonard, she constantly relied on him in her work. With little formal education, she would submit everything which she wrote to his appraisal. I suspect that, in the case of her reviews, his help was not confined to appraisal but extended to the actual writing of key sentences and even paragraphs. How much Olivia depended on his help was brought home to me when I remarked that in *The Rain Forest* she had committed the error of making a restaurant owned by Muslims serve pork. She was at once annoyed, not with me or herself but with poor Reggie – 'Reggie should have noticed that!'

It was at Olivia's parties that I used to run into Anthony Burgess. He and his first wife would lurch into the room, arms round each other, faces glistening, hair bedraggled, as though, victims of a shipwreck, they had just emerged from a turbulent sea. By the end of the evening both were often hardly coherent. Yet there was something extraordinarily touching about their dependence on each other, and I liked Burgess far more then than I do in these days when, long since rehabilitated by his tough and efficient second wife, an Italian, he shows himself so much more in command of his destiny.

Olivia told me that, only a week or two after the death of his first wife, Burgess suggested that she should marry him. She objected that she was already married to Reggie; to which he replied, 'Well, divorce him!' Whether this is true or not, I have never been able to confirm with Burgess, not knowing him well enough to do so.

Olivia enlisted me in her efforts to get an honour for Burgess, knowing that I shared her admiration for his work. Sadly and unaccountably, we were not successful.

Almost every week Olivia and I would make an excursion together. Often this would be to Kew, since she shared my love of the Gardens. We would lunch off a joint and two veg – this too was a love we shared – at the Maids of Honour and then we would wander from conservatory to conservatory. Far better informed than I about flowers and trees, Olivia seemed to derive an almost mystical pleasure from their silent contemplation. Then, suddenly, she would look at her watch. 'Oh, heavens, it's nearly four o'clock. I must get back home.'

'Must you? It's such a lovely day.'

'Yes, I must, I'm afraid.'

The reason, or excuse, was always the cat. It had to be fed or taken to the vet; she had forgotten to change its tray or leave it any water; she was afraid that she had shut it into the kitchen or the bathroom. A cat-lover, I began to hate that cat of hers, just as, a dog-lover, I used to hate Joe Ackerley's dog.

There was always this unaccountable tendency in Olivia to bring an abruptly premature end to something which had been giving her pleasure. Later, she would say, 'Oh, that was such a perfect day in Kew!', making me want to answer, 'In that case why did you have to rush off like that?' Like Roger Hinks, she always enjoyed things far more in retrospect than at the time.

This tendency to bring things to an abruptly premature end also extended to her party-going and party-giving. At a dinner-party at Herman's, in the middle of some conversation which she had patently been enjoying, she would glance at her watch; then again it was 'Oh lord, look at the time!', followed by the excuse that she had forgotten to do something or other for the cat. Reggie was never used as an excuse.

At her own parties, one usually sensed from her increasing taciturnity and restlessness – collecting glasses, patting cushions, gazing out of the window – when she wanted one to leave. When the parties were big it was, of course, more difficult for her to get this across to her guests. On one occasion, I was emerging from the lavatory of the flat in Marlborough Place, to find her in the hall, with her back to me. To my amazement she took a leap into the air to land with a loud thump. She took another leap. The thump was even louder. A third leap followed, so violent that I felt myself rocking on my feet. Then she hurried from the hall into the sitting-room: 'That's the neighbours,' she announced. 'Banging on the ceiling from downstairs. They use a broom. I can't have another show-down with them. The last time they were extremely rude to me. Threatened legal action for any noise after eleven. I'm afraid you'll all have to go.'

Everyone went.

I once told Olivia that I had a perfect relationship with my bull-terrier Joe: an inveterate fighter, he preferred humans to dogs; I preferred dogs to humans.

She crowed with delight. I was, of course, joking: I do not really prefer dogs to humans. But I think that in her affections Olivia really did put humans second to animals. She was active in a number of animal charities; she would, to my embarrassment, rush up to, say, some Japanese tourist outside Harrods to demand whether she was not ashamed to be wearing the skin of a tortured animal; and, in her will, she left most of her money to the Wood Green Animal Sanctuary, instead of to indigent friends or to something like the Royal Literary Fund.

Yet, despite this love of animals, she also had a terror of them as possible carriers of rabies. Her attitude to this disease, so rare in Europe, was totally irrational – as she acknowledged when she wrote *Artist Among the Missing*, about a man, resident in Egypt, who becomes obsessed with the idea that a lick from a stray dog may have infected him with the dread disease. When staying in the Pensione Seguso in Venice, Olivia insisted that one or other of her travelling companions should make sure that the establishment cat was not in the dining-room or lounge before she would enter either. In Greece, she forbad Epi Edwards to feed a horde of famished cats gathered round their table in an open-air taverna: 'Don't attract them here! Don't attract them!' she screamed in genuine terror. 'They might be infected.'

I eventually decided that this terror of rabies was really a fear of death. However bleak the forecast, a cancer sufferer always has some hope, however flimsy, of a cure or at least a remission. A rabies sufferer, like an Aids sufferer, has none. Rabies is not merely a cause of death; it *is* death.

Because I was a man and therefore not, in her view, in competition with her as a writer, Olivia was endlessly encouraging and helpful to me in my work. I have never in life either telephoned a literary editor to demand why no review of a book of mine has appeared or badgered writer friends to review it. Olivia, who would do both these things on her own behalf, would also do them on mine. I would beg her not to. She would not listen, telling me that I had no idea how to *push*. She was adroit and fearless at pushing.

Hearing from a mutual friend that I was, as so often in my Brighton years, floundering in debts and in the endless literary chores which I was obliged to accept in order to get free of at least some of them, she at once bestirred herself to procure me a grant from the Arts Council. Thanks to it, I was able to relinquish some of my reviewing and so concentrate more on the stories which made up *The Brighton Belle*.

In addition to our walks in Kew and the countryside round London, Olivia and I would often, like Viva and I, go round antique shops and galleries. But whereas Viva's chief interest was in the beauty or interest of an object, Olivia's was in its potential as an investment. Of course she appreciated its beauty and interest too, but that was always secondary. Was there about to be a boom in Art Deco, Baxter prints, Helen Allingham, Denby Ware, John Minton? She had an uncanny knack of predicting such booms, buying (for example) her Hockney at the bottom of the market and then seeing it go up and up in value. With an

American woman painter (name forgotten) she was less successful. 'I'm afraid I made a mistake there,' she told me some eighteen months after she had bought a picture by her. 'I'm going to take it back to the gallery and ask for my money back.'

'But no gallery will give you your money back.'

'We'll see.'

Extremely embarrassed, I entered the gallery with her. At first, the director was adamant – no gallery could be expected to take back a picture after so long a period. But Olivia persisted. Some assistant (she could not give his name or more than a vague description when the director asked for them) had assured her that, if she found that the picture did not fit in with the décor of her dining-room, she could bring it back. The director pointed out that it did not take eighteen months to decide whether something fitted in with the décor of one's dining-room. Olivia continued to argue. Eventually, to my amazement, the director agreed to give her back the full purchase price on condition that she bought another picture for the same or a greater price. Olivia bought one for a slightly lower price and managed to screw the balance out of the dealer. This picture, she informed me triumphantly a few months later, was 'going up'.

In antique shops Olivia would bargain shamelessly and ruthlessly. She would invariably ask for a special 'trade' price, and usually got it. But she was not trade, I would often protest to her, only to be told, 'Oh, you're so boringly honest. You've got to remember that I don't have your classy sort of background. My family had to live on its wits and fight for things. Yours lived on its investments and were fed things with a silver spoon.' She was equally contemptuous of my 'bourgeois morality' when I declined her offer to sign for me three pictures by Algernon Newton which hang in my house. 'A signature would add enormously to their value,' she told me. She had already appended wholly convincing signatures to two or three pictures of her own.

Despite her lower middle-class origins, Olivia was a Tory. Reggie, on the other hand, was a communist. Since his death and even before it, people have often told me, 'He was a KGB agent, of course.' Some of these people were in a position to know. One of them, a diplomat in Romania, told me of how Reggie, on a visit to Bucharest at the invitation of the Romanian government, took the Ambassador's secretary out to dinner, flirted with her and then began to question her closely about her work. She reported this. But Reggie was so indiscreet that I find it awfully hard to believe that he was a spy – even though, admittedly, he was no more indiscreet than Guy Burgess.

With her combination of discriminating taste and financial acumen, Olivia collected many beautiful and valuable things in the course of her life. These Reggie inherited. On his death he left them to his second wife, who eventually married the artist Paul Hogarth. The couple now live in Olivia's beloved flat among her beloved possessions.

I often wonder what Olivia would say about that.

*

Soon after I moved to Brighton, Viva King told me to be sure to get in touch with a friend of hers, Theodore Goodman, brother of Arnold Goodman, who lived in the same street as mine. I walked down the hill and inspected the small cottage. Then, since I was busy getting my house into order after my move, I decided to postpone doing anything about him.

Two or three days later I was taking my Pekinese dog Wang for a walk along the front when I saw a pudgy man waddling extremely slowly towards me, as though he were suffering from corns, with a Pekinese dog exactly like mine on a lead. When he smiled at me, I pointed at the dogs, which were now sniffing at each other, and said, 'Snap!'

He at once began to talk to me in his near-falsetto voice, volubly, eccentrically stressing unimportant words and slurring over important ones. He would apply the same eccentricity to his life, I would learn: making much of trivialities and slurring over what was important to him. He was extremely amusing. When he learned that we lived in the same street, he said, 'Oh, in that case you must come round soon for a *goûter*.' The word was a favourite of his, absolving him from the need to serve up a meal. So began a close friendship, which ended only with his death four or five years later.

Theodore was a man quite as discriminating and well-informed as his brother; but he had none of his brother's ambition and force of character. I always cite him as an example of how kindness and generosity are two entirely separate things – so that it is foolish to take as a criterion of a man's character his willingness, literally or metaphorically, to stand his round. Theodore was at once the kindest and stingiest man ever known to me – prepared to do anything for his friends except spend money on them. When I had a birthday he presented me with a box of the finest Irish linen handkerchiefs. 'Well, this time Theodore really has turned up trumps,' I thought. On using one of the handkerchiefs, I found that the initials TG had been embroidered on it. Clearly the gift had originated with someone else. Yet he was tireless in his efforts to publicize my work, to introduce me to people who might be of help to me, to comfort me in moments of despondency. In all this, he was the exact opposite of me: my genorosity all too often being a substitute for kindness. After all, it is far easier to order £30 worth of flowers to be sent by Interflora to a sick friend than to make a trek out to a hospital to visit him.

Stinginess is something which always interests and amuses me. If people are poor, then stinginess is justified. If they are well off and are as unwilling to spend money on themselves as on others, then it is venial. But if they spend lavishly on themselves, taking expensive holidays, eating expensive meals in restaurants, buying expensive clothes, and yet begrudge, say, a minimal Christmas bonus to a charwoman, then it is repellent.

Theodore lived surrounded by antiques and pictures and yet in extraordinary squalor. I found a Japanese student to be his au pair; and on his first day of work (Theodore was in London) the boy came up to my house and actually cried – he would never get that house clean, it was impossible, impossible. I consoled him by telling him (which was only the truth) that Theodore would never notice whether the house was clean or not. To this boy Theodore was infinitely kind, as he was to his more robust successors, also found by me, a Pole and Greek.

Through Theodore I met a number of people. One of these was the stage designer, famous in her day, Matilda Homan, a woman of great strength of character and a rebarbative manner. Liking difficult people as I do, I liked her. She was married to an eminent American economist, Paul Homan, who had been adviser to President Truman. The Homans bought a flat opposite the mortuary of Brighton General Hospital and Matilda then proceeded to embellish it at great expense. When it was ready, she invited a few friends to see the result. Among them were Theodore, Kay Dick and myself. Theodore and I had left our dogs at home; Kay Dick arrived with her dachshund. We all admired the thick, white carpeting which covered every floor in the flat – 'It cost an absolute fortune,' Matilda told us, 'but I feel it was worth it.'

After a prolonged tour of inspection, with Theodore leading us, in his shrill near-falsetto, in our exclamations of amazement and admiration, Matilda imperiously ordered Paul, old and extremely decrepit, to fetch us our drinks – 'They're all set out in the kitchen,' she said. Having taken the first orders, Paul tottered off. When he returned, shuffling along, with a tray held in shaking hands, Matilda let out a scream: 'Paul! Stop where you are! Stop at once! Stop! *Stop!*' Paul halted, blinking his eyes in confusion. 'Look what you've done.' She pointed to the floor.

By then we had all seen what he had done; or, rather, what Kay's dachshund had done. All along the thick white carpet which led down the hall from the kitchen to the drawing-room, there were indelible brown footprints.

When his health began to fail, Theodore sold his Brighton cottage and moved into the flat in Ashley Gardens which, he was delighted to tell one, he had for a bargain rent. There I would often visit him not so much for a *goûter* of tea and an exceedingly dry slice of one of Mr Kipling's cakes as for the encouragement and amusement of his company. A lover of music, he died exactly as he would have wished: in the middle of a concert in the Festival Hall. I still miss him.

After his death, Arnold Goodman wrote to tell me that he had left me the choice of one of his pictures in his will. Would I like to come to University College, where the pictures were housed, in order to make the choice? Of all the people whom I have met in public life, Arnold is the one whom I most admire. This is partly because he is so witty, partly because he is so adroit, but chiefly because he is so *sensible*. He now welcomed David and me, offered us a cup of tea, and then, when we had had that, waved a hand round the room. 'All Theo's pictures are hanging here. Choose which you like.' In pride of place over the chimney-piece I saw Graham Sutherland's famous portrait of Arnold. I pretended to inspect all the pictures, then pointed at the Sutherland. 'I think that's the one I really like best.' Arnold looked acutely embarrassed: 'I'm sorry. I'm afraid that belongs to Lord Rayne. It's on loan to me.' I laughed. 'I was only joking!' I then chose the Duncan Grant portrait of Vanessa Bell which hangs in my hall.

It was in the company of Theodore that, in a murky Brighton junk-shop, I picked up a portrait of a fisherman by Henry Tuke. As I extricated it from a pile of rubbish and, with an attempt at indifference, asked its price, Theodore suddenly squealed beside me, 'It's a Tuke, it's a Tuke!' I scowled at him to be quiet, and managed to buy the picture for £1. It is reproduced in Emmanuel Cooper's book on the painter.

Wholly different from Theodore was Godfrey Winn – or Winifred God, as we used to call him, not to his face. Along with Beverley Nichols, he was one of the last of the sob-sisters, writing highly lucrative rubbish for an adoring readership of women. He was extraordinarily industrious, ambitious, ruthless, courageous, fly. People would often ask me how I could be friends with such a monster; and I suppose that I should then have replied that, as Jonathan Fryer observed, I like people more for their faults than for their virtues.

Godfrey lived out near the campus of the University of Sussex, in what had been the dower house of Stanmer Park. With the charm which he could so potently exert when he wanted something, he had persuaded the dowager Lady Chichester to give him a life tenancy, at a small rent. Not surprisingly, after her death, her immediate descendants were vexed – particularly since Godfrey was constantly telling people, 'It's *the* most wonderful bargain.'

Godfrey frequently entertained me there, on the first occasion to a large cocktail party, which spilled out into the garden ('You *must* have a look at the Albertine on the far wall!' he admonished everyone). For him, it was essential that each of his guests should be important, since that importance would then add to his own. So it was that he introduced me as 'Francis King – in my view the best novelist of his generation', Brian Fothergill as 'our leading biographer' and David Tomlinson as 'that outstanding comic actor'.

Eventually a distinguished-looking man in a beautifully cut grey suit, purple socks and purple watered-silk tie appeared. Godfrey was, for once, nonplussed. 'This is Alex Kellar. I don't know what he is.' Alex Kellar was in fact Deputy Director of MI5. He was later to become a neighbour and close friend of mine.

On another occasion, Godfrey telephoned to me on a Sunday morning to ask me to come over for luncheon and to make a fourth at bridge. He had two women friends – both widows of South African millionaires, he hastened to tell me – coming over; but Lord Gage, who was to make up the fourth, had unfortunately fallen ill. Knowing that Godfrey played bridge, as he had once played tennis, to championship standard, I demurred: 'Oh, Godfrey, my bridge is appalling. It's kitchen bridge. And in any case I must get a review written for the *Spectator*.' He would hear none of it: it was to be only a friendly game; he knew that I would love the two South African women – one or other of whom might well eventually invite me to stay with her in Johannesburg; surely I wouldn't refuse to help out an old friend in a jam? My will always crumpled at any collision with Godfrey's. It did so now.

After an exceptionally tedious luncheon, we settled down to our bridge. Unfortunately I drew Godfrey as my partner. 'You don't *still* play a forcing two club, do you?' he asked me petulantly after the first hand. After the second, eyes narrowed, he said, 'I don't think you quite understood my lead of that Jack of diamonds.' By then I had already forgotten that he had led a Jack of diamonds. In the middle of the third hand, he suddenly flung down his cards. 'I'm sorry. I'm very sorry. But I really cannot continue to play with a fool like you.'

The women tried to calm him – it was only a game, what did it matter?

But Godfrey rose to his feet. 'No, I'm sorry. If one's a first-class player, one really cannot play with a total amateur. It's altogether too painful. And boring.'

We spent the rest of the afternoon admiring his Albertine and the other roses in his garden.

One such rose, a pale mauve, was named after Godfrey. He gave me one as a birthday present and I then planted it in my garden. A few months later he asked me, 'How is your Godfrey Winn doing?' I had not the courage to tell him that it was dead. 'Oh, very nicely,' I answered.

Godfrey, having had some bruising reviews for the first volume of his autobiography, asked me to help him with the second. Short of money, as so often then, I agreed. From then on, he always referred to me as 'the Prof'. He would also often say to other guests in my presence, 'I feel so embarrassed about employing a writer as distinguished as the Prof as an editor. But the sad thing is that, whereas an old hack like myself earns an average of sixty thousand a year, a novelist as fine as the Prof is lucky if he earns six thousand.'

One of my tasks in editing the book was constantly to remove the phrase 'Little did I then know . . .' A typical passage would describe how, invited to a party by Lady So-and-so, he had noticed a beautiful young girl, standing lonely and lost, by a window. He had hurried over and chatted to her. 'Little did I then know that I was chatting to someone who was eventually to achieve immortal fame as Scarlett O'Hara.' Another of my editorial tasks was to remove every other adjective, eventually causing Godfrey to complain, 'You're cutting me *to the bone.*'

My task completed, Godfrey summoned his editor at Michael Joseph, Peter Day, to Stanmer for a working luncheon with me. Peter, as so often when nervous, arrived in pain from his ulcer and sat on the edge of a chair in the conservatory, hugging himself, his face pale. When Peter left the room to go to the lavatory, I said to Godfrey, 'He's obviously ill. Why don't you send him back to London? Early next week I can go up to see him there.'

'I'm surprised at your suggesting anything so unprofessional. No, I'm afraid the two of you must get the work done today. I've promised Edmund Fisher [then editorial director of Michael Joseph] that he will have the typescript tomorrow.'

On the morrow Edmund Fisher had the typescript.

The autobiography is, in fact, an interesting one, particularly when Godfrey is writing about the war, in which he showed shining courage while accompanying, as a journalist, our perilous convoys to Russia. The second volume was far better received than the first, with one review beginning, 'It is not often that, in his fifties, a writer can drastically improve his style. Godfrey Winn has succeeded in doing so.' I was pleased with that; Godfrey less so.

One review – or lack of it – particularly annoyed him and was almost the cause of his casting me off, as he had cast off so many friends before me. Godfrey had convinced himself that, as a result of sending the book with a personal letter to Raymond Mortimer, Raymond would give it one of his lead reviews, then so influential, in *The Sunday Times*. Raymond did not oblige. When we were having a drink with Alex Kellar in a pub in Eastbourne, Godfrey suddenly started on the subject. 'When I think what I've done for Raymond in the past! After he had annoyed the Rothschilds by staying with them and scandalously undertipping, who put in a good word? I also drew the attention of Stephen Potter to Raymond as a possible broadcaster. I once lent him money. You know, I even once slept with him, after he had insisted and insisted. A ghastly experience, worse than Willy Maugham.' I tried to defend Raymond by saying that he could not be expected to review every book written by a friend, he had too many of them; but Godfrey would hear none of it. 'You see him, don't you?' he suddenly demanded of me.

I agreed that I did.

'Well, ring him tomorrow and ask him to do it. Tell him I'm *extremely* hurt. And annoyed.'

'I'm sorry, I can't do that.'

'What do you mean – you can't do that?'

'I wouldn't even do it for one of my own books.'

Godfrey was furious. 'You're a nice sort of friend, I must say. One has only to ask a small favour of you –'

Fortunately Alex then intervened. 'Godfrey, you're being unreasonable. Francis is right.'

The judgement, cool but authoritative – by then Godfrey knew Alex's occupation – put an end to the tirade. Our friendship was saved.

It was through Godfrey that I got another editing job. This was for a billionaire tycoon, still alive, whose name I cannot give, since it was part of our agreement that I should never reveal it. He wanted someone to 'knock into shape' (as he put it) his extremely long and extremely tedious autobiography. But at each knock, he would set up a wail: 'I merely want you to get the English right!' No reputable publisher would look at it, and it eventually appeared with a disreputable one, at his own expense.

At our first meeting, this tycoon asked how I wanted to be paid: would I like a fee or would I like a used car?

'May I see the car?'

'Certainly.' He then took me out of the house to the stable block which had been converted into garages. The first thing that I saw was a Volkswagen. I at once assumed that this was the car. Then he pointed to a Daimler. 'There she is! What do you think of her?'

'I'll take her,' I said, in a moment of reckless madness such as overwhelms me from time to time even today.

'Good! What I suggest is that you drive her back to Brighton now, and tomorrow my secretary can see to the legal side of things.'

'But I don't drive.'

He was amazed. 'Then why do you want a car?'

'I'm going to learn.'

The next day David went over and fetched the car. I then took driving lessons, passing my test at the first try. 'My God!' my instructor exclaimed, clutching his head and goggling, when he heard this. There followed a number of near-accidents and a number of nightmares in which I dreamed that I put my foot on the accelerator instead of on the brake and mowed down a screaming horde of schoolchildren. (This recurrent nightmare was the genesis of one of the better of my short stories, 'Children Crossing'.) Eventually I decided to sell the car; but since that was during the petrol crisis, I got only £300 for it. It had already cost me far, far more than that in repairs.

Godfrey was still an excellent tennis-player; but my Italian friend Giorgio was an even better one. Hearing of Giorgio's prowess, Godfrey invited me to bring him out to Stanmer for a game. The two began by holding their services; then, gradually, by dint of his greater agility and brawn, Giorgio began to gain the upper hand. 'Out!' Godfrey called, as one of Giorgio's cunning lobs fell just within the base line. 'Yes, that was out, I'm afraid, no doubt about it, no doubt at all,' he said firmly, when Giorgio questioned the verdict. 'Out!' he called again to a serve. Giorgio was far too polite to argue.

Godfrey won the match.

Later, when Giorgio had gone inside to shower and change, Godfrey said to me, 'Well, that was a lesson to you in the tactics of tennis. The important thing is not to win every point but to be sure of winning the vital ones. Do you see?'

I saw only too well.

Godfrey had a wonderful servant called Bardwell, whom he housed, along with his wife and offspring, in a pleasant house in Brighton. 'I've told Bardwell that if – if – he is still in my employment when I go, then the house will be his.' Godfrey was not always an easy employer; but, not surprisingly perhaps, Bardwell never showed the slightest inclination to leave him.

When Godfrey was going on a visit to Finland, I gave him an introduction to my old friend, Willy Huttunen, now headmaster of a Helsinki school. Willy entertained him to a tête-à-tête dinner in a modest restaurant and, at the weekend, took him to stay with a GP friend of his in his small cottage by a lake. One of my aunts later showed me the article which Godfrey had written about the visit in *Woman's Own*. 'The well-known novelist Francis King had kindly given me an introduction to Finland's leading educationist Willy Huttunen. Mr Huttunen gave a delightful dinner-party for me, at which I met all the leading people in his field. At the weekend he took me to stay with a famous brain-surgeon in the splendid manor house which he owns in the countryside outside . . .' So it went on.

Godfrey and Beverley Nichols had once been friends. Then there had been a rift between them. I enquired about the reason for this rift. 'Well, he behaved most offensively,' Godfrey replied. 'We were both at a party and I said, most generously, to the woman to whom I had been talking, "That's Beverley Nichols over there. He has more talent in his little finger than I have in my whole body." Then I went over to Beverley and I said, "I've just been telling that woman over there that you have more talent in your little finger than I have in my whole body." Beverley looked me up and down. Then he said, "Yes," turned on his heel and walked away. Well, I ask you!'

Godfrey had also quarrelled with that least quarrelsome of men, Arthur Marshall. Godfrey had written a play and Arthur had apparently been less than flattering about it. Godfrey then learned that Arthur had been spending Christmas with another of his friends, the former actress Adrienne Allen, now Mrs John Witney. Godfrey wrote her a letter of remonstrance: he was amazed that she should have Arthur in the house after the monstrous way in which he had behaved to him. Adrienne Allen replied, most sensibly, that she could only judge people as she found them; that she was sorry if Arthur had caused Godfrey offence; but that to her his behaviour had always been impeccable. This letter sent Godfrey into a towering rage. 'I left her my Bonnard in my will. But that Bonnard is never going to hang on her walls. I'm going to leave it to you.'

Sadly I never had the opportunity to hang the Bonnard on the walls of either Sotheby's or Christie's, since Godfrey died before the will had been changed.

Two or three days before his death, Godfrey had been to dinner with my mother and me. To my mother, who, in his eyes, must have been a woman of no importance, he was extraordinarily kind and friendly. This was one of his virtues: at a party he would at once pick out someone who was clearly ill at ease, and then set about charming him or, more often, her. He had done this to my mother when first they had met. On that last evening he told us how he had just spent a fortnight at Forest Mere, undergoing a cure. 'Look what it's done for me!' He jumped up from the dining-table and began to pirouette, hands on narrow hips, in front of my mother. 'I've lost almost a stone. Anyone would think that I was not a day over thirty-five – wouldn't they, Mrs King?' My mother agreed: 'Yes, you look wonderful, Godfrey, wonderful.' Godfrey pointed at me: 'Mrs King, you must do something about Francis, you know. His figure's all over the place. He should go to Forest Mere. In fact, I'll treat him to a fortnight at Forest Mere. It's extremely expensive but I'll treat him to one. If he isn't careful, he'll drop dead of a heart-attack. It's thoroughly unhealthy to carry round all that blubber.'

In the event, it was Godfrey who dropped dead of a heart-attack, while playing a game of tennis. He was clearly exhausted when the score stood at one set all; but, determined to be the winner, he refused to abandon the match. In death he found an opponent whom, for once, he could not cheat out of victory on the court.

*

Although I had been tipped off by a mutual friend that Alex Kellar worked for MI5, I assumed that this was something that I should on no account mention to him. I was therefore astonished that, when I arrived early for a dinner-party given by him at his flat in Clanricarde Gardens, he should tell me that a former colleague, the novelist John Bingham (Lord Clanmorris), would be among the guests. Later, Alex would gossip to me about such things as his work at Blenheim and Wormwood Scrubs during the war (one of my cousins had worked for him at Blenheim) and sharing a room with Anthony Blunt ('I never really liked him').

Like Olivia, Alex was essentially a serious figure, and yet at the same time a preposterous one. A tremendous snob, he pursued anyone with a title; insisted that one should wear a black tie to his dinners (particularly annoying for me, since I had long since outgrown my dinner-jacket and used to feel that I was about to suffocate in it); and employed handsome hunks, off-duty from the Household Cavalry, in white monkey jackets, to wait at his table. All too obviously a homosexual, he blissfully thought that no one was aware of this.

When I had moved to Gordon Place in London and he had moved, on his retirement, to a flat in Sheffield Terrace, I saw a great deal of him. He had clearly taken a shine to David, whom he would often summon on the telephone to do the sort of practical job at which David was so adept: mending a broken wireless, moving a telephone, changing a plug. After we had known each other for two or three years, he suddenly said to me, when the two of us were alone together, 'Forgive me for asking this question, Francis, but would I be right in thinking you were homosexual?' It amazed me that someone who had risen so high in MI5 should not long before have intuited the answer to this question. In fact, I was so amazed by it that I failed to say, 'And would I be right in thinking that you also are homosexual?'

Alex performed one extraordinary kindness for me. He had asked me how my novel *Act of Darkness* was progressing; and I had then told him that I was obliged to do so much reviewing in order to keep my head financially above the water that it had come to a standstill. The next day I found a brown envelope lying on my mat. Inside was £500 in £50 notes, with a brief letter to say that he could not bear to think of my not getting on with my novel; that he would like to lend me some money; and that he was giving it to me in notes and not as a cheque, since I had spoken of an overdraft. Eventually, when *Act of Darkness* appeared, sadly after his death, I dedicated it to him 'For that rarest of things, an act of totally disinterested kindness.'

Alex endured his final illness with remarkable valour. Once, walking up Church Street after nightfall, I saw a figure slumped in the doorway of an antique shop called The Lacquer Chest. I thought that it was one of the pathetic vagrants then increasingly common in the district; but, approaching nearer, I realized that, smartly dressed, his shoes gleaming, it was Alex. Was he all right? I asked. Through bloodless lips he told me that he had had 'a nasty turn' on his way back from a cocktail party. I helped him to his feet; took him home, where I poured him some brandy; and then, having been told that, no, he did not want a doctor – 'I don't think a doctor could do much for me' – I left.

A few days before this he had told me of an incident when he was spending a weekend, alone, in his cliff-top house near Eastbourne. In the middle of the night, he had been woken by a sound of tapping. Realizing that it was coming from the window of the bedroom, he had got out of bed and gone to it. Outside was a huge black bird. For a while they stared at each other. Then the bird flew off. I took this as an omen of imminent death. Whether he also did so, I did not have the courage or heart to ask him.

By then *Act of Darkness* had been completed and accepted. On receipt of the advance, I at once sent him my cheque for the £500. Months later – by this time Alex was very close to death in the Edward VII Hospital – I realized that the cheque had never been cashed. On my next (and last) visit to him, I said, 'Alex, you've never cashed that cheque of mine.' He closed his eyes and sighed. 'Oh, let's forget it. I don't need it now. I'm happy that it helped you.' At that, he seemed to go to sleep. Then he opened his eyes and whispered, 'Do you know who's sharing this room?' He raised an emaciated hand to point across at the figure asleep in the bed opposite. 'Lord Redmayne. He was once the Government Chief Whip.' That he and a peer should be dying in the same room was clearly of comfort to him.

Shortly after Alex's death, I received a letter from one of his two nephews. Among Alex's papers he had found an uncashed cheque of mine. He would be obliged if I now made out a new one, payable to the estate. I wrote and told him of my last conversation with Alex. He wrote back that he 'must insist' on my sending the new cheque.

I sent the new cheque.


Shortly before his horrendous death by hara-kiri, Yukio Mishima visited me in Brighton. The British Council sent him there by car.

'Is it all right for my driver to join us for lunch?' he asked as soon as I had greeted him.

Having invited some Brighton writers and academics, I was disconcerted. 'Oh, I'm sure he'd much rather go off on his own. I'll give him some money for his lunch and tell him to come back at six. I can take you around Brighton in my own car.'

The driver appeared to be delighted with this arrangement.

When Mishima was subsequently saying his goodbyes in the London office of the British Council, the woman who had been responsible for his programme asked him, 'Mr Mishima, who was the most interesting person you met in the course of your visit?' She expected him to name someone like Stephen Spender or Angus Wilson. But without a moment's hesitation he replied, 'Bill Brown.' The woman was puzzled. After Mishima had gone, she asked her secretary, 'Who is Bill Brown?' The secretary was also puzzled. Then she remembered that Bill Brown was the name of the chauffeur who had driven the writer to Brighton.

During our hours together in Brighton, Mishima spoke at length about his daily visits to a health club in London. He described the exercises; he spoke proudly of the weights which he lifted; he told me of the casual friendship which he had struck up with a policeman. Subsequently he complained to me about the behaviour of the poet Anthony Thwaite. He had always regarded Thwaite as a friend, he said. But after they had had dinner together the night before, Thwaite had failed to take him to a gay bar. But Thwaite was not gay, I protested. 'No, he is not gay. I know that. But he knows I am gay. In Japan we do everything possible to give our guests what they want.' It was useless for me to counter that Thwaite probably did not even know where to find a gay bar. 'He should have made enquiries,' Mishima replied implacably.

Mishima fascinated me, as one of those people who succeed in totally remaking themselves, turning himself from an effeminate weakling, who had dodged military service, into a modern samurai warrior. A similar person was Muriel Spark, who changed herself from the dowdy, dumpy, douce little Scots body whom I had first met in her Poetry Society days, into a glamorous woman of the world. So too was James (Jan) Morris, who changed himself into a replica of my beloved Aunt Amie.

When I first met Morris, before his transformation, I at once saw a physical resemblance between him and Mishima. Both were small, wiry, tough men, with a strong feminine component. Both, obsessed with turning private fantasy into public reality, went to extremes. But the extremes were the exact opposite of each other, Mishima determined to tear out whatever was feminine in his nature and Morris whatever was masculine. Each, in a sense, made a choice which involved death. But whereas James died, more happily, to be reincarnated as Jan, Mishima died to become a legend.


Joe Ackerley was a frequent visitor to me in Brighton. There was now a terrible aimlessness about his life. After his departure from *The Listener*, he had little to do but booze. When asked to produce a review, he could still do so with all the old trenchancy and elegance; but editors rarely asked him, and he was too proud to approach them. After his death, when I told Terence Kilmartin of this, he exclaimed, 'Oh, if only I had known that he *wanted* to review. I never realized!' In June 1965, Joe had had a return of one month to *The Listener*, in a brief interregnum between one literary editor, Anthony Thwaite, and his successor, Derwent May. The recall had had an astonishingly vivifying effect on him; but when he was once again back, as he put it, 'in the junk-yard', his spirits seemed to sink even lower than before.

Now all his love seemed to be concentrated on Queenie, his irascible, possessive bitch; and when, after agonizing far too long, he realized that the time had come when he must have her destroyed, the blow was mortal to him. From that time, I noticed a slow but inexorable deterioration in both his spirits and his health.

Joe did not as a rule care for small dogs; but he was fond of Wang. 'Funny little thing,' he would say, as he stroked him on his lap. Once he asked my mother, 'How do you suppose that he has sex with legs as short as that?' Unfazed, my mother replied, 'He doesn't have sex. He doesn't seem to be interested in it. But a breeder of Pekineses once told me that you stand the back legs of the male on a telephone directory.' Inevitably, Joe coaxed Wang, who had been trained to sleep in a basket in my bedroom, on to his bed. After Joe's departure, my daily called me into the guest-room. 'Look what's happened here! That naughty dog!' There was a large, damp stain in the middle of the bed. Strictly house-trained before he had come to me, Wang had never before done anything of that nature. I took him over to the bed, pressed his nose on to the stain and then slapped him. He squirmed in my grasp, gave a little whimper, and then looked up at me with reproach in his bulging eyes. He had every reason to be reproachful, since I learned later, from Joe's diaries, that he intermittently suffered from enuresis.

Not long before Joe's death, the designer John Drummond, then a lecturer at the Royal College of Art, lent him his elegant house, almost opposite mine in Montpelier Road, for a fortnight. Joe brought his sister Nancy with him. Of Nancy, beautiful, neurotic, demanding, I once remarked to E.M. Forster, 'She loves Joe, doesn't she?', to receive the emphatic reply (like many of Joe's friends, Forster did not care for her), 'Nancy is *in love* with Joe.' Joe clearly loved Nancy and was perhaps, in some measure, also in love with her; but since that love and that being in love both frightened him, they were transformed, in the later years when I knew him best, into what often seemed to be cruelly near to hatred.

During that stay in John Drummond's house, I said to Joe, met in the street with Nancy, 'Why don't you come to lunch tomorrow?'

'That would be lovely, darling. But what about Nancy? Do you want Nancy?'

'Of course.' How could I say No in front of her, even if I wished to do so – which I didn't?

'Are you sure, darling? She doesn't have to come.'

By then, Nancy and I had become fond of each other and I had begun to see her through my own eyes and the shrewd and sympathetic ones of my mother, and not merely through those of Joe and his often misogynistic friends.

Having always showed a pathetic eagerness to share in all Joe's activities, however uncongenial, Nancy had now come also to share in his boozing. Almost every morning of that holiday, the two would make their way down to the local, the Temple Bar, just before it opened; and just after it had closed in the afternoon, one would see them dragging their slow way up the hill again, back to the once spotless house which Nancy so rarely cleaned and then only perfunctorily.

Once, when they were making this slow progress home, Clifford Kitchin was standing in the bow window of my first-floor sitting-room, an after-luncheon cup of coffee in one hand. He looked down, and saw Joe, whom he did not like, and

Nancy, whom he did. 'Charles and Mary Lamb,' he murmured. Joe was leading Nancy, as though she were reluctant to follow, walking one step ahead of her, while his left hand grasped hers and his right arm hugged a wine bottle. There was a terrible pathos about them at that moment. Both had once been so beautiful and so high-spirited; and now they looked so shabby and so dejected.

Conscious, I am sure, of the imminence of death, Joe was now working intermittently on two tasks. One was to make ready for the press his last memoir, *My Father and Myself*; the other was to negotiate with the well-known firm of Bertram Rota the sale of the many letters which E.M. Forster had written to him. About both these projects he often spoke to me as his literary executor. *My Father and Myself* was to be published posthumously; but it was only to be published if Nancy and his two surviving half-sisters, Diana Petre and Sally Westminster, gave their assent. I was to complete the sale of the Forster letters and was then to persuade Nancy to invest the money, £6000, as otherwise 'the silly old dear' would only fritter it away.

Nervous about how much he had betrayed of his secret life and the secret lives of others, Forster had made some half-hearted attempts to recover his letters; but Joe had foiled him. As always in such cases, a moral problem was involved: the letters contained things that the writer wished to conceal from posterity and that the recipient felt that posterity should learn. There was also, understandably but less creditably, the question of the financial value of the letters to a man subsisting on a niggardly pension and worried that he had no capital to leave to the sister who, for so many years, had depended almost entirely on his support. Joe sometimes took a high-minded view of his refusal to let Forster have back the letters, writing on one occasion to Sonia Orwell:

How good he is. He would have felt safer, even in his death, to have had his letters returned, he thinks he is not a good letter-writer and betrays himself and others. It may be that he is *not* a good letter-writer, but whether he is or not, his letters, and his friendship, have been the major influence in my life from Cambridge onwards; and if I gave up his letters I should give up one of the foundations of my life. I expect he knows that, he knows everything; he tried it on out of nervousness, and has easily let it go.

He was being less high-minded when he wrote to Sonia:

I am interested . . . in securing for them [the letters] a sum of money which will enable Nancy and me to drink ourselves carelessly into our graves.

The irony here is that Forster, who disapproved of alcoholism in general and of Joe's alcoholism in particular, would have hated to think that the sale of his letters might enable anyone to drink himself carelessly into his grave.

Whether Forster ever found out about the sale of the letters is, in the view of his biographer, P.N. Furbank, uncertain. In moments of morbid guilt, Joe was sure that he had; and he would then seek from his friends some assurance that he was doing the right thing, not merely by himself and Nancy, but by Forster and posterity. Certainly it is odd that in his will, made before Joe's death, Forster should have left his once beloved friend only £500 out of a large estate. (The bequest was of course invalid – as I had to point out to a disappointed Nancy when, by mistake, the solicitors forwarded a cheque.) But Forster may well have decided to show so little generosity because he had already shown so much – responding to Joe's ill-judged request that the older and richer man should settle an income on him by giving him £1000, and financing trips to me in Greece and Japan, of which he approved, but also a lot of hard drinking, of which he did not.

It was with Joe that I invariably met Forster, usually in the Senior Common Room of the Royal College of Art, of which they had both been appointed honorary fellows. By this time people would often say of Forster, as they would say of L.P. Hartley, that he was 'a sweet old thing'. But under his courteous, gentle manner, I was always aware of the tungsten. When people exasperate or shock me by their behaviour, I go off them for a while and then return to them. In such cases, Forster went off them for ever. So it was with Harold Nicolson, who, as a BBC governor, had failed to support Ackerley against his editor, the Director-General and the other governors, in his attempt to publish a poem by Sidney Keyes considered by all of them – how long ago it seems now! – too obscene for *The Listener*. So it also was with Cyril Connolly. 'That wretched Cyril Connolly insists on coming here to see me,' Forster announced peevishly, when Joe and I joined him in the Senior Common Room. 'He wants me to sign some of my books for him.' Connolly arrived, with all Forster's works, pamphlets included, under an arm and proceeded to make Forster not merely sign but inscribe each as well. Forster, who loathed to sign copies of his books unless he had presented them, scratched away with a weary politeness. Then the waiter arrived to take the order for our drinks. I asked for sherry. 'A double sherry,' Forster told the waiter. Connolly also opted for sherry. 'A *single* sherry,' Forster said to the waiter, with a just perceptible emphasis. As soon as we had finished our drinks, Forster rose to his feet and said frostily to Connolly, 'I'm afraid that I must now take my friends in to lunch.'

People often found Ivy Compton-Burnett formidable; but I found Forster much more so. Once one had become her friend, Ivy was infinitely understanding and forgiving of one's sillinesses and sins. But with Forster one knew that if those sillinesses and sins became too frequent, he would have no hesitation in casting one into outer darkness – where one would stay.

In my Brighton years I saw Cyril Connolly from time to time, since he was living not so far away, in a house intended for the Gages's bailiff, on the estate of Firle House. I realized the extent of his mania for books when he was having a drink with me in my house in Montpelier Villas, not long before that meeting with Forster and Ackerley in the Senior Common Room of the Royal College.

Connolly told me that he had all my novels bar one. This was my first, *To The Dark Tower*. He had, he said, looked everywhere for it, without success. Could I perhaps let him have a copy? I pointed to a shelf: 'I'm afraid that's my only copy. Somehow all the others have gone.' 'What a pity, what a pity!' he said, suddenly looking mournful. A few minutes later, he said, 'I wonder if I could have a glass of water, just ordinary water, water from the tap.' Since there was no water on the drinks tray, I went out to the kitchen. When Connolly had gone, I found that the copy of *To The Dark Tower* had also gone – presumably slipped into the brief-case which he had with him. I was then in a dilemma. Should I telephone and demand it back? The situation was too much fraught with embarrassment. I did nothing.

On one occasion, Connolly invited me over to Firle to dinner with Elizabeth Bowen. He loved food and wine and knew a great deal about both. 'I think this is rather a good Beaune. Clos de Mouches.' He sniffed at the opened bottle, then poured a small amount into a glass for himself and then a half-glass for Elizabeth Bowen. He sipped, rolled the wine round his tongue, and sipped again. He pulled a face. 'Do you think this wine is corked?' he asked Elizabeth Bowen. She sipped. 'Oh, no,' she replied politely. 'It's wonderful.' He poured me some. 'What do you think, Francis?' I tried it. I know little about wine. But there was certainly something wrong. With great daring, I said, 'Yes, I think it must be corked. It tastes decidedly odd.' 'Of course it's corked!' Momentarily he sounded furious. He rushed over to the sink and emptied the bottle down it. I felt that he had planned to test the two of us. I had passed the test, Elizabeth had not done so. But he was equally angry with both of us.

At that period Connolly was attended by two women, his long-suffering and charming wife Deirdre, and another, whose name I have long since forgotten. On one occasion, when my friends and neighbours Peter and Albert and I were having tea with Duncan Grant at Charleston, Connolly and the two women also were there. We sat down to tea, a lavish one, spread out over the dining-table. Unfortunately, Peter and Albert and I had little chance to eat anything, as either one woman or another solicitously pushed every plate on the table in Connolly's direction and he then proceeded to demolish everything on it.

On form, Cyril was the most wonderful talker. But this form, like that of some temperamental tennis-player, a Virginia Wade or a McEnroe, would suddenly wobble and collapse. A morose look would come over his face; he would fall silent. Once, at luncheon with Herman Schrijver, he had kept Herman, Edouard Roditi and myself enthralled with an account of the scandal which eventually furnished James Fox with the material for his book *White Mischief*. When the time came to go, I offered him a lift in my taxi – since he was on the way to the London Library, I to the National Gallery. For a while during the journey, he continued to talk with all the brilliance he had displayed over the luncheon table. Then he stopped, staring moodily out of the window beside him. When I tried to question him, he answered with monosyllables. At the Hyde Park Corner traffic lights, he suddenly announced, 'I think I'll get out here,' and left the taxi. Perhaps I had annoyed him in some way? But Herman reassured me. 'He suddenly succumbs to that kind of *cafard*, and then he wants only to be alone.'

Soon after Connolly had become a father, for the first time, in his sixties, I remarked to him, 'I envy you, having a child.' 'Oh, do you?' he all but snarled. 'It means that I shall now have to slave away until I drop.'

I was in my house in Brighton on the morning of 4 June 1967 when Nancy rang to tell me that she had found Joe dead in bed. I at once rushed up to London. By the time that I had reached the dilapidated top-floor flat, 17 Star and Garter Mansions, above a cavernous pub overlooking the Putney towpath, both Sonia Orwell, who had hurried round to be with Nancy, and the doctor had gone. Nancy, who was surprisingly calm, told me how she had gone into Joe's bedroom, when he had not appeared for breakfast, and had then gone out again, imagining him to be asleep. It was only when she had gone in a second time that she realized that he was dead. She asked if I wanted to see him; and, though in fact I had no wish to do so, I said yes, since I guessed that that was what she would like.

Joe lay on his side, sheet and blanket drawn up over his shoulder – but whether by him the previous night or by Nancy or the doctor that morning, I could not know. There was no sign of struggle or distress on his face; but I did notice that the lips had a bluish tinge to them, as had the nose. It was easy to see how going into the curtained room in the morning, Nancy had supposed him to be asleep. Beside his bed, there was a half-drunk glass of whisky on a table. (When he stayed with me, he would always take a glass of whisky to bed with him; and the next morning I would often find it with an inch or so still in it.) Nancy pointed to his desk, many of its drawers now open. 'I found his will there. You'll want to see that.'

A close friend of Joe's, John Morris (at a dinner-party at my sister Elizabeth's, Clifford Kitchin, learning that John was a mountaineer, asked with languid indifference, 'Have you climbed any mountain of which one might have heard?', to receive the answer, 'Well, you may have heard of Mount Everest') had remarked brutally to me, when I had told him that I had agreed to be Joe's executor, 'All you'll get for your pains will be Nancy.' As, over a cup of tea and some wholemeal biscuits (Nancy was a great one for roughage), we went over the will and she began to put innumerable questions and requests to me, I remembered that ominous warning. Joe had often said resignedly, 'I'll never be free of Nancy until one of us dies.' Would I now find myself in the same position? Selfishly, I kept asking myself that question as I travelled back to Brighton.

In fact, after a few weeks, when I had been constantly obliged to explain to her such everyday actions as how to make out a cheque, how to pay a gas or electricity bill, how to arrange for a window cleaner, she ceased to be any trouble to me. Having kept afloat for years by all but strangling the brother around whose neck she had flung her arms in convulsive panic, she had now learned, if not to swim, at least to tread water on her own. Often the worst thing that you can do to people is to do too much for them; the crutch creates the invalid.

In this process of achieving independence, Nancy was greatly helped by Sonia Orwell, best of foul-weather friends. Sonia, always quick to perceive methods of helping people more effective than merely writing a cheque, arranged for an interior decorator friend to supervise, at her expense, the total rehabilitation of a flat that had for so long gathered dust and grime. This renewal of her home seemed to become for Nancy a personal renewal; so that her pride, as of a young bride, in showing the home off to her friends was also a pride in showing off her rehabilitated self.

I concluded the deal with Bertram Rota for the sale of the letters. Trickier was the publication of *My Father and Myself*. The anthropologist Geoffrey Gorer, one of Joe's oldest and most trusted friends even though he had often got on his nerves, had been clearly amazed and hurt that I, not he, should have been appointed executor. From the moment that he heard of Joe's death, he began constantly to telephone me with instructions about such things as the funeral, probate and the lease of the flat. I bore with all this patiently. Then, when he began to issue similarly peremptory orders about how I was to proceed with the memoir, I surprised myself, no less than him, by losing my temper. 'Look, Geoffrey, get this into your head once and for all! I'm perfectly capable of dealing with the matter without your constant interference.' A coldness followed. But eventually I was once again invited down to his Sussex mansion, full of pictures by Braque and Rouault which he had sagaciously bought in Paris in his Twenties youth. After luncheon we sat out on a terrace, our conversation interrupted on each of the many occasions (it was a Saturday and the summer weather was perfect) when walkers would stray even a step from the public footpath which bisected his grounds. Geoffrey, waving his stick – he was by then very lame – would heave his bulk out of his deck-chair and, accompanied by his dog, would stagger down the lawn. 'You're trespassing!' he would shout to some middle-aged couple. 'Get back on to that path or I'll have the dog on you.' The dog, an otherwise placid Labrador, would at that begin obligingly to bark. Eventually Geoffrey would return to his deck-chair: 'As I was saying, Francis . . .'

I knew that one of Joe's two half-sisters, Diana Petre, would make no objection to the publication of the memoir, with its revelations of how their father had started his life as a guardsman, had been befriended by at least one rich homosexual, had himself grown rich as the Banana King of England, and had then fathered two families, one legitimate and one illegitimate, which he kept in houses conveniently close to each other. Indeed, she herself was later to publish a memoir, *The Secret Orchard of Roger Ackerley*, quite as good as that of her half-brother. But Sally Westminster presented a problem. In marrying the man who was later to become the Duke of Westminster, she had invented for herself a pedigree more conventional than her true one. With her ambition, alas never realized, to become a lady-in-waiting to the Queen, would she really want that less conventional pedigree to be revealed? If she decided that she did not, then I should be obliged to follow Joe's instructions and withhold the book from publication.

In all this Diana proved, as in so many other difficulties in my life, an invaluable help. Thanks largely to her, Sally finally agreed that, provided that her name was changed, the book could appear. It did so, to critical acclaim.


Another of Sonia's acts of imaginative generosity was to pay for Jean Rhys to spend a week at the Royal Crescent Hotel in Brighton. She wrote to ask me to 'keep an eye on the old dear'.

I had already met Jean Rhys at a dinner-party given by Herman Schrijver. On that occasion she had spoken at insistent length about the way in which she was persecuted by the other inhabitants of the West Country village in which she was settled. She was particularly upset that the children, having decided that she was a witch, threw stones at her. After she had gone, Herman dismissed all this as paranoia. I could not be sure.

During the week of her stay in Brighton, I called round three times, at hours fixed by Jean – once at midday, twice at six o'clock – at the Royal Crescent Hotel. On each occasion, although the weather was perfect, I was asked to go up to her bedroom, where she lay out on a large double bed, not sleeping, not ill, doing nothing. I had always been an admirer of her novels and short stories; but she proved, unfortunately, far less interesting than them. Conversation was sticky. On the midday visit, the first of the three, she eventually ordered lunch to be brought up. She did not ask if I myself wanted anything to eat. I had already been despatched to her wardrobe to fetch out a bottle of gin, which stood beside a bottle of whisky; but had foolishly declined any. 'Perhaps I'd better leave you to eat in peace,' I said; to be told, 'No, no, stay and talk to me.'

When I eventually left for my own belated luncheon, Jean asked me whether I would be a dear and bring her another bottle of gin on my next visit. I did this. I also brought her a bottle of whisky, again at her request, on the visit after that. She never offered to repay me. I got the impression of one of those people (Diana Duff Cooper was another) with whom it is all too easy to fall in love but whom it is difficult to like. In her mauve bedjacket, her head back on the pillows, she certainly looked beguiling, even in old age; and the voice, with its soft, West Indian intonations, was also beguiling.


In helping Jean, Nancy and many other writers and their dependants, Sonia clearly felt that the money which she derived from the Orwell estate was, in a sense, hers only in trust. She was yet another difficult woman but also a kind and generous one. The difficult side of her nature was revealed to me at one of her parties, which I attended from Brighton. At half-past eleven, I told her that I was leaving to catch the last train home. This seemed to be a perfectly reasonable thing to do at that hour. But it drove her – she was clearly drunk – into a fury.

'Well, how's that for bloody cheek! This party was *intended* for you!' (This was the first that I had heard of this.) 'There were people I wanted you to meet. That's why I gave this fucking party. Well, fuck off if you want! Fuck off to your bloody Brighton!'

The next time I saw her, at a publisher's party, I felt a trepidation. But she come over to greet me – 'Francis! Lovely to see you!' The previous scene might never have occurred.

Sonia's last years were darkened not merely by illness but by an increasingly acrimonious conflict between herself and her accountants. Whether they had cheated her, as she maintained to me on more than one occasion, I had no way of judging. It was they whom she had recommended to me – 'You couldn't do better. They really are *marvellous*' – to handle the investment of that £6000 received for the Forster letters. I had no reason to complain.

When Sonia's illness and her unhappiness were both at their worst, Hilary and John Spurling were wonderfully supportive to her.

An American professor called to see me.

'Where are you staying?' I asked.

'Oh, I've been lent a part of their flat by the Spurlings. They're away, you know. The only problem is that they've lent the other part to an extremely difficult woman. In fact, I think her quite mad.'

The woman proved to be Sonia.


A woman as radiant in her youth as Sonia in hers, as gallant, intelligent and generous, and with the same ability to be difficult, is my old and beloved friend Kay Dick. When, after a rift between her and her partner Kathleen Farrell, I lured her down to Brighton, finding for her a small but attractive basement flat in Arundel Terrace, she jokingly told people that I had got her there with a promise of marriage and had then abandoned her. Had we indeed got married, we certainly should not have been happy, each of us being so wilful. But for many years we have enjoyed a relationship that can often be no less close than marriage – that, in effect, of brother and sister. Scarcely a week passes when we do not communicate.

Kay's dominant characteristic is extravagance. I myself am extravagant, as I have already indicated; but hers is extravagance of a totally different order, extending, admirably, beyond money to her own self. Of that inimitable self there is no holding back or hoarding; she will sparkle as brilliantly for some dreary old man or despondent old woman seated next to her in a restaurant, in a pub or on a train, as for someone famous.

Our first encounter was typical of this generosity of spirit. My then publisher, Bertie Van Thal, had invited me, a shy twenty-two-year-old, to a party his firm was giving at Grosvenor House. When he told me, 'Everyone who is anybody in the literary world will be there,' my blood froze. I almost did not go; and having arrived, wished that I had not done so. Bertie introduced me to Hannen Swaffer, and then at once moved away. Within a minute or two, Hannen Swaffer had also moved away, with a cry of 'Oh, there's Nancy [Spain]! I must speak to Nancy!' I stood alone, a glass of champagne in my hand. Then I realized that a woman was weaving her way through the crowd towards me. I was stunned by her elegance. Above a narrow black skirt, reaching to below her knees, she was wearing a white silk shirt, with black bow tie, and a dinner-jacket. A monocle was screwed into one eye. Her sleek blonde hair was closely cropped.

'Hello! Who are you?'

I told her.

'Oh, Bertie says I must read your novel. Must I? Is it any good?'

She had rescued me at the moment when I had seemed to be drowning in a sea of totally indifferent people. I felt a surge of gratitude. That gratitude intensified when she went on talking to me for several minutes on end and then, with enviable social adroitness, drew person after passing person into our conversation, introducing me to each.

Kay has never lost this social adroitness, whether at a literary party of that kind or in circumstances far more humdrum. Boldly she addresses people totally unknown to her; and such is her easy charm that, instead of being affronted or shy, they at once unfold like previously pinched buds to her sun.

Life for her is always a drama, even a melodrama; and of this drama or melodrama, she is always the protagonist. As she relates a clash with some neighbour, a confrontation with some tradesman, or some such domestic tragedy as the collapse of a ceiling or the blockage of a lavatory, one's own tribulations – an illness, a vituperative review, even a bereavement – suddenly appear so trivial that one hardly dares to mention them. Whereas my attitude is always a feeble one of 'Anything for peace,' hers is a forceful one of 'Anything for my rights.' Those rights seem constantly to be infringed; and no less constantly she fights like a lion for them.

Such is her generosity – once, when I took my sister Pamela to a meal with her, she served up enough prawns to feed a party of twenty – Kay is all too often broke. Like me, she believes that the function of money is to buy things; and the things (here she differs from me) must always be the best available.

Like another, no less talented woman writer friend of mine, Isobel English (June Braybrooke), Kay is one of those unfortunate people who have no difficulty in starting a book but often are unable to finish it. This inability derives, I should guess, from a terror of submitting to judgement. All writing is a confidence trick: one must have confidence in one's ability; but, even more important, one must have confidence in the ability of other people to believe in one. If one does not have that confidence, then, like a tight-rope walker who loses his nerve, one crashes to disaster.

After I had written a short book, *E.M. Forster and His World*, for Thames and Hudson, Kay was commissioned to write a similar short book on Colette. Indefatigably she then set to work: reading everything Colette had ever written, reading everything written about her, making contact with her daughter, who, clearly charmed by Kay as everyone else has always been charmed by her, was prepared to give her all the help that she could. 'But Kay, you're not writing a full-scale critical biography,' I protested. I then pointed out that I had written my own little study – favourably received and even today still earning me modest royalties – in less than six months. Kay would not listen. She went on with her research. Eventually the publishers succumbed to an all too natural impatience. What had happened to the book? 'Kay, give me all your material and I'll write it for you!' I eventually urged. At last the publishers issued their ultimatum: either they must have the book or the advance must be returned. Honourably but with great difficulty, Kay returned the advance. The book would, I am sure, have been far superior to anything else written about Colette.

When I published my novel *Punishments*, I dedicated it to Kay 'for valour'. Why valour, she asked. I then explained to her that, indomitably and cheerfully battling on against now indigence, now illness and now some injustice or injury perpetrated against herself or a friend, she was one of the most valorous people I had ever encountered.


Near to Kay, and a friend of hers, lived the then nonagenarian drag-artist Douglas ('Dougie') Byng. Master (or mistress) of the *double entendre*, he had had particular success on the Thirties stage with his impersonation of a plaid-skirted Flora Macdonald boasting 'there were risings in the highlands, there were risings in the lowlands', as she described her gallivantings around Scotland with Bonny Prince Charlie. Dougie's kind of sexual innuendo was no longer in fashion – 'People have become so *crude*,' he would often complain – and it was only rarely that he now performed except for friends in private.

Afflicted with a nervous tic – or, rather, a variety of tics – he could be a social hazard as well as a social asset. Seated beside me on a sofa, after he had given a zestful performance to the guests, most elderly and many of them theatrical, at a party given by Colin Campbell-Johnstone, he was grimacing and jerking his head from side to side, as so often when not on the stage. Then, all of a sudden, his leg shot out, kicked Flora Robson, then chatting to Zena Dare, on the elbow, and so precipitated an accident in which her glass of red wine emptied its contents all over the two women's party frocks. Flora looked around amazed, literally not knowing what had hit her; and Dougie, apparently oblivious, went on talking to me as I jumped up off the sofa to fetch a cloth.

Dougie was full of entertaining anecdotes, my favourite being one about the French actress Alice Delysia – whom, now elderly and plump but still enchanting, I would sometimes meet in Brighton. Apparently, on her first appearance in England, in a revue with Dougie, she was so much terrified of the audience's reaction that he had been obliged literally to drag her on to the stage for their first number together. As they left the stage, there was thunderous applause. Delighted she turned to him and squealed, 'Oh, Dougie, Dougie! We have got the clap!'

He himself was no less delighted when I recounted to him how a woman friend of mine, a neighbour of his in Prince of Wales Drive during the war, had spoken admiringly of him: 'Oh, he's a wonderful man! Really wonderful! So kind! Not a night seems to pass when he doesn't give some homeless serviceman on leave a bed! Yes, I see him come in night after night with some soldier, sailor or airman. He must go out and pick the poor things up.'

Even worldly people could really be as innocent as that then.


During my Brighton years I would often go over to Charleston to see Duncan Grant. Although then approaching his nineties, he was, like Dougie Byng, full both of zest for life and of interest, often malicious, in everyone around him.

I had always admired one picture of his, a nude, seen from the back, of David Garnett lying on a bed. Eventually, having received an unexpected and unexpectedly large payment for a short story from American, I asked him, with my usual extravagance, if he would sell it to me.

'Well, I shouldn't really,' he answered. 'Much though I'd like you to have it. You see, I have to sell everything through my gallery. That's our agreement.' He then pondered. 'Well . . . since you're a friend . . . And since I know you're certainly not rolling in it . . . With the commission, you'd have to pay much more to the gallery. But I could let you have it for . . .' He named a sum rather higher than I had hoped.

I bought the picture.

Some time later, I visited an exhibition of Duncan's work. Not one picture cost more than I had paid for mine. His shrewdness in this matter amused me and did not in the least upset me. I thought in admiration: Wonderful old boy!

This admiration increased when Godfrey Winn, seeing my Grant, decided that he must have one too. I wrote a letter to Duncan: might I bring Godfrey to tea one afternoon to see his pictures?

Duncan wrote back in uncompromising terms: He did not want 'that man' in his house, and he certainly did not wish to sell him a picture.

Even in his old age Duncan amused himself by producing erotic drawings and pictures. Clearly attracted by my friend David, he asked him if he and a black friend of his would pose for him. When the two young men went out to Charleston, they were soon invited to strip off and to glue themselves together in increasingly provocative embraces. This, with a lot of giggling, they did. Meanwhile, Duncan sketched away.

The next time that they went out, Duncan asked them, when once more stripped, whether they had any interest in flagellation. David said that he had none at all. The black boy was not sure. Duncan then produced a cane and asked first the black boy to give David 'a whack' and then David to give the black boy one. Again, both of them giggled. Meanwhile Duncan was sketching frenziedly.

Finally Duncan got to his feet and, lowering his trousers, asked David to give him 'a whack' too – 'But mind my balls,' he added. To receive this 'whack', he bent over the back of a chair. David was extremely reluctant; but, at Duncan's insistent urgings, eventually complied. He gave a small tap. 'Ouch!' Duncan let out a gasp. His body was briefly convulsed. Then he straightened up. 'Oh God! Look what I've done to that loose cover!'

When David recounted all this to me, I was not in the least shocked or annoyed. Rather, my reaction was once again one of 'Wonderful old man!' But from that time on, I noticed a change in Duncan's attitude to me. He was always slightly sheepish. Clearly he was wondering how much David had told me. On David's first visit he had asked him, 'Does Francis know that you are out here?'; and, when David had replied Yes, had said, 'Pity. You shouldn't have told him.'

Transformed into a philosopher, Duncan appears in my novel *A Domestic Animal*. The portrait is a flattering one. But I heard from mutual friends that Duncan was not at all pleased to find himself (as he put it to one of those friends) 'being read about in a book'.

Years later a friend of mine, Roland Stark, a South African writer resident in America, saw my nude and told me that he had an accompanying one, also of David Garnett, but from the front. I had a vision of having the two nudes framed back to back, with a hinge which would enable me to exhibit first one and then the other, and almost asked Roland whether he would sell me his. But I knew that the price would be far beyond my means. By then a Grant was selling for far, far more than the price that Duncan had so cunningly upped.

Every visit to Charleston reminded me that the Bloomsberries, for all the accusations of effeteness, were a tremendously hardy lot. Except in Duncan's studio, where there was a Potterton stove, every room was damp and cold. The dining-room, the rising damp extending for two or three feet up its walls, was the worse of all. Eating luncheon there, I had to go out so often to pee that, concerned, Duncan once remarked, 'You're young to be having prostate trouble. Oughtn't you to have it seen to?' I thought it would be discourteous to say, 'It's not prostate trouble. I'm just dying of cold.'

What I loved about Duncan was that, even in extreme old age, his face was always set to the future. I often questioned him about the Woolfs, Vanessa and Clive Bell, E.M. Forster, Maynard Keynes; but he was not really interested in answering and did so perfunctorily. He wanted to talk about the morrow – and the day after that.

I also loved Duncan for the joy that he took in his work. As he aged, the quality of that work, always erratic, became more and more so. But the important thing for him was not whether he was producing masterpieces but whether he could hold a brush, a pen or a pencil, gaze out on the world which he still found so interesting and beautiful, and record something of it.

# — 5 —

# *Home and Away*

While looking for somewhere permanent to live in London, I rented the furnished two-roomed flat in the basement of Elizabeth's and John's house in Sydney Street, Chelsea. The Japanese au pair who had been working for me in Brighton – a youth whose will was as powerful as his physique – insisted on accompanying me there. There was, in effect, no work for him to do; and sleeping in the sitting-room until ten or eleven in the morning – he had an astonishing capacity for sleep – he was a continual nuisance to me, accustomed as I am to get up at six or even earlier. I was reluctant to dispense with him until I had found somewhere else for him to go, because he kept telling me that he had no money other than what I paid him. One morning, however, I rushed into the sitting-room to grab a manuscript before consigning it to a taxi sent round by Penny Hoare, to find him seated, still in his pyjamas, on his bed, with one of his suitcases open before him. The suitcase was full of dollar bills, in neat bundles. Where had the money come from? Perhaps he had brought it with him from Japan; perhaps, since he consorted largely with Arabs – met, so he told me, at the language school which he attended – there was some other provenance. At all events, I now had no compunction in telling him that, since there was really nothing for him to do in a flat so small, I should have to give him two weeks' notice.

My days were largely spent in viewing houses and flat. Since I had by now disposed of the Daimler, this entailed a lot of wearisome trekking about London, from Hampstead to Hackney, from Battersea to Balham, from Camden Town to Campden Hill. But I am one of those people (I met an exasperating number of them while trying to sell my Brighton house) who love to view a property even if at a first glance it is clear that it is totally unsuitable. Facing Tooting Common, there was a fascinating Edwardian house, seemingly unchanged but for an antiquated refrigerator, since the day it was built. To my shame I must have misled the elderly, arthritic couple who limped round after me from one sombre, capacious room to another, with my cries of 'Oh, this is wonderful! I love that lincrusta!' or 'Oh, look at that William Morris paper and the curtains to match!' I had no intention of acquiring a house so large and so obviously in need of repair; or indeed of going to live in Tooting. But that night, in bed, I started to imagine what it would be like to be the owner of that house. I wished that I had had the nerve to ask the owners all the questions which now crowded in on me: Had they inherited the house or had they bought it? How long had they lived there? Had it once been full of relatives, children, guests? And why were they moving? And where were they going?

In one flat, in Little Venice, overlooking the canal, the harassed-looking, middle-aged woman who was showing me round opened the door on a bedroom in which an emaciated young man, in nothing but Y-fronts, his black, tangled hair reaching to his shoulders, squatted in a corner, back to the wall, humming to himself on a single high, extremely loud note, his eyes shut. She said nothing to him, not even 'Excuse me' or 'I'm showing this gentleman round the flat.' She walked to the window: 'There's a nice view of the canal from here.' She pointed to the wash-basin: 'Hot and cold.' She opened a built-in cupboard: 'I had this put in last year.' The youth went on humming.

I liked the flat, which was remarkably cheap for the area; but somehow the whole visit had unsettled me. 'I'll think about it. I'll let you know,' I said, as I had said, and was to say, to so many other people. I did nothing of the kind.

One house which I almost bought belonged to the playwright Anthony Shaffer. Queen Anne in period, with eight beautifully panelled rooms, all of the same small, rectangular size, it was cheap because of its appalling position: in Wandsworth, on an extremely busy corner, with traffic constantly passing. At once I fell in love with it. But just before contracts were to be exchanged, I began to have doubts. Without a car, it would take me almost as long to reach central London as it had done from Brighton. There were no decent shops or restaurants to hand. The noise would madden me, and it and the fumes would prevent me from ever sitting in the garden – which in any case was minuscule. Not surprisingly Shaffer was annoyed when, at the last possible moment, I cried off.

As soon as I mounted the steps of the house, off Church Street Kensington, in which I still live, I knew at once: 'This is it!' Inhabited by three elderly women, two of them living together and one separately but all sharing the same kitchen, bathroom and lavatory, it was in an appalling state of disrepair. The one who showed me round was Mary Chamot, who had been born in Russia and who was an expert on Russian art – of which valuable examples hung on the walls. Her friend Loulette, a Russian, had taught the language to a friend of mine, Peter Davies. By yet another of those coincidences so common in my life, Peter had actually lodged in the house for a while. Loulette now suffered from heart disease, which necessitated a move to a flat.

Mary Chamot was amazed when, after about five minutes, I said, 'Yes, I'll buy it.' (What, in fact, I was buying was not the freehold but a sadly short lease.)

'Are you sure?'

'Yes, absolutely sure.'

'But you haven't seen the kitchen – or the garden!'

'Oh, that doesn't matter. I want to buy it.'

Later, when I called round to discuss the purchase of some of the carpets and curtains, Mary said to me, 'Don't you want to show the house to your mother before signing the contract?'

Without thinking, I replied, 'Oh, no! She has absolutely no visual imagination. She'd be horrified and try to dissuade me.' Then I was aghast. What *had* I said? But if I had upset Mary, she did not show it.

Mary produced an old builder who had been looking after the house for, literally, decades. He was very choosy, she explained. He would have to talk to me before deciding whether he wanted to work for me or not. I was nervous at our interview; but he gave his approval. He executed all the work – removing the perilously rotting boards of the basement floors, putting in a hot-water system in place of a wood-burning stove, totally rewiring the whole house – impeccably and at remarkably little cost. When I moved in, I felt that I had come home. I was back in Kensington, where I had spent so many happy years in my teens; and I was in precisely the sort of house, with none of the grandeur or beauty of the Brighton one but none the less comfortable and comely, which suited me best. I have lived in it ever since, becoming a statutory tenant, on an ever-soaring rent, when the leasehold expired.

I was fortunate to find a young German au pair when I moved in. Immensely efficient and willing, Erwin hung the pictures, placed the books on shelves, hacked down the straggling privet bushes which choked the garden. He was always quiet, always respectful, always well-behaved. Years later, he visited me with his English wife. Where had they met? I asked them. 'Here,' he replied. 'In London. When I was working for you.' They exchanged glances and both began to giggle. Then he told me how, at night, he would smuggle her into the house. He would leave the side-gate into the garden open and they would then enter by the back, not the front, door.

'Does this news upset you?' he asked.

'Not at all! But how is it I never heard you?'

Again they both began to giggle. Then she said, 'Well, it was often difficult not to make a noise.'

Eventually David disposed of his Brighton flat and joined me, thus obviating any need for an au pair. But of that I shall write later.

After I had been living in the house for six months or so, Loulette had a fatal heart-attack. The move from the house which she and Mary loved into a flat had, in effect, not been necessary. In the garden Loulette had planted some lily-of-the-valley, which still come up each year, some twenty-five years later. Since Loulette loved these flowers more than any other, Mary asked me if she could have some from the garden to place on the coffin. Unfortunately the lily-of-the-valley had been early that year and there were none in bloom. After some hesitation, I then decided on what was, I hope, a justifiable deception. I went to the local flower-shop and bought some bunches, and then pretended to Mary that they had come from the garden.

In London I was at last free of the burden of lodgers, since the house was too small for them; but, looking back, I am none the less amazed by how much I did – writing my own books, reading and editing other people's books for Macdonald, reviewing, broadcasting, lecturing, entertaining. I suffered from a strange superstition: if I ever said No to any offer of work, I might never again receive one. As a result I would trek off to, say, Worthing or Ilkley or St Albans, to speak for a pittance to some tiny audience most of whom had never heard of me. Nowadays I am far more selective. Occasionally my friend Tom Wakefield persuades me to do a reading with him; but whereas the vanity of some writers is flattered by the presence of even a dozen or so people eager, as they see it, to touch the hems of their garments, I return from such occasions wondering why on earth I ever went.

From time to time Giorgio, on a visit to England for Olivetti – he had been appointed their economic adviser – would come and stay. My turbulently obsessive passion for him had now become a tranquil, wholly undemanding love. Looking at him over the breakfast table before each of us started out on a busy day, I still used to think: How beautiful he is. But I might have been thinking of my Duncan Grant nude, a beautiful work of art but one with no power to stir me sexually.

Now began close and rewarding friendships with a number of women, of a kind achieved only rarely in the past. Intense but platonic, they were made possible by two things: firstly, an increasing toleration of homosexuality and a freedom to talk about it; and secondly the fact that I had now entered middle-age. When, as a young man teaching in the British Institute in Florence, I had been so devoted to my colleague Anita Ryan, or when in Japan I had become no less devoted to my pupil Setsuko Ito, I had constantly felt, 'What can she be thinking of me? I ought to be *doing* something.' There was now no longer any pressure to do something. None of these women expected a pass from me; they were (I hope) as happy in our asexual friendship as I was. I have always preferred the company of women to that of men; and I was glad that I could now go away on holidays with them, even share cabins, or sleepers, or hotel bedrooms with them, if that was unavoidable, without any embarrassment or guilt about falling below their expectations.

At this period the British Council often sent me on lecture-tours abroad. Some of these would take me to Iron Curtain countries. In one of the two novellas which make up my book *Flights*, I write of the strange relationship, at once intimate, combative and wary, between visitor and native interpreter-guide in a communist state. In many instances these guides were out of sympathy with the regime which they served; but their well-being and that of their families depended on that lack of sympathy never being revealed. One such interpreter-guide, an attractive and highly intelligent woman, has since told me of how, after my departure, she had to fill in an elaborate form about me: what were my political affiliations, what were my sexual preferences, with whom had I made contact while in the country? 'If I had refused my family would have suffered. I knew that nothing that I wrote could cause any trouble to you. So I filled in the form. ... Please forgive me,' she concluded.

'There's nothing to forgive,' I replied. I meant it. In similar circumstances, I should no doubt have filled in a similar form. One can demand decency from others but not a heroism which it is extremely unlikely that one would show oneself.

The amount of money expended on such pointless surveillance contrasted cruelly with the general poverty of the countries in which it occurred. Some English friends of mine had for many years employed a Bulgarian daily called Lily. When this woman had retired, she had decided to return to her native Sofia, to be with what remained of her family. When my friends heard that I was about to leave for Bulgaria to lecture for the British Council, they asked me if I would take some presents to Lily who – they had gathered, reading between the lines of her stilted, laconic letters – regretted that she had ever left England.

One afternoon I was free of all engagements. I then decided to look Lily out. 'What will you do this afternoon?' my interpreter-guide asked. 'Oh, I think I'll have a rest,' I replied. Luncheon over, I set off on foot, with the aid of a map, for the area in which Lily lived. I eventually came on a drab block of flats. The lift was out of order, and so I mounted innumerable dirty stairs. I might have been in some tower block in a poor quarter of London. When the door to the flat creaked open, I at first mistook one of the sisters for Lily herself. Then, bowed and limping, wearing a shabby dressing-gown and slippers, Lily appeared. When I explained my errand, she was delighted to see me. She hurried off 'to make myself a little more respectable' (as she put it in her excellent English).

In a small room, crowded with furniture and knick-knacks – the divan on which I was asked to sit clearly did duty as a bed for one of the trio at night – Lily began to question me not merely about her former employers but about life in England. 'Things are not good here,' she said more than once. Between them, the sisters produced some coffee and biscuits. Among the gifts from my friends were packets of Fortnum and Mason tea.

We were all happy together. Then, suddenly, there was a ring at the bell. The three sisters looked at each other in alarm. One said something in Bulgarian, raising her pencilled eyebrows – although old, she was still a pretty woman, certainly the most glamorous of the trio – and Lily, in a whisper, made some reply. The pretty one got up and went to the door. It was my guide-interpreter. 'Oh, here you are, Mr King! I thought you would not want to walk so long a way back to the hotel and so I came in the car to fetch you.' As I rose to my feet, she put out a hand: 'There is no need to hurry. Please take as long as you wish.' She drew off first one glove and then the other. The three women, clearly terrified, were soon scurrying around to clear a chair for her, to bring her some coffee, to offer her a biscuit.

There followed some minutes of stiff conversation before we left.

In the car I wanted to ask the interpreter-guide how she had known what I was doing and where I was. Even more I wanted to demand, 'Why the hell couldn't you leave me alone?' But I feared that my visit might have done the three sisters enough harm already. I must say nothing to make things worse.

When on a visit to Romania for the British Council, I found myself in room 403 in the Athenée Palace Hotel – then the best in Bucharest. One night, when I was already in bed, there was a knock on the door. I got up to unlock it. There outside stood an attractive, well-dressed woman. She smiled at me. 'I think you've made a mistake.' She continued to smile at me. I repeated the words in French. She replied, '*Pas de méprise. Pas du tout! Puis-je entrer? Je voudrais parler avec vous.*' '*Non merci.*' I closed the door and relocked it. She knocked twice again. Then I heard her voice: '*Monsieur King! Monsieur King! Je voudrais parler avec vous.*' In any country other than a dictatorship, a combination of politeness and curiosity would have impelled me to let her in – after all, she might have merely been either a tart, admitted by the porter in return for a bribe, or one of those writers who badger any foreign literary guest in the hope that he can somehow effect publication of their books in his own country. But I was not taking the risk.

Some four years later, I was with my friend David on a tourist visit to Romania, where we had booked rooms for three nights in the same hotel before setting off on a tour by car. David was accommodated on the second floor. My room was once again room 403. At an Embassy party I commented on the coincidence of this to a young British diplomatist. He laughed: 'Oh, it's no coincidence! That's one of the bugged rooms.' What could anyone eavesdropping on my conversations with David hope to learn of importance?

It was this young diplomatist, a married man with children, who said to me *sotto voce* at the same party, 'Have you found any places where gay people go?' He had read my *A Domestic Animal* and from that knew that I shared his sexual interests.

'No,' I replied. 'But David has chummed up with three charming students, met at the swimming-pool.'

'Oh, do let me meet them!' the diplomatist said. Reluctantly I then invited him to join us the following evening in what was, in effect, a Greek taverna in the heart of the city. *Emigré* Greeks – the father of one of the boys was one, from the period of the Greek civil war – frequented it.

The boys were merely eager to meet foreigners and (I guessed) to be invited abroad; there was nothing more to it than that. But the encounter demonstrated the fatuousness of the Foreign Office and British Council edict that no homosexuals should serve in Iron Curtain countries. Suppose the boys had been *agents provocateurs*? Had there then been any attempt to blackmail David or me, we should simply have said, 'So what? We don't care who knows we're homosexuals.' But the diplomatist, with his wife and his children, might have been far more vulnerable.

When, two days later, David and I arrived in the once German city of Sibiu, we parked our car, hired from the Touring Club of Romania, with its rear to the hotel, so that on our departure we had only to get into it to drive off. When the next morning we saw it, it was parked facing the hotel. No doubt everything which we had left in its boot had undergone a thorough search.

Later, as we progressed further northwards, we became aware of a battered little Volkswagen, containing three large men all wearing trilby hats, behind us. 'Do you think that car is following us?' I queried.

David pooh-poohed the idea: 'This is the main highway north.'

From time to time, we stopped to pick up a hitch-hiker. Most of these spoke some English or, more often, French. Settled in the car and discovering that we were foreigners – our car had a Romanian number plate – they would begin to ask us what we thought of the Ceausescu regime and, in some cases, themselves begin to complain about it. I was extremely wary and urged David to be equally so. The hitch-hikers might be trying to provoke us; and if they were not, there was still the possibility of a bug in the car, which could land them in trouble.

The three men put up in the same hotel in which we stayed that night. Once again David laughed at my suggestion that they were tailing us – 'Where else would you expect them to stay? This is the only half-way decent hotel for at least fifty miles in all directions. Don't be so paranoid!'

The next morning, when we were viewing some Roman excavations, there once again was the little Volkswagen. The three men in their rumpled dark suits tumbled out of it, adjusted their trilby hats in the high wind, and then put on a perfunctory performance of inspecting the remains.

'Perhaps they're archaeologists,' David said. 'Or they may be tourists – just like us.'

When we arrived at Tulcea on the Danube Basin, the three men once again checked into our hotel.

Our plan had been to hire a boat to explore the Basin for its vegetation and birds. In a café that evening – by now the trio had vanished – a group of men at the next-door table got into conversation with us, in a mixture of French and German. We mentioned our wish to hire a boat. *Pas de problème*! One of them was a fisherman; he could take us out. We agreed to meet him down on the docks the following morning at seven thirty.

When we arrived at the docks, he was apologetic: his boss had given him another job to do. The night before he had said nothing of a boss; he had told us that the boat was his own. We approached a number of other fishermen, apparently idle; they all made excuses. Then a large, bossy woman – well-dressed in as far as any Romanian at that period could be said to be well-dressed – stepped out from a café overlooking the docks and told us that there was a large boat, with a group of East German tourists aboard, which was about to leave for an all-day cruise of the Basin. If we hurried, we could get on that. We did as she suggested. The Germans were jolly, noisy, friendly. We saw little, because all at once, as often happens on the Danube Basin, a thick mist rose up off the murky waters and wrapped itself around us.

For lack of single rooms in the Tulcea hotel, David and I were sharing one. In the middle of the night, it was apparent that the food which I had eaten on the boat was about to disagree with me. I got out of bed and rushed to the lavatory. As I switched on the light, I realized that there was someone standing out on the terrace, looking in. To hell with him! I lowered my pyjama trousers, squatted. The resulting explosion presumably blew the watcher off the terrace. At all events, he vanished.

At long last, David was prepared to acknowledge that, yes, we were being watched.

The next day, he behaved with what I thought childish recklessness. After we had left Tulcea and had entered a smaller, neighbouring town, the Volkswagen once more in pursuit, he began to act as though in a car-chase in a James Bond movie, swinging the wheel now to the left and now to the right and then screeching at speed down some alley almost too narrow to admit us. I kept telling him to stop – we should only make the three louts even more suspicious of us. But he would not listen.

'Anyway, we've lost them,' he eventually announced to me in triumph.

But the triumph was short-lived. A few miles along the road, I looked back and once again saw the dumpy Volkswagen. David, who knew more about these things than I did, opined that our car carried a directional bug, which enabled our followers to know precisely where we were. Some fifty miles from Bucharest, the Volkswagen vanished.

That night, we had dinner in an attractive hotel called Maniuk's Tavern. The elderly waiter who first dealt with us spoke not a word of any language but Romanian. He was soon succeeded by another waiter, an extremely handsome youth, who spoke both English and French. Apparently responsible for no table but ours, he kept asking us about ourselves and our travels. Eventually, when we had paid our bill, he suggested that the next day we might like him to take us sightseeing. 'Don't you have to work?' I asked him. He could take the day off, he replied.

He was an excellent guide and a charming companion. But his questions became more and more intrusive. We parried these as skilfully as we could. Our sightseeing over, I gave him a tip large by Romanian standards. 'Why did you do that?' David demanded. 'He must get a good screw from the secret police.' David of course was right. But the boy was extremely attractive.

Surveillance of this kind was totally absurd: neither David nor I had any secrets to impart and we had no wish to abstract any. But it was also extremely sinister. Some injudicious hitch-hiker might well have landed up in gaol because of a remark made to us. The fisherman who had offered us his boat might well have also been in trouble.

It was during a British Council lecture-tour in South America in 1979 that I met Jorge Luis Borges, a writer whom I revered, in Buenos Aires. The person who brought about the encounter was an old and trusted friend of his, Alicia Jurado, the dominant Argentine woman writer of the time and a person who combined great force of character with great kindness. She had taken me in hand (the phrase is the right one, since I sometimes felt that I was merely her glove-puppet) during my stay, introducing me to the sort of people – writers, painters, composers, authors, museum directors – whom, puzzlingly, I was seldom meeting through the Council.

While we were travelling to Borges's house in a taxi, Alicia told me something of his past and present life. After he had been struck down with blindness, his beloved mother, who lived on into her nineties, would read endlessly to him. On her death, Borges married a surrogate mother. According to Alicia, he had fallen in love with this woman when a young man; then, remeeting her half a century later, he was able to imagine, in his blindness, that she was still the beautiful girl whom once he had known – 'very far from the reality', Alicia added. Whereas he had always had a child's indifference to money, this wife proved unusually sharp about it. On one occasion, Borges, having lectured at an American university, was afterwards chatting in one corner to a group of academics, while in another the Dean of the faculty discreetly handed Borges's wife an envelope. Indiscreetly she opened it in front of the Dean and examined the sum. Then she protested vehemently: It was not enough. Why, Borges had received far more for lectures at X and Y. The Dean tried to explain about allocations and authorizations, but she would not relent. The money must be increased. Now. Eventually embarrassed professors were emptying their own wallets in order to make up the sum demanded.

Separated from this dragon, Borges now lived in an orderly flat, with an orderly peasant woman to act as his housekeeper; and a number of other orderly women – to whom, according to Alicia, he behaved with the capriciousness of a child favouring now this aunt and now that – took him out and read to him.

Having sat Alicia down in an armchair, Borges sat me down on a sofa and then, literally, almost sat on top of me. Since the blind soon learn their way about their own premises, I presumed that this contact was intentional. I was embarrassingly conscious of his arm along my own, of his knee against mine, and of the side of the sofa digging into my ribs. At once he began to ask me questions: never about myself or the England which he told me that he so much loved, but about this or that English author. Did I read Kipling? Did I admire Browning? Did I feel that Stevenson was too smooth to be a truly great writer? But, like Pontius Pilate, he did not stay for an answer. I would start to say something and he would cut me off with a lecturette. Since each lecturette was erudite, lambent with a playful irony and often barbed with wit, I had no complaint.

From the first he struck me as projecting all the winsomeness of a supremely gifted child. The chief joy of this child was to make brilliantly intricate constructions, not out of such real materials provided by life as, for example, the intrusion of an English novelist into his home, but out of a seemingly inexhaustible Lego-kit of books read and remembered. It was a matter of indifference to him whether I was English or Argentine; male or female; old or young. Even if he could have seen me, with those disconcerting, because seemingly healthy, eyes of his, always focused on some spot just above and beyond my head, I doubt if he would have *noticed* me. I was merely someone fresh to watch him at play. 'Sit down, look at me, see what I can do,' he seemed to be saying, as, swift as thought, he joined one piece of Lego to another and another to that.

Nothing, it was clear, had been added to this Lego-kit since about 1930. When he spoke of Kipling's knowledge of Old English poetry and its influence on him – his hand patted my knee to emphasize the rhythm of the Kipling verse that he quoted – I mentioned Auden. Silence. I tried to persuade him that he would enjoy J.G. Farrell's *The Siege of Krishnapur*. No response. I told him that William Shand's translations of some of his poems reminded me of Cavafy. Who? Cavafy, I repeated. Cavafy? Oh, yes ... Yes ... Well, yes, perhaps ... Obviously he had heard of Cavafy and might even have read him; but no less obviously his name and work were not nestling down there in that Lego-kit of his. As I sat on, uncomfortably feeling that frail, long, bony knee against mine, I suddenly thought of Nabokov's remark that *Lolita* was the result, not of an infatuation with a young girl, but of an infatuation with the English langue. Clearly Borges's masterworks were the result of an infatuation not with life but with literature.

The telephone repeatedly rang and, summoned by the peasant maid, he would totter out to answer it. Why, I wondered, did he not have an extension placed near to hand? Two shabby, slightly furtive men were shown into the room, whispered briefly and vanished. A plump, panting young man with a pinkish face arrived, a number of books under an arm. He had apparently come to read Old English with Borges. Borges explained that he was busy and asked the young man to return the next day. But before he went, he must recite some Old English to the visitor. (Never once did he either address me by my name or refer to me by it.) The young man put his pile of books down on to the table, stood to attention, cleared his throat, wiped the sweat off his forehead with the back of a hand, and then began in a surprisingly loud, high-pitched voice. *Beowulf? The Wanderer?* I could only guess. It was strange to hear those sounds high above the noise of traffic in a flat in Buenos Aires.

Eventually Borges asked me to read to him: he would like to hear an English voice. But again the telephone rang and again he shuffled out. Returning, he gave precise instructions to Alicia: the first volume of Burton's translation of *The 1001 Nights*, third shelf down, five books along from the left. She fetched the book and handed it to him. He then handed it to me. 'Page eleven,' he said. 'Second paragraph.'

I began to read; and as I did so, I realized that my voice had developed a tremor and that my hands, in which the heavy volume was resting, had begun to shake. For a moment I wondered at this. Then I realized: this was the first time, throughout our meeting, that this great writer, whose work I so much admired, had really paid attention to anything that had issued from my mouth.

After I had finished, he sighed and patted my knee. 'That was nice, very nice.'

Alicia and I both knew – though he gave no indication more definite than this – that it was time to leave. Outside the flat I looked at my watch. He had told me to come at ten and that he had another appointment at eleven thirty. It was precisely eleven thirty. I wondered how a blind man had been able to judge the duration of my tutorial so exactly.

Eerily, throughout the rest of my stay, I kept coming on Borges: in the street, in a shop, in a restaurant, in the foyer of my hotel. He was invariably in the company of a woman, never the same one. Each time I used to wonder whether to go up to him and announce myself; each time I did not do so. I felt sure that, if I were to do so, he would have absolutely no idea who I was.

Another much admired novelist met at about the same time was Edith de Born. In her case a first encounter, arranged by Alethea Hayter, developed into a valued friendship.

Edith, who had been born in Austria or Hungary, who had been educated in Germany, England or France, who was or was not Jewish, who had been married once, twice or three times, and who might, when I first met her, have been any age from fifty to sixty-five (she was extraordinarily evasive when I attempted to question her about her past), was one of those writers, like Conrad and Nabokov (both greatly admired by her), who opt to write in a language other than their own. That she should have opted for English was particularly odd, since she spoke French so much better and was resident in Belgium.

Her husband, cultivated, worldly, rich, was a banker called Bisch. Their house in Brussels, at which I stayed on a number of occasions, was staffed by a butler, an excellent cook and a maid. The kitchen, which out of curiosity I once inspected on a Sunday afternoon when everyone was out, was totally devoid of such modern devices as electric kettle, toaster or dishwasher; the central heating was erratic; and from the guest-room it was necessary to descend two floors to an antiquated bathroom. This, I imagine, was how the rich lived in the Edwardian age.

Edith was tiny, chic, forceful, sympathetic, tolerant. In the smartest club in Brussels, to which, without her husband, she would take me to luncheon, she was imperious to the waiters: we had been waiting too long for our drinks; there was far too much vermouth in her martini; what had become of the promise of a table by the window? To the staff of Durrant's Hotel, where she would stay on her London visits, she was equally imperious. But hers was an imperiousness, as of some member of royalty in exile, to which no one took exception.

Since Edith was precisely the sort of woman to attract Evelyn Waugh, it was no surprise to me to learn that he had once been a friend of hers. A guest at the Brussels house, he had gone out of his way on a number of occasions to ingratiate himself with his host and hostess by comparing the 'Frogs' (as he referred to them) un-favourably with the Belgians, in particular remarking at almost every meal on the superiority of Belgian to 'Frog' food. It was only at a dinner-party on the last even-ing of his stay, when he overheard the English Ambassador say something about 'you French' to Monsieur Bisch, that Waugh had suddenly realized, to his shame and chagrin, that his host was not a Belgian, as he had always imagined, but a Frog.

Edith's books deserve to be far better known; but my attempts to persuade Virago to reissue at least the two or three best of them came to nothing. Perhaps the most remarkable of the many remarkable things about them is the beauty of the style in which they are written. This contrasts piquantly with the style, sometimes grammatically incorrect, sometimes even gauche, of her letters. I remarked on this to her, to receive the reply: 'Well, I take much more trouble over my books.'

It was only after her death that her and my close friend Jonathan Fryer

discovered that somewhere in East Anglia there lived a clergyman's wife (or it may
have been widow) who, over a period of many years, had corrected almost every
other sentence of every one of Edith's books for her.


A lesser but far more popular writer, Cecil Roberts – Graham Greene's first job
was to work under him on the *Northampton Gazette* – also had an amusing story
about Evelyn Waugh. But for poor Cecil the story was a source not of amusement
but of indignation and pain.

   For many years Cecil, who had made a lot of money with his books and who was
also conducting an *amitié amoureuse* with an extremely rich American widow, had
been living at the Excelsior Hotel in Rome. Learning that Evelyn Waugh was
putting up there, he wrote him a note, which he asked the hall porter to put in his
pigeon-hole. He was an old friend of Waugh's brother, Alec, Cecil wrote; he had
always been an admirer of Evelyn's work; he would like to invite him to a meal or a
drink.

   The next morning the note was in Cecil's own pigeon-hole. Across the opened
envelope was scrawled: 'Not known. Return to sender.'

   That same evening Cecil found himself in the same lift as Waugh. 'Oh, Mr
Waugh,' he said. 'It *is* Mr Waugh, Mr Evelyn Waugh, isn't it? I think there's been
some kind of misunderstanding. I'm Cecil Roberts, I sent you a letter.'

   Waugh stared at him in pop-eyed amazement. 'Good God! You're Cecil
Roberts! I thought you were in the nick in Patagonia for buggering Bobo Dunkley!'

   At that the lift reached the ground floor. Waugh stepped out and disappeared.

   Telling the story to David and me, Cecil concluded, 'What's so mysterious is
that I've never been in Patagonia . . . and I've never been in prison . . . and I know
no one called Bobo Dunkley . . . and I've never really gone in for buggery . . .' He
shook his head in bewilderment. 'Do you think that Waugh is absolutely *mad*?'

   Although Cecil may never really have gone in for buggery, he claimed to have
had affairs with a lot of famous men. These included Laurence Olivier, Ivor
Novello, Baron von Cramm (the tennis-player), Somerset Maugham and the
Duke of Kent. For Cecil, snob that he was, the last of these represented the highest
achievement.

   It was Cecil who gave me an explanation (true or false I do not know) of why Sir
Charles Mendl, of no great distinction as a diplomatist, had come to be knighted. A
South American gigolo, resident in Paris, was blackmailing the Duke of Kent over
some indiscreet letters. Mendl, then serving at the Paris Embassy, was given the
task of retrieving them. This he did by employing two *apaches* to burgle the South
American's apartment.

   Cecil longed for a knighthood, which he unaccountably felt to be overdue. Since
I was Chairman of the Society of Authors at the time, he asked me to intervene.
Although I took the view, confirmed by some subsequent honours, that a discreet
word to the right person at the Athenaeum or the Garrick (of neither of which I
was a member, being the least clubbable of people) would be far more likely to

achieve his objective, I did what I could. But, sadly, not even an MBE (an OBE was the most for which I had hoped) came his way.

After Cecil's death, I was asked to give the address at his funeral at St Margaret's Westminster. Among a number of distinguished people present was John Betjeman, who shuffled over to me (he was already stricken with Parkinson's) at the end of the service, to congratulate me on the address. Then he went on, 'You know, dear old Cecil was always very grateful to you for getting that offer of a knighthood for him. He always hoped that you would understand his refusal. He just felt – as he told me only a month or two ago – that he was not worthy of it. Silly of him to be so modest. But rather touching, don't you think?'

I did not tell Betjeman the truth.

In his egotism, vanity and snobbery, Cecil resembled Godfrey Winn. But, unlike Godfrey, he was benevolent, generous and affectionate. I do not think that his novels will now find many readers. But, blessed (or cursed) with total recall, he produced some volumes of autobiography which are wonderfully entertaining and not at all ill-written. Some publisher should reissue at least a selection from them.


During the Seventies I was, along with Brigid Brophy, Maureen Duffy, Lettice Cooper and Leo Garfield, a founder member of WAG (Writers Action Group).

The battle for Public Lending Right for authors had been conducted in a succession of waves, each repulsed by a combination of librarians and civil servants. In that battle people as various as John Brophy (Brigid's father), A.P. Herbert, Arnold Goodman and Michael Holroyd had, at one time or another, played important parts. The feeling among the members of WAG was that the Society of Authors was mistaken in not backing a loan-based scheme and less than energetic and efficient in pursuing a scheme of any kind. We saw ourselves, in effect, as a ginger group; and, like most ginger groups, we made ourselves unpopular with the sort of people who say, 'Just leave us alone to get on with it,' when getting on with it is something of which they are totally incapable.

Without Brigid Brophy and Maureen Duffy, two remarkable women prepared to sacrifice their own writing to a cause which for a long time seemed hopeless, I often wonder whether even today writers would be receiving PLR money. A loan-based scheme would be both difficult and hugely costly to administer, the librarians and civil servants constantly told us. It was Maureen, with her grasp of how computers could be made to work at a time when only a few experts were familiar with them, who conclusively demonstrated the fallacy of this argument. Meanwhile Brigid was winning over a number of influential people in the Commons – Michael Foot, Robin Cooke and Airey Neave at once come to mind – and Ted Willis in the Lords.

At one point Pauline Neville and I were despatched to persuade the then Minister for the Arts Hugh Jenkins (later Lord Jenkins) of both the desirability and the feasibility of PLR. 'You can do the speaking,' Pauline told me. 'I'll just give you moral support.'

Jenkins, who had aspirations to be an author himself, proved to be a charming man but one lacking, I thought, in 'bottom'. He sat me down in one chair and Pauline in another. 'Persuade me,' he said.

I drew my notes out of my pocket. Pauline, beautiful and elegant, sat back in her chair and crossed her long legs, the skirt above the knees. I began to lecture Jenkins. For a while he nodded or interjected a 'H'm', 'Yes' or 'I see'. Then I was conscious that I had lost his attention. I ploughed on.

What he was doing, I eventually realized, was gazing at Pauline's legs.

At the close of my speech, he beamed: 'Well, you have my full support.'

As we left his office, Pauline turned to me, delighted, and threw her arms round me: 'Well done! You won him over!'

'No, Pauline. *You* won him over. Or, at least, your legs did.'

We were less successful with some other politicians. Two particularly vehement opponents of the scheme were called Moat and Sproat. It gives me some satisfaction that their parliamentary careers never came to anything much. Douglas Hurd, although himself an author, frigidly withheld his support. But this did not subsequently prevent him from registering for PLR, once it was achieved.

Maureen and Brigid were extraordinarily close at this period. Then, sadly, they fell out. It always struck me that they were the perfect complements to each other: Maureen extrovert, jolly, practical; Brigid introvert, moody, impractical. At meetings Maureen would be eloquent; Brigid would brood. Then, when everyone had given an opinion, Brigid would at last speak out. What she had to say was always far more intelligent and incisive than anything said before.

One evening, after her split with Maureen, Brigid and her husband Michael Levy came to a dinner-party at my house. They arrived a little late because, they told me, Brigid had had an unaccountable fall on their way up the hill. I had never known Brigid to be so brilliant. She surpassed herself. The next morning, ringing up to thank me, each of the other guests said in effect, 'Wasn't Brigid wonderful?' Brigid herself did not ring up. The reason was that she had started the terrible illness, multiple sclerosis, which eventually forced her first into a wheelchair and then into a nursing-home. What was particularly distressing was that she appeared to blame Maureen for the disaster: it was the shock of the 'betrayal' that had precipitated the illness, she insisted to everyone.

I made some attempts to go and see her, but she fended them off – as she did when all but the closest friends made similar attempts. 'Write to me or telephone to me,' she said.

Brigid is a remarkably intelligent, shrewd and witty writer; and she is someone to whom, along with Maureen Duffy, every other writer owes a debt. Her fate has been a ghastly one.


In 1976, I served on the Booker Prize jury. Since my two fellow judges were Walter Allen and Mary Wilson, my sister Elizabeth, having looked through the newly arrived piles of submissions on my sitting-room floor, at once told me that the winner would be David Storey, with his *Saville* – 'More than five hundred pages, North Country working-class life, lots of brooding passion, no humour. They'll both go for that and outvote you.' She was absolutely right.

That was a hot summer. As I sat out in my garden, I would repeatedly drowse off, with the result that my lawn was pockmarked at the places where novel after novel had slipped from my nerveless fingers. Storey's made a large hole. Walter Allen was in a wheelchair as the result of a stroke. Mary Wilson's knowledge of fiction was embarrassingly narrow – so that when, after she had praised one novel, I remarked, 'But surely Kafka has done that sort of thing far better already?' she asked me, bewildered, 'Who is Kafka?' There was the additional problem that she immediately rejected any book which had too much of what she called 'PD' – physiological detail or, to put it more brutally, sex. My favourite, a novel by Julian Rathbone, contained not too much PD but, even less admissible in her judgement, cannibalism. It was with difficulty that I wrestled it on to our short-list.

During drinks before the Booker dinner at Grosvenor House I saw Rathbone standing alone in a corner of the bar and went over to talk to him. I then approached Mary Wilson: 'May I introduce Julian Rathbone?'

She shied away from me. 'Oh, I don't know ... I don't think ...'

'It's all right. He won't eat you.'

She then consented to my bringing him over.

I liked Mary Wilson for many things, not least her total lack of any kind of pretension. At one of our meetings, we were guests of Martyn Goff at an expensive and fashionable Italian restaurant in Bond Street. Having examined the menu, Mary Wilson announced that all she wanted was some cold ham and salad.

'Sure, madame, sure!' the proprietor told her. 'Some delicious *prosciutto crudo* from Parma, with some salad dressed with balsamic vinegar and the best virgin olive oil!'

'Oh, I don't want any of that *raw* ham. I meant some cooked ham. And please no dressing. Just some salad cream if you have it.'

To his credit the proprietor sent out for boiled ham and a bottle of Heinz's salad cream.

At that period it was impressed on us Booker jurors that our deliberations must be wholly confidential. This is therefore the first time that I have written of them. Nowadays jurors write or talk on television or radio of their anguish in reaching a choice – an anguish which, I must confess, I myself never suffered – even before the result has been announced.

# — 6 —

# The Drama of My Life

That my twenty or so years of working for the *Sunday Telegraph* were such happy ones was due to something increasingly rare in journalism: trust. The people for whom I worked trusted my capabilities, and I in turn trusted in their judgement and support. I had occasional arguments when, for reasons of limited space on the arts and books pages, my copy was cut; but I never had a row.

In those days the books pages were, I am convinced, the best to be found anywhere on a Sunday. This was largely due to the formidable presences of two reviewers, Rebecca West and Nigel Dennis. I might be uninterested in the books under review by them, I might disagree with what they had to say; but none the less I always had to read them. Today, only John Carey of *The Sunday Times* is of the same stature. Both Dennis and West were exacting contributors. In the case of Dennis, an epileptic and living on Gozo, the problem was one of delivery: would he be well enough and would the posts be efficient enough for copy to arrive? In the case of Rebecca West, the problem was one of worthiness: not whether she would be worthy of the book but whether the book would be worthy of her. 'Oh, I can't be bothered with that sort of piffle,' she would say. Or 'Is there nothing more substantial?' A succession of literary editors – Anthony Curtis, Rivers Scott, Duff Hart-Davis, Nicholas Bagnall – were constantly cosseting and coaxing her. The strain and effort were well rewarded.

It was useless to ask Rebecca for a fixed number of words. She wrote for as long as she wished to write. This meant that from time to time the literary editor of the day would ring me up with apologies: 'I'm afraid I'm going to have to hold your piece over until next week' or 'I'm afraid I'm going to have to cut your last paragraph.' Bloody woman, I'd think murderously. But then I would read what Rebecca had written. It so much surpassed anything else written in the *Sunday Telegraph* or anywhere else that I realized that the literary editor had been absolutely right.

I became the *Sunday Telegraph* theatre critic entirely by accident. I had never thought of myself as suitable for the job, I had never wanted it. What I had thought myself suitable for and what I had wanted was the job of Director of the British Institute in Florence. For this I had been short-listed out of a vast number of applicants. All went well at my interview with the board of governors until the most vocal of them, Michael Jaffe, Keeper of the Fitzwilliam Museum, asked me if I spoke Italian. 'Yes,' I replied, and added, 'I used to speak it well but now, after so many years of absence from Italy, I'm afraid it's rather rusty.' In Italian he then asked me, 'Where did you stay when you were living in Florence?' For some reason annoyed that he should so blatantly put my Italian to the test instead of taking my word for it, I replied in English, 'First I lived in the Via Parioncino, then at Poggio Imperiale.' He put another question in Italian. Again, foolishly, I answered in English. I could see that this second refusal to undergo his test annoyed him. I later learned that, when it came to making a decision, he was against me.

I am glad now that I did not get the job. As so often in my life, a seeming disaster in the end worked to my good. The threatened libel action had forced me to move from Brighton to London and from a large house into a small one. In the end, both suited me far better. Now not going to Florence meant firstly that I became a drama critic and so was able to save up something, however small, for my old age, and secondly that I could interest myself increasingly in the work of the writers' organization PEN, eventually becoming, as I shall later relate, its International President.

A few days after my rejection by the board of the British Institute, I was summoned to see John Thompson, the shy, self-effacing but capable editor of the Sunday Telegraph. Like many people not themselves at ease, he always made me feel ill at ease. But I had a liking and admiration for him. Did I know anything about the theatre? John asked me. I told him that in my youth I had gone to the pit or the gallery two or three times a week. What I did not tell him was that, because of claustrophobia, I now rarely went to the theatre at all, and then usually suffered agonies.

'Good. Very good. The problem is that Frank Marcus is ill and we need someone to take over from him next week. How do you feel about that?'

I told him that I felt enthusiastic.

The week extended to another week, and then to another, and then to yet another. Then John told me that Frank Marcus, still ill, wished to relinquish the post. Would I be prepared to continue in it? I said Yes.

This meant that I now had to spend four or five evenings each week in the theatre. It also meant that I was involved in an embarrassing situation. Frank Marcus had had a deputy, Rosemary Say, who now became my deputy. Like all deputies, she had hoped to succeed her boss; and like most deputies, she had failed to do so. Not unnaturally she was at first prickly towards me, a newcomer to a profession in which she had worked for so many years, and I, having been told of her expectations, was defensive. But hers was such a sweet nature that we had soon become allies and friends. I suffered a similar embarrassment with that excellent critic Eric Shorter. He had applied for the job, as he was later to apply, also without success, to succeed John Barber, whose deputy he was, on the Daily Telegraph.

My first months in the job were often excruciating because of my claustrophobia. I used to tell the PR girls that, on account of an arthritic leg, I must have seats on a gangway. But whereas some, like Sue Hyman, the beautiful and capable wife of my fellow critic Michael Coveney, always ensured that I did so, others, notably at the National and the Barbican, would tell me brusquely as they handed over the tickets, 'I'm sorry, I know you wanted seats on the gangway, but the *Sunday Telegraph* allocation has always been in the middle of Row E' – or wherever it was.

I had spoken to my doctor, Michael Rowan, of the problem and he had then prescribed for me a minuscule dose of valium. One reads constantly now of people whose lives have been ruined by this drug, so that doctors have become reluctant to prescribe it. But, like alcohol, it only ceases to be beneficial if not properly used. Those people who claim that it has induced in them a variety of psychiatric ills, far worse than the original one for which it was prescribed, would probably have succumbed to those ills in any case. Before giving a lecture, going to the dentist or embarking on a flight, I usually take my 2 mg dose. It is always helpful, it has never proved in the least addictive.

I have memories of sitting through plays, in the middle of a row at the Barbican or the National Theatre, with my heart pounding and the sweat running off my body on even the coldest night. The fact that, since I was there to review the play, I could not possibly quit the auditorium, made the ordeal even worse. Often as I left the theatre, I used to tell myself, 'You've got to give this up.' But I went on with it, week after week; and, as I did so, the panic attacks became fewer and fewer and less and less severe. In the eight years of my theatre-reviewing, I never missed a single performance – on one occasion even sitting through a tedious play (everything about it now forgotten) at the Tricycle Theatre when I had just undergone a cystoscopy from which, embarrasingly, I began to ooze blood in the middle of the first act.

There are two kinds of drama critic: those, like that dear man John Trewin, now dead, for whom theatre is in effect the whole edifice of their lives, and those, like Charles Morgan, Bernard Levin and James Fenton, for whom, usually temporarily, it is only an ante-room. I belonged to the second category. Both kinds have their advantages. I could never aspire to the knowledge of John – 'Didn't Michael Redgrave once play Andrew Aguecheek?' I would check with him and he would reply, Yes, it was on such-and-such a date, at such-and-such a theatre, and the other leads were X, Y and Z. On the other hand, my knowledge exceeded that of James Fenton – who, nonetheless, proved, during his brief spell on *The Sunday Times*, to be excellent at the job. When we were about to see a performance of *Peer Gynt* at the Other Place at Stratford, James asked me over a drink, 'Do you know anything about this play?' Yes, I replied, amazed by the question. 'Well, tell me something about it.' I told him what I could. His subsequent review was the most interesting that any of us produced. This was because, never having seen Ibsen's masterwork or even read it or read about it, he came to it absolutely fresh, with no preconceptions.

The relationship between drama critics is an odd one. One sees one's colleagues more frequently that one sees one's closest friends; but encounters are usually confined to theatre bars or, if one is out of London, to restaurants. One rarely meets one's colleagues' families or visits their homes. One theatre critic was almost always accompanied by an attractive young woman. With him and her I often used to chat in the interval. Eventually I referred to her as 'your wife'. There was immediate embarrassment. 'Well, actually,' he said, 'this is – this is – a – er – friend.' Later I met his wife. She told me that she hated the theatre and wished that her husband had never decided to work in it.

I have affectionate memories of Milton Shulman, who managed to drop off to sleep intermittently throughout a performance but would then, by some miracle, give an absolutely accurate account of it in the *Evening Standard* the next day. I have equally affectionate memories of Benedict Nightingale, one of the best of the fraternity, who was always delightfully vague – 'I expect I'll see you tomorrow evening at Chichester,' he would tell me, for me firmly to correct him, 'No, Benedict, Stratford, *Stratford*. Chichester is next week.' Ned Chaillet, then on *The Times*, would invariably arrive at the theatre in a hat. He would sit on one of his two seats and place his hat on the other. When I saw announced the publication of Oliver Sachs's *The Man Who Mistook his Wife for a Hat*, I assumed that this study of neuropathology must be about Ned. A later *Times* stringer was, briefly, a young man called, somewhat unfortunately, Morton Crapper. He would bustle into the theatre, all sharp nose, knobbly knees and angular elbows, like some hoity-toity nurse summoned from her knitting to bring a bedpan to a patient. His attitude to the eventual contents of the bedpan was usually a sniffy 'Pooh!' Then, suddenly, overnight it seemed, he vanished from our scene. I have often wondered what has happened to him. He had a rare gift for a derisive phrase, such as nowadays often by itself ensures a critic of success.

I suspect that, unlike Crapper and like Michael Billington of the *Guardian*, a man whose personal sweetness of nature spills over into his reviews, I was often too kind. Soon after I had started to be a theatre-reviewer I had been unnerved by a letter from an actor (name now forgotten) whose performance, in a play at the National, I had described as 'pitifully inadequate'. His letter ran (I quote from memory): 'You may care to know that, until I got the job at the National, I had been out of work for eight months. I have a daughter with spina bifida and my wife has just had a nervous breakdown. My invalid mother is living with us. I hope that you are satisfied.' I wrote back that I was extremely sorry about his circumstances but that they were totally irrelevant to my review. None the less, I felt uneasy, even guilty. I hoped to see him act again, so that I could at least describe him as 'that greatly improved actor X'. But I never did.

Equally disquieting were a series of postcards which I received from John Osborne after I had given what I thought an, on balance, favourable review of the revival at the Royal Court of his *Inadmissible Evidence*. One of the young secretaries at the *Sunday Telegraph* told me, 'Oh, Mr King, a horrible postcard has arrived. I don't think I'd better give it to you.'

'Don't be silly. Let me see it.'

With extreme reluctance she handed it over.

It was addressed to 'Francis Shit-house King' and the message consisted merely of telling me what a fucking cunt I was.

I replied to suggest that, if Osborne really wished to change my opinion, then a reasoned argument was more likely to do so than abuse.

A letter of more abuse followed. At the same time a postcard arrived for the editor, declaring 'King must go', followed by the disturbingly metaphysical question 'Has he ever been?' Neither of us answered. I received another abusive postcard.

I then thought of a solution. I wrote politely to Osborne. I was extremely worried, I said, by my correspondence with him, but not for the reasons that he might think. What worried me was the state of his mental health. I begged him to go and see Dr William Sargent, who had had miraculous success with a friend of mine (this was true) who had been suffering from paranoia. I appended Sargent's Harley Street address and telephone number. I heard nothing more.

When I subsequently told Irving Wardle of the letter and the postcards, he said blithely, 'Oh, I have a whole stack of those. One day I'll sell them at Christie's. With luck, the proceeds will keep me in my old age.' Such is Osborne's present reputation, I somehow doubt whether they will do that; but they may buy Irving a bargain weekend break.

The correspondence with Osborne was the occasion of a successful practical joke played on me by my old friend Jeremy Trafford. The telephone rang and a voice, exactly like Osborne's voice, demanded, 'King? Is that you, King?'

'Yes,' I replied. 'This is Francis King.'

'Osborne here. I just want to tell you one or two things. The first is that you're an absolute fucking shit.'

'Oh, don't be so childish!' I slammed the phone down. Then I removed the receiver, certain that Osborne would ring back. After half an hour, David, who was expecting a call, replaced it. At once the telephone rang. I told him to answer. On the other end was Jeremy, laughing at my gullibility.

During this period of theatre-reviewing, I myself had a play, *Far East*, produced at the Belgrade Theatre in Coventry. It was a bruising but salutary experience. For the young director Peter Wilson this was the first time that he had been entrusted with a professional production. Not unnaturally he was wary of both his author and his actors. Those actors themselves were, with one exception, unremarkable. I used to go to Coventry from time to time and be overcome by dismay. Everything that everyone was doing seemed almost right; but nothing was wholly right. Foolishly I now see, I said nothing – Yes, everything was fine, fine, I kept telling Peter when he asked what I thought. I suspected that, like me, he knew that everything was not fine, fine, but lacked the courage to tell these hardened old pros what was wrong.

The one exception to the general mediocrity of the performances was a Pakistani actor called Renu Setna who, for lack of a Japanese actor whose accent would be intelligible to an audience, had been cast in the key role of a Kyoto professor. During rehearsals Setna gave a wonderful performance, a gentle, benevolent spirituality glowing at the centre of the character. He gave an even more wonderful performance after the first night. Unfortunately, on the first night itself a lapse of memory caused him to make total nonsense of a long, key speech. Eric Shorter, unaware of my presence, was sitting just in front of me. During this speech, he began to do what I used to do when bored in the theatre: read the biographies of the actors in the programe. At that moment I knew that the play would never gain a hoped-for transfer.

Some of my colleagues were generous; some were merely patronizing. Sheridan Morley – a writer whose assiduity in recycling would satisfy the most fanatical of ecologists – managed to review the play unfavourably four times: in *Punch*, in the *Herald Tribune* and twice on the radio. This struck me as a little excessive.

Setna was clearly desolate at having, as he saw it, let me down. If the critics could have seen his subsequent performances, things might well have been different both for the play and for him. He was a character remarkable for his unworldliness, goodness and charm.

This experience as a dramatist, which I vowed never to repeat, was a salutary one because it demonstrated to me how much writer, director and actors are all at the mercy of each other. Actors have always seemed to me particularly vulnerable. Many was the time when an actor would write to me: Yes, I was absolutely right in my criticism of the way in which he had done or spoken this or that, but that was how the director had wanted it and so that was how it had had to be.

What eventually persuaded me to retire from theatre-reviewing was the serious illness of which I shall write later. By then changes had taken place at the *Telegraph*, with Lord Hartwell being obliged to sell out to Conrad Black and John Thompson being succeeded by Peregrine Worsthorne. Inevitably a new editor wants new people around him. Perry removed an outstanding literary editor, Nicholas Bagnall, and replaced him by Derwent May, who also became arts editor. I had liked and admired Derwent for many years, first meeting him when he had taken over the literary editorship of *The Listener*. But there were now times when our relations were strained. For this I was at least as much to blame as he was.

Throughout my period as drama critic I had been given virtual *carte blanche* by John Thompson and his urbane and witty deputy Desmond Albrow. Derwent, understandably, wanted to exert more control. But the problem here was that, although he knew a great deal about music and literature, he knew virtually nothing about the theatre. Before a play opens, an experienced drama critic hears rumours, favourable or unfavourable, about it. Derwent heard few such rumours. When an adaptation of Zola's *Nana* was about to open at the Mermaid, he telephoned to me: I was going to make it my lead review, wasn't I? 'Oh, no, Derwent!' I responded in anguish. 'I hear it's no good at all! I want to lead with the play out at Greenwich.' No, he wished me to lead with *Nana*. We had an argument, at the close of which he huffily conceded that I could lead with the

Greenwich play. No doubt, just as I thought him unnecessarily interfering, so he thought me unnecessarily obstinate.

When I did retire, Brenda Madox, a neighbour of mine and always a good friend, suggested to Perry that, after so many years of service with the *Telegraph*, I should receive some kind of handshake. Eventually I was sent a cheque for £2000, with a note to inform me that this was not legally due and was merely an *ex gratia* payment. At the time Perry expressed the wish that I would maintain my connection with the *Sunday Telegraph* by continuing to write the reviews which, in the past, Nicholas Bagnall had so often commissioned from me, even when I was drama critic. But fewer and fewer books came my way.

Perry has always struck me as a brilliant columnist. Like Bernard Levin, he has grasped that the secret of his kind of journalism is to start off with a single idea, often not original, and then, like a virtuoso violinist, to extemporize a series of fizzing variations on it. He never struck me as a particularly accomplished editor, being far too self-absorbed. In personal dealings he is always so charming, tolerant and kind that the ugly tone of some of his writing, particularly when he is dealing with the disadvantaged, never ceases to shock me. How can someone so civilized in his social behaviour be such a barbarian when he gets a pen in his hand? Auberon Waugh, a man to whom I at once warm each time that I meet him, poses the same riddle; but in Waugh's case I suspect that when he is at his most entertainingly outrageous, he is merely having one on.

# — 7 —

# *PEN Friends – and Enemies*

From the publication of my second or third novel I had been a member of the international writers' organization PEN. I had become one on receiving a letter from the President of the English Centre, Veronica Wedgwood, then unknown to me, urging me to join. I was, she said flatteringly, just the sort of promising young writer that PEN needed to revivify it. I did not then realize that she was sending out innumerable such letters as part of a recruiting drive – as I myself was similarly to do when, many years later, I in turn became President.

When I was living in Brighton, the then Secretary, David Carver, invited me to join the committee of management. Once again flattered, I agreed. David, with his great height and girth and his handsome, choleric face, was a remarkable figure both in physique and in character. The son of a butcher – I was once present when he and Ronald Bottrall, also the son of a butcher, had an argument as to which of them came from the humbler origins, with Ronald clinching the argument by shouting, 'But your father was a *master* butcher!' – he looked like some aristocratic ambassador, a Lord Lothian or a Lord Halifax, of the old school. Although PEN's finances were always shaky, it was as an ambassador that he insisted on travelling – first-class, a chauffeur-driven car at his disposal, a suite in all hotels. Fortunately he had a number of well-to-do female admirers, who would from time to time contribute funds and who, after his cruel death from motor neurone disease, would confide, 'I was really the only one, you know.' So many of these women claimed to have been present at his death-bed that I can only assume that the room was the size of the Albert Hall. Whether he slept with any of these admirers I very much doubt. Originally a singer, he had become Secretary of PEN in succession to Herman Ould chiefly because the two of them had been lovers. During the war, when he was ADC to the Governor of Bermuda, Sir John Boles, he persuaded Boles's wife Blanche to leave Boles and marry him. After the marriage he would refer to her as 'Lady Blanche'. I felt some surprise that he did not ask people to call him 'Sir David'.

Because of the grandeur of his manner, David was extremely successful with all the foreign centres, other than the French. He cut a distinguished figure; he was totally at his ease with rectors of universities, foreign ministers and ministers of culture. He was also totally at his ease in the smartest and most expensive of restaurants and hotels.

In choosing Presidents of the English Centre, he ensured that all real power rested with him by opting for writers who either, like Alan Pryce-Jones, were rarely in the country, or, like L.P. Hartley, were only too happy to be told what to say and do. My first committee meeting was with Leslie in the chair. He did little other than announce each item on the agenda, after which David at once assumed control.

I have noticed that the members of literary committees are always totally docile about finance but enter into furious arguments about the wording of any document or letter. It was perhaps for this reason that David erupted into one of his volcanic rages when, mildly and totally without malice, I questioned some item of office expenditure on the balance sheet. His already ruddy face becoming purple, he jumped to his feet and towered over me: 'Are you suggesting that some dishonesty has taken place? In that case, I'll have no hesitation in resigning. Yes! Either you withdraw that imputation or I shall resign! Now! At once!' Leslie began to twitter, 'Oh, David, I'm sure that Francis had absolutely no intention of suggesting for *one moment* . . .' while I tried to make it clear that I had merely been puzzled by the figure and was making no accusation against anyone. David simmered down. Soon he was even beaming down at me from the dais, in a placatory way. Such scenes, played with all the brilliance of a Finney or McKellen, were frequent at meetings both in England and abroad. Over-awed, even terrified, people would then give way to him – the one notable exception being the distinguished French writer Pierre Emmanuelle, who could effortlessly match one of David's tempests with one of his own.

Since it soon became evident to me that David was an autocrat and that the committee therefore had little function other than to agree with him, I eventually resigned – pleading the distance from Brighton to London (which, as David rightly pointed out, was not really all that great).

I returned to the committee, on the invitation of his successor Peter Elstob, after David's death. The affairs of PEN were then discovered to be in a parlous state. The lease on Glebe House, the beautiful and capacious premises in Chelsea, bequeathed by the writer Henrietta Leslie, was coming to an end; and there was no way of renewing it, since David had drawn so heavily on funds during his last years that there was a vast overdraft. Another unfortunate legacy was a young man who David had agreed should rent a flat in the building. As a sitting tenant, this youth now demanded compensation for quitting the flat.

Peter Elstob, a resourceful, much-travelled and enigmatic character – right-wing writers were constantly telling me, 'Of course he's a member of the KGB,' left-wing writers, 'Of course he's a member of the CIA' – must be credited with saving PEN at this juncture. A successful businessman as well as a successful writer, he showed great skill in his dealings with the landlords, the Church Commissioners, over dilapidations, with UNESCO over funding, and with the membership over a sharp rise in their subscriptions. It was he who wooed me back on to the committee, where – since his approach differed from David's by being wholly democratic – I was happy to serve.

There was one invaluable lesson which I tried to learn from Peter but which, for reasons of pride and obstinacy, I never wholly mastered. Faced with criticism by members, English or foreign, for some contravention of the PEN charter or some other mistake, Peter would show abject contrition: 'Yes, I'm sorry. It was totally wrong of me. I can't think what came over me. Please forgive me. I don't know what else to say.' This was quite as effective as David's threats to resign – Peter's self-humiliation being so embarrassing to everyone present that there were immediate protests of, 'No, no! You were probably right in doing what you did. It's so difficult for us to know the exact situation, etc., etc.'

Peter was a superlative judge of people. When he decided to give up the post of Honorary Secretary of English PEN, in order to concentrate on being International Secretary, he chose as his successor, despite some vigorous opposition from the old guard of David's admirers, one of the most remarkable women I have ever met, Josephine Pullein-Thompson. Josephine was already a successful writer of stories about horses for children. Her chief qualification for the PEN post was that, herself an intrepid horsewoman, she had run a pony club. She was absolutely right in seeing little difference between the running of such a club and the running of a club of writers, since the methods she had used for the former proved equally successful for the latter. As confirmation of this, I can only quote from my own experience. During a PEN congress in Puerto Rico, a group of us travelled on a Sunday from the capital of San Juan to the appealingly named Ponce. We had planned to have luncheon in Ponce; but, as we trailed up one dusty street and down another equally dusty under a broiling midday sun, it was clear that every restaurant was shut for the sabbath. 'Oh, God!' I eventually wailed. 'We'll *never* find any food.' Food at regular intervals has always been important to me. Josephine halted in her tracks and glared at me. 'Now stop grizzling! Stop grizzling at once! That's enough of that grizzling!' I might have been some fat little boy, astride his Shetland pony, who had started to grizzle that he did not like hacking in the rain. I stopped grizzling. Soon after that, Josephine announced that she could see a restaurant which was actually open. 'There, you see!' she triumphantly told me. 'There was absolutely no need for that grizzling.'

From her pony club days Josephine had also learned that writers, however spavined their figurative mounts and however maladroit their figurative equitation, nonetheless like to show off. Whereas I soon become impatient with the vanity of writers, she is indulgent to it.

As President of the English Centre I was constantly attending PEN conferences and congresses as an official delegate. Unfortunately, the Central European delegate who told Julian Barnes, then reporting on an English congress for the *New Stateman*, that people only attended such congresses for the screwing, was far wide of the mark. One attractive female delegate certainly used screwing on more than one occasion to screw the courage of some wavering delegate to the sticking-point of support for an otherwise unpopular American resolution, and one German delegate certainly made it a routine to turn up at every congress not with his wife but his mistress – disaster eventually overtaking him when, for once, he did turn up with his wife and another delegate innocently asked him where was Lotte (or Inge or whatever the mistress was called). But in general these congresses were – and still are – lamentably staid.

None the less I found much to enjoy in them – the conversations late into the night at bedroom parties given by that redoubtable and ever generous Scottish children's writer Lavinia Derwent; the visits to palaces, museums, art galleries and gardens not usually open to tourists; some brilliant paper by someone like Mary McCarthy, Czeslaw Milosz or Michael Holroyd.

Unfortunately too many delegates at such conferences suffer from the delusion that they are taking part in proceedings at the United Nations. They produce defiant resolutions requesting or even demanding that this or that government should not merely release this or that writer but should refrain from harassing its minorities, destroying its heritage of old buildings, or cutting down its forests. When I was International President, I was constantly reminding delegates that PEN had no power, only influence. But I was rarely heeded. I was also constantly reminding delegates, with similar lack of success, that if PEN ceased to be a writers' organization, limiting itself to fighting for writers, then that influence would be dissipated. Deplorable though we might all find starvation in Ethiopia, apartheid in South Africa, civil war in Lebanon, and the oppression of women in the Muslim world, these were general concerns, not the concern of PEN, which existed firstly for the exchange of literary ideas and secondly for the defence of writers against censorship, persecution, imprisonment.

I can truthfully say that, just as I neither expected nor worked to become a theatre critic, so I neither expected nor worked to become International President of PEN. That I was approached first by a Vice-President, an ancient and to me far from likeable Dutch writer called Bob den Doolard, and then by the Croatian Centre, to allow them to put my name forward for election, was, I am sure, because of three things: firstly, at assemblies of delegates I had been effective in producing the kind of compromise resolution that two warring sides would accept; secondly, I had been forceful in my criticism of what was going on behind the then Iron Curtain, at a time when there were a number of writers who were constantly coming up with extenuations and excuses; and thirdly, unlike my predecessor Per Wastberg, whose habit it was to pose the question, 'Do you think he (or she) is Nobel Prize material?' before deciding how to behave to his fellow writers, I all too frequently found an obscure delegate from, say, Colombia or New Zealand far more companionable than, say, a world-famous one from Germany or the States, with the result that I could now rely on the Colombian, New Zealand and similar votes.

International Presidents fall into three categories: those who are Nobel Prize material (as Wastberg would put it); those who are capable administrators and chairmen; and those who are both Nobel Prize material and capable administrators and chairmen. Heinrich Böll and V.S. Pritchett fell into the first of these categories; Wastberg and I into the second; Mario Vargas Llosa and Arthur Miller into the third.

I was elected to the International Presidency at a New York congress in 1986. I had never before visited the States, for some reason having always dreaded to do so. I was surprised by what I found there. Firstly, I had always supposed the Americans to be the most efficient people in the world; but if this congress was anything to judge by, they were clearly among the most inefficient. Even the St Moritz Hotel, facing Central Park from the South Side, failed to live up to its reputation as a luxury hotel. Each morning, as delegates tried to descend for their breakfast, they would hold long conversations with each other as they waited for the lifts. Some of these lifts were out of order; others moved creakingly with a geriatric slowness. When I tried to procure breakfast in my room, it arrived some forty minutes late. My second surprise was at the provinciality of the American writers taking part. At the Tokyo congress, the Japanese had been eager to hear what their foreign guests had to say. But the Americans were totally uninterested. Even Claude Simon, who had recently won the Nobel Prize, went virtually unnoticed. What was absorbing the attention of all the American participants was a battle between Norman Mailer, then President of American PEN, and a horde of feminists who felt that their presences were being ignored. These women disrupted every meeting, demanding to be heard. But since their voices were invariably raised, it would have been impossible not to hear them. Mailer sported a black eye, which made him look like a disgruntled panda. He claimed that he had received this in the course of a boxing (or it may have been judo or karate) session; but an official of American PEN told me (with what truth I do not know) that one of the maenad women had socked him one. Had she done so, no doubt with his usual chivalry he had then socked her back.

Although I was International President elect, Mailer totally ignored me, as did the rest of American PEN even when I took to my bed with a bout of influenza. It was then that I learned how extraordinarily kind Americans can be. In London I had met an American banker, who, now hearing that I was at the St Moritz, telephoned to ask if we might meet. I croaked that I was ill. He at once rushed round, bringing me some cold chicken, salad and fruit from his local delicatessen and a bundle of dollars — 'in case you haven't had time to cash any money'. After my recovery, he gave up a whole day to taking me round the city.

After my election, I thought that I had better introduce myself to Mailer. I approached him as, in jeans, T-shirt and sneakers, he lolled in a chair, slurping at a can of beer. 'Oh, Mr Mailer, I don't think that you know me. I'm Francis King. I've just been elected International President.' He slurped once more at the can. He looked me over. 'Yeah. They wanted me to stand for International President, but I decided that I wanted that like a hole in the head.' He said nothing more. I said nothing more.

At my election, Per Wastberg made a speech, in the course of which he graciously told the delegates, 'Anyone who reads Francis King's books will know that he is not nearly as nice as he seems.' I was tempted to respond, 'Anyone who

reads Per Wastberg's books will know that he is not nearly as nasty as he seems.'
But I restrained myself. Although neat, the riposte would not have been fair.
Wastberg would never have seemed nasty to anyone.


Unfortunately, throughout most of my Presidency, I was involved in an acrimonious, never resolved debate. This was over a congress eventually held in South
Korea. The decision to accept the invitation of the South Korean Centre was
taken, under the Presidency of Wastberg, during a congress in Tokyo. I was myself
not present at the relevant meeting, from which I had had to absent myself in order
to be interviewed on Japanese television. Subsequently, after I had succeeded
Wastberg, the American Centre decided that, because there were some half-dozen
writers in prison in South Korea, it would be 'obscene' (the word figured frequently in their vocabulary at that time) to hold a congress there. In this they were
supported by Wastberg. Since there were now fewer prisoners than when the
decision to go to South Korea had been taken, and since both the American Centre
and Wastberg had supported that original decision, I was puzzled. What had made
them change their minds? I never got a satisfactory answer. At every congress, the
Americans, their allies and Wastberg would once more bring up the issue. A vote
would be taken, which would confirm that the congress should take place; but this
democratic outcome only fortified the losers, who would bring up the matter again
and yet again. The South Koreans were fascists, these people declared; and since
Peter Elstob's successor as International Secretary, Alexandre Blokh, and I were
both in favour of the congress on the grounds that, if it did take place, then it was
much more likely that the writers would be released from prison as a gesture of
good will, we too were fascists. Through all this I found staunch allies in the
French – a nation which I have always admired for its rationality and lack of cant.
     Eventually I arrived in South Korea, to find, to my surprise, that all the people
who had declared that they would boycott the congress had either already turned
up or were about to do so. The Korean Centre, under its dignified and generous-
spirited woman president, Madame Chung, explained to me and Alexandre the
strategy for obtaining the prisoners' release. The President of South Korea would
be giving a party for the congress, and I should there be presented to him but
should on no account raise the subject. Two days later he would grant me a
private audience. I should then plead for the prisoners' release, which they
thought that he would grant.
     Unfortunately, before this strategy could be put into effect, Susan Sontag, the
chief American delegate, had arrived. At the airport American PEN had
organized a press conference for her. She there denounced the Korean
government and 'demanded' (this word, like the word 'obscene', often featured in
the vocabulary of the American Centre) that the prisoners be released. The
President, not used to having foreigners demand things of him, at once cancelled
both his party and his private meeting with me. The prisoners stayed in prison, to
be released at a later date.

This maladroitness of the Americans was sadly all too typical. It was useless for Nancy Ing, the charming and sage Chinese-American President of the Taiwan Centre, to explain to them the importance of face in the Far East. The conception of face did not exist in the United States, and it was therefore absurd to them that it should exist anywhere else in the world. If something was obscene, then one must denounce it as obscene. There was no place for pussy-footing.

It was equally useless for me to explain the dangers of moral indignation. To vent their feelings of outrage was less important, I told them, than to obtain the prisoners' release. At this point I used to draw a parallel with judicial punishment. Punishment imposed merely as a release for moral indignation was the worst kind of punishment. The best kind of punishment was remedial and deterrent.

Susan Sontag, both then and on other occasions, set a problem. Was this still attractive, always intelligent and slightly grubby-looking woman so energetic in PEN out of altruism or out of self-interest? With her press conferences and her adroitly managed appearances at precisely the right moment at the side of precisely the right person at precisely the right party, reading or debate, she struck me as being in large part motivated by vanity and ambition. But then I used to begin to examine my own conduct. Certainly I was dedicated to all for which PEN stood – genuinely wanting to fight against censorship and to help my fellow writers. But, if I were truthful, I had to admit that I was flattered by being interviewed for television and the newspapers, by being received by government ministers, by hobnobbing with world-famous writers. All that I could say in my defence was that, for no financial recompense whatever, I sacrificed hours and hours each week to the usually tedious business of PEN, often typing my own letters and often also paying for the postage on them.

The Americans and their allies could never forget that they had been defeated over the decision to hold the South Korean congress. Much later, after I had ceased to be President, it was proposed that Madame Chung should be elected to the honorary office of Vice-President. At once the Americans began a campaign to have this proposal defeated. Once more there was a great deal of acrimony. Madame Chung was elected but by so small a majority and after so many hurtful things had been said or implied about her, that so far from being delighted, she was all too clearly desolated. I felt profoundly embarrassed and ashamed, since I had been one of those who had put her name forward and had campaigned on her behalf.

The other cause of turbulence during my three-year 'reign' was a dead German writer called Blunck. While I was nursing David through the terrible illness which eventually killed him and was myself in constant discomfort or pain from what was belatedly diagnosed as cancer, I received a letter from a German lawyer in impeccable English. The centenary of the birth of his uncle, the famous writer Hans Friedrich Blunck, was about to come up and some of his friends and disciples were preparing a *Festschrift*. Since Blunck had been a devoted supporter of PEN and since I was the present International President, would I be prepared to write a brief foreword to the book? I groaned, vacillated and eventually said yes.

Consulting a History of International Literature on my shelves, I learned that Blunck – a kind of Teutonic J.R. Tolkien, from what I could gather – had won a number of prestigious prizes. I then cobbled together some 500 anodyne words.

When the *Festshrift* appeared, it somehow got into the hands of the PEN centre, based in London, of the German-speaking Writers Abroad. Why this centre should still be in existence so long after the end of the war was something which had always puzzled me. Surely its members could join either the West German or the East German Centre; or, if those alternatives did not appeal to them, the English Centre? At all events, these dozen or so German exiles seized a wonderful opportunity to stir up a fuss. Blunck, they announced by way of a circular letter to all PEN centres and Vice-Presidents, had been an enthusiastic supporter of the Nazis. I was all too clearly, they implied, a Nazi sympathizer for having written my foreword. At once I received a number of self-righteous letters from people important – or self-important – in PEN. One, to my surprise, came from Wastberg. Another, not at all to my surprise, came from Bob den Doolard, who had originally proposed me for the Presidency but had then been disillusioned when I had started to make efforts, eventually crowned with success, to establish a PEN centre in Moscow. How could I have done such a thing? den Doolard demanded.

Having decided to adopt Peter Elstob's ploy when under a barrage of criticism, I wrote back both to him and to everyone else that I was deeply embarrassed, deeply ashamed, should have been more careful, could not forgive myself, did not know what had come over me to be so careless etc., etc. To den Doolard I added the information that my judgement might have been affected by the fact that, when I received the request for the Foreword, I was nursing a dying friend and was suffering, though I did not then know it, from cancer. Den Doolard replied, 'I am sorry to hear of the death of your friend and of your illness. But I am afraid that these two things are totally irrelevant.'

This confirmed me in my opinion of den Doolard. In PEN he was the administrator of what was called – and is still called – the foundation PEN Emergency Fund, set up to aid any writers or their families in desperate circumstances because of official persecution. Neither I, as President, nor Alex Blokh, as International Secretary, could find out anything about the workings of this fund except in the vaguest and most melodramatic terms. As though he were parodying a John le Carré novel, den Doolard would recount to us how he had travelled secretly to a certain city of the Soviet Union to meet a certain contact who would act as conduit for money to be given to the wife of a certain writer in the Gulag. He was never more precise. As soon as he had arrived at the rendezvous, he had realized that he was being followed. How much of all this was fantasy, how much truth? I never knew. At all events, he was immensely pleased with his role as intrepid cold war warrior.

My dog-rolling-over-on-to-back-paws-in-air act had absolutely no effect. It only made my assailants that much more ravenous to sink their teeth into the soft underbelly thus exposed. Equally without effect was my discovery, through a

German well-wisher, that Blunck, although he had feebly and culpably gone along with the Nazis to the extent of being fined a small sum after the war as a 'sympathizer', had certainly been no monster (as Wastberg had actually called him in a letter to me). The Germans in Exile simply would not let the matter drop. One of their number, puffed up with pride and disapproval, even visited my house during my protracted convalescence to make known his displeasure.

However, if some people behaved badly in this matter, others behaved impeccably. Peter Elstob wrote to assure me that I had his full support: I had made a mistake but of my integrity he had no doubts at all. Far more surprising was a letter from the then President of East German PEN, a writer called Heinz Kamnitzer. Since he was the staunchest of communists, he and I had often argued both privately and at PEN assemblies and at a CSE Cultural Forum in Budapest, at which I had served as a British delegate. Despite these political differences, I had always liked and admired him – feelings which I think that he reciprocated. A Jew, who had been a refugee in England during the war and who had lost many of his family in the Holocaust, he had every reason to detest a man such as Blunck. But he wrote to tell me that he thought that the protesters were making a lot of silly fuss about nothing, and that the sooner that the whole matter was forgotten, the better.

Near the close of my three-year period of office, a number of centres gave me private assurances that they would vote for my re-election. One of these centres even claimed to have made soundings and to have confirmed that I commanded a sufficient number of votes. But it would have proved a close-run thing; and in any case I had reached the conclusion that enough was more than enough. Had I had the energetic support of the International Secretary, Alexandre Blokh, I might have felt differently; but his distinguished career in UNESCO had given him the international civil servant's dread of any kind of open conflict. For people to argue hotly in the assembly of delegates struck me as democratic and therefore always welcome; he, on the other hand, was constantly pleading with me, 'Let's try to get this settled in private. We don't want any public show of division in PEN.' A fiercely contested election was the last thing that he wanted. Although I had often given him unequivocal support, even against my better judgement, when he had made unpopular decisions or said unpopular things in the past, I knew that, despite our happy private relations with each other, I could not now in turn count on such unequivocal support from him. I therefore thanked my would-be backers and bowed out, giving my recent operation as my reason.

The search for my successor then began. My own wish, supported enthusiastically by the English Centre, was that this should be the Nigerian writer Chinua Achebe. He was both a novelist of indisputable stature and a man of total integrity. There was the further consideration that there were too few PEN centres in Africa and that the persecution of writers was lamentably common there. A few weeks after the English Centre had sounded out Achebe, I was stunned when, at a dinner given by my friend Peter Day, the President of French PEN, René Tavernier, announced his own candidature. Witty, gallant, forceful, capricious, influential, René had been unstinting in his loyalty to me during my Presidency. I had come to regard him not merely as an ally but as a friend. The sad truth, however, was that he was visibly dying, his ample frame so shrunken that his clothes hung about him and his face grey and glistening. There was a terrible silence when he made his announcement. Peter and Josephine looked at me and I looked at them. Then I summoned up my courage: 'René, I must tell you that, at this moment, Achebe would be the best choice. I'm sorry. You know how fond I am of you and how much I admire you. But it should be Achebe.' My opposition resulted in a coldness between us, fortunately only temporary.

The French at once set to work, rallying their votes. The fact that the Americans supported Achebe meant that a number of centres decided not to vote for him. I was perturbed when one of the Polish delegates, a man whom I greatly admired and liked, asked me, 'Why are you so enthusiastic about this Achebe? Isn't he a – er – little *unsophisticated*?' 'No, not at all,' I could reply with total truthfulness. 'If you read his novels, you will see just how sophisticated he is.' By *unsophisticated* I guessed that the Pole meant uncouth, uncivilized, *black*.

By a narrow margin René won the election at Maastricht, where I was presiding at a congress for the last time. Sadly, this delightful man had no opportunity to show whether he was a good President or not. Within a few months he was dead. (His last illness is depicted in a moving film directed by his son Bertrand Tavernier.)

He was then succeeded by the Hungarian writer György Konrad. Konrad is certainly Nobel Prize material. But he shows as much talent for chairing a meeting as I would show for refereeing a Rugby football match. That that disability should have made no difference to the efficacy of PEN demonstrates, perhaps, that its President is not really all that important.


When I look back on my PEN experience, I must at once differentiate between my seven years as President of the English Centre and my three years as International President.

The seven years were wholly happy ones. Apart from the unfailing support which Josephine gave me, I invariably received the support of the committee of management and the members. Often, the older and frailer a writer, the more willing he was to turn out for some demonstration. In particular, I remember how on an icy winter's day, Victor Pritchett, Stephen Spender and Angus Wilson all stood shivering outside the Polish Embassy, before we were admitted to present a petition on behalf of Polish writers in prison. I thought then that the gallant trio deserved their knighthoods as much for what they were prepared to do to help their fellow writers as for their writings. Some younger writers whom we had approached had declined to come; some had promised to come but failed to turn up. Among other writers totally selfless in their commitment to PEN were Harold Pinter and Antonia Fraser, Michael Holroyd and Margaret Drabble, Timothy Mo, William Boyd, Graham Swift, Kazuo Ishiguro and Salman Rushdie.

The annual PEN Writers Day was always a particularly happy occasion. On one such Day, when I was presiding in the Queen Elizabeth Hall over a discussion in which Harold Pinter and Tom Stoppard were taking part, I suddenly glimpsed Arthur Miller in the audience. Would he be prepared to join the panel? After some hesitation he accepted my invitation. I was then able to tell the audience, 'Now you have before you the three greatest living dramatists of the English-speaking world.'

Gore Vidal was a waspishly entertaining guest at another Writers Day. During luncheon, I introduced the critic Philip Friend to him. 'Are you the father of someone called Sean French?' Vidal asked. Philip replied that he was. 'Oh, he once wrote a short story about me,' Vidal said. Philip said that he did not think that possible, his son did not write short stories. 'Well, admittedly it was called an interview,' Vidal conceded, 'but it was fiction from beginning to end.'

Vidal's named cropped up at the CSE Cultural Forum in Budapest, which I have already mentioned. At one session, one of the French delegates made a protest about the persecution of homosexuals in the Soviet Union. I then spoke out in support. Purple in the face, a member of the Soviet delegation rose to deliver a tirade. How could writers of our distinction ally ourselves with degenerates? Many of the ills of the Western world could be ascribed to lax sexual morals. Homosexuality was a contagious disease.

The session over, the Soviet delegate showed absolutely no animosity towards me, even inviting me to sit down to luncheon with him. During luncheon, he told me how he shared my love of Italy. He had just been there. He had been staying with the American writer Gore Vidal.

I wish that I had had the courage to ask him if he had caught the contagious disease of homosexuality from his host.

At this same CSE Cultural Forum, I also complained – at the prompting of David, a jazz-buff and jazz-player – about the persecution of jazz musicians in Czechoslovakia. Two days later I was bidden to a party at the Czechoslovakian Embassy. The Ambassador and his wife, having courteously greeted me and said a few words, invited me to enter a room behind them. It was so small that the little band of musicians in it almost wholly filled it. As soon as I had joined them, along with some of the other Western delegates, the band struck up. I have never heard jazz played worse or more noisily.

After some minutes, unable to endure the cacophony any longer, I retreated. The Ambassador approached me, smiling. 'I hope you enjoyed the jazz, Mr King. I know that you are a jazz lover. We flew in this band from Prague specially for this party.'

I liked the ingenious, albeit expensive, reply to my protest.


Looking back on my Presidencies first of the English Centre and then of International PEN, I am grateful that they obliged me to acquire a skill which previously I lacked: the making of impromptu speeches. 'Would you perhaps say a few words, Mr King?' was something repeatedly urged on me at congresses abroad – not merely at a dinner or reception but during a visit to a museum or art gallery, on an excursion by boat, even once when I stepped through from the customs into the arrival hall of Osaka airport. At a congress at Lugano, I found myself holding forth three or four times a day. On one occasion during that congress, I was standing in front of a table loaded with a resplendent buffet luncheon. As I spoke, I was aware that everyone present was surging past me and behond me. By the time that I had finished, the table was bare. After that, Josephine would always collect some food for me, as well as for herself. On such occasions the French were invariably the greediest, piling their plates so high that chicken legs, meatballs and hard-boiled eggs would topple off them, to be trodden underfoot by the crush. On one such occasion in Lugano, René Tavernier remarked to me, with the portentousness to which he was prone, 'Despite my age and despite my state of health, I am still hungry for life.' Looking at his plate, I felt like remarking, 'Yes, and you're still hungry for food.'

Another lesson which I learned from my Presidency of International PEN was the extreme good fortune enjoyed by writers of the Western democracies. We grumbled about the smallness of our royalties, the inadequacies of our editors and the obtuseness of the people who reviewed us, but none of us had suffered the kind of persecution common in many other parts of the world. When I expressed this surely uncontroversial view at an Edinburgh Book Fair symposium three or four years ago, I was at once attacked by the Scottish writer James Kelman. Writers in Britian were in a fooking situation, he shouted, with their sales constantly falling. Who fooking cared about writers in other countries? I was like a mother telling her children to be happy with the mook they were given to eat, because in other parts of the world children were starving. The small but derisively vocal claque which Kelman had brought along with him applauded these sentiments. No doubt encouraged by them, he then asked the seemingly irrelevant question why no Scottish writer had won the fooking Booker. I could have made one of two answers, which would have enraged him equally: either that, yes, it was a fooking scandal that the Prize had never been awarded to Allan Massie, or that no Scottish writer had won the fooking Booker because so far no Scottish writer had been fooking good enough. But by now a terrible weariness had paralysed me. It was therefore left to Marina Warner, also on the panel, to argue with Kelman. Despite her logic and eloquence, she did not, perhaps predictably, get very far.


I take pride in the sole real achievement of my Presidency. This was the creation, for the first time, of a centre in the then Soviet Union. In the past there had been a single stumbling block to this: the demand by the Soviet authorities that any centre would be, in effect, a subsidiary of the then state-controlled Writers' Union. With the beginnings of *glasnost* a second stumbling block appeared: those writers who had previously been banned refused to join in a centre with officially approved writers. To solve these two problems, Alexandre Blokh and I decided to make a trip to the Soviet Union together.

On the day before we were due to depart, my major operation only two or three months behind me, I was suddenly seized with agonizing stomach pains. Was I to go or was I to cancel? That night, a consultant friend of mine telephoned to me: he had heard that, though ill, I was about to leave for the Soviet Union; he begged me not to go; if I became worse and needed another operation, it would be disastrous not to have my own surgeon, one of the best in Europe, to perform it.

After sleepless deliberation, I set off for Moscow still feeling ghastly. On my arrival, I was rushed to a banquet, at which caviare and vodka were both in liberal supply. To hell with it! I consumed vast quantities of both. Amazingly, the next morning I felt absolutely marvellous.

Our negotiations were prolonged, complex and tough, but eventually successful. Alexandre, with his charm, negotiating skills and fluent Russian, and I, presenting the image of a well-intentioned, high-principled ignoramus, proved a good team. We eventually got agreement that the proposed centre should be independent of the Writers' Union, and that the two conflicting groups of writers should collaborate in it.

On my return to England, I recounted to my doctor the story of my miraculous recovery. She told me that unfortunately she could not prescribe caviare and vodka for me on the National Health.

# — 8 —

# *Darkness Falls from the Air*

As soon as I arrived in Brighton, ideas for the short stories which eventually made up my collection *The Brighton Belle* began to jostle in my head. In the forefront was the idea for a short story about a charming, negligent, amoral deck-chair attendant, who devises an ingenious means of cheating his employers, the council, out of part of his daily takings in order to save up for a journey, often dreamed about, to Las Vegas. The problem was that I had no idea of how he was to do this cheating. Had I been a bolder writer, I should simply have walked down to the seafront and got into conversation with one of the deck-chair attendants who, often in no more than ragged shorts and gym-shoes on a fine day, could be found perched on railings or lolling in their own deck-chairs while waiting for custom. As it was, I put an advertisement in the *Brighton Argus*: a novelist wished to meet a deck-chair attendant in order to acquire some information.

Having received three answers, I arranged interviews on consecutive evenings.

The first to come was an Etonian of about sixteen or seventeen, the son of a Brighton solicitor, who was working for the second consecutive year on the deck-chairs in order to save up enough money to buy himself a motor bicycle. Skinny and extremely tall, with the kind of stoop, one shoulder higher than the other, which extremely tall people often adopt in order not to be conspicuous, he had large glistening lips, a large glistening nose, and strangely tiny hands. No doubt from nervousness, his manner was one of vague affront. No, he didn't want a drink, thank you, he never drank. No, he didn't want a Coke, thank you, he didn't really want anything. He stared at Wang. 'I've never liked Pekes,' he said. 'My mother had a Peke. Dead now.' I felt that its deadness was the only thing to recommend it in his view.

When I asked him about the possibility of a deck-chair attendant cheating the council, the vague affront turned to indignation. 'Oh, yes, yes, it's perfectly possible. In fact, I think most of them are on the fiddle. Yes, I'd say sixty or seventy per cent. You may not believe this, but they actually *boast* of it. Yes, if I were prepared to do the same sort of thing, I'd have that motor bike by now. I'd have had it long ago.'

'How exactly do they do it?'

'Do what?'

'The fiddling.'

He drew back from me, on the sofa facing my chair, as though I had made some indecent proposition. 'I've no idea. I've absolutely *no* idea at all. I don't want to know. I think that kind of behaviour *quite disgusting.*'

I could see that he was going to be of no use to me at all.

The second desk-chair attendant was all too clearly gay. Middle-aged, plump, with continually pursed lips, he wore a number of bracelets up a bare arm, had thick, tousled black hair with golden spikes, and was soon calling me 'Sugar' with an American accent which must, I was sure, be put on. He all too obviously thought that my advertisement had merely been a pretext for a date.

When I asked him about the fiddling, he yet again pursed his lips, tipped his head backwards, eyebrows raised, and told me, 'Oh, it's a doddle, easy as can be! Well, with the amount that those skinflints pay us, why shouldn't we make a little on the side?' People had their different methods, he went on to explain. Then he told me of his, concluding, 'Now, Sugar, you do promise me you won't breathe a word to a soul, won't you? I mean, I could get myself into trouble – and a whole lot of lovely boys into trouble too.'

That subject dealt with, he held out his glass for another Pimm's. 'I shouldn't really. These things go straight to my head, and then I start doing things I oughtn't to do.'

He began to question me about myself: Did I live in such a lovely home all my myself? Didn't I feel lonely? Did I have lots of adventures? Did I go to the Spotted Dog, the Forty-two, the Champion? Did I know of that new bar which had just opened in Peacehaven? Yes, in *Peacehaven*! Would you believe it? By now he was on his third Pimm's. He began to tell me about himself. He and a friend had opened up this boutique, men's clobber, and first it had gone well, wonderfully well. But then the friend had fallen for this businessman, who lived in Sheffield and was really *not at all nice*, and the friend spent all his time with him in Sheffield, it was heart-breaking really, they had been so close to each other, and of course the boutique had been just too much for one to manage on one's own . . .

So it went on; and all the time, as he got drunker and drunker, I realized that he thought that the evening would end up with the two of us in each other's arms. Eventually, desperate, I said, 'The dog's getting restless. I must give him a little walk before an accident happens. Would you like to come with us?'

Reluctantly, unsteadily he rose. 'Oh, all right, dear. Since it's a nice evening.'

I walked with him to the top of Montpelier Road – 'He does pee a lot, doesn't he?' he said of Wang; and then I said, 'Well, I'd better say goodnight to you here. I'll go back to the house now. You did say that you lived off the Dyke Road, didn't you? It was so kind of you to come and help me.'

I knew that I was behaving ungratefully, even ruthlessly. But I could take no more of the inane chatter, which would, I knew, go on and on and on, unless I was prepared to find something else to distract him.

When I opened the door to the third informant, I experienced an immediate shock. As a boy of fourteen, visiting Paris for the first time, I had become obsessed with a Titian portrait in the Louvre, *L'homme au gant*. Here on my doorstep was someone who looked uncannily like that man with the glove, with the same pale narrow face, the same slightly aquiline nose, the same high forehead, the same elegant hands. He told me that his name was David Atkin. I never thought for one moment, so virile was he, that he might be gay; and oddly, he exerted absolutely no sexual attraction on me, despite his good looks.

From the first we got on well. Yes, of course the deck-chair attendants fiddled their takings, he said. He fiddled them himself. He then told me – an interesting parallel to my projected story, which in fact I never published, since I never got it right – that he fiddled them because he was trying to save up enough money to visit India. He had always dreamed of visiting India. On my telling him that I had spent my childhood there, he began to question me eagerly.

When he got up to go, I asked him if he would like to have dinner with me one evening.

'Why not?'

We met at Wheeler's. Years later, he told me how terrified he had been. He had never before eaten at that class of restaurant and he feared that somehow he would betray this. I had asked whether he would prefer a Muscadet or a Chablis and he had had no idea which to say. But I had guessed nothing of all this. He had seemed to be wholly at his ease. Once again, despite the differences in our ages, upbringings, educations and interests, we got on remarkably well.

So began a friendship. Then, as we became increasingly frank with each other, I realized that he was bisexual. He had, of course, long before realized that I was gay. One evening, returning a little drunk from having had dinner together once more at Wheeler's, we quite naturally, without any forethought or fuss, went to bed together. After that, I still regarded him as no more than a handsome and companionable friend. This was demonstrated by the fact that, when I succumbed to the madness of my obsessive love for Giorgio, I told David all about it. 'I bet you wish I was Giorgio,' he said to me on one occasion when we were in bed together. I laughed and did not answer. He was teasing me, in no way jealous or annoyed.

Then, slowly, Giorgio by now back in Italy, I began to fall in love with David. Before, I had made no great efforts to see him; and, if he failed to telephone me for days on end, I did not really worry. Now all that changed. 'What happened to you? You promised to ring me,' I would reproach him. Or: 'I thought you were going to call round after the theatre.'

By now he had ceased to be a deck-chair attendant and, since he was a superb swimmer, had become a life-guard. He would often tell me of how both men and women would chat him up on the front – 'It's amazing how brazen they can be,' he would say. I used to feel a devouring jealousy. Sometimes I would go down to the front and would sit myself in a deck-chair not far from his station. Pretending to read (he did not like me to talk at length to him while he was working) I would watch, with surreptitious malevolence, as, say, two teenage girls would boldly accost him with a lot of giggling and squeals of shocked delight, or some elderly man, dog on lead, sidled up to him to say some shy, mumbled words.

Whenever he had an afternoon free, he would drive me in the Daimler, which I had by now acquired, either up on to the downs, where we would go for a walk, or over to Worthing, where he would swim and I would go round the antique and junk-shops. (I chose Worthing because so many elderly people went there to die, their goods and chattels eventually ending up in the hands of dealers or in the local auction rooms.) He loved the Daimler, as he loved all large and powerful cars.

When Richard Attenborough began to film what I consider his one indisputably great film, *Oh, What a Lovely War*, in Brighton, David managed to get himself taken on as an extra. Then, since he had soon become friendly with a number of people in the company, he graduated to a small speaking role as the private who tells John Mills's Haig that it is 'Six o'clock, sir. Time for the attack.' So it was that he started on his career as model and actor. Totally without ambition, he was content if it brought him in enough money to survive without the dole. He had a contempt for other young people, even friends of his, who regarded the dole as preferable to work. This was odd in someone so anarchic, who was constantly chiding me or laughing at me for being, as he would put it, 'so boringly honest'. I remember one occasion when, in the back of a London taxi with him, I found a wallet containing £25, with no indication of who was the owner. I handed it over to the taxi-driver, who said that he would 'see to it'. 'I bet he'll see to it,' David said, when we had left the taxi. 'He'll keep it. What a wimp you can be!' When I was paid some small sum for a lecture, he would ask me in astonishment, 'You're not going to declare that, are you?' When I said yes, that I thought that I should, he would tell me, 'But there's no way they'll ever find out about it.'

Unlike me, David was extraordinarily reticent about himself, so that it took me many years, literally, to learn his full story. His father, a Jewish furrier from Latvia, and his mother, a lower middle-class Gentile, had both been married before. Each had had one child by these previous marriages but, since one had emigrated to Canada and the other to Australia, David had never met either and, oddly, had no wish to do so. His father had done well on migrating to England, so that he was eventually able to buy a farm in Sussex, with the result that David had been born in a maternity hospital in Guildford. His father, much older than his mother, had died when David was eight or nine. His mother, who had inherited the farm and a substantial amount of money, had soon after remarried. This stepfather came from Yorkshire; and in consequence left David with a profound distrust of anyone from there. During their honeymoon, mother and stepfather farmed David out with the stepfather's family, who were then beastly to him. When David was reunited with the stepfather, he was equally beastly. Worse, he persuaded the mother to invest the inherited money in a number of harebrained schemes and so lost almost all of it for her. After four or five years, the couple separated and eventually got divorced.

David's mother, clearly an astute businesswoman once she had got rid of the incubus of her second husband, entered the catering business with a woman partner, whose lover she also became. David told me how, returning home from school, he would often come on the two women seated on a sofa together, their arms around each other, as they read the same newspaper. They used to take baths together and sleep in the same bed.

Such a history does much to explain David's attachment to me. I represented first the beloved father whose death had precipitated his expulsion from a childhood Eden into the hell of his adolescent years; and secondly the stability, financial and emotional, which he had always craved but so seldom known.

Oddly, despite the unconventionality of her own life, David's mother could not stand male homosexuals. As a consequence, David, who was devoted to his mother, decreed that we should never meet. On one occasion we were in the car, he driving and I seated beside him, when she saw us in a Brighton street. She stared, and David then hooted and waved. 'Oh, God! How am I to explain who you are?' He did not really need to ask that question. He was always resourceful. When questioned, he told his mother that I was an antique dealer, to whom he had sold some things picked up in an auction sale. He was driving the car because the antique dealer had been disqualified.

Not long after, when I was attending Godfrey Winn's fiftieth birthday party, I saw her, a tiny, energetic, highly competent figure, dashing about in charge of the catering. Passing me, a plate of canapés in her hand, she gave me a long, surprised look, no doubt identifying me as the man she had seen with her son in the car. That evening she said to David, 'That antique dealer friend of yours was at Godfrey Winn's party.'

'Which antique dealer friend?' David asked, with assumed vagueness.

'The one whose car you were driving.'

'Oh, that one! Perhaps Godfrey Winn buys things from him.'

David had worked in the antiques business for a while as a knocker. This had meant travelling around the country in a small, dilapidated van which his mother had bought him, sometimes attending auction sales but more often knocking on doors. On one occasion he knocked at the door of a large house in Sussex. He heard someone shuffling down the corridor to open the door. Then at last the door creaked back. Peering round it was Harold Macmillan.

David stammered out that he wondered whether there were any antiques in the house which Macmillan wished to sell. Clearly lonely, Macmillan asked him in. He offered David one or two unexceptional pieces, which David bought, and then suggested a glass of sherry. They talked for some time. David was extraordinarily knowledgeable about foreign affairs. When one of my foreign PEN contacts arrived at the house, he would cause amazement by knowing the names of all the chief ministers in the country, however obscure, from which that contact came. He caused similar amazement to Macmillan by knowing the names of all the chief ministers who had ever served under him. When he finally left, Macmillan presented him with an ivory paper-knife, with his initials H.M. on it. After David's death I gave this to my friend Peter Day, in return for all the care which he had lavished on David during his last, prolonged illness.

Before I had known him, while still in his teens, David had emigrated to America. He had travelled the country, working briefly at one job after another. In Miama he had been an 'oil boy' at one of the leading hotels – rubbing oil into the flaccid bodies of usually ancient men and women. 'It was like lubricating tortoises,' was how he once described it. One of these ancients, a millionaire, suggested that David should go up to his room from the pool. He would make it worth his while, he said. 'But I couldn't face it, he was so old and ugly,' David said.

David had also hitch-hiked around most of the world. Like me, he had a passion for travel; unlike me, he liked the travel to be as arduous as possible. That was one reason why we usually had separate holidays. The other was that, when out of England, he was eager for what he called adventures, i.e. sex with either women or men.

After I had moved to London, he would come up from his little Brighton flat to visit me almost every weekend. The weekends grew longer and longer. Eventually I said to him, 'Why do you waste your money on that flat? You could have a room here free.'

'May I think about it?' He would often criticize me for the speed with which I came to decisions, only to regret them later.

He thought about it for several weeks. Then he made up his mind.

He had an extraordinary tact, knowing precisely not merely when I wished for his company but when I wished for conversation and when I didn't. My friend Jeremy Trafford always attempts to share his own interests – literature, theatre, art – with anyone with whom he is in love. This is typically generous-hearted of him but sometimes unwise. People often do not wish to be changed from what they are. I made no attempt to make David share my interests and he made no attempt to make me share his. But eventually, from accompanying me to the theatre, he became infected with my love of it; and from listening to jazz with him, I in turn became infected with his love of that.

There was a brief period when, uncertain of his love for me (he was totally undemonstrative, 'I love you' was something that he probably never said to anyone), I was jealous and possessive. Then an extraordinary thing happened. I calmly accepted that, young as he was, he would wish to lead the same sort of life which I had lived at that age. This he did with the same tact with which he always knew when I wanted his company and when I didn't. There were many of his friends whom I never met until his death; there were some of whose existence I did not even know until then. Occasionally, however, he would introduce me to someone with whom he had had sex. One of these was a delightful black woman. I have no idea whether she had any inkling of the relationship between David and me. I liked her and we got on well.

One day the bell rang and there, on the doorstep, was a world-famous pianist, whom I immediately recognized, having attended, with Theodore Goodman, a concert of his at the Festival Hall only a few days before. 'Oh!' He seemed astonished to see me. 'Doesn't David Atkin live here? Have I come to the wrong house?'

'Yes, he lives here. I'll call him.'

I shouted up the stairs.

David descended half-way and squinted down at the man. 'I'm sorry. I'm busy at the moment.'

'Yes. Yes, I see.' Suddenly the pianist was embarrassed. 'Well, ring me,' he said. 'You have the number.'

David said nothing, still squinting down, his hand on the banister.

The man turned to me. 'Thank you,' he said. 'I'm sorry to have disturbed you.'

After he had gone, David was furious. 'I told him not to come here. I told him! Not once, not twice, three times! Bloody fool! That's the last time he'll see me.'

'It doesn't matter.'

'It does matter. Bloody fool!'

The man had infringed a rule of undeviating discretion.

There were some of my friends whom David liked and was prepared to visit with me. There were others to whom he was polite and even friendly if he came across them, but whose invitations he invariably refused. In general, like me, he was irritated or embarrassed by anyone who was camp. For that reason he loathed gay parties and could rarely be persuaded to attend one.

His secrecy and the difficulty which he experienced in showing any deep affection or tenderness I ascribed to his bruising early years. He was convinced that the expression of feeling, indeed feeling itself, made one vulnerable. Yet, in addition to his close attachment to me and his mother, he was also attached, hardly less closely, to my family and to a small circle of friends.

David had always been extraordinarily healthy. With his vitamins, his daily swimming, his avoidance of sugar and fats, his breakfast of muesli, his disapproval of smoking, the rarity of his drinking, he was constantly chiding me: 'Why do you have to eat that kind of poison?' or 'No, no! *Don't* have another vodka. You don't realize how bad it is for you.' I was the one who was intermittently ailing; he the one who seemed impervious to colds, headaches or stomach upsets.

Then, suddenly, he began to have one minor ailment after another: acne suddenly pitting the clear, sunburned skin of his muscular back; a fungal infection; sore throats; a persistent cough; diarrhoea. At first he was reluctant to go to the doctor – 'No, it's nothing, nothing.' Finally I persuaded him. Eventually he had some tests and told me, 'I have something wrong with my blood. That's why I get these infections. It's to do with the platelets.'

'Can't they do something about it?'

He shrugged. 'They're doing what they can.'

He became irritable when I tried to question him further. 'I don't know. I just don't know. You know what it's like when you see a quack on the National Health. He's not prepared to tell you all that much or to have a long conversation with you. He's far too busy.'

For a few days after that he was oddly preoccupied and quiet. I assumed merely that he was not feeling all that well.

At that period, when little was known about Aids and there was so much speculation, it was often a subject of conversation at dinner tables. It was at my dinner table that a woman guest, an American, began to speak about it. What was happening to the gay community in New York and San Francisco was terrible, really terrible, she said. It was such a mysterious illness, no one really knew where it had come from. Her husband gave his opinion that it had obviously been brought back from Haiti by gay American holiday-makers. Someone else produced the conspiracy theory that the virus had escaped from some secret laboratory at which scientists were conducting research into germ warfare on behalf of the CIA. Why not Soviet research on behalf of the KGB? the American woman indignantly demanded.

Suddenly David, who tended to sit silent at such dinner-parties, said in a loud, strained voice, 'Might we change the subject?'

I put in, 'But, David, it's interesting. And important. Important to everyone, not just to homosexuals.'

'Might we change the subject?' he repeated.

We changed the subject.

Later, the guests gone, I asked him, genuinely puzzled, why he had been so insistent that we should not talk about Aids.

As he went on collecting glasses and putting them on a tray, he said, 'It's so morbid constantly to talk about illness and death. Aren't there more interesting things to talk about?'

'Illness and death are facts of life,' I protested. 'One can't ignore them. They come to us all.'

He picked up the tray of glasses and walked out of the room.

That night I was doing the *Times* crossword in bed – as I still do it every night until either sleep takes me or I have completed it – when the door opened and he came in. He looked down at me. Then he said, 'Hold me. Hold me for a moment.'

It was so unlike him to say something like that, with such intensity, that I was astonished. I put out my arms. Briefly he lay on the bed, my arms around him. Then he disengaged himself and, without a word, left my room.

It was a few weeks after that that there came a telephone call from America, from the lover of a New York architect whom both of us had known. David, who had first met him, must, I had concluded, have had an affair with him. He had even visited the architect and his lover in New York. Metro – that was his nickname – was a vivacious, boyishly handsome man, with a passion for Lutyens. It was this passion that had brought him more than once to England.

As David spoke to the lover and I listened, an extraordinary change came over him. He seemed to diminish in size; his face became grey. When he put down the receiver, he put his head back in the chair in which he had been sitting and drew one deep breath and then another. 'Oh, Christ!'

'What's the matter?'

'Is he crazy?'

'Is who crazy?'

He then told me that Metro was dying in a New York hospital of Aids. There was little hope for him. His lover had telephoned to give us the news and also to ask David if he would ask our friend Graham Storey if he would ask the then Archbishop of Canterbury, Runcie, to offer up prayers for Metro. Graham had been Runcie's best man, as he had happened to tell Metro when Metro had been staying with him. 'Is he crazy?' David repeated angrily. 'Why should Runcie pray specially for one particular person whom he's never met? There are thousands and thousands of people dying of Aids. Metro isn't even a believer.'

'It does seem rather dotty,' I said.

I did not then know that, when someone whom one loves is dying, one is prepared to try any expedient, however preposterous, to save him.

In the event we never got on to Graham. As we were still deliberating whether we should do so or not, we heard that Metro had died. At the news David ran up to his room. I knocked on his door. He did not answer. I left him alone. It was only the next morning, at breakfast, that I saw him, and then he was once more his usual self. We never again spoke of Metro.

Suddenly David began to run an extremely high temperature. I begged him to let me call the doctor but he rejected the idea. 'What can a doctor do? It's only a bout of a virus. It'll pass.' Day after day he lay in bed, a woolly skiing cap pulled over his head and blankets piled on top of him. He took huge doses of aspirin and paracetamol. Constantly he sweated, drenching his pyjamas and sheets. I used to try to change these sheets for him, but he would not let me. From time to time he would stagger out of bed, go out to the linen-cupboard and fetch new sheets.

'Please let me help you.'

'No! You have enough to do already.'

Even for me to carry food up to him was something to which he objected. 'I'll come down,' he would say. 'I'd like to come down.'

As he sat huddled opposite to me in his dressing-gown at the kitchen table, he would shiver and his teeth would chatter.

Then, suddenly, the temperature fell. The next day, although pale and weak, he set off early in the morning, long before I was up, for a film job at Pinewood. Gradually the colour came back into his cheeks, he began to put on weight.

'You're your old self again,' I said to him, delighted.

'Yes, I am better, aren't I?' He sounded dubious.

It was shortly after that that he went away on a holiday to Spain with a friend. He returned from it looking even better.

Then once more he was running a temperature. This time I was even more insistent that I must summon the doctor.

'No, no! You can't expect her to turn out. She's far too busy. I'll go over. It's only a five-minute walk.'

I stood at the sitting-room window, watching him make his way up the hill. He strode out with all his old, easy athleticism. No one passing him would have guessed that he had a temperature of 104.

When he returned it was to tell me that the doctor had told him that he must go to hospital. 'It's an awful nuisance. I was hoping for that part in *The Two Ronnies*. I'd all but been promised it.'

He allowed me to help him to pack; but he would not allow me to accompany him to the hospital. 'That's the last thing I want! Having you around, fussing and with that long face, will only make things worse.'

I argued; but eventually he set off in a taxi alone, after I had dissuaded him, with difficulty, from driving the car.

David was always extremely adoit in working the National Health Service. He had persistence, he was young and handsome; but, more than that, he had a jaunty courage which instantly appealed to doctors, nurses and administrators. When I therefore found him in a room to himself, it did not in the least surprise me. I assumed that he had charmed himself into it. Even the notice 'Barrier nursing' did not make me suspicious.

I had gone to the hospital, Charing Cross, on the afternoon of the day of his admission. I took a 27 bus and then walked down Fulham Palace Road, surely one of the dreariest in London. Whenever David was in hospital, I walked down that road day after day. I used to call it, an acrid joke, my *via dolorosa*. After David's death, my publishers moved into offices in the same road. Even now I hate to visit them there. As, once again, I walk towards the hospital, a terrible depression descends on me. On one occasion I even found that tears were running down my cheeks.

'What do they think is the matter with you?'

I am now amazed by my innocence in constantly putting that question to him. Could it be tuberculosis, leukaemia, malaria picked up during his travels in Africa? 'They don't know, they just don't know,' he would tell me wearily.

'But they're doing all the tests?'

'Yes, they're doing all the tests.'

Aids was something which happened to other people; it was not something which could happen to us. For a long time the possibility never entered my mind; so that when Robert Liddell wrote to me from Greece, 'I do so hope it is not the Dread Disease,' I actually felt affronted. No, I wrote back, of course it wasn't.

One day I left David's room in the company of one of his closest friends, also an actor, called Geoff Whitestone.

'I wish they could discover what was wrong with him.'

Geoff said nothing.

'One would have thought that with all the resources of modern medicine . . .'

Geoff said nothing.

Suddenly, I do not know why, I said, 'You don't think he has Aids, do you?'

Geoff still said nothing. Later I was to learn that at that time he himself was HIV positive.

A few days later I said to David, 'I think I'm going to ask to see the doctor in charge of you. It's absurd that they still have no idea of what's the matter.'

He stared at me. Then in a quiet, conversational voice, he said, 'They know what's the matter.'

'What do you mean?'

'They've known for a long time. And I've known for a long time. I have Aids.'

He might have been telling me that he had a cold.

That I was not stunned may have been because, somewhere deep in the recesses of my being, dreaded and unacknowledged, this possibility had been lurking.

'Why didn't you tell me?'

For a while he was silent. Then he smiled. 'Well, it's obvious, isn't it?'

'What do you mean?'

'Well, if you'd known, you might not have wanted to have anything more to do with me.'

That did stun me. It was the cruellest thing that he had ever said to me.

'How could you have imagined that of me? How could you?' I was furious. He shrugged and smiled.

Later, I walked back up the *via dolorosa* and boarded an empty 27 bus. The driver-conductor must have seen my face in his mirror, as I sat on the bench closest to the door. He called out, 'Cheer up, guv! It may never happen.'

'But it has happened – you bloody fool!' I wanted to shout at him. But I merely forced myself to give him a smile.

Later I went to see my mother.

'How did you find David?'

I burst into tears. She looked on, appalled. Then I managed to control myself. 'Oh, I think there's some small improvement.'

'It's a terrible strain for you.'

'Yes, I suppose it is.'

Two or three days later David said to me, 'Don't you think you ought to have a test?'

'A test?' I had already been thinking distractedly about the subject. If I did not have the test, I would keep worrying, hypochondriac that I am, 'Maybe he has infected me.' But if I did have the test and learned that I was HIV positive, could I bear to go on living?

I dreaded going to see my doctor, who was also David's doctor and the wife of my agent. But she was extraordinarily sweet. No less extraordinarily sweet was the young nurse, a New Zealander, who took the sample of my blood. The extraordinary sweetness of such people, often women, threw into vivid contrast the vileness of people like those journalists, among them Peregrine Worsthorne and Paul Johnson, who wrote of Aids as though it were a punishment sent by God. How could a merciful God inflict on young people so terrible a punishment and yet smile benignly on the adultery, fornication, alcoholism, hypocrisy, uncharitableness so common among the people who took this self-righteous line?

There followed a week during which I lived in a state of mental agony which I could reveal to no one. Diana Petre may perhaps have guessed at it, asking me, 'Is anything on your mind?' No, nothing, nothing really, I answered, just David's illness.

Eventually my doctor's receptionist rang me. The test had been negative, Negative? For a moment I thought: negative means bad. Then relief surged through me.

When I visited David, he at once asked me, as soon as I had entered his room, 'Have you heard the result of the test?' He knew that on that Tuesday I would hear it. I nodded. I felt suddenly stricken, ashamed.

'Well?'

'Negative.'

'Negative!' He jumped out of his bed and threw his arms around me. He hugged me in joy. 'That's marvellous. Oh, I am glad, I am glad! What a relief!' A moment later he was telling me to ask the nurse on duty for the bottle of champagne, a present from a friend, which she had put in the refrigerator.

But, oddly, I could not share in his joy. Indeed, it seemed as if the very selflessness of that joy destroyed any that I myself might feel. I was on the verge of tears.

Eventually David had another remission. What, I asked him, did he want me to say when people asked me about his illness? He was vehement. On no account did he wish anyone to know that he was suffering from Aids. I went down to Kensington Library and eventually decided on a disease the symptoms of which were not all that different from those of Aids. I told everyone that David was suffering from leukaemia. This explained the frequent blood transfusions which he was obliged to endure after he had started to be treated with AZT.

David's mother died. In her forties she had had cancer, from which she had made a miraculous recovery. Now in her eighties she had it again. Fortunately its progress was quick and relatively painless. Repeatedly David travelled down to Brighton to be with her. I am sure that the acute anxiety and then the no less acute grief of bereavement hastened his own death.

I have often wondered how things would have turned out if she had survived him. At his death or even before it, she would have learned of the nature of his illness; and she would also have learned of our relationship. Her going was merciful: for me and even more for her.

A friend of ours, Terry Madely, arrived at the house to tell us, calmly, that he had Aids and did not expect to live for more than a year or so. He had no inkling that David was similarly afflicted; and David, to my surprise, did not tell him. Terry, while at drama school, had worked as a hairdresser, coming to the house to cut and shampoo my hair, as he did for many of my friends. He had a camp wit which always amused me. Snip–snip–snip went his scissors and snip–snip–snip went his tongue, as he sliced up the reputations of directors, actors and mutual friends. David could not bear to listen to him, much less to have his hair cut by him.

Terry went public about his Aids, even agreeing to appear on television on a number of occasions. I admired him for this. But David was bitter: 'He always wanted a starring role and now he's got it,' he said.

I tried to explain that each person must find his own way of coming to terms with imminent death. For Terry that way was one of talking freely about it; for David, a stoical silence. David would not accept this. He thought Terry's behaviour, discussing his illness in detail even with women friends, disgusting. He was even more disgusted by Terry's televised funeral, with 'There's no business like show business' being played as the coffin was carried out of the church.

During this period of remission David and I had the last and the happiest of all our holidays together, in Dublin. He seemed to be full of energy; also full of hope, though there was no reason for it. Only one thing marred the long weekend. Since he had told me that he had Aids, we had made two or three attempts to make love; but though my spirit was totally willing, my body somehow refused. In Dublin I initiated another attempt. Once more it failed. I felt angry with myself, humiliated, ashamed. David put his arm around my shoulder. 'It doesn't matter. It doesn't matter.' But to me – and I think also to him – it did. We never tried again.

Soon after that David began to go blind in one eye. Once again showing extraordinary persistence and resourcefulness in working the National Health, he managed not merely to see one of the leading eye-surgeons in England but to persuade him to attempt an operation.

Now it was to Moorfields that I trekked out to see him. I had planned to have an hour with him there, before going on to the Barbican to review a play. But on the way the underground train was halted. Someone had apparently thrown himself (or herself) on to the line. I remember thinking in my anxiety and rage: How can people be so totally inconsiderate? Why choose such a public method? And why choose the rush-hour?'

Eventually I arrived at Old Street and literally ran to Moorfields.

'I can only stay ten minutes,' I gasped. I explained about the play to be reviewed and the delay on the train.

That was the only time, throughout his illness, when David was unreasonable. So that was it! he shouted at me. So all I could spare him was ten minutes of my time.

'I'll come again tomorrow.'

'But I wanted to see you today. You don't know how bored I've been. I was so much looking forward to talking to you.' He was like a petulant child.

The eye-operation was not a success – a likelihood of which the specialist had warned him.

Now David could no longer drive his beloved car. 'I'll have to sell it,' he told me at breakfast one day.

'But why? Why? Your sight may get better.'

'No chance. And you'll never drive it. And when I'm no longer here, you won't be able to get the price you ought to get. You know how hopeless you are at selling anything.'

With his usual efficiency, he set about selling the car. In answer to an advertisement in the *Evening Standard*, a sinister-looking little Cockney, with long, greasy hair and long, dirty finger-nails, appeared. He was a chauffeur at one of the Arab embassies. He and David argued loudly – I could hear them from the kitchen – and then a deal was struck. The next day, the man arrived with a battered suitcase. Inside was the money in £50 notes. David and he carefully counted it out together.

When the man drove off in the car, David and I stood on the steps watching him. David turned to me as the car disappeared from sight. 'That's that,' he said. There were tears in his eyes. It was the first time that I had ever seen him shed any.

Eventually David went into hospital for the last time. Once again he had a room to himself and once again each afternoon I used to make my way down the *via dolorosa* to visit him. It was terrible to watch the gradual disintegration of that once strong and beautiful body.

Because the inexorable deterioration of his sight made reading increasingly difficult for him, I looked out a powerful magnifying glass which I had stowed away in a drawer of my desk. This glass I had given as a present, many years before, to a Japanese friend, Norikazu Fukushima. Having for some months studied on a British Council scholarship in England, Norikazu had had to be hospitalized with a long-standing kidney complaint. Since I was virtually the only friend he had in England, day after day I used to visit him in St Mary Abbott's. Those were days when dialysis was still in its infancy, and there was an acute shortage of machines. Seeing his rapid deterioration, I eventually asked to see the specialist in charge. Couldn't he possibly be put on a machine? The specialist sighed and wearily covered his face with his hands. 'There are just not enough machines to go round. In the bed next to your friend's I have a young man with three children. In the ward next door there is a seventeen-year-old girl. I couldn't let your friend jump the queue.'

'What if he went private? I'm sure his English and Japanese friends would subscribe.' In retrospect I see that this suggestion was immoral. But when one is desperate about someone whom one loves, one forgets about morality.

'There are just not enough machines to go round,' he repeated.

Norikazu began to go blind. It was then that I bought him the most powerful magnifying glass I could find. I took it to him. In an emaciated hand, he raised it before him and then peered through it at the copy of *The Times* which I had also brought. Then, with a small sigh, he let the glass drop from his nerveless hand on to the bedclothes. Two days later he was dead.

Exactly the same thing happened with David. This time it was over a copy of *The Economist* that he raised the glass. There was the same small sigh; the same nerveless dropping. The incident had a terrible double resonance for me: its own and that, jangling discordantly, from a past half forgotten.

David and I had never in the course of our whole relationship made any demonstrations of love to each other. We were both too reticent. But there came a day when suddenly, on an impulse, I jumped off my chair, crossed over to his bed, and took him in my arms. As I rocked him, my lips on his forehead, one of the sisters, a middle-aged Irishwoman, walked in. She looked at us both in amazement. David had always told everyone in the hospital that I was his uncle. Then, lips pursed, she said in a harsh voice, 'Would you leave the room please? I have to do one or two things for Mr Atkin.'

I left the room.

From that time onwards the attitude of this sister, previously friendly, even coquettish, totally changed. She became silent, disapproving, grim. All the other nurses were marvellous. She was the one exception.

Eventually David went blind; and it was then that Peter Day demonstrated that he was the best of foul-weather friends. Each day he would set aside an hour in a busy life, in order to bicycle over to the hospital and read from the *Telegraph* or *The Times*.

I had to travel to Glasgow to review Peter Brook's seven-hour *Mahabarhata — or Megaborata*, as I called it.

'Do you have to go?' David pleaded.

Of course I did not have to go. But my ludicrous sense of duty impelled me to do so. 'Yes, I must.'

He sighed. 'You will telephone me?'

'Yes, of course I'll telephone. First thing tomorrow morning, before I set off for the show.'

For some reason the first performance was on a Sunday. So preoccupied had I been with David's illness that I had totally forgotten that that was the day on which the first reviews of my novel *The Woman Who Was God* would be appearing. With my early breakfast in my room, the waiter brought me a copy of *The Sunday Times*. Turning over the books pages as I munched at my toast, I suddenly saw my name and the title. The review was by Peter Kemp and, in retrospect, it now seems the least just that I have ever received. But at that time, so distracted was I by thoughts of David that it meant absolutely nothing to me. I could have been reading a review of a book by a stranger.

Breakfast over, I tried to telephone to David. But there was no answer from the hospital. I rang and rang again, constantly looking at my watch in my anxiety that I should not arrive late for the performance. Eventually I had to give up. Then I could not get a taxi. Fortunately one of the actors, a Turk staying in the hotel, had ordered one the night before and he gave me a lift.

In the theatre I found myself sitting behind a new colleague, whom I had still not identified. When, after many hours on extremely hard seats, we eventually filed out of the auditorium for the first interval, I asked the colleague next to me, Jim Hiley, 'Who is that man in front of us?' He told me that it was Peter Kemp. At any other time I might have then felt an upsurge of rage – a feeling of 'Oh, how I'd like to kick him!' But, like Kemp's review, Jim's revelation now had absolutely no effect on me whatever.

While my colleagues rushed towards the buffet offered to them by the management, I rushed off in the opposite direction in search of a telephone. There was none to be found in the tram shed doing service for a theatre. Someone directed me to some public telephones down the street. All of them had been vandalized. In a small sweet-shop I begged with a woman in a sari to allow me to use her phone. In a voice empty of all expression, she repeated, 'Sorry. Phone is for private, not public, use.' I was no luckier anywhere else.

When I returned to the tram shed, there was virtually no food left. I bought myself a double vodka on ice and gnawed at a slice of bread and cheese. Then it was time to dash back into the auditorium. The play was excruciating in its boredom; but even more excruciating was my anxiety. I had promised to telephone David; I had failed to do so. I knew how much my daily telephone calls meant to him.

When I rang that evening, he sounded hysterical. 'What happened to you? I was terribly worried. You said you'd telephone. I kept imagining that something had happened to you.'

I tried to explain all the difficulties of the day, but he kept reiterating, 'What happened to you? You said you would telephone.'

I learned later that he had even telephoned to Elizabeth to say how worried he was about me – it was so unlike me not to call when I had promised to do so.

It was only a few days later that he telephoned to me, early in the morning, to tell me that he felt so strange, he wondered if he had had a stroke. In fact, his brain was now affected. I rushed to the hospital but by then he could hardly speak and then only in disconnected phrases. I held his hand. He lapsed into a coma.

While he was in the coma, I asked the Irish sister, when she came into the room, 'How long can he last?'

Imperiously she beckoned me out of the room. Then she hissed angrily at me, 'Don't you know that you should never say anything like that in front of a patient?'

'But he's unconscious.'

'The sense of hearing is the last thing to go. I thought everyone knew that.' She swept off.

I sat with David for hours on end. Sometimes I tried to talk to him, reminding him of all the wonderful times that we had had together and telling him how much I had always loved him, but it was like talking to myself.

One midday I rushed home to dash of my *Sunday Telegraph* review. As I was seated at my computer, amazed that at such a time I could still write something coherent – something that would not make my readers say, 'He's badly off form this week' – the telephone rang. It was Peter Day, to tell me that David had died. Peter had been with him. I could not bring myself to ask Peter for details. I have never done so.

Elizabeth and I went to the hospital. Later I was to feel as much relief that David's long torment was over as grief at his going; but now I felt only grief. I went in to see him but could not bear to look at him. When I came out, one of the nurses – small, young and pretty, she had been David's favourite – began to cry. The Irish sister arrived. She stared at me. Then in a totally different voice from the one she had so often used to David and me, a voice warm with sympathy, she said, 'Sit down' and, when I had sunk into a chair, 'I'll bring you a cup of tea.'

The next day Elizabeth and I returned to get the death certificate. The young doctor was visibly embarrassed as he asked me, 'You know the cause of death, don't you?'

'Yes ... yes, I do.'

'I'm afraid I have to put it on the death certificate. Does that make things difficult for you?'

'Put whatever you want.'

When I signed the book which he held out to me, I saw that, by a strange coincidence, the name above mine was also 'King'. The death recorded was that of a four-year-old girl from leukaemia. Later, in the women's lavatory, Elizabeth heard a woman sobbing in one of the cubicles. When she emerged, Elizabeth tried to comfort her. She was the mother of the four-year-old girl.

I wondered how the official at Fulham Town Hall would react when I handed over the death certificate to him. Would he look disapproving, shocked, disgusted? In the event, he behaved admirably.

At first grief induces a strange exaltation. That exaltation stayed with me until after the funeral. I debated whether to ask Gerard Irvine, who had officiated at the funerals of so many of my literary friends, or Charles Sinnickson, an American clergyman long resident in England, to take the service out at Putney Crematorium. Both were close friends of mine and both had known David. Gerard, as I have related, bought my first Brighton house. Charles I had known, long before he had taken holy orders, when he was a well-to-do, witty *flâneur* on a visit to Greece when I was working there. I had lost touch with him for many years; then, walking through Soho, I had seen him swishing towards me in clerical garb reaching to his ankles. I assumed, to his displeasure, that he was on his way to a fancy-dress party. He was, in fact, then curate of St Anne's Soho. Genuinely eccentric in his views – he once maintained to me, in what appeared to be all seriousness, that Harold Wilson was the anti-Christ – he was also, I soon realized, a genuinely good man. Eventually, after much thought, I opted for him. The choice proved an excellent one. He spoke of David with true affection and understanding.

The service over, I was the first to leave the chapel. I went and stood under a tree. No one came near me, no doubt not wishing to intrude on my grief. I then realized the loneliness of bereavement.

In the days that immediately followed David's death, I rushed to clear up all his belongings, as though to rid myself of any reminder of the horror of the last months. Recklessly I stuffed valuable things – an almost new Braun electric razor, a similarly almost new Armani jacket, some Hermes ties, some Gucci shoes (as an actor, David spent a lot of money on clothes) – into black plastic refuse bags. Some of these bags I lugged over to Oxfam. Others I merely put out for the dustmen. The last of these bags, stuffed chiefly with his papers, split as I heaved it down the narrow stairs, scattering its contents everywhere. Then I sat down on the steps and, for the first time since his death, burst into tears.

Apart from three legacies, to his friends Geoff Whitestone and John Gonezi and my niece Cathy, of whom he was particularly fond, David left everything which he possessed to me. This included the money which he had so recently inherited from his mother. I had so often worried about my old age and about what would happen to him when, after my death, he would be told to leave the house. I need not have worried about either. Against all my expectations he had predeceased me; and, thanks to the hard work of a woman who had never met me and would certainly have disapproved of me had she done so, I had enough to yield not a large income but one that would keep me from any possible penury.

David had an uncle, his mother's brother. When David had been in hospital, this uncle had never visited him; the two men were clearly far from close. On David's death, I rang this uncle to inform him. He at once asked who was the executor of the will. I said that I was. I told him about the funeral and, on the assumption that he would wish to come, asked him to have luncheon with me, my sister and Charles Sinnickson in my house before it. He accepted the invitation. Then, as an afterthought it seemed, he asked me, 'What did he die of?'

'Leukaemia,' I said, as I had said to so many other people. I have never been a good liar; but during those months I came to understand how people who have committed some crime can lie to protect themselves with total conviction. Eventually one not only fools others with the lie, one all but fools oneself. I think there were times when I really did believe that David was dying of leukaemia.

The next day I was telephoned by a solicitor. He was speaking on behalf of David's uncle, Mr S. Would I please inform him of the contents of David's will? I replied that I thought it premature to talk about the will only two days after David's death; but that if Mr S. was really in such a hurry, then the solicitor could tell him that I was the executor and that, three small legacies apart, I was also the sole beneficiary. I then went on, 'Mr Atkin was ill for a long time. His uncle never once visited him in hospital. I visited him every day, as did one of our friends. My sister and other friends visited him two or three times a week.'

'Please, Mr King! I have Mr S. here with me. He can hear what we are saying.'

'I've no objection to his hearing what I am saying.'

Clearly rattled, the solicitor then asked me if I could send him a photocopy of the will. I said that I should be happy to do so.

In the event, the uncle never came to the funeral. There was a place laid for him in the dining-room and a place kept for him in the hired car. He did not even telephone to warn me of his absence.

Later still, not wishing to be on bad terms with him, I wrote him a letter. David had brought from his mother's flat many family photographs and documents. Would he like to have these, since they concerned his family, not mine? He telephoned to thank me and to say that one of his sons would pick up the things 'in due course'.

I heard nothing more. The suitcase full of them is still in my attic.

David left me a letter. It was written in a curiously stilted English, as though it was tremendously difficult for him to say all the things that he wanted to say after so many years of reticence between us. 'I did love you,' he wrote: the word 'did' underlined no doubt because whenever I had asked him (which was only rarely), 'Do you love me?', he had never replied. Then he went on to urge me to believe, as he did, in an after-life. During those last months spent intermittently in Charing Cross Hospital, he had derived great comfort from the remarkable man who was – perhaps still is – the hospital chaplain. Sadly I have been unable to follow David's urgings. Belief is not a matter of the will.

With his letter to me was another, sealed letter to a friend of his, an elderly man, with the instruction: 'To be posted after my death.' I speculated about its contents and all but decided to steam it open. David's friendship with this man was an odd and touching one. Originally, the man (whom I shall call Ted, since he may still be alive) had been the friend, perhaps even lover, of one of David's closest friends, Tristram. Tristram, a handsome Old Harrovian constantly in debt or in some other kind of trouble, had always exerted what I thought a baleful influence on David, who was tempted to emulate him. Together, before I had met David, the two boys (as they then were) had been involved in a number of near-illegal activities and, I suspect, some illegal ones, while trading with American forces in North Africa and Spain. Subsequently, Tristram had acquired a yacht, which he had used for smuggling. David told me that Tristram had never smuggled anything other than cigarettes and booze; but I had doubted this.

While his yacht was in some Spanish harbour, Tristram was found aboard with a bullet hole in his temple, a revolver lying beside him. The eventual Spanish verdict was that he had killed himself; but David was convinced that, having in some way cheated his Arab bosses, he had been murdered.

Tristram had often turned to Ted, who was in love with him, in times of need. Now David became a friend – though not, I am sure, lover – of Ted, who, as he grew older and frailer, relied on him for all sorts of services, from running errands to Harrods to helping him have a bath.

Having received the forwarded letter, Ted telephoned to me from the country. I had already told him of David's death.

'I don't understand about this letter.'

'I'm afraid I know nothing about it.' I explained how I had found it, along with David's letter to me and a copy of his will, after his death, and that I had never read it.

'Well, it's all rather odd.'

He then told me that, in himself making a will, he had told David that he was leaving him a flat which he owned in Caterham. In the letter, David begged him to change the will and leave the flat to me.

'Of course you don't have to do that,' I said. 'He shouldn't have asked that of you.'

'Well, I don't know . . .' He sounded bewildered and wary.

I was extraordinarily embarrassed and yet at the same time touched that David should have been so worried about my future. I have never heard again from Ted and I have no doubt that, as I should have done in similar circumstances, he ignored the request.

It was some time after reading David's letter to me that, re-reading it, I noticed the date. He had written it some two years before his death. With nerves of steel, he had acknowledged the inevitability of what was going to happen to him and had then made all his dispositions and written his farewell.

For the first weeks after David's death, I constantly felt that he was somewhere in the house. Crazily I used to think that, if I searched long enough and thoroughly enough, I would find him somewhere. More than once I would enter the house on my return from reviewing a play and call out, 'Hello!', as I used to do when he was alive. Then the silence would descend on me like a suffocating blanket.

I have always had an astonishingly acute sense of smell, often amazing David by asking, when I returned home, 'Has so-and-so been here today?' Now I could hardly bear to go into his former bedroom, because it still carried his odour.

Everyone was extraordinarily kind to me at that time, Peter, Josephine and Diana especially so. They were constantly inviting me to meals, suggesting outings, telephoning me to ask how I was. But there were times when, like some stricken animal, I wanted only to be alone.

I am still awed by David's courage. In similar circumstances, my health inexorably deteriorating as I progressed towards an inevitable death, I should certainly have killed myself. David never for one moment (as far as I know) considered that option. Often I used to think in anguish, 'How can he bear to go on?' Had he asked me to help him to precipitate the end, I should have done everything in my power, regardless of a possible prison sentence.

Recently in the *Spectator* I read a peculiarly disgusting article by Paul Johnson. Johnson regretted that in a new book on etiquette Drusilla Beyfus had included suggestions of how to deal with homosexual guests and their partners. Johnson asked, 'Why should a hostess ... invite them in the first place? After all, other guests may not like living in the same house with people who could have Aids.' I wonder whether, in the fell clutch of some circumstance similar to David's, Johnson would show the same bravery, selflessness and grace.

The most terrible and fruitless aspect of bereavement is guilt. Guilt haunted me in the immediate aftermath of David's death and still, intermittently, haunts me, albeit not so acutely, even now. One memory in particular stays with me. This is of occasions when I would be working on my computer on the novel which eventually became *The Woman Who Was God* and suddenly would become aware of David standing in the doorway of my room, looking at me.

I would glance up. 'Yes?'

He would continue to look at me, saying nothing.

'Did you want something?'

He would shake his head.

'I'll be with you in a moment. I must just finish this page.'

He would go away.

If I have learned anything from those last terrible years, it is that writers, myself of course included, put far too high an estimate on the importance of their work. Not long ago I was staying with a writer friend in the country. As I sat in the guest bedroom reading a book, the writer's children played happily and, yes, noisily in the garden. Then the writer's wife went out to them: 'Sh! Do be quiet! Daddy's trying to write.' A moment later the writer himself was shouting out of the window of his study, 'Stop that bloody din!' Tolstoy's work justified his cruelty to his wretched wife; but nothing that that writer has ever produced justifies that stifling of his children, and nothing that I have ever written justifies my not having jumped up from the computer and run to David.

The truth is that from time to time the whole situation became so unbearable to me that the only effective way in which I could escape from it was into the increasingly unhinged world of the heroine of *The Woman Who Was God*. Seated before my computer, I would brace myself like a diver; then I would plunge into the waters framed by its screen, immersing myself deeper and deeper until I was wholly shut off from the outside world. It was a novel which seemed to write itself; so that each time that I read over a passage I had written, it would surprise me – 'Where on earth has this come from?' I would think. When it finally appeared, I suffered a profound discouragement that the reviewers, even when they were approving, so totally misjudged it – its ambiguities and its complexities equally lost on them. Then I received a letter from a young Australian academic Bill Taylor, never met, and he analysed the book so brilliantly, peeling off skin after skin, that my discouragement at once turned to relief and even joy.

There is one other terrible memory which still haunts me. This is of the early months of David's illness, when he knew its nature but I still did not do so. He had been extraordinarily and uncharacteristically gloomy and silent for several days. 'What's the matter with you?' I eventually burst out in exasperation. 'It's so depressing to have to live with you when you're in this kind of mood.'

'Sorry,' he said. Then he repeated, 'Sorry.'

Even today I cannot prevent myself from wondering who it was who infected David and in what kind of circumstances. What does it matter? But an insane, never to be satisfied curiosity gnaws away at me, a rat in the belly. Usually, reliving that telephone call from New York, I eventually decide that it must have been poor, vivacious, charming Metro. How can I blame him? Someone fucked up his life and he in turn fucked up David's and, to a lesser degree, mine. In any case, as I have already noted, blaming is such a sterile occupation. But in this case I cannot help blaming.

I also often speculate on whether, before he knew that he had Aids, David infected anyone else. It is not impossible that he might have infected some unsuspecting woman and that she in turn infected some other man. I want to jump off the sickening roundabout of such thoughts but cannot do so.

The danger of bereavement is that one starts to idealize the dead loved one. I hope that I have not done that here. There were things that were unattractive about David: a toughness of spirit, as well as of body, so that he could be indifferent and even callous about people weaker than himself; an impatience with eccentricity, inefficiency, effeminacy; a flyness which sometimes verged on dishonesty. But his courage, dignity, vivacity, zest for life in the most horrible of circumstances still fill me with admiration.

I was extraordinarily fortunate to have had twenty years with him, in a relationship far happier than many a marriage that I have witnessed. When I think back on those twenty years and their terrible aftermath, I remember what Ivy Compton-Burnett wrote to me, in the very different context of my libel problems: 'It is better to be drunk with loss and beat the ground, than to let the deeper things gradually escape.'

Near the close, I think that both David and I had found one satisfaction in the otherwise unrelieved tragedy in which we were participating. We were seeing the terrible thing through together, remaining true both to each other and to something deeply buried within us. Looking back, I still find that satisfaction. It is, in some small part at least, a solace for my loss.


By an eerie coincidence, a close friend of mine, Adam Johnson, died at the age of twenty-eight on May 16, 1993, exactly five years to a day after David's death. A poet of extraordinary promise, Adam succumbed to an abscess of the brain, caused by Aids, just as David had done. Like David's, his funeral was at Putney Crematorium. I was surprised by what a terrible ordeal that occasion proved to be for me. There was my grief for Adam; and, ferociously intensified, there was my grief for David. The two griefs became almost insupportable. I dreaded that I would burst into tears. Perhaps it would have been better for me if I had done so.

# — 9 —

# *Shadows of the Evening*

1988 was the worst year of my life: David died near its beginning and near its close I myself almost died of cancer.

For almost a year before David's death, I had been suffering continual discomfort or pain. After I had been to see my doctor three times, she referred me to a consultant gastroenterologist. I at once took to Dr. X, who struck me as a cultivated and sympathetic man.

After examining me, he said that he did not think that there was anything seriously wrong and prescribed some pills.

My symptoms worsened. Again I went to see him.

'Are you under any kind of stress?' he asked me, as he had asked me on the previous visit.

Now, instead of denying that I was, I said Yes.

'What kind of stress?'

I saw no reason not to tell him about David. At once he showed what I am sure was a genuine, not a professional, sympathy. 'Yes, I know exactly the sort of hell you must be going through. Well, that could make you have all these symptoms. I think I'd better put you on to an antidepressant.' His abstracted, nervy manner made me wonder if he should not also put himself on to an antidepressant.

The antidepressant which he prescribed produced such a ferocious allergy that I ended up in the Cromwell Hospital for almost a week. He then put me on to a different antidepressant.

David kept telling me, 'There's nothing wrong with you mentally. There's something physical wrong with you. Tell him you must have a barium enema.'

'I can't tell a famous specialist what to do. He knows what to do.'

'That's what you think.'

I had by then persuaded myself that the gnawing pain was merely a physical manifestation of the anxiety which, even in the theatre or at a party, would suddenly have me in its grip. Later, after David's death, I decided that this gnawing pain, now so much more aggressive, was merely a physical manifestation of my sense of loss and loneliness. However, when during my travels in South Korea after the Seoul Congress and during subsequent travels in Taiwan,

324

otherwise so enjoyable, I sometimes found myself actually doubled up in an attempt to relieve the pain, I decided that I must return yet again to Dr. X. On this occasion, he decided that I might be suffering from a recurrence of the duodenal ulcer from which I had suffered some years before. He therefore performed an endoscopy, after which he told me, 'I am happy to say that I found absolutely nothing amiss.'

Some weeks later I was back in his consulting room. As though David were prompting me, I at last told him that I wished to have an X-ray of the bowel.

He sighed. 'Well, if you really want one. If it will put your mind at rest.'

My mind was far from at rest when I saw the expressions on the faces of the woman doctor and her male assistant as the X-ray proceeded. Before they had been jolly. Now they exchanged ominous glances, did not address a word to me except to give instructions, and never looked into my eyes.

'Is everything all right?' I asked at the end, knowing full well that it wasn't.

'You'll have to wait for Dr. X to get in touch with you.'

This he did that same afternoon. He told me that a polyp had been revealed, and that there was a possibility that it might be maligant. 'I think that you should have an operation without delay.'

The surgeon to whom I was despatched at first spoke not of a possibility but of a probability of malignancy. Later, after an extensive examination, this became 'a near certainty'. I realized that this was how, gently but inexorably, medical men break such things to their patients.

During the week in which I was waiting to enter the Lister Hospital, Geoff Whitestone came to see me. He was emaciated and grey. Within a few months he was to die of Aids. 'What exactly is the matter with you?' he asked me.

I told him that I had cancer.

'Oh, but that's terrible, that's terrible!' He jumped off his chair, facing mine in the kitchen, and put his arms around me, hugging me to him.

I thought that for a man who knew that he was dying to do such a thing showed an extraordinary generosity. I had some hope of recovery; he had none.

When I arrived in the hospital, the anaesthetist told me, 'I can promise you that you're not going to have any intolerable pain.' He kept his promise. I had no intolerable pain, indeed hardly any pain at all. But I had a great deal of discomfort, particularly from constant, uncontrollable vomiting.

On the night after the operation, I was given a pain-killer, by way of a spinal drip, which I now realize must have been either morphine or heroin, since the next night, when I asked if I were to be given it again, the doctor told me, 'Oh, no! We only give that on the first night.'

That first night I had the most wonderful and also the most terrible dreams. One of these was of a huge fire such as I had never seen since the blitz. Out of it David walked towards me, smiling, totally unscathed. I held out my hands to him. He grasped them. Later, by then half-awake, I looked across the room and there he was standing, in nothing but a pair of dark blue shorts. This time he did not move. He was staring intently at some spot just above my head.

Dr. X came to see me. He was clearly mortified and embarrassed.

'What is my chance of survival?' I asked him.

'Well, the average survival rate is five years.'

'Is that all?'

'You *are* sixty-five. You can't expect to live for ever.'

'I know. But, even though it's impossible, I think that we all want to be immortal.'

He smiled. 'I'm afraid that no doctor can give you immortality.'

My surgeon, Meirion Thomas, has proved a better psychologist. Each time that I have a check-up, he tells me, 'The longer you're in the clear, the less likelihood there is of a recurrence.'

Lying alone in my hospital room, I longed for company. But when the company came – friends were extraordinarily solicitous – it so much fatigued me that I longed to be alone again.

Among those who visited me were two American friends, on holiday in England. They told me, as other Americans were to tell me, 'You must sue this doctor for negligence.' It was not negligence, I told them; it was merely a failure of professional judgement, such as I myself had shown on many occasions. Had I not advised George Weidenfeld against publishing the subsequently best-selling (under another imprint) *Games People Play*? Had I not been convinced that Nina Epton's book about the daughters of Queen Victoria would be a best-seller? Had I not predicted that *Les Misérables* would not run for more than six weeks? In any case, if I had decided to be litigious, it is unlikely that I should have succeeded. When I told Meirion Thomas that it was a pity that the polyp had not been diagnosed before it became malignant, he told me, 'The two problems were that you did not have the usual symptom of bleeding, and that you did have all the symptoms associated with a duodenal ulcer.'

In the next-door room was a young Greek girl of sixteen or seventeen who had had the same operation as I had. Her door was always open to reveal a vast number of people crowded about her bed. Sometimes these people even spilled into the passageway, to dusturb the other patients with their chatter and laughter. Whereas I had started to walk up and down the corridor two days after my operation, this girl absolutely refused to leave her bed even to go to the lavatory. In this refusal her entourage supported her. The physiotherapist asked me to have a word with her, telling her of my own experience. I went into the room and, to the amazement of everyone present, spoke to the girl in Greek. It was useless. Her relatives were all noisily vehement: after such an operation it would be madness to walk for at least a week, they had never heard of such a thing, did the hospital wish to kill her?

When I came out of hospital, various people asked me to go and stay with them. But I decided that I wanted to go home. Peter Day then showed his usual kindness. Each evening for a week he would bicycle over in order to sleep in the house.

In the immediate aftermath of the operation I had experienced a euphoria, thinking, 'Well, at least I'm not dead!' But now depression descended on me. The house seemed even more empty than before; and I kept asking myself, 'How long have I got?' It was then that I conceived the idea of writing a comic novel, about my PEN years, to cheer myself up. But I should have far more effectively cheered myself up if I had embarked on a tragic novel. Each day I would write some pages of what was eventually to be *Visiting Cards*. The next morning I would read those pages and ask myself, 'Did you really imagine that all this was *funny*?' But I pushed on. As I have related, at the same time I was passing through all the troubles over Blunck.

Once again, as after David's death, I was overwhelmed by the kindness of friends and even strangers. One neighbour, hardly known, asked me in the street where I had been – it was so long since she had seen me. I told her of my operation. Spontaneously, she cried out, 'Oh, you poor dear!, threw her arms around me, and kissed me on the cheek. The little son of other neighbours brought me a bunch of late roses, which he told me he had picked in Holland Park. 'I really stole them,' he confessed.


In May of 1992, I went to Lake Bled in Slovenia for a literary conference. Hating the sea, I love lakes; and of all lakes, Bled is for me the most attractive. I at once felt happy and at peace there. It therefore surprised me when, one night, I had a series of nightmares, one after another, each with David at its centre and each more terrible than the one before it. In particular, I remember one in which, having arranged to meet him in Victoria Station (when he was alive, I would often meet him there, on his return from a weekend with his mother), I could nowhere find him. Then I glimpsed him, across a crowd, in the far distance. I tried to fight through to him, people jostling, shoving and cursing at me. When I got to the spot, he had vanished. Once again I glimpsed him; pushed through the crowd; was shoved and jostled and cursed at. Once again he vanished.

I got out of bed feeling hideously depressed. What had caused such a night? Then I remembered: that morning was the anniversary of David's death. I have always been puzzled by people who mourn for their loved ones on an anniversary; surely one mourns for them all the time? But on this occasion my subconscious had forced me to a rite of remembrance which I had tried to ignore.


Looking back on my life, I realize how extraordinarily fortunate I have been. For most of it I have done the one thing, writing, that I most wanted to do; and for most of it I have fulfilled Henry James's definition of being rich: I have been able to turn most of my dreams into reality. Admittedly those dreams have not extended to owning a yacht, a private plane or a country-house, employing a large staff of servants, or building up a world-famous collection. But I have had one completely happy 'marriage', I have travelled to most of the places I have wanted to see, I have bought such pictures as I have coveted and felt to be within my means, and I have lived in a series of enviable houses.

If I have one regret, it is that there has been too little joy in my life. There was joy in David's life, until his illness first clouded and then destroyed it; but, as I dedicated myself more and more to the writing of books, so joy, as distinct from contentment and even happiness, seeped out of my life. If I was enjoying myself, I also felt guilty.

I have often said that I am never happier than when I am writing. That is true. But it might have been better for me and for those close to me if it had not been so.

# INDEX